FUSILIERS

Fusiliers

Eight Years with the Redcoats in America

MARK URBAN

faber and faber

First published in 2007
by Faber and Faber Limited
3 Queen Square London WC1N 3AU

Typeset by Palindrome
Printed in England by Mackays of Chatham, plc

A CIP record for this book
is available from the British Library

ISBN 978–0–571–22486–9

2 4 6 8 10 9 7 5 3 1

To those who serve honourably
in unpopular wars

Contents

CONTENTS

Illustrations

A 1776 sketch by Richard Williams showing a proposed light
company uniform for the 23rd. Courtesy of the Colonial
Williamsburg Foundation.

The opening engagement of the wars in Lexington Green, where poor
British troop discipline may have contributed to the outbreak of
hostilities. © Corbis.

Frederick Mackenzie in later life. © Royal Welch Fusiliers Museum,
Caernarfon.

George Baynton, painted in the mid-1780s in splendid Fusiliers dress
uniform. © Royal Welch Fusiliers Museum, Caernarfon.

Thomas Saumarez, one of the longest-serving officers of the 23rd
during the American war. © Royal Welch Fusiliers Museum,
Caernarfon.

Caricature of Robert Donkin. © National Portrait Gallery, London.

Earl Cornwallis, admired by many of his officers for his aggression on
the field and his desire to protect the army's honour. © National
Portrait Gallery, London.

George Washington was not a great battlefield commander but a
superior strategist to William Howe during the key campaigns of
1776–7. © Corbis.

Harry Calvert, painted in his twenties. © Courtauld Institute of Art,
London.

Britain's failure at Bunker Hill lampooned. © Library of Congress,
Washington DC.

The opening of the battle of Germantown, with British troops around

Cliveden Manor (detail). © Valley Forge Historical Society, USA;
The Bridgeman Art Library.

A detail from a Richard Williams sketch of Boston during the siege of
1775. © The British Library, London.

British troops seizing Rhode Island in 1776 (detail), one of the
impressive amphibious operations launched by the Howe brothers.
© National Maritime Museum, London.

The French flagship, *Languedoc,* dismasted in a storm and left at the
mercy of British ships, here the *Renown.* © Library of Congress,
Washington DC.

A later view of British soldiers storming one of Yorktown's outer
redoubts. © Delaware Art Museum, Wilmington, USA, Howard
Pyle Collection; The Bridgeman Art Library.

The taking of the British ship *Romulus* in Chesapeake Bay.
© National Maritime Museum, London.

The march to Yorktown's surrender field, drawn by an artist who
witnessed the scene (detail). © Chateau de Versailles, France,
Lauros, Giraudon; The Bridgeman Art Library.

Maps

Preface

The British army's struggle to prevent American independence was undoubtedly one of its most significant campaigns. Not only did the outcome produce one of the great seismic shifts of global history, but it also marked a vital learning experience, the necessary shock required to launch the defeated forces on a path towards reform.

I freely confess that studying the battle for America has been a passion since childhood. It even motivated my first real steps in historical research, clutching a newly issued National Army Museum reader's ticket at the age of sixteen. The fact that the contest ended in the British losing thirteen colonies simply increased its romance to me. And, if the fighting took place on a much smaller scale at Brandywine or Saratoga in 1777 than at Waterloo thirty-eight years later, this simply served to underline the intimacy of those earlier battles.

While the epic victories of Wellington's army in the peninsula have long riveted British readers, an understanding of the carnage of Bunker Hill or triumph at Camden is in fact a vital prerequisite to discovering why the redcoat did so well against Napoleon's armies. The fact that the narrative of Fusiliers continues until early 1809, when that of my earlier book, *Rifles*, begins, is quite deliberate.

Whereas *Rifles* described the campaigns of that elite and rather unusual corps, the 95th or Green Jackets, the story told in these pages is that of a red-coated regiment of the line, the 23rd or Royal Welch Fusiliers. In this sense the experiences of those soldiers fighting in America is more representative of the late eighteenth-century army and soldiering as a whole than that of the riflemen.

Many readers may ask, why the 23rd? There are two reasons. First, the Fusiliers were involved in the first fight, at Lexington in 1775, and campaigned right through to Yorktown in 1781 when the British venture finally came to grief. Their campaigns therefore provided a narrative that mirrors the wider story. The second is that there are enough first-hand accounts emanating from the 23rd to bring the regiment to life, and this is a very rare thing for that period. Some regiments, such as the 5th, boast excellent archival material rarely used by historians but left the American battlefield halfway through that conflict. One or two others, such as the 43rd, served as long in America as the 23rd but left no substantial personal accounts to speak of.

Two soldiers of the 23rd are very well known to specialists of this period: Serjeant Roger Lamb, one of the earliest British rankers to publish memoirs, and Frederick Mackenzie, adjutant of the Fusiliers at Lexington. I knew that in order for this account to be worth writing I would have to find much more than these two accounts – for in any case Lamb only entered the 23rd three years into the war, and Mackenzie left regimental service soon after the war started, being employed in a series of staff jobs.

There were many times, as I began the process of digging into the 23rd's campaigns, when I wondered whether the necessary weight of historical documents still existed, and whether my quest would end in failure. For while Wellington's campaigns against Napoleon produced literally hundreds of printed memoirs or journals from survivors, there is no more than a handful from the much smaller number of men who fought across the Atlantic.

An initial success gave me the incentive to carry on. For while searching for material on another subject, I discovered that at a country seat north of London the Verney family still possessed an unpublished journal and autobiography of an officer named Harry Calvert. He served as a young subaltern in the 23rd, joining the regiment in 1779, fighting through the Carolinas and ending up captured at Yorktown. Here was a start then, an account unknown even to historians specialising in this subject. The lesson of the Calvert find was that dozens of haystacks would have to be searched to produce some more glinting needles of testimony.

Little by little the search of obscure archives began turning up letters – documents more useful in many ways than journals since they are more immediate and less dry. I discovered some prolific letter-writers like the lieutenant colonel who commanded the 23rd for most of the war, or a captain who ran its recruiting operation in Britain. Many of these messages were dull or businesslike of course, but some gave vital insight into the hopes and fears of the men I wished to write about. As one find grew upon another, the Duke of Northumberland's papers yielded a string of letters from a young officer on service with the 23rd keen to do his duty, while the National Archive at Kew yielded up a correspondence with a disillusioned old Fusilier equally determined to avoid it. So I ended up with dozens of letters from officers in the regiment that are not only previously unpublished but have been little if ever used by other historians.

In the course of searching for letters, I encountered some great runs of them from men not in the 23rd: Richard Fitzpatrick, a foppish Guards officer; Francis Hutcheson, a lugubrious staff man; or Richard Dansey, a fire-eating light-infantry officer. Their insights have been used to illustrate more general points about service in that army.

The result of this research is an account that I hope readers will find quite different from any published before, providing depth in getting under the skin of one regiment as well as breadth in consulting a great range of testimony. I tried in setting out on this task to read every first-hand British military account of the American War of Independence that I could find. Of course some more may lurk in archives, but I pursued every journal or letter I became aware of. When examining the 23rd's campaigns, naturally I used primary accounts from the American side too or from the point of view of Britain's German mercenaries. Nevertheless, this is unapologetically a British-army-centred version of these events.

Inevitably there are differences of perspective between a Briton and an American investigating this conflict. Its history has usually been written by the victor. The story of the revolution is a font of national mythology for writers in the United States. Sadly, even the better ones tend to stick to the enemy-image of the redcoat as a brutalised robot, marching on inept orders. They tend to overestimate British military efficiency at the beginning of the war, and underestimate it at the end. Inventive leadership, enthusiasm, and bravery are virtues that many American writers expect to find only in the ranks of Washington's army. Consequently they have never looked particularly hard for material in the British archives that challenges their stereotype of the enemy. Certainly, I found myself frustrated during years of searching for a book that addressed the redcoats' experience of the war, telling me about the fortunes of a single group of men or the effect of this long painful fight on the army's development.

As for the distortions in British telling of this history, these tend to emerge from political and class dynamics. Since the war was a cause supported enthusiastically only by ultra-Tories it has often been portrayed by the Whig or liberal school of history as a gigantic act of folly. More recently, social antagonism has guaranteed a ready reception for representations of the British officer-class in this period as useless upper-class twits. All of this ignores the subtle workings of the eighteenth-century army. The story of the 23rd reveals them – how senior officers arranged the promotion of those who could not afford to purchase higher ranks or that the dividing line between the ranks and commissioned class was a good deal more fluid than it became later, in Wellington's times.

When writing I was at first tempted to quote these protagonists with their eighteenth-century spelling intact, but at length I realised it would just be too confusing. I have allowed myself the odd exception, such as 'serjeant' rather than the 'sergeant' more widely used today. The 23rd's title provides a case in point about inconsistency in period spelling. Some spelled it 'Welsh', whereas others used the archaic 'Welch' that the regiment considers correct today. As for 'Fusiliers' it can be found as Fuziliers, Fuzileers and even Fusileers. My editor did not share my early enthusiasm for giving this book the title 'Fuziliers'.

Unearthing the story of this regiment has required a far larger archival research project than that needed for the 95th Rifles. Those kind members of the Royal Welch Fusiliers regimental family – Major General Jonathon Riley, Major Nick Lock, as well as archivists Brian Owen and Anne Pedley – who wanted to help could only do so to the limited extent that the archive at their disposal permitted. Instead I would have to investigate dozens of archives, and in some cases rely on a legion of researchers to undertake those tasks that geography or time prevented me from carrying out in person.

Those that I engaged professionally were: Brendan Morrissey (an author on this period in his own right, who collated the information in the 23rd's regimental muster lists for me); Susan Ranson, who copied out the important finds in the Verney Papers; Ellen Poteet, who spared me the journey to the important Clements collections in Ann Arbor Michigan; Jayne Stephenson, who worked on Lancashire records; and Roger E. Nixon, who topped up my research at Kew. I must thank Sir

Hugh Verney and the Clayton House Trust for giving permission to reproduce those important Harry Calvert finds.

A further contingent gave freely of their expertise: John Montgomery at the RUSI Library; John Spencer; Gary Lind; William Spencer; Duncan Sutton; David Brown; Donald Graves; Scott Miskimon; Ron McGuigan; and James Collett-White. During my visit to the 23rd's southern battlefields Charles and Judy Baxter were fabulous hosts; Nancy Stewart, Diane Depew and Chris Bryce also gave generously of their time. Among that great band of living history enthusiasts in the States, Will Tatum, Jay Callaham, Robert Sulentic and Don Hagist gave great support.

In getting the job of writing done Peter Barron was very helpful allowing me leave from *Newsnight*, Jonathan Lloyd did his magic as my agent, as did Julian Loose and Henry Volans at Faber and Paula Turner. Behind the scenes, trying to talk the author out of his study and back into the twenty-first century were my beloved wife Hilary, daughters Isabelle and Madeleine and son Sol.

The March From Boston, 19 April 1775

Or the Anxious Mission of the 23rd Fusiliers

It was around 9 a.m. when the long column of redcoats snaking its way out of Boston crossed the Neck. The British were late and, in the business they had been ordered to do that day, an hour might make the difference between success and disaster.

Soon they were over the Neck and into the rebellious hinterland, leaving behind their base, a city almost surrounded by its watery moat where they had come to feel secure. They were plunging into a country where alarm bells rang, calling thousands of men to arms, ready to oppose the King's troops.

There were 1,200 soldiers in the British column. At its head, the brigade commander sat astride his horse. After him tramped two regiments of foot, a battalion of marines and, near the back, the 23rd Regiment, perhaps the most celebrated British corps on the American station, also known as the Royal Welch Fusiliers.

Lieutenant Frederick Mackenzie, adjutant of the 23rd, was not in the best of moods that morning. Orders to assemble the brigade at 7.30 a.m. had in one case been delivered to the wrong officer, resulting in the marines arriving one hour late. Mackenzie did things by the book, a middle-aged officer confined in low rank but with all the wisdom of thirty years' hard service. He knew how important the delay might prove, since they were being sent to support another British column that was already fifteen or sixteen miles away at a place called Concord, deep in territory controlled by their most ardent opponents.

The eight companies of Fusiliers marching beside Mackenzie that bright morning mustered around 350 men of all ranks. Two other

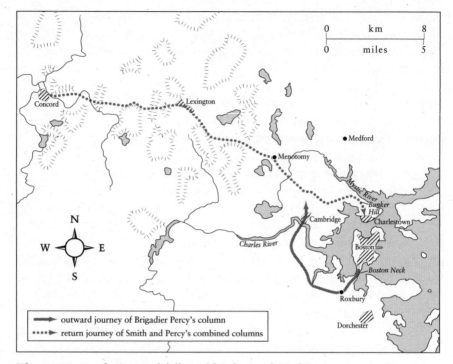

The route towards Concord followed by the 23rd Fusiliers

companies of the 23rd had left Boston the previous night on what was meant to be a secret mission. Mackenzie was already worrying that the preparations made to seize weapons from the rebels inland had been conducted so clumsily that the entire countryside would be alarmed.

Mackenzie's fears were confirmed as the redcoats marched through Roxbury, the first village on their route towards Concord, for he realised that 'few or no people were to be seen; and the houses were in general shut up'. Word had indeed been spread by the rebels of the impending British expedition to Concord, and the people of Massachusetts awaited the outcome with dread.

The soldiers passed white clapboard houses, pleasant groves of trees, duckponds and taverns. Their brigade commander, on a previous outing, altogether less fraught, had admired the landscape, believing that nature and hard work had produced something in New England that excelled even the work of England's most celebrated gardener: 'It has everywhere the appearance of a park finely laid out. Mr ["Capability"] Browne here would be useless.'

On this particular day, though, landmarks that had previously symbolised the bucolic idyll of this American scene took on a very different meaning. The many houses of worship dotted about the Puritan settlements were still except for those where a tolling bell signalled the alarm. Many preachers were that day far from their pulpits, out among the people stirring up rebellion. As for the village greens, more often the setting of peaceful assemblies, these had become the rallying points for militia companies. Farmers, mechanics or smiths arrived with hastily grabbed weapons, ready to put into action the drills and marksmanship they had spent months practising.

On the soldiers tramped, west to Brookline then turning north towards Cambridge. They crossed the Charles River without incident. Bridges were a source of concern to Earl Hugh Percy, the brigade commander. There had been several excursions into the countryside during the preceding months, for the British commander-in-chief wanted to improve his men's stamina while getting the rural people used to the sight of marching troops, so that they might be complacent when the day for fighting arrived. But would a battle be necessary, that 19 April?

Less than three weeks before, the Americans had brought two cannon to one of the spans across the same river as Percy's redcoats approached. For a few tense moments it had seemed as if they were prepared to massacre the soldiers as they were squeezed into that bottleneck. The rebels, though, had run off, leaving the loaded artillery pieces behind them. Percy knew as well that those seeking to thwart the King's troops might also pull up the planking on bridges.

The brigadier, the thirty-three-year-old heir to the dukedom of Northumberland, was a highly professional officer, widely respected within the Boston garrison. Some of those marching behind him that morning were of a hotter disposition. They believed that incidents like that with the loaded cannon in March showed that the colonists were full of talk but would not fight. Among the regimental officers and soldiers there were quite a few who believed that the British army would smash any vagabond militia the rebels could bring against them. 'Never did any nation so much deserve to be made an example of to future ages,' one angry young officer of Percy's brigade had written to his father, 'and never [was] any set of men more anxious to be employed on so laudable a work.'

This bitterness had arisen by the spring of 1775, because the army had been exposed to months of abuse and scorn. It took the form of seditious handbills, spitting or insults in the streets and the formation of militia or 'minutemen' companies in dozens of villages. On previous trips through the countryside, British soldiers observed these citizen soldiers armed, drilling and making ready to fight. Even six months earlier, in the autumn of 1774, Brigadier Percy had written to his father, 'This country is now in as open a state of rebellion as Scotland was in the year '45.'

While many soldiers favoured a Scottish solution to American disobedience – scourging the rebellion with fire and bayonet – such views did not hold sway in the higher command. By April 1775, however, even the moderates felt something had to be done. The smouldering tension around Boston had come to a head, as British generals ordered the seizure of rebel cannon in Concord.

Percy led his troops into the New England countryside with colours flying and bands playing. Whatever doubts or disagreement might lurk within the hearts of his officers, Percy wanted the brigade to make an imposing sight for the Americans. They knew they were being watched through shuttered windows or quiet orchards as they marched, so they pressed on proudly to the tune of 'Yankee Doodle', a favourite with the redcoats, complete with its lyrics ridiculing the colonists.

Some of the Fusiliers, the grenadier and light companies, had gone to Concord with special battalions of the army's picked troops. The main body of the regiment marched out to support them behind its two standards: the King's Colour, a union flag, snapping and dancing in the spring breeze, and the Colonel's Colour, with a union in one corner, but royal blue in its other three fourths and the Prince of Wales' feathers in the centre. The Fusiliers' allegiance was symbolised by these two flags – to their monarch naturally, and to the army in which their place was precisely fixed by the number, colour and badges on the Colonel's Colour.

The men following those flags understood that they were being asked to uphold the fine reputation that the 23rd had garnered during its first eighty-five years of service. Captain Lieutenant Thomas Mecan marched with the colonel's or senior company. An Irishman (these days his name would be usually written McCann), he was, like Mackenzie, a veteran of the Seven Years War that produced epic battles in Europe where the 23rd had burnished its reputation thirteen years earlier. Although the Irish Mecan was, at thirty-six years old, somewhat younger than the Scots Mackenzie (forty-four at this time), both men had endured long years in their lowly ranks, lacking the money to buy their way up the promotion ladder. They had aged in the service, but many of their rank and file were callow.

Robert Mason, beating out the signals of command on his drum, was just nineteen years old. If he had not been in action before, at least he had lived his entire life within the Fusiliers. He was 'a child of the regiment', having been born to a father within it and a mother who followed it. Most of Mason's short life indeed had been spent in uniform, for he had been just nine years old when taken on as a drummer boy.

Corporal Jeffrey Grimes eyed the ranks of his company, looking for the man who stepped out of place or might fail in his duty. Grimes had been in the regiment for less than five years but had been promoted just after the regiment arrived in America. His new rank had brought him higher pay and the right to wear the knotted woollen cord on his right shoulder that denoted a corporal's status. He was a keen soldier who kept his nose clean, and might look forward to further promotion – if he survived.

Not long after 1 p.m., fifteen or so miles into their march, a man driving a horse and chaise had stopped at its head, and Earl Percy peered in to see a seriously wounded young officer of the 4th Light Company, one of the men who had left Boston the previous night. From this casualty, the brigadier learnt that the fighting all of them had expected for so long was indeed under way, and that the King's forces were getting the worst of it.

At this moment, anyone in Percy's brigade who might have doubted that they were about to go into action was at last disabused. Mecan had tasted battle before and hungered for a chance to show his mettle again. Mackenzie was also a veteran, but his wife back in Boston was heavily pregnant with their third child. If the slender support of his lieutenant's pay was cut away, she might soon become destitute. Drummer Mason had grown up amid the tales of old soldiers; the moment in which he would see whether he was brave enough to join their company would soon be upon him. As for Corporal Grimes, the eyes of his superiors would be upon him, looking to see whether his rapid promotion would be justified in action.

The Fusiliers had entered an odyssey of war that would last eight years, carrying them thousands of miles through countless battles.

Some of the men who would play vital roles in the regiment's story were serving elsewhere that day. Others were just boys sitting by their hearths in England. As for Mackenzie, Mecan, Mason and Grimes, only two would survive, one would prosper and the other face disgrace.

The Royal Welch Fusiliers on the Eve of Revolution

Or Lieutenant Colonel Bernard's Troubled Family

Several weeks before the regiment marched out of Boston on its vital mission, the 23rd had marked one of the most hallowed dates in its calendar.

The delights awaiting those who filed into the dining room on 1 March 1775 were more than anyone on foreign service had a right to expect. The table groaned with delicacies, fine wines as well as liquor flowed freely, and the band accompanied the hubbub of conversation with pleasant airs. It was the custom of the Royal Welch Fusiliers to mark the anniversary of Wales's patron saint with a dinner fit for any person of rank or nobility.

Among the guests that evening in Boston were General Thomas Gage, commander-in-chief in America, Brigadier the Earl Percy and several other gentlemen of quality, accompanied by their secretaries or staff. The seventeen guests were ably hosted by twenty-one officers of the Royal Welch Fusiliers who were present and who had subscribed the cost of the event from their meagre pay. Those who partook of the regiment's hospitality were rarely disappointed. Indeed the officers of the regiment had so impressed one prominent New Yorker (the regiment had stayed one year in that city after being sent to America) that he enthusiastically recommended them to a friend in Boston: 'As respectable a corps of gentlemen as are to be found in the uniform of any crowned head upon earth. You may depend upon their integrity. They have not left the least unfavourable impression behind them, and their departure is more regretted than that of any officers who ever garrisoned our city.'

At the head of the table sat the lieutenant colonel, Benjamin Bernard, a pleasing embodiment of the 23rd's traditions and service. His father John has been wounded while leading a company of fusiliers during the celebrated battle of Fontenoy, fighting the French thirty years before. The commanding officer himself had served his sovereign on the field of a victory even more hallowed in the regiment: Minden, where a small force of redcoats fighting under Allied command in Germany on 1 August 1759 had defeated thousands of Frenchmen. At the other end of the table, the lieutenant colonel could spy his own son, also called Benjamin, a second lieutenant barely twenty years old. Thus three generations of the Bernard family had escaped the poorer fringes of the Anglo-Irish gentry, served their King and graced the annals of the 23rd.

Half of the officers dining that night in Boston were able to boast that they were Minden men. Even those who were not proudly called the regiment 'Old Mindonians'. A couple still bore the scars of wounds that they had received on that celebrated field of the Seven Years War where the British line had repulsed the flower of the French army. During the blaze of musketry 218 of the Royal Welch Fusiliers had been killed or wounded, but they had not buckled.

The wars of 1756–63 had been global, producing plenty of epic feats in America too, not least the capture of Quebec by General Wolfe. This separate theatre had been given its own name – the French and Indian Wars – but many people in Boston or New York had imbibed the military prejudice that events in Europe, involving the greatest professional armies of the epoch, represented a higher form of soldiering. So even Americans, particularly those sympathetic to the King, were well aware of the distinction of Minden – for the 23rd was the only one of the six regiments that gained laurels on that German field serving in the colony of Massachusetts. One American newspaper had even published a verse extolling the Royal Welch's valour in that faraway battle:

> Such ease and expertise these Fusileers shew,
> You'd think each man a Fusileer born;
> Their *manoeuvres* so just, and their fire so true,
> Wou'd delight you 'till evening from morn.
> Twice ten thousand Gauls formed in battle array,
> Would not dare two such regiments come near.

Some mystique still attached even to the title 'fusiliers' that had been given to troops chosen decades earlier to carry an advanced firearm, the *fusil*, even though they had long since lugged muskets like any other regiment. Those who looked to the army to quash any rebellion therefore expected much from the 23rd. They saw them as a picked regiment, as deadly on the field as their officers were charming in the drawing room.

When the meal was finished, the table was cleared and bumpers charged for the first toast of the evening, to the Prince of Wales. The order in which these tributes were drunk was prescribed by custom, but once the boozing started it could go on for hours and it was not uncommon for more than twenty toasts to be drunk.

A visitor gazing around the table that evening at ruddy-cheeked officers imbibing so diligently for their country could have been forgiven for thinking that the gentlemen of the Royal Welch Fusiliers were a picture of contentment. But beneath the superficial cheer, all was not well. Indeed, these officers were, for the most part, desperate to quit their stations as soon as possible. Some of them had grown old in their lowly ranks and yearned for promotion, hoping that they would gain it in the American war they now all expected. Others wanted nothing to do with such a fight.

One captain had told all and sundry before they sailed from England two years earlier that 'nothing should induce him to go to America'. The exigencies of the service had left him with no choice. The captain commanding the regiment's grenadiers was another malcontent who would reveal soon enough his desire to get out of that country.

There were many officers gathered around that Saint David's Day table who, by contrast, were quite ready to do their duty against the rebels. Even among them, though, there were strongly diverging views about what methods might be used to subdue the sedition that they had witnessed during preceding months. These differences were exacerbated by the officers' own political differences, for the schism between Whig and Tory ran deep within the army. It was matters of royal power and religious toleration that defined this divide among Britons, and increasingly also their crisis with the colonists.

One of the fusiliers at that dinner, Lieutenant Richard Williams, thought that the rebels calling themselves Whigs 'quite reverses our characters', implying a sympathy with those back in Britain who would keep the king in check by non-violent means. Indeed, Williams believed very few of the things that American 'Whigs' claimed. His intolerance for cant was clear in his journal, when he observed that Boston boasted 'no such thing as a play house, they were too puritanical a set to admit of such lewd diversions, tho' perhaps no town of this size could turn out more whores than this could'.

Williams considered the situation that was emerging in Boston to be 'civil war'. The danger – religious-based anti-monarchism – had previously been exported from Britain but now once more endangered the mother country. An officer in another regiment wrote home candidly confessing his mixed feelings about the impending campaign: 'Though I must confess I should like to try what stuff I am made of, yet I would rather the trial be with others than these poor fellows of kindred blood.' In the coffee house or across the Fusiliers' mess table these relatively liberal views would have received support from some, like Captain Robert Donkin (the veteran officer commanding the 23rd's Light Company), but brought a lively response from others.

Major Henry Blunt, Lieutenant Colonel Bernard's second in command, took a tougher line. He believed settlement in America had created a different nation, writing home to one friend, 'These people, most of them originally Scotch or Irish, have united in marriage with French, Germans and Dutch and from them have sprung the high-spirited race that boast so much of British Blood and British Liberty, and who have had the folly and impudence to talk of *chastising* Great Britain.' The Major noted bitterly that 'man as well as every thing else transplanted here degenerates'.

This debate, about whether the Americans were 'brothers' or not would continue for years to come. It would inform British views about whether to accept or fight the colonists' movement towards independence, as well as their opinions on the degree of force that might be used to suppress it.

All of those celebrating that 1 March 1775 were approaching the moment when they would have to decide whether they were ready to fight. As if the looming battle against those who shared their language was not enough, Lieutenant Colonel Bernard's regiment also contained many older officers who were anxious to leave.

Captain Grey Grove, who had a reputation as a drunken sot, was coming up to thirteen years in that rank and was embittered by the promotion of younger men; and three other captains had been petitioning unsuccessfully for removal to a staff job. One of those letter writers,

Captain Robert Donkin, the regimental savant keen on quoting Plutarch and Caesar, was, after years of petitioning his superiors, about to be rewarded by removal to the staff of General Gage. Of the 23rd's seven captains, indeed, only the youngest was reckoned by his mess-mates to be cheerful about his duty. The other officer who did a captain's job, Thomas Mecan, was not present at that dinner. Mecan could doubtless have raised a glass to Saint David along with the best of Irishmen, but that night some officers of his rank were required to do duty in the garrison, and, in a telling portent of what was to come, Mecan showed by doing this duty that he was never a man to shirk his responsibility. Mecan indeed was married to the job for the soldier's life and meagre pay had never allowed him to find a wife. Mecan's odd-sounding title, 'captain lieutenant', indicated that he still received a lieutenant's money while commanding a company.

The officers who ran the 23rd, its captain lieutenant, seven full cap-tains, major and lieutenant colonel, had, excepting the most recently promoted captain, grown old in their rank. In an age when a gifted and well-connected officer could aspire to a lieutenant colonelcy by the age of twenty-five, Bernard and Grove were well into their forties and other captains in their late thirties. Even some of the subalterns present that evening cut the forlorn figure of middle-aged men with grown-up children living on the pittance of a lieutenant's pay – Frederick Mackenzie, the adjutant, being only the most shocking example, having served in this lowly rank for nearly half of his forty-four years.

Those men, who knocked back toast after toast, understood that the keys to promotion were money and patronage. None of them was heir to a title, although some were only one or two degrees removed from the aristocracy by family connection. Quite a number, like Bernard himself, were the sons of officers, and lacked money. Those who raced up the army in this epoch were those who combined cash with 'assisting friends'. One or two of the officers could call on considerable reserves of family cash, but were not well connected. Donkin, on the other hand, had some powerful friends, but lacked the money for his next step of rank. Lieutenant Colonel Bernard backed Donkin's claim for advancement, and was also favourably disposed towards William Blakeney (the grenadier company commander) – the three men forming an Anglo-Irish bloc in the regiment – but he had shown himself to have limited influence in the higher reaches of the army.

Several of the officers partaking of that Saint David's Day feast not only doubted that their pretensions to promotion were about to be gratified, but suspected instead that the coming of war would bring an influx of wealthy young bloods who had sidestepped the tedium of garrison service but would be spoiling for the opportunity of distinction in battle. Good manners and a sense of their own lowly status would have prevented these officers making their case directly to General Gage over dinner, but just three days later captains Grove and Blakeney joined with ten other officers in sending their commander-in-chief an impassioned letter.

'Many young officers lately acquired the rank of major by purchase,' the old captains complained, adding that others who had only recently become captains 'are likely soon to succeed to the same preferments'. Could not the general do something about their claims for promotion after such long service? Another hard-done-by captain who had written to the general complained that 'nothing is more mortifying to an old soldier, than to be commanded by a number of inexperienced young boys (which is often the case on our service)'. Gage, it would transpire during the following weeks, did nothing to address the concerns of these old warriors. Instead the eighteenth-century promotion bazaar would get under way in earnest with the first shots of war, and the fears of the 'hard bargains' would prove justified, for it would be a case of every man for himself.

As for the wives and children of those officers who risked life and limb in the name of their sovereign and parliament, they were not present that evening. Across Boston, in the candlelit parlours of modest rented rooms, Major Blunt's Molly or Captain Blakeney's Sarah found their own suppers. Lieutenant Mackenzie's wife, Nancy, 'Mrs Mac' as he affectionately called her, was expecting a late addition to their family. Dozens of soldiers' wives too awaited the expected campaign. Any fears they may have stifled – that they would soon be called upon to wash their husbands' wounds as well as their shirts, and to follow the drum, acting as the army's unpaid auxiliaries – were about to be realised.

The Saint David's Day dinner followed its ritual late into the night. The spurs of Toby Purcell, the second in command who had stepped into action when his commander was killed during the Irish campaign of the Boyne back in 1690, were toasted, and honours done to Shenkin ap Rice, by legend a simple soldier of the regiment.

Matters came to a noisy and inebriated climax when the regimental goat, its mascot, decorated with appropriate garlands, was brought into the dining room, led by the drum major and with a drummer boy mounted, rather unsteadily, on his back. It was the drum major's solemn task to lead this unlikely pair three times around the table, while the room resounded to the acclamations of the company. Alas, in 1775 he did not make it. One of those present recorded that 'the animal gave such a spring from the floor, that he dropped the rider upon the table, and then bouncing over the heads of some officers, he ran to the barracks'. Some of the ensemble spilled out into the cool New England night hallooing and cheering the goat, passers-by joining in. The officers of the 23rd had marked their special day and retired to the comatose sleep of over-indulgence, while those who despised the army's presence in Boston prepared their rebellion.

The congregation that filled the pews five days later on the sunny spring morning of Sunday, 6 March 1775, at the Old South Meeting House close by General Gage's quarters was, to put it mildly, one of a more sober and serious disposition than that which had honoured Saint David. Many of the most articulate advocates of resistance to British power were there to hear the annual oration in com-memoration of a confrontation five years earlier in which five locals had been killed by redcoats. This sad event had been dubbed the 'Boston Massacre' by enemies of the British Ministry or government.

Although the great majority of those attending this service were clad in their Sunday best, there were red coats too visible in the hall. The last ties of civility had not yet been cut between the King's servants and their enemies, and indeed some of the officers, including Frederick Mackenzie, who had come to this puritan place of worship were the self-same men who had participated in the excess and hilarity of 1 March. These officers and their more ardent foes regarded one another with suspicion and dislike, expecting a riot might break out at any moment. Many concealed cudgels and sticks.

Joseph Warren, a noted Presbyterian minister and friend of Liberty, went to the pulpit. He began by reminding the congregation that their ancestors had come to America to escape persecution:

Our fathers having nobly resolved never to wear the yoke of despotism, and seeing the European world, through insolence and cowardice, falling a prey to tyranny, bravely threw themselves upon the bosom of the ocean, determined to find freedom or perish in the glorious attempt.

[13]

Outlining the colonists' grievances against ministers in London, Dr Warren excoriated them for sending regiments to enforce their decrees on America, adding that 'standing armies always endanger the liberty of the subject'. Warren could not openly call for revolt, for he must have suspected that some of those red-coated gentlemen were there simply to goad him into words that might see him clapped in jail charged with treason. Similarly the officers suspected that Warren might taunt them, in Mackenzie's words, 'to act improperly, and strike or lay hands on some of the party, which would have been the signal for a battle. It is certain both sides were ripe for it.' Mackenzie was no fool though, far from it: he impressed superiors with his intelligence. His appearance also – strong brow, clear blue eyes, a beak of a nose – reinforced the sense of an experienced man who would not easily succumb to provocation.

Some of Warren's statements produced hisses from the officers. As they looked around they could see John Hancock, president of the Congress challenging British power, and Samuel Adams, regarded by many of the officers as an uncouth, corrupt rabble-rouser, and certainly someone who longed for the revolt to begin. As Warren came to his peroration, he called for a new equality in the relationship between Britain and the American colonies, and his audience heard him come as close as he dared to publicly advocating rebellion:

if these pacifick measures are ineffectual; and it appears the only way to safety is through fields of blood, I know you will not turn your faces from your foes, but will undauntedly press forward until tyranny is trodden under foot.

Warren stepped down, having somehow harangued his divided audience without the expected riot. Sam Adams stood up and thanked him for the speech before proposing a vote on who should deliver the 1776 oration commemorating the 'Bloody Massacre'. At this, several British officers signalled their disgust at this language by shouting 'Fie!' A general commotion ensued, as some of the congregation could hear the fifes and drums of a regiment marching nearby and thought the officers inside had called out 'Fire!'

One British officer approached Adams to remonstrate that the captain commanding the soldiers in 1770 had been tried and acquitted. Adams tried to brush him off by saying he would settle the matter with General Gage. 'You and I must settle it first,' replied the determined redcoat, and at this moment violence might easily have broken out. Adams, however, backed down and made his way out of the Meeting House. People dispersed and, for a matter of weeks at least, the sword remained sheathed.

Even during these fateful weeks, officers like Earl Percy remained on good terms with men such as Adams and Hancock, sharing dinner with them sometimes. It may be that they hoped to play upon the earl's political sympathies, for they knew that, as Member of Parliament for Westminster, he had aligned himself with the Whig opposition that questioned the Ministry's policy of sending troops to enforce the British writ in America.

If the Select Men – the colonists' senior representatives at Boston – hoped that calling themselves Whigs and allying themselves with those who wanted to the limit the King's powers in Britain or Ireland would help them divide the army and win their argument, they were mistaken. While it is true that quite a few officers in Boston in 1775 might have considered themselves, like Earl Percy, to be Whigs, they did not feel they had anything in common with those whom Dr Warren urged into 'fields of blood'. Indeed, Percy's familiarity with the likes of Warren, Hancock and Adams produced contempt for them, as he wrote home in blistering fashion: 'The people here are a set of sly, artful, hypocritical rascals, cruel, and cowards. I must own I cannot but despise them completely.' Indeed a suspicion of dishonesty on the part of the Americans tainted the views of many a British officer who might otherwise have been sympathetic.

Dr Warren had, during his oration on the 6 March, insisted that 'an independence of Great Britain is not our aim'. Nonsense, thought Lieutenant Williams of the 23rd, an educated young officer with a lively interest in history who had toured Europe and painted well with watercolours in quieter moments. He believed the very origins of the Massachusetts colony, as a haven for religious zealots who had disturbed the peace of England in the seventeenth century, meant that 'these people have not in the least deviated from the steps of their ancestors, always grumbling and unwilling to acknowledge the authority of any power but what originated among them. They certainly have long looked forward to the day of independency.'

One thing, though, could be divined clearly from Dr Warren's words or those of his foes in British uniform. Violent language and vigorous debate would define the coming conflict because the protagonists were united by a common tongue. It would be a war of words from the outset, one of unending argument between those within each camp as well as continuous attempts to convince those who tried to take a middle way.

In March 1775 Gage's view about dealing with the increasing verbal violence of the King's foes prevailed. The commander-in-chief pursued a policy of trying to persuade the colonists even as some prepared for armed rebellion. Earl Percy and many other officers felt that Gage's approach simply emboldened the Americans to go further. Both sides struggled to convince the uncommitted by appearing righteous. Even a lowly, if shrewd, officer like Lieutenant Mackenzie had understood the importance of not striking the first blow on that Sunday at the Meeting House.

Many of the King's men believed that the colonists, like Sam Adams on 6 March, would walk away from a fight if it was offered to them. Surely the martial prowess of the British army would still have the power to intimidate?

If the officers of the 23rd were uneasy about the coming fight, what about the other ranks? Most days the Fusiliers could be seen marching about the cobbled streets, returning from some work detail or going out to the quays to practise shooting at floating casks.

The Fusiliers defied easy generalisations. Few were Welsh, despite the regiment's title, which derived from the patronage of the Prince of Wales. The bulk, something like three-quarters, were English and half of them were in their twenties. Although largely illiterate, with many labourers skimmed from the land, there were a good many who had formerly had trades. A small number, indeed, were highly intelligent men capable of scaling the ranks to become serjeant major or even follow the example of Richard Baily, a former ranker who served as a lieutenant in their regiment.

Why had they joined? 'My chief intention', wrote one soldier, 'being to travel and traverse the seas occasioned my inlisting.' Sometimes, a row or debt triggered the decision to join. One seventeen-year-old who later matured into a serjeant in the 23rd lost money gambling with dissolute friends and 'afraid to return and tell my father of my indiscretions . . . I shrank from my best hope, parental admonition, and formed the resolution of entering for a soldier.' Men who joined on impulse or when cornered drunk by the recruiting party at a tavern often bitterly regretted their decision. When put on transports for America, some tried to escape or even leapt to their deaths in the sea, a shocking sight that, thankfully, had not afflicted the 23rd when it left Plymouth in 1773.

Scores of new recruits had been thrown into the ranks prior to the regiment's sailing to America. The rank and file were certainly a more callow bunch than the officers. Fewer than one quarter of them had served long enough to be 'Minden men'.

Since arriving on those shores two years earlier, two dozen soldiers of the Royal Welch had absconded. In one or two cases, it had been a matter of drink, no more, and they had returned, receiving lenient treatment from Colonel Bernard. A somewhat larger crop had gone when the regiment was ordered from New York to Boston. Many old campaigners regarded this as normal, since soldiers residing in a large city often lost their hearts to local girls from whom some could not bear to be parted. Those intent on desertion often went with a messmate or friend from another company.

Thomas Watson and Jacob Jones, for example, had disappeared from Boston together on 7 March. Private Watson was a ladies' man who had struck up a relationship with a woman in New York.

In other cases, though, there were motivations that would have caused officers more disquiet. The rebels were trying to seduce soldiers into breaking their oaths, offering them money for their muskets and material rewards if they would join the cause of Liberty.

William Hewitt, who deserted the Fusiliers with another man on 17 March, had made his way to the nearby village of Ipswich in New Hampshire. Hewitt was no boy, thrown into uniform when the 23rd got its orders for America; rather he had been serving in the regiment for nearly nine years, prior to which he had worked for a time as an apprentice weaver in his native Lancashire, and was literate. Once in Ipswich, he enlisted in Captain Ezra Town's militia company, ready to fight his former comrades.

Such sympathies were unusual in Gage's army, but definitely motivated some. One Irish soldier who subsequently deserted the 49th, wrote that he had tried to abscond as soon as he got to Boston, 'finding they were striving to throw off the yoke under which my native country – sunk for many years – induced me to share the same freedom that America strive for'. Irish soldiers were to prove particularly susceptible to the appeals of American Whigs, but fortunately for the 23rd the number in its ranks formed a small minority. The more common reasons for desertion were the entreaties of a woman, arguments with messmates or a feeling of injustice resulting from some punishment.

When a private of the 52nd had been caught trying to desert on 3 March, he had been sentenced to death by general court martial – the means of dealing with serious offences among soldiers, including all capital ones – on the 9th but pardoned five days later. Despite the draconian statutes embodied in the Articles of War and Mutiny Act, General Gage rarely allowed executions. The commander-in-chief's apparent unwillingness to use capital punishment worried many officers. 'The lenity shown', wrote Mackenzie in his journal, 'has not had the effect the General expected, as some soldiers have deserted since that event.'

As the rebellion gathered pace in America, harsh punishment was out of fashion in the British army. Gage's judge advocate, the officer who ran his courts martial, stated, 'I disapprove of making capital punishments too familiar . . . when great punishments are inflicted only for great crimes, it will be the more easy to reform abuses.' Too frequent a use of the gallows, he argued, would lead to officers concealing crimes in order to save both lives and regimental reputation. The judge advocate also thought that the lash should be 'sparingly made use of'. The alternative for drunkenness, insolence and other non-capital offences could be fines, extra duty, spells in the 'black hole' and reduction to the ranks for serjeants or corporals.

Lieutenant Colonel Bernard's instincts were similar to those of General Gage and his judge advocate; he was known to believe in showing mercy towards miscreant Fusiliers. The frequent floggings with hundreds of lashes known in his father's time of service were a rarity in Boston. Apart from anything else, those in command on the American station knew that it was all too easy for a man who considered himself hard done by to desert.

For many officers, Gage's softness towards the army's criminals was all of a part with his treatment of the rebels; they thought their commander-in-chief lax and ineffectual. They wanted to be able to punish their men properly in order to strengthen discipline; there was a need for forthright leadership from General Gage; most of all they wanted to show toughness to the colonists. On previous marches into the countryside the militia had run away upon the appearance of the King's troops, convincing many that the rebellion could be nipped in the bud. These illusions were exploded at Lexington and Concord on 19 April.

The Fight at Lexington and Concord

Or Adjutant Mackenzie's Observations on American Warfare

The march of Earl Percy's brigade had barely begun as redcoats of Major John Pitcairn's battalion deployed at the trot on Lexington Green. The late departure of that relief force meant that the 700 men of the British flank battalions sent out from Boston the previous night would have to face that morning's crisis on their own. In their path were American militia of Captain Parker's company. Like many of the country people of Massachusetts they had talked for months of confronting the government.

Faced that morning with the sight of picked troops moving swiftly into battle order, many of the Americans were no longer quite so sure. The odds were not good either; more than 300 British soldiers facing 130 local volunteers, men who had tilled the soil or tended the forge until a few hours earlier.

As the regulars formed, Major Pitcairn came forward on his horse and bellowed out to the armed villagers in front of him, 'Disperse! Disperse you damned rebels!' Captain Parker decided that discretion was the better part of valour. The command was given to file off the green.

Officers on both sides had given absolute orders to their men not to open fire first. At Lexington, early that morning of 19 April 1775, it seemed for a moment that they would be obeyed and civil war averted. Pitcairn signalled his soldiers to move forward and disarm the locals.

The sight though of the Americans lowering their weapons and moving off touched some nerve of contempt among the British soldiers. For months the local people had abused and taunted them.

Where was their courage now, when it came to a fight? Instead of a deliberate, orderly walk forward, many redcoats started shouting and cheering, running towards the Americans with fixed bayonets. Facing this onslaught, one or two of those villagers opened fire.

It took just a few moments for the British response. Without orders from Pitcairn, one of the formed British companies levelled its weapons and let fly a crashing volley. Several villagers went down. There were a few straggling shots in reply, one wounded a redcoat in the leg, another hit Pitcairn's horse, but within moments bonds of military discipline dissolved and the British soldiers were careering in all directions, chasing after the minutemen as they fled through gardens and groves, desperate to save their lives.

Colonel Francis Smith, Pitcairn's superior in charge of the 700 or so British troops sent out from Boston the previous night, heard the shots and came running to the head of the column. 'Finding the Rebels scamping off (except those shut up in houses),' the colonel wrote several weeks later, 'I endeavoured to the utmost to stop all further firing, which in a short time I effected.' Smith, an infantry officer in his early fifties, was thought of as a relic by many, but had the benefit of long service in America and thus a knowledge of its people.

The cooler-headed among the British officers and serjeants then began scouring the fields and farmsteads, collecting up their men. 'We then formed on the Common, but with some difficulty,' one young lieutenant noted, 'the men were so wild they could hear no orders.' Some of the soldiers were shouting and pointing out buildings which they said were being used by the rebels to fire at them. Colonel Smith dreaded what might happen if his outraged troops entered Lexington's homes or its Meeting House, 'knowing if the houses were once broke into, none within could well be saved'. Strict instructions were issued to block the men, and they were successfully rallied under the colonel's eye.

Some sort of regularity had been restored, but several Americans had been killed and the remainder of Captain Parker's company had scattered into the country, carrying breathless reports of the bloodshed to neighbouring villages. What to do? Colonel Smith had his orders, which were to push on to the village of Concord, a couple of miles further on, and destroy some cannon and other military supplies gathered there by the rebels.

After what had happened in Lexington, he was determined to press ahead in a disciplined formation. Marching towards Concord, the road was commanded to the right by some ridges. Setting off once more, Smith used his light infantry, Pitcairn's men, trotting along the high ground to deny it to the enemy and protect his right flank. He marched meanwhile along the road at the head of his grenadiers, tall men in bearskin caps who were, by repute, the steadiest troops of the British regiments in Boston.

A couple of shots were fired at the British but none returned, Colonel Smith noting with satisfaction that his troops moved on Concord 'with as much good order as ever troops observed in Britain, or any friendly country'.

All the time, though, the American militia was gathering. Men from Acton, Bedford and Lincoln set off to join their brethren in the Concord companies. Some watched from heights, as the British column snaked through the New England farmland. Others ran along to one side or other of it, puffing away, glimpsing the redcoats occasionally between the trees or clapboard houses.

The alarm bell had already tolled in Concord, summoning men to arms, when some militia marched into the village, fifes and drums playing loudly, on the road from Lexington just a few minutes ahead of the enemy.

It was around 10 a.m. when Colonel Smith's advance guard entered the sprawling township that was their objective. Their enemies for the moment left them to it, gathering by the hundreds on nearby slopes of Punkatasset Hill as Colonel Smith broke the British force into parts. The village was bounded on several sides by waterways, most importantly, the Concord River to the north and west. While searches were carried out, this stream would form a natural barrier against any attack by the colonists, so Smith deployed his men accordingly. Each of his battalions – grenadiers and light infantry – was formed of companies picked from the regiments stationed in Boston. They were meant to be the best men, taken from their parent regiments and formed into combined battalions for special tasks. After their wild behaviour in Lexington, Smith might have doubted their reliability, but he had no choice but to break the light infantry battalion into several smaller parties.

Three companies from Pitcairn's battalion (an impressive-sounding total, but actually only around a hundred men in these peacetime establishment regiments) were sent to the south bridge over the Concord, a similar detachment to the north bridge, and a third group of light infantry continued beyond that crossing to the home of the local colonel of militia. This last detachment contained the Light Company of the 23rd Fusiliers. Their captain was not with them that day, so the Fusiliers and others were placed under Captain Parsons of the 10th Regiment. His small force moved more than one mile beyond the north bridge, and became the farthest-flung element of Smith's force, having gone deepest into enemy country, as thousands of armed men converged around the district.

In the village itself meanwhile the grenadiers set about searching houses. Some of the musket balls and cannon shot had been dumped hours before in a pond by locals, because Colonel Smith's arrival came as no surprise to those who led the rebellion. Other items, like the cannon themselves, could not be easily concealed or indeed removed. So once found, British soldiers smashed the trunnions off those three artillery pieces, making it impossible to mount and therefore use them. To put the matter beyond doubt, they also set fire to the wooden gun carriages themselves.

There was symbolic violence too, directed in this case towards Concord's Liberty Pole and the flag that fluttered from it. These had appeared in scores or even hundreds of settlements across the Thirteen Colonies of America, they were manifestations of the colonists' desire to decide on their own affairs, free of interference by the King's faraway ministers and of their desire to throw off 'taxation without representation'. A few short minutes with an axe brought down the Liberty Pole in Concord.

While barging through the Town House, one of the village's principal structures, some of the soldiers had started a fire. It took hold quickly, sending a column of smoke into the sky. Another plume snaked its way up from near the south bridge, where the British had fired the wooden gun carriages. Colonel Smith hastened towards the burning building. His soldiers joked that the old colonel was too heavy a man to get anywhere quickly. As the flames licked around the windows of the wooden Town House, thousands of militia saw the smoke. Smith's 700 men were heavily outnumbered, and where was Percy's brigade? They had failed to make an appearance.

Among the companies watching from the nearby Punkatasset Hill the word went around that 'the British were burning the town'. They could not stand idly while the brutal arm of the Ministry in London destroyed their homes.

Down below, Smith organised a line of soldiers to pass buckets of water, trying to staunch the flames. He would later claim to have saved much of Concord from being consumed by fire, but no matter, the locals had drawn their own conclusions. A force of around 500 Americans moved down the hill towards the Light Infantry guarding the north bridge. About sixty or seventy light infantry had been posted on the far side of that bridge, but, faced with hundreds of advancing Americans, they ran back across the span and fell in behind another company that had remained on the Concord side.

The hot flush of fear now carried off the judgement of the British officer at the north bridge. His foes had reached the other end of the span, cutting off the three companies sent beyond it with Captain Parsons. The militia took the wooden construction without a shot, for they too were under strict orders not to fire first and had gained their success simply by marching down the hill. It was the British commander who ordered his men to open up, and as the rebels returned this firing with interest, the two companies that had run back across the bridge moments earlier were unable to shoot, because their comrades were in the way. The superior enemy fire began cutting down redcoats, bowling them over with a gasp or a scream. Within moments four of the eight British officers at the bridge were hit, and three men were killed. The light infantry began running away.

With crackling of musketry audible for miles around, Captain Parsons abandoned his own search and hastened towards the bridge, finding hundreds of rebels between himself and the rest of Colonel Smith's force. They were cut off. As for the weighty warrior himself, he was on the other side of the Concord River, leading reinforcements towards the scene of the firing.

Fortunately for Captain Parsons's detachment, there is no monopoly on stupidity in war, and the militia who were in a position to block his retreat to the north bridge simply fell back and watched instead. One young officer with the British column noted in his journal that their enemy 'let Capt. Parsons with his three companies return and never attacked us; they had taken up some of the planks of the bridge, but we got over'.

With the British troops once again forming a single body in Concord, and the colonel's original orders discharged to the best of his ability, it was time to leave. They had been in that village for something like four hours, and their enemy had not been sitting idle. The British had seen for themselves the enemy militia converging on them, but other reports were gabbled among the frightened soldiers: of a wounded redcoat near the north bridge scalped by the Americans (bludgeoned it would transpire later by a boy with an axe). Outrage ran through the ranks, an emotion that would undermine what remained of their discipline and therefore success of what they had yet to do.

Smith intended to take his men the two miles back to Lexington in much the same formation as they had come up: grenadiers in the centre, on the road, with strong parties of light infantry covering his flanks. But within a few hundred yards of the column setting off, at a bend on the road called Merriam's Corner, it became obvious that the return would not resemble their orderly outward journey in any way. They would be fighting for their very survival.

More than 1,000 rebels were waiting. They had no intention of forming line, by the European drill book. 'They hardly ever fired but under cover of a stone wall, from behind a tree, or out of a house', noted one British officer, 'and the moment they had fired they lay down out of sight until they had loaded again.' Marching through the hail of whizzing, cracking balls at Merriam's Corner, a few men fell but the column pressed on.

The light infantry, running along the hilltops and engaging the rebels behind their cover, were soon nearly spent. 'We at first kept our order and returned their fire as hot as we received it, but when we arrived within a mile of Lexington, our ammunition began to fail,' wrote one officer, 'and the light companies were so fatigued with flanking they were scarcely able to act.'

A dread realisation spread through Colonel Smith's force. If they fired and used most of their cartridges and exhausted themselves in the first mile or two of their journey, how could they possibly make it the fifteen further miles back to Boston? They felt they were beyond salvation. 'We had been flattered ever since the morning with expectations of the British brigade coming out, but at this time had given up all hopes of it, as it was so late,' wrote one of Smith's force.

Panic was running through the light infantry: 'We began to run rather than retreat in order', wrote one British subaltern, another confessing it was a 'critical situation'. Reaching Lexington Green once more, several officers from the light battalion got ahead of their men and formed a little line, preparing to confront them. The captains and lieutenants turned about to face the redcoats running towards them, 'and presented their bayonets and told the men that if they advanced they should die'. Even this desperate expedient did not restore the order of a properly formed line, although it checked the headlong rush of Pitcairn's mob. At this moment of despair, deliverance appeared on the ridge just beyond Lexington.

For on the high ground leading elements of Percy's brigade, marching out from Boston, had finally appeared.

Lieutenant Frederick Mackenzie of the 23rd described the practised ease with which 'we were ordered to form the line, which was immediately done by extending on each side of the road'. But the New England landscape of meadows, fences and trees was no parade ground, and Mackenzie soon noted, 'by reason of the stone walls and other obstacles, [the line] was not formed in so regular a manner as it should have been'.

Percy himself was under no illusions about what he saw unfolding around Lexington, as soldiers from Smith's column fled up the road towards him. Late he may have been, but, as Percy would write to his father, the duke, 'I had the happiness, however, of saving them from inevitable destruction.' It was about 2.30 p.m.

Some of the exhausted light infantry and grenadiers dropped to the ground gasping for breath, others glugged water from their canteens or looked to the reinforcements to refill their empty cartridge pouches. While Smith's men were brought back into some kind of order, the chorus of muskets or sporting guns carried by the minutemen and militia companies resumed once more, the enemy was swarming around them. Some casualties from the fighting at Lexington had been brought on commandeered wagons or horses, but several had been left behind.

The Fusiliers, formed according to the regulation, presented their muskets and fired some big, ripping, volleys into the undergrowth, trying to nail their skulking enemy. 'Our men threw away their fire very inconsiderately,' thought Mackenzie, 'and without being certain of its effect.' Whatever training these soldiers had received, it had been in levelling and firing their weapons on the words of command, not choosing their moment against fleeting targets. Most of them, furthermore, had not been in action before.

In the European mode of warfare one line of infantry gave fire to another at close range, sometimes as little as forty or fifty yards, much like ships pummelling one another with broadsides. At Lexington, the enemy were not so considerate as to form shoulder to shoulder, right in front of the Fusiliers, in such a way that would have allowed even the most mediocre shot a chance of finding a target. So hundreds of musket balls, produced with billows of smoke, did little damage to the Americans.

Percy had brought with him two cannon, six-pounders, and these were now fired at the rebels. This bought the British some moments of peace, less by the effect of the ball than by the panic caused by the shocking, unexpected, boom of artillery. Seeing that some of the buildings saved by Smith that morning were being used by sharpshooters, Percy gave orders for them to be torched and flames soon began consuming them.

About an hour after arriving in Lexington, he issued orders for the march back to Boston. Smith's men would take the lead, flankers would be sent out from the fresh battalions to surprise those lying in wait along the road, and the Fusiliers would bring up the rear. The whole force was ordered to move away from the village slightly before the march got under way.

'We immediately lined the walls and other cover in our front with some marksmen,' wrote Mackenzie, who as adjutant was the 23rd's drill master, watching the Fusiliers with professional satisfaction as they 'retired from the right of companies by files to the high ground a small distance to our rear, where we again formed in line'. This elaborate piece of military choreography saw each of the regiment's line of eight companies falling back simultaneously from one point to another.

Once the new line was formed, the regiment's commanders went along it, checking its arrangement. Captain Lieutenant Mecan watched them deploying with a practised eye. Drummer Mason beat out the signals of command and Corporal Grimes would have been ready to correct any man who stepped out of place.

By the time the head of Earl Percy's brigade began its march, though, the men of the 23rd were simply intent on living through that day. It took about half an hour, one regiment falling in behind the other on the road, before their turn came to join the rear. All the time, while the 23rd waited, they spotted rebels moving through the undergrowth, trying to follow the column and get around their flanks. Finally they were moving too.

As they marched along, the crackling of musketry moved with them.

Percy pushed his soldiers 'as fast as good order and not blowing the men would allow'. But he noticed, all around, the rebels followed them 'like a moving circle'.

Percy's flank guards tramped along, cresting the higher ground or crashing through the farmyards on each side of the main column. This precaution paid dividends in many places, surprising the New Englanders, looking one way as they awaited their enemy but receiving instead the last and most hideous surprise of their lives; a bayonet plunged into their flank or a musket going off, point blank, in their face. These men died to the curses of enraged redcoats, as did dozens who fired from windows.

'We were now obliged to force almost every house in the road, for the rebels had taken possession of them and galled us exceedingly,' noted a lieutenant with one of the flanking parties, 'but they suffered for their temerity for all that were found in the houses were put to death.' Although the soldiers had noticed on their way out to Lexington that women and children had apparently disappeared from the villages along the Boston road, it is obvious that not all of those killed in those frenzied moments in passageways, larders or on stairs had been firing at the King's troops.

After quite a few of these ghastly encounters, the soldiers helped themselves to pewter plate, rings or clothing before bursting out of the doors and catching up with their mates. In some, though, greed defeated survival, and those who looted more systematically met their end at the hands of the enraged citizenry.

About half way back to Boston, seven miles into the march, Earl Percy was obliged to replace the 23rd at the tail of the column. The task of keeping at bay the mob of pursuing enemy militia was not an easy one, and many of the Fusiliers were running low on cartridges. Not for the first time that day, officers bemoaned their soldiers' wild, often panicked, shooting. Their muskets were largely inaccurate in firing at anything further than a hundred yards away, it was true, and even those described by Mackenzie as 'marksmen' would have had only the most rudimentary idea of how to hit their target. In fairness to these soldiers, the men of Percy's brigade had been issued with only thirty-six rounds each, and his two cannon had just twenty-four shot between them.

In the village of Menotomy, just a few miles short of Boston, there was another gauntlet to be run in the form of militia. Once again the firing came from all around them, musket balls whizzing and cracking about their ears. Here the 23rd's commanding officer, Lieutenant Colonel Benjamin Bernard, was wounded, his thigh shattered by shot.

Two miles further on, as the head of the column approached Cambridge, Brigadier Percy made an important decision, to turn left where the road forked, taking the road to Charlestown, near Boston, rather than returning directly to the city by the route they had followed out in the morning. This proved a wise choice, for the rebels had pulled up the planking on a bridge over the Charles River, just beyond Cambridge, one that Percy's brigade crossed earlier in the day, and were lying in ambush there.

It was 7 p.m. before the redcoats marched over Charlestown Neck, on to a peninsula facing the city. The local people in Charlestown had heard reports of that day's fighting. Although many supported the insurrection against ministerial power, they saw that evening in the powder-blackened faces of the British soldiers a mood so ugly that they did everything possible to assist them back across the bay to Boston. The people of Charlestown came out by candlelight to help wounded soldiers into rowing boats and skiffs. That process would last long into the night, and it took until the early hours for the Fusiliers to get back in the city.

Mackenzie, the serjeant major, company commanders and others went among the ranks, tracking down men who had been wounded or asking after those seen disappearing into some house or yard. They calculated the 23rd's loss at four killed, twenty-six wounded and six missing. Of the latter, three would soon turn up as prisoners of the rebels. They were men of the light and grenadier companies who had been detached under Pitcairn and Smith during the morning's actions. As for British losses overall, sixty-eight soldiers had been killed, 167 wounded and twenty-two were missing. Among the officers, a couple had been killed (both light infantry officers) and fifteen wounded, a few of the latter being captured by the rebels.

The British soldiers who retired that night in Boston had no way of knowing how many Americans they had accounted for. They tried to console themselves that they had faced 5,000 enemy, perhaps more. Casualties among the many companies that had taken potshots against the King's troops were slight, almost certainly fewer than a hundred men, between forty and forty-five of whom had been killed.

Among the colonists exchanging experiences of that day's fateful events there were vivid impressions of panicked redcoats, faces flushed as they ran for their lives; of an entire brigade of the King's troops racing its way back to Boston as fast as its legs could carry it; and of those who faltered – through wounds or because they went off to steal – being left to the mercy of an enraged people.

William Gordon, minister of the Congregational Church in Roxbury, one of those divines who had done so much to inspire the spirit of righteous resistance in the colonists, wrote to an English friend of the day's events. 'The Brigade under Lord Percy marched out, [playing] by way of contempt, "Yankee Doodle",' noted Gordon. 'They afterwards told that they had been made to dance to it.'

'They pillaged almost every house they passed by, breaking and destroying doors, windows and glasses &c and carrying off clothing and other valuable effects,' wrote the impassioned correspondent of the *Essex Gazette*. 'It appeared to be their design to destroy and burn all before them; and nothing but our vigorous pursuit prevented their infernal purposes from being put into execution.'

British officers and men smarted from what had happened. The expedition was 'as ill planned and as ill executed as it was possible to be', according to one officer, while another felt the soldiers behaved with 'great bravery but little order', and another, more laconic, letter-writer called Lexington and Concord 'the little fracas . . . between us and the Yankee scoundrels'. Some shuddered at the recollection of how the light infantry had broken ranks at Lexington, opened fire without orders and later been so fearful that their own officers had to check the soldiers' headlong flight with levelled bayonets.

Farmers, blacksmiths and mechanics had managed by adopting an irregular form of warfare to give a costly lesson to the army. By adopting these lilliputian tactics they had brought down the redcoats' Gulliver-sized reputation. After 19 April 1775, revolt was open and general throughout the Thirteen Colonies – Britain found itself confronting the spectre of a strange and unwelcome war on the other side of the world.

It took a matter of hours for the troops in Boston to realise how much their situation had changed on the day they marched back from Concord. The rebels had chased them to the edge of the city, and within days thousands were congregating in armed camps in Roxbury, Cambridge and other outlying settlements. General Gage ordered troops manning positions in the Neck to stop communication with the countryside across that narrow isthmus. This rule was soon relaxed in favour of hundreds of families who, sympathising with the Whigs, piled up their wagons and fled the city. A lesser number of Tory Americans who still felt loyal to their King came in the other direction, from some scattered communities where they felt in danger.

In many places across America, officials on royal service fled, magazines or stores were seized and Committees of Public Security established. Ugly scenes were repeated across the continent where mobs calling themselves 'Sons of Liberty' converged on the homes of noted loyalists to barrack them, break their windows and, in some cases, tar and feather them for public ridicule.

Boston remained the only sizeable garrison south of Canada. Gage's army of around 3,500 men able to do duty was soon besieged by several times that number of Americans. Initially some 20,000 answered the call to arms, but as the weeks wore on this figure dropped somewhat. In May, following a skilful *coup de main*, the colonists took Ticonderoga on Lake Champlain, one of America's principal fortresses, and by doing so seized a train of heavy siege guns that could be used to hit Boston.

Rhetorical artillery was also pressed into service, that hard-hitting preacher Dr Warren finding himself commissioned as a Major General in the militia. Many who actually knew the business of a soldier, veterans of the French and Indian Wars, also flocked to the Patriot cause. Some of these New Englanders had been part of Wolfe's legendary march on Quebec back in 1759, and there were sufficient men of this species among the company, regimental and brigade commanders to instil some sound judgement into the American camp.

Initially, after the night of 19 April, British soldiers held positions across the water from the city at Charlestown. This was one of two places where headlands jutted into the bay sufficiently close to the city of Boston for artillery to pose a potential threat to British shipping at anchor. In the weeks following Lexington, British commanders gave much thought to conquering the heights both of Charlestown and Dorchester.

The British could not, however, decide quickly what they wanted to do about securing these two places and actually withdrew their forces from the heights above Charlestown. General Gage was nervous about a general rising within the city, an attempt to massacre his troops. He did not want to post large detachments across the harbour in Charlestown or Dorchester, where there might be problems – for example during bad weather – ferrying them back, or indeed reinforcing them. Gage did not have enough troops to defend his situation. The chief engineer later decreed that Britain's first big mistake of the war had been 'taking post at Boston – a mere libel on common sense – being commanded all round'. Like many others, he would have preferred New York, a city abandoned after Lexington, but also in fact requiring the defence of a very large garrison.

Gage was required to re-think his position after 25 May, when the frigate *Cerberus* brought three British major generals to his assistance. All would prove significant in the struggle ahead. John Burgoyne was a cavalry officer, playwright and notorious gambler with excellent political connections. Henry Clinton, born in New York, had garnered much valuable experience in Germany during the Seven Years War. William Howe, having served in a key role in Wolfe's attack on Quebec, was considered an authority on tactics to be used in America.

Hemmed in and outnumbered, the officers of Gage's army entertained some disturbing reflections on what had happened at Lexington and Concord. Burgoyne, soon after arriving from England observed 'men still lost in a sort of stupefaction which the events of the 19th of April had occasioned, and venting expressions of censure, anger, or despondency'. Some railed about the bad planning of that expedition. Others, like Mackenzie, also worried about the thieving and wild behaviour of many soldiers.

Lieutenant Barker, who had been with the 4th Regiment light company at Concord bridge, remarked: 'Our soldiers the other day showed no want of courage, yet were so wild and irregular, that there was no keeping them in any order.' As for their thieving, there was another issue at stake: 'The plundering was shameful; many hardly thought of anything else; what was worse they were encouraged by some officers'. The problem of indiscipline, in other words, had been exacerbated by men in command who believed that the Americans deserved to be 'scourged' for taking the path of rebellion.

As the days following their first, unpleasant, experience of American warfare passed, the anger was directed away from internal recriminations and back towards the enemy, one lieutenant speaking for many when he wrote home early in June, 'our troops I believe would be very glad to give them a good drubbing'.

By early June, a couple of weeks after the three new major generals had arrived, Gage had been persuaded to approve an offensive plan. The British army would take the heights of Dorchester and the Charlestown peninsula before moving on rebel headquarters at Cambridge. How, though, would they attack an enemy that skulked behind walls and fences?

Humphrey Bland was probably the most widely read of the many tactical theorists whose books informed British officers. He had summed up the army's approach to war from the Duke of Marlborough's great victories, seven decades before, to Minden and the Seven Years War. Bland distilled this experience to describe the formula for a perfect attack.

As you advanced your battalions in line, the enemy would be encouraged to waste their fire by opening up when their targets were still too far away. The redcoats would bide their time, answering with a single close-range volley, which would be followed instantly by a bayonet charge before their foe had a chance to re-load. Bland understood well the psychology of the defenders' situation, noting that victory would often be won before the attacking line had reached the defences, for 'when troops see others advance, and going to pour their fire amongst them, when theirs is gone, they will immediately give way'.

It was vital, in this description of the perfect assault, not to allow your troops to be stalled by the enemy and get into a running firefight, for in the thick smoke and frenzy of re-loading the attack would lose all momentum and fail, as the French had learned at Minden. Such episodes led Bland to give the following warning to any officer leading an assault: 'If you do not follow your fire that moment, but give them time to recover from the disorder yours may have put them into, the scene may change to your disadvantage.' These words could have been read as a portent of what was about to pass.

Benjamin Bernard would hear reports of the great drama that was unfolding in Boston from a sickbed. The ball that had shattered his leg on the 19 April had in fact finished his career as a soldier. Bernard, however, was not a man to relinquish command of the 23rd without a fight. He entertained hopes of convalescence and a return to duty, as the army prepared to confront the vast rebellion brewing in the country.

On 17 June 1775 the Boston garrison received a rude awakening. One of the Royal Navy ships in the harbour had opened up. The shot were directed at Breed's Hill, an eminence on the Charlestown peninsula where, overnight, thousands of rebel soldiers had seized the hill and by throwing up a system of trenches shown their intention of holding this ground. General Howe would claim in a letter home that they had pre-empted by a single day the launch of the British offensive. Howe, Gage and the others attending a hurried council of war 'instantly determined' to launch their plan, only to start at Charlestown rather than Dorchester. If the rebels were willing to stand there and defend themselves, then the British were ready to administer the bayonet, and give them a lesson in the realities of warfare.

Bunker Hill

Captain Mecan's Trial By Fire

There was a purposeful bustle on the Boston quay during the late morning of 17 June. Soldiers stepped gingerly from terra firma into the longboats arrayed in front of them. Encumbered with weapons, blanket, cartridges and knapsack, a fall into the water might easily have drowned them. Once aboard, the men of ten light and ten grenadier companies crowded knee to knee on the benches provided as tars from the fleet pushed off and rowed out towards Charlestown peninsula.

As regards the 23rd Fusiliers, the quarrelsome Captain Blakeney had on this day placed himself at the head of his grenadier company. Thomas Mecan joined the boats in command of the regiment's light company. Although Captain Donkin was nominally responsible, he was absent, and Mecan, sensing a great day in which some feat of daring might bring the approbation of great men and with it a chance for promotion, had volunteered immediately to go in his stead. The main body of the 23rd, the eight so-called battalion companies, were not destined to see action that day.

The splashing of oars was accompanied that morning by the mad timpani of British guns. A battery of artillery in Boston itself was firing at the redoubt, some Royal Navy ships had joined in for good measure, and shallow-draught gun barges manoeuvred into place so that they could shoot at the Americans as they crossed the narrow neck connecting Charlestown peninsula to the mainland. It certainly occurred to some that cutting off the Americans by landing at this same narrow isthmus, behind their main position, might be the wisest plan of attack. But there were some navigational impediments – a dam

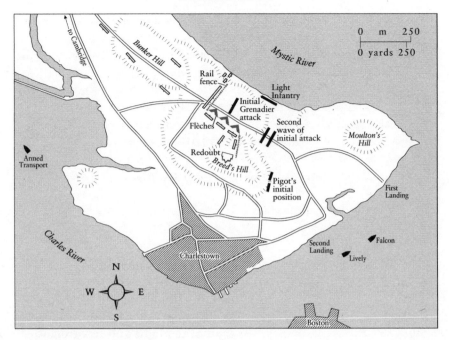

The battle of Bunker Hill

blocked passage to the neck's southern flank and sand flats hindered (but did not completely prevent) landing to the north, on the shore of the Mystic River. Instead the generals at that morning's council of war eschewed lengthy manoeuvres by boat that might have given their enemy time to escape and opted to land on the head of the peninsula.

Light companies and grenadiers, or flank companies, the 'flower of the army', would be deployed as elite battalions, a strike force under the hand of Major General William Howe. They landed at about 2 p.m., which coincided with high tide, so the boats could clear the sand banks. Four regiments of the line (the 5th, 38th, 43rd and 52nd) had been ordered to support them.

There were only enough rowing boats to carry 1,100 men across at once, so two trips were needed before the two flank battalions and four regiments totalling about 1,550 men were assembled on the tip of the Charlestown peninsula, some 500 yards from the top of Breed's Hill with its rebel earthworks. In addition to leading the flank battalions, Howe would have to take personal charge of the entire unfolding operation.

General Gage, commander-in-chief, did not intend to lead his troops on the field. This poor personal example was naturally followed by his staff, which gave rise to Captain Donkin of the 23rd's absence, he having been appointed as Gage's aide-de-camp.

Howe at least brought the reputation of a fighting soldier to the enterprise. He had commanded Wolfe's light infantry, playing a key role in the capture of Quebec in 1759. He was a big man, over six feet tall and broad too, and projected a considerable presence. Howe had gone over to Charlestown with a definite plan of how to take the rebel position. The landing of his first wave complete, he began to study their lines at close quarters.

As he looked up, the town of Charlestown was on his left. The ground rose just over a hundred feet from the fenced gardens of that settlement to the crown of Breed's Hill, where the main rebel redoubt stood. The gap between the houses and that fort was about 200 yards, and much encumbered with obstructions; too tight, Howe reasoned, for his battalions to manoeuvre. As for the main rebel work, shot lobbed at it during the course of the morning had done little damage. A similarly thick rampart – Howe called it a breastwork – with a ditch in front extended for about 80 yards to the right of this redoubt, covering what remained of the hilltop. To the right of this, below the hill and a couple of hundred yards further away from the British, ran another defence line, which extended about 300 yards from the side of Breed's Hill down to the Mystic River. This area, on the right of the general's view, was where Howe intended to win the battle.

The general's instinct was good in one particular at least – the works on that side of the peninsula were far less formidable, allowing a chance to bypass the main defences. American commanders there had simply pulled down some pickets, piled them on to an existing rail fence and filled in the gaps with brushwood and clods of earth. As he stood making his final appraisal, though, Howe overestimated the strength of this rush job, thinking it cannon-proof. There were also some additional small works, called flèches (because they resembled arrowheads) that connected the enemy line at the rail fence with the position on top of the hill. Since these flèches were aligned perpendicular to the hilltop breastwork and the rail fence, troops manning them would be able to shoot right down the line of any regiments attacking the rail fence, or, in military parlance, enfilade them.

Whether or not Howe grasped the importance of this extra element of fortification (since it would have been largely hidden from him by Breeds Hill itself), he soon reckoned that the force he had brought over was insufficient to the task. The general might also have readily observed that there were two or three times as many Americans as British troops. So, with his first-wave troops standing impatiently in line, Howe sent a messenger by boat back across to the city to ask for reinforcements.

On top of the hill, the defenders watched these comings and goings with bemused nervousness. 'When we saw our danger,' wrote Peter Brown, a soldier in Prescott's Massachusetts Regiment, 'being against ships of the line, and all Boston fortified against us, the danger we were in made us think there was treachery and that we were brought there to be all slain.' Brown's commander, Colonel William Prescott, had placed his soldiers inside the main redoubt.

The colonel, a veteran of the Seven Years War and Indian campaigns, was noisily seconded by his nominal superior, Major General Joseph Warren. The Presbyterian minister fully intended to be at the hottest part of the action. Warren's type of spirit was all very well, but something more thirst-quenching was needed too, as Private Brown noted: 'We began to be almost beat out, being fatigued by our Labour, having no sleep the night before, very little to eat, no drink but rum.'

To their right (or the British left) were more Massachusetts regiments, others from Connecticut and, down on the rail fence, two strong regiments from New Hampshire. These were placed under Colonel John Stark, perhaps the most impressive leader on the lines that day, a one-time member of Rogers' Rangers, the elite American battalion of the French and Indian Wars. Stark moved his men on to the peninsula shortly before Howe's troops landed. As they approached Charlestown Neck, the thump and whoosh of British cannon balls increased in pitch. They claimed lives too, one shot cutting three men in half. 'The veteran and gallant Stark harangued his regiment in a short but animated address,' wrote one New Hampshire officer, adding that their colonel ordered them through the gauntlet of enemy fire, 'directed them to give three cheers, and make a rapid movement to the rail fence'.

Once Howe's reinforcements were in place – some additional flank companies as well as the 47th Regiment, field artillery and 1st Marine battalion – the general began his attack in earnest. There were more than 3,000 British troops in play. He had placed the 38th and 43rd centrally, in front of the redoubt, under Brigadier Robert Pigot. The recently landed elements were put initially behind Pigot's brigade, and formed a reserve of kinds, for it was still Howe's intention to take the position by attacking the rail fence rather than frontal assault on the redoubt itself.

Howe ordered the light infantry to move up the beach, on the shore of the Mystic River, in a column. The grenadiers would move up next to them, forming line and attacking the rail fence frontally at the same time. Howe trusted that although the light infantry would only have a matter of feet to work in, they would break through the enemy at the waterside, and then 'take them in the flank'. In expectation of a rebel collapse, the 5th and 52nd would be drawn up in line, moving up behind the grenadiers in order to exploit their success.

At about 3.30 p.m., the flank company men began to move forward. The soldiers who ought to have been Howe's steadiest troops were skittish and nervous; the light infantry in particular knew an unpleasant truth – that they had run away during the fighting at Lexington and Concord. They and the grenadiers had been standing under arms for more than an hour, and wanted to get the business over with. The grenadiers did not wait for orders, but started off on their own initiative, some men crying out 'Push on! Push on!' As they got closer to the rail fence, they heard the odd crack and whine of a musket ball, but the rebels were under strict orders. Stark had placed himself near the flèches where 'his men were directed to reserve their fires until they could see the enemy's half gaiters'.

Tramping forward, the grenadiers ran into some fences. The battalion stalled momentarily as men clambered over or tried to kick their way through. When they got closer to the line of the Americans at the rail fence some of the grenadiers and light troops 'began firing, and by crowding fell into disorder'. This was an obvious violation of the very sound tactical advice given by Humphrey Bland and others, for he directed that the enemy should be encouraged to give the first fire. In the moments that followed, pretty much every feature of his ideal attack was disregarded too.

The redcoats advanced a little further but when the New Hampshires let go their first crashing volley, it was terrible. One of Stark's officers saw that his enemy 'received a volley which mowed down the whole front ranks'. With the flank battalions staggered under this heavy fire, the 5th and 52nd advanced into the back of them, causing further confusion.

Rushing forward through the hail of musket balls to see what was wrong, Howe had an awful realisation. His favourite corps, the men sent along the beach, were actually falling back: 'The Light Infantry . . . being repulsed there was *a moment that I never felt before.*' The general's plan had been foiled and he did not have another.

One disaster followed another, for the light troops, rallied by Mecan and their other officers, pulled up behind the grenadiers. Turned back towards the Americans, but confused by the smoke and fear all around them, the light infantry opened fire on the grenadiers to their front left. The officer commanding the grenadier battalion and many of his men were thus killed by British fire, as they struggled to organise themselves for a further attack to their front.

Bereft for the moment of any new directive, grenadier and light infantry officers had halted their men in confused huddles and were trying to lead them forward again. They came on in small clumps rather than the neat lines of the parade ground. There was an answer to this kind of ragged attack and the Americans soon realised it: 'Our men were intent on cutting down every officer they could distinguish.'

Several failed attempts separated the brave soldiers from those who hung back. Captain Blakeney, commanding the 23rd's grenadiers, was shot, as were both of his subalterns. Mecan somehow made it through unscathed, but both of his light company subalterns were also hit. Around two-thirds of the Welch Fusiliers engaged that day became casualties. Two serjeants, one drummer and eleven men were killed by the American fire, and thirty-six wounded by it. Only five of the grenadier company remained fit at the end.

The Americans meanwhile loaded and fired into the crowd in front of them. For those aiming down from the flèches, enfilading the British, pretty much any shot where the musket was levelled right had a good chance of finding a target, for if it went to the left or right of some fellow immediately to their front, it would travel another 200 yards, parallel with the rail fence, through the floundering mass of redcoats. Some of the British tended their stricken comrades, others gave vent to their fury, loading and firing for all they were worth. But this kind of shooting, in the midst of smoke and mayhem, had little effect. One New Hampshire man noted contemptuously, 'The fire of the enemy was so badly directed, I should presume that forty-nine balls out of fifty passed from one to six feet over our heads.'

It took some time – perhaps half an hour - for Howe to conceive a new plan and put it into effect. If his attempts to go around the works on top of Breeds Hill had failed, then he would have to force the strong-point itself. Two of his aides were shot down next to him, slowing the delivery of orders. But eventually word reached Brigadier Pigot. While an intense battle had been going on in front of the rail fence, Pigot had already move a little closer to Charlestown and the redoubt. He had been greeted by sniper-fire from the edge of the town that had killed, among others, Major Pitcairn, the marine officer who had commanded the light companies at Lexington. The British had, by way of response, pulled back and got their warships to fire carcass (incendiary shells) into the town, and it was soon burning fiercely.

On a hillside in Boston Major General John Burgoyne and numerous other sightseers were watching. The soldier-dramatist was alive to the awful grandeur of the unfolding scene, writing that the

prospect of the neighbouring hills, the steeples of Boston, and the masts of the ships as were unemployed in the harbour, all crowded with spectators, friends and foes, alike in anxious suspense, made background to the piece; and the whole together composed a representation of war that I think the imagination of Le Brun never reached.

Under the new orders Pigot was to skirt around the inferno of Charlestown and Howe would pull together the 5th and 52nd, extricating them from the confusion in front of the rail fence and attacking the hilltop from the right. Major General Henry Clinton, who had been watching events alongside Burgoyne, was so worried by what he could see that he made his way to the quayside and crossed by boat. There he put himself at the head of some further companies of men who had been sent across from Boston as reinforcements.

As the British threw new forces into the bloody struggle for a little hill that hardly any of them would have previously noticed, the Americans too brought new companies to bear. Although the troops earmarked to defend the peninsula may have numbered as many as 3,000 early that morning, many had decided they would rather be elsewhere, particularly once the British cannon had begun bombarding in earnest from around 11 a.m.

It was not simply a matter of desertion by startled individuals here and there. In some cases, the officers ordered entire companies to march off, across the neck towards the backcountry. Peter Brown, in the redoubt, watched in contempt as one artillery captain, possessing the only American guns deployed on the hilltop, 'took his pieces and returned home to Cambridge with much haste'. Brown wanted court martial and the death sentence for such a coward.

Worried by the hundreds of men streaming off the peninsula, American commanders called forward additional men from the outlying villages. Captain John Chester led his company of militia from Wetherfield, Connecticut, and marched his men on to the peninsula at the height of the battle. He saw frightened groups running in the opposite direction 'retreating, seemingly without any excuse, and some said they had left the fort with leave of the officers'.

This produced fury in Chester, who prided himself on the steady discipline and smart appearance of his own volunteers wearing blue coats with red cuffs and lapels, unlike the great majority of Americans that day who simply came in working clothes. The captain was particularly angry when he saw groups of men marching away from battle under the leadership of their officers. Exasperated at trying to reason with one such hero, he wrote, 'I halted my men and told him if he went on it should be at his peril. He still seemed regardless of me. I ordered my men to make ready. They immediately cocked, and declared that if I ordered they would fire.' The threat of oblivion at last convinced the fleeing commander to do his duty.

Chester's men threw themselves into action at the rail fence, 'every man loading and firing as fast as he could. As near as I could guess, we fought standing about six minutes.' His militia had arrived near the end of the action in this sector.

About one hour after Howe's initial attack had begun, the second assault got under way, with redcoats attacking the Breed's Hill redoubt from two sides. Pigot's men had the smouldering houses of Charlestown close to their left. Howe directed the remnants of the grenadiers, 5th and 52nd, towards the place where the flèches met the breastwork on Breed's Hill.

Many more British soldiers ascending the slope went down with that distinctive slap of bullet hitting body, some in silence, others with a scream of anguish. Prescott's men in the fort saw the marines and others under Pigot heading towards them. Once again the redcoats did not plough on regardless but began to open fire with musketry as they neared the top. 'Finding our ammunition was almost spent,' wrote Colonel Prescott, 'I commanded a cessation till the enemy advanced within 30 yards when we gave them such a hot fire, that they were obliged to retire nearly 150 yards before they could rally and come again to the attack.'

Lieutenant Waller was one of the Marines on the receiving end of this unequal firefight. Seeing his men throwing away their shots at an entrenched enemy, he tried at first, bellowing above the cacophony, to improve their aim but soon gave up: Waller realised that 'at length half mad with standing in this situation' they must push on, the 47th forming 'upon our left in order that we might advance to the enemy with our bayonets without firing'.

On the other side of the hill, British troops had reached the corner where the flèches met the breastwork. Some men who had mounted these works were shot down and repulsed, leaving the majority pressed flat on the ground just a few feet from the Americans on the other side of the earthworks. One officer of the 52nd explained: 'As soon as we got up to the works we were not nearly so much exposed to their fire as we were then in some degree covered.'

Having got to the very lip of the American works, the redcoats stayed in cover, unwilling to try their chances with the metal flying overhead. Only the officers would stand and scramble up to the top of the embankment. Captain Harris of the 5th, twice encouraging the men to follow him, felt the sickening sensation of finding himself alone. '[I] was ascending a third time, when a ball grazed the top of my head, and I fell deprived of sense and motion.' Harris was caught with his head wound by Lord Francis Rawdon, a lieutenant in his regiment. Rawdon got four men to carry Harris away from the fight: leaving cover to go downhill proved as dangerous as going forward, three of the casualty-bearers being wounded.

Rawdon summoned up his courage and, exhorting his men to follow, stood up and pushed on. He got a bullet through his cap, but fortunately not his skull. Some men, at least, followed him. The American defences were crumbling as the first brave attackers scrambled over their ramparts.

On the other side of the hill, the Marines had finally pushed forward too. But whereas those on Rawdon's side conquered the breastwork, Waller's men entered the main work. 'I cannot pretend to describe the horror of the scene within the redoubt when we entered it,' Waller wrote home, ''twas streaming with blood and strewed with dead and dying men the soldiers stabbing some and dashing out the brains of others.'

The few dozen Americans who had remained inside until the last minute fled out of the back, redcoats trying to bayonet them or taking potshots as they went. It was here, just behind the redoubt, that Major General Warren was killed. Taking his place alongside Prescott earlier that morning, the preacher turned soldier had said he was there 'to let those damned rascals see that the Yankees will fight'. He had made his point.

With militiamen streaming back across the neck, the British mopped up, chasing their enemies from one fence or wall to another as they withdrew. It was dusk as the redcoats began digging in, the Charlestown peninsula behind them strewn with casualties. The British had lost 226 dead and about 900 wounded – there was particular shock at the loss among officers, nineteen killed and seventy wounded. American casualties amounted to about half those of the redcoats.

In their official dispatches, messages for public consumption, the British tried to make the most of their conquest, emphasising the valour of their soldiers in expelling such large numbers of enemy men 'entrenched up to their chins' upon such a strong position.

The battle, named after Bunker Hill, a rather larger eminence just behind Breed's Hill, had provided the stand-up fight that many British officers had longed for, but instead of giving the rebels their 'drubbing', the outcome caused the most profound shock and dismay.

Writing home privately, Howe gave vent to dark feelings: 'The general's returns will give you the particulars of what I call this unhappy day – I freely confess to you, when I look to the consequences of it, in the loss of so many brave officers, I do it with horror.'

In explaining their grievous setback, senior officers pinpointed indiscipline. The redcoat had earned a reputation for courage and steadiness during the Seven Years War and earlier conflicts. At Bunker Hill they had in fact proven nervous and disorderly. So shocking was this discovery that Henry Clinton jotted his notes about what had happened in cipher, lest others read it: 'All was in confusion, officers told me that they could not command their men and I never saw so great a want of order.'

Some of those at Lexington and Concord had already noticed the soldiers' 'wild' behaviour, but its consequences had not been so ruinous. At Bunker Hill, men had pushed forward without being ordered to, had then stopped to open fire in front of the rail fence – causing the whole plan to falter – and fallen into such confusion in front of that obstacle that they had killed one another by mistake, and had later proved for a time immovable in front of the earthworks on Breeds Hill itself. The American defenders of the redoubt would later claim that they had only lost it because they ran out of ammunition.

'As I am certain that every letter from America will be opened at the post office, I cannot in general give you my thoughts freely upon the situation of our affairs,' Lord Rawdon wrote to England a few weeks after the battle, expressing a widespread fear that discussing the reasons for the army's disaster might cause one's loyalty to the Crown to be called into question. The nub of it, Rawdon nevertheless went on to explain, was that 'our confidence in our own troops is much lessened since the 17th of June. Some of them did, indeed, behave with infinite courage, but others behaved as remarkably ill.' Certain officers, he conceded, had not done their duty either.

When news spread about the battle, many felt that the very heavy loss in British officers had resulted from American skill with firearms. This view was propagated in particular by those who had not been close to the fighting and who wanted to extol the prowess, and by extension the invincibility, of born frontiersmen. One British Whig who was visiting New York at the time of the battle wrote home breathlessly, 'There are amongst the provincial troops a number of surprising marksmen, who shoot with rifle guns, and I have been assured that many of them at 150 yards will hit a card nine times out of ten.'

John Burgoyne, talking to his friends after the battle, came up with a different and rather more credible theory for the loss among the army's leaders:

The zeal and intrepidity of the officers, which was without exception exemplary, was ill seconded by the private men. Discipline, not to say courage, was wanting. In the critical moment of carrying the redoubt, the officers of some corps were almost alone.

Officers were bound to suffer disproportionately when the men refused to follow them forward. Burgoyne, like Rawdon or Clinton, found these truths so disturbing that, with the playwright's fitting melodrama, he told his correspondent in London, 'Though my letter passes in security, I tremble while I write it; and let it not pass even in a whisper from your Lordship to more than *one* person.'

American news-sheets recited with glee the losses of 'the regulars' after 17 June, but in what sense were the militia any worse as soldiers?

Most of the British men had not been in action before Bunker Hill either. Their training, in the *Manual Exercise* (how to fire their muskets) or in drill (the necessary skill in marching required to deploy the regiment in various formations) was, in many cases, no greater and conducted with a good deal less enthusiasm than that of the militia amateurs preparing constantly on their village greens during preceding months. 'We have learnt one melancholy truth,' one of the British officers wounded at Bunker Hill reflected on his sick bed, 'which is, that the Americans, if they are equally well commanded, are full as good soldiers as ours, and, as it is, are very little inferior to us even in discipline and countenance.'

The idea, though, that an American imbued with a love of Liberty could face down the professional soldiers of a European power was too good for Whig scribblers to resist. In providing details of the battle, the Provincial Congress issued a dispatch trumpeting, 'The Welch Fuzileers were nearly all cut off, and one captain only remains alive of that regiment.'

It may be surmised that the Fusiliers were one of the few regiments that many readers of the newspapers printing this statement had heard of. The regiment epitomised the British army's humiliation and, never mind the facts, the Minden men had been wiped out. The inconvenient truth that eight out of the Royal Welch Fusilier's ten companies had not even fought at Bunker Hill had clearly escaped the American dispatch writers. The single germ of fact in this was that Thomas Mecan was the only one of the six officers in the 23rd (i.e., those in its light and grenadier companies) to make it through the day uninjured.

In the days following the battle soldiers on the Charlestown peninsula faced the grim task of recovering the wounded, burying the dead and sweeping away the detritus of war. Major General Howe was given the command there as the British fortified their hard won conquest.

Thomas Mecan was one of those who served in this unpleasant duty. The Irishman was a tough old soldier less interested in reflecting on what had gone wrong than in seeing whether he could turn it to promotion. Sitting in his tent on the heights above Charlestown, Mecan began a letter-writing campaign, seeking the promotion that he knew he could not afford to buy. Just two days after the battle, he petitioned General Gage with a memorial written in a finer hand than his own. Was he not an old soldier who had served through the

German campaign and volunteered to lead the light infantry at Bunker Hill? 'The events of that day made several vacant companies in the Army under your command,' argued Mecan, anxious to step into the shoes of one of those dead captains, hoping, 'Your Excellency will be pleased to consider his pretensions, and grant him such reward as you think his services merit.' Mecan canvassed powerful men in London too, one of whom, the commander-in-chief at headquarters in Horse Guards, replied that he should trust in General Howe who would 'do everything that he can to contribute to the happiness of deserving officers'. Words of this kind, so often written to fob off a jaundiced old soldier, would in this case happily be proven right long before Mecan even received the reply from London.

There was at least promotion to be gained in all that bloodletting, and it was in this theme that the army more widely took some comfort. In the desperate struggle at the rail fence or redoubt one or two heroes had emerged. 'Lord Rawdon behaved to a charm,' Major General Burgoyne wrote home to his wife, 'his name is established for life'. This passage formed part of his letter published in British newspapers. Quite a few aristocratic young blades would soon be finding their way to America in search of similar reputation.

Those whom Howe remembered, doing their duty manfully amidst the smoke, cacophony and confusion at Bunker Hill, would have a head start over any newcomer. Captain Lieutenant Mecan was one. In the days after the battle, proving himself in the fortification of Charlestown heights, Mecan was given several assignments by the general as well as an assistant engineer's acting title and pay.

Captain Nisbet Balfour had also came to Howe's notice on 17 June. He was leading the 4th Regiment's light company in the bloody maelstrom in front of the rail fence. In the race for promotion Balfour was better placed than Mecan but well behind Rawdon. While the young peer was just twenty-one years old, Balfour was thirty. He had family connections with the landed gentry of his native Galloway in south-west Scotland but Balfour would rise through bravery, diligence and ruthlessness. The Scottish captain had carried on fighting despite being wounded at Bunker Hill and was already being entrusted with independent errands by his commanders. Nobody could have known it at the time, but Balfour's fate would become tied to that of General Howe and indeed the Fusiliers.

For a few weeks following the battle, the British held on to the trenches, ditches and bastions that they had placed on Charlestown peninsula at such terrible cost. General Gage, never the most aggressive of commanders, had lost his will entirely to attack the Americans. Any idea of proceeding with the plan to drive towards Cambridge had 'been entirely set aside'. The shock of 17 June had been too great. Instead Mecan eyed the American lines from his little fortress. The British were besieged.

FIVE

Boston Besieged

Why Lieutenant John Lenthall Bid Adieu to the 23rd

Service on the lines offered few prospects for distinction. Instead there were hours of tedium and a small but distinct chance of ruin.

Just after midnight, in the early hours of 27 July, Lieutenant John Lenthall of the 23rd was nearing the end of his duty and looking forward to being relieved. He and a couple of dozen Fusiliers were manning the outposts just ahead of British lines on Charlestown Neck. The guard's job was to provide early warning of any attack and prevent rebels approaching the newly dug trenches to their rear. This particular evening was a warm summer's one, but particularly dark. Taking advantage of the poor visibility, a party of Virginia riflemen crept towards the British posts.

The first Lenthall knew of the danger was when the night calm was shattered by an explosion of musketry. One of his sentries had opened fire on the infiltrators. Shouting above the noise, he rallied his men into formation and ordered a volley towards a group of riflemen. It quickly became apparent that enemy parties were moving about him in large numbers, the lieutenant writing, 'the rascals called out to us several times to surrender'.

Fortunately for the Fusiliers, their relief appeared at this moment out of the darkness. Hastening towards the sound of shooting, the second subaltern's party began to fire in support of Lenthall's men. Both British and American troops took their chance to break off the night action, falling back to their respective lines. 'Their intention was to have taken all of us prisoners,' the Fusilier lieutenant wrote, adding it was 'a narrow escape', since the American party had far outnumbered them.

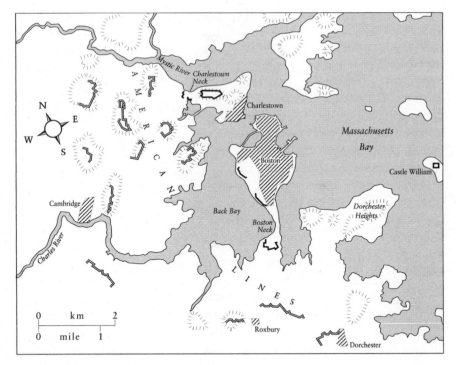

The Boston siege lines

Lenthall was the acting commander of the 23rd's grenadier company. By late July he had already been in action at Lexington and Bunker Hill, where he was wounded. The twenty-five-year-old subaltern had quickly returned to his duty, unlike his captain who was still indisposed. Having been an eyewitness to the confusion of those two actions, Lenthall knew all about the defects in British discipline.

When the army launched a raid in retaliation for the night attack of 27 July, it turned into a fiasco. Lenthall was sent ahead of British lines at the head of a party with orders to move several hundred yards north to Penny Ferry, where the Mystic River narrowed to a crossing point, and then push up the riverside road, wreaking further vengeance. Their intention was to creep forward with the same stealth that the Americans had shown, burn down some houses used as guard posts and take prisoners. What happened is best described in the lieutenant's own words:

We burnt Penny Ferry House . . . and should have taken the whole guard and burnt the barns up Mystic road, had our men behaved like men and soldiers and obeyed orders, which were upon no account to fire even if fired upon. They fired and to mend the matter ran away without even having their fire returned.

Lenthall managed to collar a few of his panic-stricken soldiers to carry off a captain of marines. It was the least the Fusilier lieutenant could do, since it was his own fearful grenadiers who had shot the poor man. The raid ended without prisoners and cost the life of that British captain who later died of his wounds.

Lenthall's affair was no isolated incident. Lieutenant Richard Williams could have brought his own example to the 23rd's mess table. One month before, at the same spot on the lines, he had also been involved in a chaotic action. When a patrol had been sent out from one of the two bastions on the Charlestown Neck defences, men in the other strong-point had not known anything about it and 'gave a general fire of small arms on them'. The two British companies had blazed away at one another until calm had been restored. Williams blamed, in part, the officer leading the patrol, for he had not informed those along the line what he planned to do.

However, Williams, like Lenthall, reserved his toughest invective for the soldiers, criticising 'the hurry and inattention natural to young troops . . . who never having seen service, foolishly imagine that when danger is feared they secure themselves by discharging their muskets with or without aim'. Williams believed that matters would get better as experience built: 'Theory is nothing without practice, and it requires one campaign at least to make a good soldier.'

While much of the 23rd had not been present at Bunker Hill, it was clear then that its soldiers were guilty of the same indiscipline that Burgoyne, Rawdon or Howe had lamented at that battle. Invested by vast numbers of rebels, the garrison's morale had slumped. The regiment was a shadow of its former self, its Minden self. What could be done to curb its men and make them worthy Fusiliers?

Most were agreed that some tough steps had to be taken to restore discipline. This was easier said – in some General Order put out by Headquarters – than it was done by the young officers who bore the brunt of actual duty. The lieutenant or captain who tried to grab some running soldier or prevent another from looting an American's house could receive volleys of abuse in return. Williams or Lenthall suffered many handicaps in trying to get their men to do as ordered. An officer who allowed soldiers to insult him would risk losing all authority, whereas one who wielded the rod too readily might meet with unpleasant reprisals.

Several days before the incident on the lines, Lenthall had brought a grenadier of the 4th to a general court martial. The man was charged with mutiny and insolence following an altercation with the lieutenant. Mutiny was a capital charge, but General Gage's aversion to the death penalty would have been well known to the court and in the end it had found the grenadier guilty only of insolence. The outcome was duly announced in Orders, and the offender 'sentenced to receive 500 lashes at such place and time as the Commander-in-chief shall think proper'. Even in this particular though, Gage left himself free to release the soldier without further punishment.

Not only was the outcome of charging a soldier uncertain, but there were also risks for the officer who attempted it. Boston had heard the rumours about poor Lieutenant Hull of the 43rd. After being wounded at Concord on 19 April, he had been captured and placed under guard of several deserters. One of these former redcoats swore revenge on Hull, who had previously brought him to a court martial. Hull had died in captivity. Whether the rumour was true or not, its currency showed officers' awareness that a soldier who considered himself wronged might find opportunities for revenge.

During the Boston siege the rank and file might also have cursed the incompetence of those supposed to lead them. The raid on Penny Ferry was followed in August by a general plan to 'alarm' the enemy conceived by Major General Clinton. The main effort was launched at Boston Neck, where he led hundreds of troops on a mission to beat up the enemy camps around Roxbury.

Clinton recorded that 'the detachment I was with succeeded to my utmost expectations'. The raiders soon found themselves in the middle of Roxbury, having caused the American militia to flee. Once there, Clinton did not know what to do. He later blamed Gage for ordering him back but some officers wondered why they had not at least burned Roxbury. The answer, farcically, was that those planning the enterprise 'had forgot to bring any combustibles'.

Following these raids, the Americans embarked on a frenzied bout of pick and shovel work, throwing up redoubts and batteries so as to thwart the chance of more British sorties from the city. Although the execution of Clinton's attack had been poor, the general's reasoning was right in one particular at least; an active scheme of defence could have helped maintain morale and denied the Americans various opportunities for mischief.

Instead, Gage allowed an acceptance that no further strategic initiatives would be possible in 1775 to blind him to the tactical requirements of holding Boston. The headland of Dorchester, for example, had been an object of British designs earlier in the summer but remained unoccupied. Their failure to secure this land was all the more puzzling given senior officers' acknowledgement that an American appearance there would reproduce the crisis of 17 June and call into question their very presence in Boston. On the lines or waters surrounding the city, meanwhile, the enemy carried out raids, taking prisoners and prize ships alike.

For those not taking their turns on the defences, the city offered a depressing prospect. When they had arrived in Boston before the war, many of the British officers had been struck by the beauty of its setting. 'The entrance to the harbour,' wrote one, 'and the view of the town of Boston from it, is the most charming thing I ever saw.' The isthmus upon which the town was built was hilly, creating a pleasing panorama of rising and tumbling roofs.

After war broke out, the blockade changed everything. Streets that had previously thronged with townsfolk echoed only to the march of redcoat companies. As the days grew shorter, hundreds of houses stood unlit, their Whig inhabitants having fled. Food and other necessaries became extremely expensive because trade with the backcountry had been entirely severed. Ravenous soldiers awaited the arrival of each new vessel in the hope that it might bring something tasty to eat. Their dislike for Admiral Graves, already blamed for not throttling the rebel naval privateers, reached a new pitch when he was discovered to have kept a consignment of delicacies from the West Indies – turtles and pineapples, no less – to himself.

Most days officers and men alike chewed their way through vile salt pork or other preserved rations that caused all manner of fluxes and agues. Dozens of redcoats' wives had been pressed into service as nurses, first to treat the huge number of casualties from Bunker Hill in makeshift hospitals and later to look after the growing number stricken by bad rations and disease.

Throughout the late summer and autumn of 1775, the soldiers watched a procession of civilians packing up their conveyances and quit the city. The blockade meant they had to share the army's unhealthy diet and one letter writer recorded in August that 'every inhabitant that can get away is going'. The population dwindled from 17,000 before the war to as few as 5,000 civilians. Those who tried to sell their possessions found prices for luxurious furniture or fine horses tumbling.

Many soldiers might have envied the Bostonians who passed their sentry posts on the neck and headed into the lush New England hinterland. But the siege had made desertion far more difficult, notwithstanding generous offers that were being made to seduce redcoats.

Soon after Lexington, handbills had begun circulating promising the men land and a new life if they defected. 'If you will quit the service, and join your American brethren,' read one such paper, 'you shall be kindly received as brothers and friends, and provided with a comfortable subsistence among us: you shall be sent with a proper escort to any part of the continent where you choose to retire, together with your wives, children and effects.'

It was hard though to sneak past the lines. Even taking the ferry to the Charlestown peninsula required a special permit, a measure designed to thwart would-be deserters. Only the ingenious could defeat these precautions, and on 27 July, Thomas Machin of the 23rd succeeded.

Machin, a soldier of Blunt's company, was literate, intelligent and Irish – a troublesome combination in those times. He had been ordered to do duty with another soldier as lookouts on one of the boats anchored in the harbour as a precaution against enemy attack by water. Machin waited until his partner was asleep before paddling off in the canoe that they used to get to and from the guard boat. He had the foresight to take both muskets with him so that if the other man woke, he would be powerless to stop the desertion. An officer in the Fusiliers noted, 'This fellow will give them good intelligence of our works.'

The Machin case, though, was one of only a handful in the months since the war had begun. Preventive measures by the army, as well as the nature of the siege, made it harder but there was also an important change in attitudes. Soldiers, in common with their officers, had smarted after the battlefield debacles. The private with his pot of grog, no less than the captain sipping wine, gave vent to deepening anger, damning the rebels' eyes, cursing their mouths or describing in blood-curdling terms what they would do to any Yankee rascal they came up with.

'The next campaign will be carried on with an inveteracy unparalleled in the histories of modern wars,' Lord Rawdon predicted in a letter back to England. The young officer shuddered at the idea of war without mercy: 'Both sides hold each other in such detestation that which ever party is victorious it will not, I fear, use its power with moderation.'

In these difficult days amusement centred around drinking, gaming and whoring. Younger officers, like Lieutenant Colonel Bernard's son, formed an Ugly Club at the Bunch of Grapes, a tavern on King Street, one of Boston's main thoroughfares. There they drank rum or madeira, and it was considered the height of poor form to fall behind in the consumption of tumblers of alcohol. Others favoured the British Coffee House.

Among soldiers there were many unofficial drinking dens or 'dram shops' that did business in outbuildings and darkened doorways. Quite a few of these were run by soldier's wives, and various attempts by General Gage to restrict their activity proved ineffective. In one General Order, he had spoken of 'most scandalous drunkenness at this critical time among the troops', and he ordered that they stop women selling liquor or they would be 'immediately seized and put on board ship'. But soldiers and officers alike could sniff out bluff, and Gage retained little authority.

'There was an order of this kind some time before,' recorded one jaundiced observer in his journal, 'but was taken little notice of notwithstanding the word *immediately*, which scarce a General Order has been without since we came to the Continent.'

Such were the grim realities of life in Boston during the latter months of that year. The man placed in charge on the other side of the lines though had a bewildering set of difficulties of his own to deal with.

On 3 July George Washington had arrived in the American camp to take command. He was to prove a figure of tremendous stature in every sense: broad and well over six feet tall he was physically commanding; as a veteran of earlier conflict on the continent he understood very well the qualities of the fighting men as well as their opponents; and being a wealthy Virginia landowner, he was steeped in the tangled political realities of colonial life.

At Bunker Hill, Burgoyne had written of the British army that 'the zeal and intrepidity of the officers . . . was ill seconded by the private men'. Washington, appearing in the American camp shortly after that battle, diagnosed the precise opposite: 'The principal failure that day, was in the officers . . . but the soldiers generally showed great spirit and resolution.'

These two perceptive generals had between them formulated one of the defining truths of the emerging conflict. A rebellion launched under the banner of 'Liberty' – quite literally, since many of the early flags simply carried that word on a plain-coloured cloth – opened a utopian panorama for the mechanic or indentured labourer hoping to transform his life. The 'haves' could not gain from such an upheaval, merely struggle to preserve what they had, or so many of the gentry who sided with the King in opposition to the revolution believed. The messages of the Patriot party could therefore inspire their own rank and file more easily than British officers could raise the men through exhortation.

As Washington toured the lines, at first he found many of the militia companies called to arms after 19 April. These were packed with enthusiasts – many wore the red 'liberty cap' or had the words 'Liberty or Death' stitched on the fronts of their shirts. In forming their bands, they elected officers, and those men usually came from the same strata as their soldiers. As the excitement of the early weeks gave way to the hardship and boredom of siege lines, the limits of that initial spirit showed themselves too. Many of these men began to think about going home, leaving their officers unequal to the task of maintaining discipline.

In his dealings with militia commanders, Washington saw 'an unaccountable kind of stupidity in the lower class of these people'. This statement revealed a whiff of landowner prejudice even if it was grounded in a sound observation:

There is no such thing as getting officers of this stamp to exert themselves in carrying orders into execution – to curry favour with the men (by whom they were chosen, and on whose smiles possibly they think they may again rely) seems to be one of the principal objects of their attention.

One month followed another on the siege lines and the militia started to drift off. Many had only enlisted for short periods and they insisted on going when their time was up. Their officers generally went with them. In their place, Washington marched new regiments of the

Continental Army, a force summoned from across the thirteen provinces by the Continental Congress. The character and skill of these detachments varied a great deal. Prescott and Stark's veterans of Bunker Hill were transformed into regiments of the new army without too much difficulty, but some of the others left much to be desired.

Consternation had been caused by the arrival at Boston of several hundred riflemen from Pennsylvania and Virginia. These were the troops who attacked Lieutenant Lenthall's Fusiliers in July. Loud, hard-drinking and violent, they embodied frontier spirit and proved almost impossible to discipline. The arrest of several for insolence led to a general mutiny on Prospect Hill in September 1775.

Washington's ability to curb such excesses was initially stymied by the ethos of enthusiastic amateurism that had brought many of his soldiers to the colours. His political masters were loath to permit flogging and it took more than one year for a proper scheme of punishments to be set in place. Until then, lashes for any offence were limited to thirty-nine, although desertion carried the death penalty from November 1775 onwards. Dozens of mutinous riflemen from Prospect Hill received no more than a fine.

Problems of keeping order competed for the commander-in-chief's attention with a host of others, from finding enough powder to procuring clothing and rations. After a few weeks, though, it dawned on Washington that 'the enemy, by their not coming out, are, I suppose, afraid of us'. Gage's inactivity created opportunities for an enterprising enemy commander to serve his own cause. A large detachment was sent north, to try to snuff out the British garrisons in Canada. Washington stepped up raids on land and at sea, giving privateers permission to stop the supplies coming in to Boston.

As the months passed, Congress appointed senior officers to its armies. Some were British-born army veterans. Others were men of property, kings of their own counties with far more wealth to their name than any officer of the Royal Welch Fusiliers. They sought to confirm their status with colonel's or general's commissions, producing squabbles and rivalries over patronage almost identical to those negotiated daily at Horse Guards, the British army's headquarters in London.

There was another category of subordinate that came to serve Washington – those who, like the ordinary soldiers, took advantage of the heady possibilities of revolution. The most impressive of these were two men who found themselves in senior positions on the basis of drive and self-education alone: Henry Knox, a Boston bookseller who read his way to the command of the American artillery, and Nathaniel Greene, a Quaker from Rhode Island who turned his back on the pacifist ideology of his sect, enlisted in the militia, and was by his thirty-fourth birthday in June 1775 appointed the youngest Brigadier General in the continental service.

By October, Washington's new initiatives to drive the British altogether from America (starving them in Boston and invading Canada) were having tangible effects. Down in the town below his lines, though, dramatic change was under way.

The *Cerberus* sailed into Boston Harbour on 6 October after a lengthy passage of the Atlantic. Information, along with many other commodities, had been in short supply and the frigate brought important news. The London newspapers carrying reports of Bunker Hill and of the response to that event were snapped up in every coffee house. Official letters, more importantly, signalled that the debacle of 17 June had cost General Gage his job. William Howe was to take over.

For those seeking advancement, the news of Gage's ouster (dismissal) launched a bewildering array of possibilities. One officer writing home noted, 'The dependents on the present commander-in-chief are down in the mouth and those who have expectations from the new one proportionately in spirits.'

Appointments, like everything else, had gone on in a slow and befuddled way since the war had begun. With Howe taking over, the scene was set for wholesale change and for dizzying displays in the black arts of patronage. Adding to the pace of change, the Ministry responded to the outbreak of war by planning a huge expansion in the army, and the miserable conditions of the siege caused quite a few officers to sell out, creating vacancies.

Thomas Mecan was one of the first to benefit. In November 1775 orders were published setting out a plan to expand the Fusiliers and other regiments doing duty in America to an establishment of more than 850 men. Given that there were only about 300 men fit for duty in Boston by that time, this would involve upheaval for the 23rd.

Two regiments serving in Boston were to be broken up, the rank and file going to others, while the serjeants and officers went home as the bones upon which new bodies of men could be built. The regiments remaining in America were asked to appoint two new company commanders, along with subalterns and non-commissioned officers, to go home for the same purpose. The creation of these two new captain's jobs allowed Mecan to get his step without buying the post. Mecan being Mecan, he traded his place recruiting in England with another officer, taking command of that man's company in America.

Advancing Mecan created a possibility for Frederick Mackenzie at last, and he took the Irish officer's post as captain lieutenant and with it also gained, after his long years of waiting, command of a company. Two other lieutenants moved on too, one worthy but penniless old officer benefiting from the Secretary at War's patronage to gain promotion into another regiment, the other getting the second recruiting captain's job in the Fusiliers and with it his ticket home.

A passage back with the recruiting parties 'pleases them not a little', wrote one of the officers forlornly staying in Boston. In addition to danger on the lines and startling rates of sickness, some men were staring ruin in the face. The annual pay of a 2nd Lieutenant of Fusiliers (the lowest officer rank, called an ensign in other regiments) was just under £67, of lieutenants a little more. Yet by the winter the price of a chicken had gone up to 6/- and of a bushel of potatoes to 12/-. Most were paying rent too and some trying to sustain wives and children. Many subalterns were unable to keep up the struggle and sold out.

On 13 December, Major Francis Hutcheson received an urgent summons to the townhouse that served as General Howe's head-quarters. Hutcheson served on the staff and as unofficial ambassador for Major General Fredrick Haldimand, formerly number two to Gage who had returned to England. Both Hutcheson and his master had been guests at the Welch Fusiliers' Saint David's dinner in March.

As the major made his way through the frigid streets, it is unlikely that he guessed the sudden order concerned General Haldimand's nephew Anthony, who, less than one month earlier, had transferred into the Fusiliers. Hutcheson was summoned into the General's presence to hear a story of woe. Howe said there was a lieutenant in the 45th for whom recent months had proven altogether too much. So indebted was the lieutenant that he asked Hutcheson to 'pay the unfortunate fellow to keep him from starving one hundred pounds'. If this *douceur* was received, then the man would clear his debts and sell out his lieutenancy. The general's nephew, 2nd Lieutenant Haldimand, might then buy the lieutenancy in the 45th for the usual price of £500.

Major Hutcheson quickly drew a bill (on General Haldimand's bankers) for £115 (the bargain proved £15 more expensive than he had expected) and the deal was completed. Young Anthony Haldimand had been promoted out of the 23rd after less than one month in the regiment, and just over one year all-told in the army. The major was gratified that Howe had asked for no favour in return, for the dispensers of army patronage were often keen on dictating a quid quo pro. Perhaps, Hutcheson reasoned, this would be requested later of General Haldimand. Hutcheson wrote to that senior officer, with more than a hint of personal bitterness, 'The respect which is due to you has gained the young man in 13 months a rank that I had three years of hard service to acquire.'

The case of 2nd Lieutenant Haldimand showed what could be achieved with connections and money. But quite a few of those engaging in the hectic traffic of commissions or appointments that autumn in Boston had no cash. In their case the support of a general or noble in England could suffice.

One of those queuing up for a passage home was Lieutenant Richard Baily. He had been commissioned from the *ranks* during the Seven Years War and made the 23rd's quartermaster. He left Boston following an intervention by the Secretary at War, Lord Barrington, who asked for him *by name* to marshal supplies for the American armies. Installed within months as the Embarkation Officer at Portsmouth, Baily would be organising dozens of ships and dispensing thousands of pounds, receiving rapid promotion to captain too, epitomising that practicality bred in the ranks so essential for operation of the British war machine.

Baily's promotion would in turn create a vacancy and there were already so many of those that the regiment would struggle to fill them. Before the year was out, Major Blunt would be gone, seizing his chance to buy the lieutenant colonelcy of the 4th – a heady transaction he could not really afford – and Blakeney, wounded at Bunker Hill, would sail for home. Of those remaining, Lieutenant Colonel Bernard became a marginal figure on the edge of his regiment, for his wounded thigh from 19 April had not healed and he remained unavailable for duty; others among the captains would also be stricken with fevers.

With winter gripping, the city became an even unhealthier place. Soldiers were laid low with fluxes, smallpox and consumption.

Occasionally, supply ships brought in fresh rations, but the diet was execrable and the soldiers increasingly reduced to pulling down houses for firewood.

In this unhealthy situation, Lieutenant Richard Williams, the well-educated Fusilier officer who enjoyed sketching the city, began to succumb to consumption. He would be allowed a passage home and permitted to sell out extra quick in order that he might be able to settle his affairs before he died, early in 1776.

Faced with this bitter hardship, those seeking to brighten the mood began putting on plays. These were staged in Boston's most important civic building, Faneuil Hall, where the first performance took place on 2 December. Lord Rawdon, the army's bright young thing, read the prologue, and other officers took leading parts in a play, *Zara*, by Major General Burgoyne. He delayed his departure from the city to enjoy that first night before taking a ship home to England.

Those who remained sometimes dined at the expense of the two generals who kept fine tables. Others borrowed from their friends or relied upon bills from home to keep the wolf from the door. Major Hutcheson was always ready when the need arose to sub his general's nephew.

As for that young man, he passed through the Royal Welch Fusiliers in little more than three weeks, and serves as an embodiment of what was wrong in the commissioning system. Anthony Haldimand had been commissioned into his uncle's regiment in 1774 as a teenager. The family were Swiss, the old general serving the King of England as a soldier of fortune. When the boy had arrived in Boston, under Hutcheson's care, he spoke no English and knew nothing of military service, despite the date on his first commission. He had attended no military academy, and indeed Britain did not have one for officers of the infantry (although there was such an establishment at Woolwich for the Artillery and Engineers).

Major General Haldimand apparently believed in the tradition that a young man embarking on the profession of arms could learn all he needed to know on actual service. Anthony had started serving with the 23rd in July, following the generals on tours of the lines and learning the rudiments of a junior officer's art.

Lieutenant Colonel Bernard and Major Blunt showed the young man every attention, placing him under the fatherly eye of Frederick Mackenzie, who had got his company in November. By the end of that month, young Haldimand had joined the regimental mess as it was deemed 'necessary he should live with the corps to become better acquainted with the language and customs of it'. Two weeks later he was off, ending his 'career' in the 23rd.

Haldimand paid another visit to the tailors, to have the distinctive colours in his uniform changed to those of the 45th and that was that. He entered his new regiment as a lieutenant with greater seniority than many of his peers, but still knowing little of his job and unable to speak English.

One more officer joined the exodus from Boston that winter. It was Lieutenant John Lenthall, who had repulsed the American riflemen's attack on the lines in July. He, like the officer of the 45th whose commission was bought for Haldimand, had run out of cash. The inflated prices caused by the siege were too much for many men. Late in November, he sold out.

It had taken Lenthall six years' service to find himself in acting command of the 23rd's grenadiers, but boys like Haldimand were daily buying their way to an equality or even overtaking him. He had struggled to stop his men running away by imposing some kind of discipline on them. The soldiers, however, carried on with their boozing and insolence, with Lenthall suffering a rebuff at the court martial when he tried to discipline one of the privates. He had to give up. So, Lieutenant Lenthall joined the generals seeking better society in London or the hobbling invalids nursing their Bunker Hill wounds, and boarded a ship for home. He turned his back on the 23rd as well as America in the dying days of 1775.

Escape From Boston

How the Colonel of the 23rd Reformed an Army

The explosions in the night of 20 March 1776 were unlike anything the citizens of Boston had heard before. Colossal blasts rent the air, shaking houses and rattling the china. The British had put dozens of barrels of powder into their own fort at Castle William and blown it sky high. The barracks on Charlestown peninsula were dealt with next. This destruction sent a clear signal to anyone who might have doubted it: the British were leaving the city.

All of this was set in motion by General Sir William Howe's orders. He had taken over from Gage as commander-in-chief five months earlier, enjoying sweeping powers. Howe had been given discretion by his masters in London to make many strategic choices; he was gathering the strings of patronage tightly in his hands so that he could make promotions as he chose and he was engaged in reforming his army. Howe had also taken a step up in one other respect, for he had, since the previous May, been colonel of the Royal Welch Fusiliers. This title, a gift of the King, amounted almost to ownership of a regiment. Howe did not run the Fusiliers from day to day, a task left to Lieutenant Colonel Bernard and his officers, but acted as a contractor responsible for various aspects of administration such as recruiting and clothing the men. In return for overseeing this work, it was accepted that a regimental colonel could pocket the difference between the money allowed for the raising of new soldiers and the actual cost of that process. Vexed by a thousand practical questions of how he might quit Boston, General Howe had little time for the minutiae of running the 23rd. However, the fact that their titular colonel was directing the entire army might shape the lives of the Royal Welch Fusiliers in many ways.

The quays had been the scene of incessant activity for days. Much of the garrison had already embarked before the 20th, but there was added urgency after that date as hundreds of tons of stores, dozens of cannon and thousands of troops were loaded on to ships. The harbour itself was crowded with scores of transports, civilian charters, and the Royal Navy squadron that would escort them on to the high sea. As the quartermasters and majors of brigade watched jibs lifting barrels or horses on board, they felt a pang of nervousness. Would there be enough room for everything and everyone – the last calculation being complicated by a thousand loyalists pleading for passage? With the waterside scene providing so much bustle and commotion, many soldiers took the opportunity to venture into side streets and break into houses to see what they might steal.

Although many had expected the army to quit Boston, the final impetus had only come on the morning of 5 March, when Washington's army had appeared on Dorchester Heights and prepared emplacements for cannon there. The British had understood for an entire year before this event that guns placed in such a position could threaten ships in the harbour or bombard Boston itself, calling into question the viability of the garrison. Despite this, the ground remained undefended.

General Howe's first impulse had been to re-take the heights by *coup de main* before heavy guns could be put into position. That evening, the 23rd, four other regiments along with battalions of grenadiers and light infantry had been carried by boat to Castle William, which sat on a small island south-west of Boston, only a few hundred yards from the Dorchester peninsula. The general meditated a dawn assault. Thus the Fusiliers and others – a force close to 2,500 men – were asked to perform a second Bunker Hill, dislodging the Americans from prepared works. It could be a desperate business, but it offered ambitious Fusiliers at least a chance to perform some heroic feat in front of their commander-in-chief and regimental colonel, thus gaining promotion.

The general had given a good deal of thought to how he might avoid a similar slaughter to that of the previous June. It cannot exactly be said that Howe was re-writing the army's tactics since no universally accepted manual existed. A drill book (one that set out the basics of how soldiers should stand, fire and form units) had been put out in

1764, but there was no text prescribing how to fight battles, although the 1762 edition of Humphrey Bland's *Treatise of Military Discipline* was widely owned and understood. It is also true that Howe did not promulgate his own written blueprint, but rather issued his ideas in disparate orders and directives. Taken together, though, they marked radical change, a distinctive 'American' way for redcoats to fight, much of it based upon his experience of fighting there during the French and Indian Wars.

Orders were given on 5 March for the grenadiers and light infantry not to load their weapons at all prior to assaulting the American position. In this way, Howe would prevent a repetition of the disaster at Bunker Hill's rail fence, where the flank companies fell into an ineffective firing rather than prosecuting their bayonet charge. Other instructions told the regiments to deploy differently to the European pattern.

At Lexington and Concord the 23rd had done its best to form three deep, with the men so close together their shoulders nearly touched. As Frederick Mackenzie had then noticed, that was not possible on American farmland; too many enclosures, trees or streams got in the way. At Bunker Hill, Howe changed his deployment to one less dense, two deep. Even then, fences, kilns and other obstacles disordered what should have been neat lines before they reached Breed's Hill or the rail fence. Following the battle, therefore, he told his officers to ensure that there would be 18-inch gaps between each 'file', a file by then being the pair of front-rank man and his rear-rank partner. This would allow them to march forward over difficult ground without bumping into one another, and allow room to side-step smaller tree-stumps or large stones. There would be further changes within weeks to many aspects of British tactics, but there had not yet been time to drill the men in these new ideas as they waited for action on that March evening in 1776.

Luckily for the soldiers sent over to Castle William, a gale blew up during the night and, the navy declaring its longboats would get swamped in the choppy sea, the attack on the Dorchester Heights was called off. Rumours ran around the men who went back into the city that thousands of rebels had been ready to face them, and that they had ingenious weapons prepared such as barrels full of rocks to be rolled down the hills as the redcoats tried to come up. The failure to attempt Howe's plan, on the other hand, decided the fate of the garrison and allowed the Americans to secure a further victory.

Within a fortnight of these events, the fleet was loading and within three weeks they were gone. Howe ensured an unimpeded embarkation by threatening to burn the city if the rebels molested his troops. Washington made a jubilant entry and the King's power in Boston was snuffed out. The British quartermasters had been right to fret for they were obliged to leave behind dozens of cannon and thousands of blankets, all of which were gratefully received by the Continental Army.

As ninety men-of-war and transports made sail, racing out of the roads on to the high seas, those who were not 'with secret' might have wondered about the destination. Some yearned that it might be home. Early on in the siege, one officer had greeted with glee a rumour that Britain might abandon the war altogether, writing home, 'I am not one of those bloody-minded people that wish only for revenge and slaughter.'

By April 1776 though, most of the informed observers in the army would have understood that the King was not planning to surrender his American dominions without a fight. Large armies were being raised in Europe – dozens of new battalions were being gathered in Britain, Ireland and on the Continent where several German princelings had agreed to provide men in return for cash. The fleet that had left Boston was therefore not going home, but to Halifax in Nova Scotia, where Howe would wait for his new army and plan the campaign.

Some officers thought Britain's best option lay in a war of naval raiding, sending parties of troops to devastate American ports. Such tactics would force the Americans to spread their little army along thousands of miles of coastline, to be strong nowhere and allow the British to come and go as they pleased, avoiding large garrisons on shore or, worse, having to penetrate the interior of the continent. The march to Lexington and Concord had left quite a few officers in fear of what might happen to British forces, far from their naval support, surrounded by thousands of Americans.

The scale of preparations under way to reinforce Howe was the surest indication though that the Ministry in London had rejected the option of a seaborne war on the cheap. Instead, the forthcoming campaign was to focus on New York and the Hudson River. An American expedition sent late in 1775 to invade Canada had been happily defeated at the gates of Quebec. The British in Canada were preparing to attack southwards, along the historic invasion route to New York, down through the lakes to the Hudson. Howe, having taken New York, would control the southern end of that great river, and could move north.

Seizing New York and, eventually, joining hands along the Hudson line held obvious appeal for the generals. Even in July 1775, Earl Percy, despairing of the Boston situation, had written, 'I confess I should have thought it a more eligible system, to take advantage of the Great Hudson's River to have carried the war into the heart of the country.' Taking New York appealed because it would disrupt the colonists' sea trade with the outside world through their principal port and, if forces could link up on the Hudson, sever overland commerce between the New England colonies and the others. Just for good measure, General Henry Clinton would be sent south with an expedition to take Charleston, the great port of the southern provinces.

Britain's strategic concept carried an aroma of insult in that it assumed the surest way to bring the Americans to bay was through emptying their pockets, rather than by defeating their ideology, but such thinking was not restricted to the King's advisers. Washington shared the view that it would be a disaster for his cause if the colonies were cleaved along the Hudson line and knew also that his political masters would insist he defend the city of New York, even if the army was not ready to do so. This offered Howe the prospect of defeating the American army in battle, and, after all, if the Americans proved incapable of defending their rebellion, how could they claim they were ready for independence? It would take months, though, before General Howe could launch this strategy, while he awaited reinforcements and re-made his army.

At dawn on 3 April, the troops in Halifax bay got their first proper view of the town. Their transports had come in to anchor the previous evening, the sailors, to their credit, performing the operation in darkness. The prospect on that morning was pretty dreadful. It was bitterly cold, with stiff winds. Streams as well as ponds were frozen over and the streets of the little garrison town remained icy. The land itself seemed barren, a wilderness of pine and rocks – the army's horses, once disembarked, had to be taken thirty-eight miles from Halifax to find some grass. In the days that followed, there were several storms, throwing everybody about in their cramped berths on the transports and carrying off several longboats left tethered to the ships' sterns.

Halifax itself was a miserable little town of a few thousand souls whose lives were defined by its function as a military base. There was a dockyard, some works, a couple of taverns and whorehouses. Once the senior officers and Boston civilians had been disembarked there was scarcely any room for the soldiers, most of whom would remain on their transports for months to come.

General Howe, though, was determined to use his time in this apparently sterile place to nurture the growth of a new spirit and discipline in his army. After Gage's ineffectual management of affairs, many officers looked to their new commander-in-chief to grip his army, curbing its wayward soldiery. Captain Lord Rawdon spoke for many when writing before the departure from Boston: 'This winter will improve them much in [discipline], as General Howe is very strict.' Within days of anchoring in the harbour, a constant shuttling of regiments to and from the transports began.

On 14 April the Light Infantry was landed, to be drilled by Major General Percy. Eleven days later it was the turn of the 23rd, 44th and 64th Regiments for the same treatment. Percy supervised the practice of these regiments in manoeuvres, and instructed them in General Howe's orthodoxies. This process, of hard days spent marching, deploying, falling back, on the shores of Nova Scotia would continue for weeks, with each regiment getting chances to exercise its men repeatedly.

The general also wanted to get regiments used to working together, so he established several brigades for the campaign of 1776. Each would be commanded by a brigadier or major general and have its own staff. This development was to provide Frederick Mackenzie with his path out of regimental service, for he was appointed major of brigade, running the little staff of the 6th Brigade, while in Halifax, a recognition of his zeal and attention to detail. Mackenzie would not serve with the Fusiliers in the field for the remainder of the war, but his new job would pay him more and make him a spectator to the doings of higher command.

There had been some thought given to the questions of how to fight dispersed enemies operating in loose formations behind cover, how to manoeuvre on American battlefields and even whether the soldiers were wearing the right clothes. The formal evolutions that Mackenzie or Serjeant Major Keens could remember from Blackheath or

Wimbledon Common, or the ideas on uniform that owed more to fashion than practicality, would be superseded.

Major General Burgoyne, back in England by this time, had jotted down his thoughts about the American enemy. He could see that their way of fighting exploited the high motivation of ordinary soldiers engaged in their cause, noting:

Every private man will in action be his own general, who will turn every tree and bush into a kind of temporary fortress, from whence, when he hath fired his shot with all the deliberation, coolness, and certainty which hidden safety inspires, he will skip as it were, to the next, and so on for a long time till dislodged either by cannon or by a resolute attack of light infantry.

Neither Howe nor Burgoyne believed in aping American tactics exactly. Rather they sensed that an enemy spread out, fighting behind cover, could be conquered easily enough by redcoats exploiting their superior organisation or cohesion, to get around or outflank their American adversaries or rush them before they could re-load. Burgoyne argued: 'Light infantry therefore in greater numbers than one company per regiment, ought to be an essential part of the general system of our army.'

When speaking of 'light infantry' these generals, in essence, meant troops who could move faster. The orders already given out respecting the use of two ranks and spaced files would help. American veterans of the Seven Years War like Howe knew that the 18-inch separation between files was just a start – if soldiers had to charge into woods or occupy a particular piece of ground, a regiment could be stretched to twice its usual frontage, opening gaps as big as two or three feet – or even more – between each pair of soldiers. But further steps could be used too: getting the men to conduct their manoeuvres faster, advancing at the trot or even running, rather than walking, forward at the regulation pace and by changing the nature of those evolutions. General Howe believed that starting all the changes from the centre of each company or battalion was more efficient than beginning from the left or right (as the 23rd had done at Lexington). If a small company, say thirty-six men, occupied a front 24 yards across, forming from one end would place the last file or pair of men 23 yards from those who had begun the manoeuvre – starting from the centre would leave nobody more than 11 yards away, meaning less margin for error and a swifter movement.

General Howe, once in Halifax, grouped all of his light infantry into battalions that would work and train together constantly, deploying as his elite advanced guard brigade in combat. But this did not answer Burgoyne's point that more light infantry relative to the number of regiments was needed. Burgoyne himself, once in command of several British battalions in Canada, would eventually convert the lot to light infantry, training them all to perform their manoeuvres at the double and dressing all of them as light troops.

Howe did not go quite this far; nevertheless, he ordered all regiments to form two deep and learn how to manoeuvre from the centre. He also used a couple of picked regiments which he thought capable of matching the pace of the light infantry to bolster his *corps d'élite*. Howe did not order all of his men to dress as light infantry, but instead accepted many practical improvements in that area.

The dress regulations stipulated the soldier's ideal appearance, but there were other texts available to guide the colonel upon the delicate matter of producing the most genteel and distinguished-looking body of men possible. Bennett Cuthbertson's work was particularly influential, gaining hundreds of subscribers including thirteen officers of the Royal Welch Fusiliers, among them Lieutenant Colonel Bernard, Thomas Mecan and Frederick Mackenzie. On matters of appearance, Cuthbertson was a pedant whose inclinations showed the short distance that sometimes separates the military camp from its theatrical variety.

Cuthbertson felt the coat should be tailored, 'always be tight over the breast (without restraint) for the sake of showing his figure to more advantage'; the soldier's breeches 'must be made to fit smooth and tight upon the thighs' and, as for socks, 'the greatest uniformity should be observed in the colour of the stockings, through a regiment, as nothing more offends the eye'. Adding to the general constriction, a tight collar, the stock, was fastened about the neck, half gaiters (with rows of buttons) were fastened over the shoes, and the hair scraped back, pulled tight across a metal ball, tied and then powdered.

Soldiers of line regiments wore a black felt hat which had the brim stitched up in such a way as to give it a fore-peak and two corners. Three regiments designated 'fusiliers' (the 7th, 21st and 23rd) were given by the regulations the distinction of wearing bearskin caps. In fact, the men of the Royal Welch had donned these prized hats when parading before the King five years before, but rarely (if ever) since. Their grenadiers continued to wear the (slightly taller) bearskin cap that distinguished these troops, officers in the 23rd often acquired fusilier caps at personal expense and wore them, and some may have been kept for General's Guards and other special detachments. But the workaday headgear of the 23rd was the black cocked hat, just like other regiments.

Quite a few officers had commented before 1775 that this regulation dress was completely impractical for campaigning. One general, writing two years earlier, had denounced the cocked hat as 'extremely incommodious', likely to be knocked off in woods, and predicted the long coat tails would snag on undergrowth; and he was disgusted at the traditional practice of dressing the hair, which he argued was likely to produce 'stagnated humours, which break out into scabs and ulcers'. He suggested instead a small leather cap on the head, 'the common tight light jacket', and one-piece trousers. This was close to the dress of the Light Infantry battalion in Wolfe's army (which William Howe had commanded) and it should therefore be unsurprising that in the first half of 1776, a similar-looking soldier emerged in his own host.

There was much needle-and-thread work going on between the cramped decks of the army's transports as they lay at anchor in Halifax, and it would go on throughout the coming campaign too. The ranks of the regiment always contained a few tailors, so these and other dab hands earned some coppers from their mates as they altered their clothes.

The results, as they moved away from regulation appearance, varied from one regiment to another, but the general trend was looser, shorter garments made more practical, as well as the jettisoning of adornment. Black felt hats were cut down or unstitched so they were less likely to be knocked off, more able to shade the eyes.

While dealing with all these pressing matters of army administration at Halifax, Howe found himself conducting an interview of the most delicate personal nature. Henry Blunt had come to the general with a problem that affected him both as commander-in-chief and colonel of the 23rd. Blunt had left the Fusiliers the previous summer on purchasing the lieutenant colonelcy of the 4th Regiment. The acquisition of this rank – the highest that could be bought and sold – set in train a chain of transactions or 'succession' that rippled down the regimental hierarchy with someone buying the vacant majority, who in turn sold his captaincy and so on. Since this sequence of deals could involve many thousands of pounds it had to be carefully timed. The officer who could not afford to buy his lieutenant colonelcy outright (regulation price £3,500) had to borrow. Blunt's undoing was that he had sold his majority in the 23rd but was so heavily overdrawn that he still could not raise the money to complete the purchase of his higher rank in the 4th.

Many officers skirted the shoals of insolvency as they bought their way up the army, but Blunt had wrecked himself. He could not go back to the 23rd as major, since that door had closed behind him when another officer, William Blakeney (still on leave in England), had bought the post. General Howe could not elbow Benjamin Bernard aside as lieutenant colonel of the Fusiliers either, since that invalid officer insisted he could still serve and, in any case, Blunt had shown suspect judgement in his transactions. What was more, the former major of the 23rd was close to Gage and other members of a set that were discredited in Howe's eyes. Blunt pleaded with the general to be allowed to return to England to raise some additional money so that he might escape the shameful limbo in which he found himself. Howe agreed, and in doing so aroused the King's displeasure: why was the commander-in-chief allowing the commanding officer of one of his regiments to go home when a vital campaign was about to begin? Howe explained it 'from a knowledge of the inextricable difficulties in [Blunt's] private affairs arising from the purchase of his present commission'.

As it would transpire, Blunt failed to find the extra cash at home and was forced to sell out of the army. He had allowed ambition to blind him to the fact that he could not really afford the promotion he craved. William Howe might have protected Blunt from this fate by allowing him acting or brevet rank on the staff or in command of the 4th but chose not to. Howe could advance those he valued without any money changing hands – thus he had obtained Thomas Mecan a captaincy and given Nisbet Balfour the prestigious job as one of his aides-de-camp. He could also facilitate back-room deals of the kind brokered for Lieutenant Haldimand. It was simply a matter of the general's whim. Little wonder that some nervous old officers decried the 'despotic power of Commanders in Chief abroad'.

Had General Howe wanted to advance the interests of his own regiment or its officers, he would have done so with the stroke of a pen. But as the grumbling old captains of the 23rd soon discovered, few of its men apart from Thomas Mecan had caught their chief's eye. What was more, Howe showed every symptom of being that species of colonel far more interested in what he could get out of a regiment than what he could put in.

When presented with the colonelcy of the Royal Welch, Howe had let it be known that he did not want it and would rather have a regiment of heavy cavalry. The high prices of commissions, uniform, horses and saddlery all allowed the colonel of such a corps to make a larger profit. Having accepted the Fusiliers with such ill grace, Howe then got into an argument with the widow of the regiment's previous colonel over which of them should pay for the 1776 issue of uniforms. To be clear, Howe *wanted* to pay since he did not want to be denied the chance to profit on the business.

By contrast the behaviour of Earl Percy as a major general serving in America and colonel of the 5th Regiment was regarded by many as a model of benign aristocratic patronage. As heir to the dukedom of Northumberland, Percy was scion of one of England's greatest land-owning families. In one letter to his father, the duke, Percy summed up his soldierly credo thus: 'I serve only for credit and not for profit.' Indeed, it was an article of faith with Percy to spend *more* on his soldiers' uniforms than the regulation allowed. He also opened his own purse to buy commissions for men who he believed would make good officers but lacked private wealth. So whereas one nobleman might create a *ferme ornée* – a gilded farm – or another fill his house with exquisite antiquities gathered on the Grand Tour, Major General Percy regarded the 5th with a passion as his vehicle for ideas about military taste and progress.

Percy would not allow soldiers of the 5th to be flogged, since the punishment disgusted him. After the regiment suffered heavy casualties at Bunker Hill, he chartered a ship at his own expense to take the widows and children of his fallen soldiers home. By this step he shamed the Secretary at War into providing a similar service for hundreds of women in an equally melancholy situation but belonging to other regiments, who found themselves evacuated to Halifax. 'Though his regiment is distinguished for its admirable discipline, he will never suffer the private men to be struck,' wrote one soldier of the 5th, 'but endeavours to win them to their duty by generous treatment, by rewards, and by his own excellent example.' Percy's attitude was unusual even if it was not unique, for Earl Cornwallis was certainly fanatical about his own regiment, the 33rd, which was also serving in America. Alas for the 23rd Fusiliers, someone like Howe, who lacked a private fortune, and was not greatly interested in his regiment, was the more usual type of colonel.

Faced with Howe's indifference, some of the 23rd's older officers gravitated towards Earl Percy, hoping his famed generosity might assist their promotion. Captain Jo Ferguson, for example, who was ambitious and had the money to buy his next step, had enjoyed Percy's hospitality while the 23rd were serving with his brigade in Boston. Ferguson began corresponding with the earl. Captain Donkin, with little money to his name and tainted by his service on General Gage's staff (all of whom knew they could expect nothing from Howe), began courting Percy too. Donkin dedicated to the earl a book he was compiling, writing fawningly in the foreword that Percy was 'the *heir* of that *illustrious family*, in whom concentrate all the *virtues* of his *glorious ancestors*'.

In their different ways, then, officers like Blunt, Ferguson or Donkin, who might once have thought that Howe's appointment as colonel could bring great things to them or the 23rd, were all disappointed. The Fusiliers got no special treatment. One of Howe's critics, an observer at headquarters, castigated him for being 'illiterate and indolent to the last degree'. If Howe could not be bothered to lavish time on regimental affairs, neither was he keen to codify his views on tactics. The general's fear of pen and paper, it is true, may have played its role in ensuring that no proper manual was ever written of the light infantry or American approach he was now inculcating in his army. The general's one positive quality was that he was certainly not indolent about effecting this change. For Howe, his moment of glory seventeen years earlier scaling a precipitous path to the Heights of Abraham at Quebec defined him as a soldier. At Halifax in 1776, Howe would start turning the light infantry into the elite and pattern for his whole army. He would restore his soldiers' faith in victory and their discipline at the same time.

As May went by at Halifax there were changes aplenty. Supply ships arrived regularly from Britain. Some brought welcome gifts too. One officer noted that month that 'the soldiers that served last campaign at Boston have each received a pair of shoes and stockings, a woollen cap and a quantity of tobacco, a donation from the people of England'. These patriotic offerings extended to one pound of superfine tobacco and ten gallons of rum – a mind-boggling ration – for each officer. There were also special provisions for the relief of women who had lost their husbands in Boston; many were shipped home and a small number per regiment allowed to remain with the army as its servants.

For soldiers, the bounty of tobacco and rum was supplemented by plentiful fresh food. Parties were made up most days to go fishing in longboats, since any fool with a hook could pluck belting cod from these waters. Officers went on trips ashore, hunting wildfowl and fishing inland streams that teemed with trout. Constitutions were fortified too by news from Canada, as it became clear when detailed reports arrived that the Americans had suffered a major defeat, their campaign costing thousands of men and degenerating into a shambles. Spirits began to lift in Howe's command.

By early June, preparations were at an advanced stage for the army to leave Nova Scotia. A vast fleet of chartered transports was assembling at Cork, Bremen and the Downs to bring over thousands more soldiers. There would be entire regiments from Britain, Ireland and the German states. There would also be thousands of reinforcements for the depleted army that had seen through the campaign of 1775.

During these final weeks, General Howe tried to take some steps to strengthen discipline. John Browning, a rogue in the 23rd, was ordered to be clapped in irons below the decks of one of the ships for striking an officer. Howe promised that this 'crime of the greatest magnitude', a capital offence, would be dealt with by general court martial as soon as the army was established further south. Three young officers caught gambling were summoned to the General's cabin on board the *Chatham* to be admonished about the dangers of such dissolute habits.

On 10 June the signal was hoisted for the fleet to sail. One by one, ships got under way, joining in line astern for a passage out of the harbour. The soldiers peering over the taffrail marvelled at the cod teeming alongside the wooden walls of their transports. Some wondered whether Washington's army, which had been concentrating around New York for weeks, would subject them to a series of Bunker Hills as the redcoats tried to land and deploy their armies. At 9 p.m. the leading ships made sail and the journey towards New York, the prize and focus of the impending campaign, began.

The Battle for New York

In Which Serjeant Grimes and Captain Grove
Were Unfortunate

For a few weeks that summer, Staten Island was the focal point of a vast global effort, a destination for hundreds of ships and temporary home to more than 30,000 troops. A place known better for market gardens and pleasant coves became the cockpit for the greatest projection of power ever attempted by Britain, or for that matter any country.

The Halifax armament, 9,300 men borne in 130 ships, had begun disembarking on 2 July. Ten days later, General William Howe's seafaring brother, Admiral Lord Richard Howe, sailed into view with a further 150 vessels carrying reinforcements from Europe. After that Lieutenant General Henry Clinton came in with dozens of sail of his own, following the unsuccessful attempt to take Charleston to the south.

Preparations for the next stage of the campaign lay in the hands of staff and special corps gathered for labour, like the carpenters who banged and sawed away, building shallow-draught assault boats. For a major of brigade like Mackenzie, it was a time of organising provisions, collecting each regiment's returns – the forms they filled out stating their strengths, number of sick and so on – or gathering working parties. Matters were not helped by his difficult relationship with Francis Smith, his brigadier, the commander of the previous year's expedition to Lexington and Concord, whom Mackenzie regarded as too overweight, old and mediocre for his job.

Below Mackenzie, the adjutants would gather information within each regiment or disseminate the brigadier's orders. Above the captain, Howe's deputy adjutant general, Stephen Kemble, collated figures for the army as a whole. The quartermaster general's department organised the camp, furnished food or forage and gathered wagons, a hundred of which were hired with their drivers on Staten Island.

For the Royal Welch Fusiliers and other regiments that had escaped the tedium of Halifax, these weeks were a time of ceaseless activity and curiosity. Each one promised a new experience, or the sight of some previously unheard-of corps.

The Ministry in London had worked unceasingly through the winter months, gathering troops in Cork, at Spithead and on the Clyde, as well as at the mouths of the Elbe and Weser. General Howe was being sent 4,400 more redcoats and 10,000 Germans, mainly from the principality of Hesse-Kassel, the hired soldiers whom the Americans called 'Hessians'.

When the German-speakers came ashore, two military cultures collided. The princelings had copied the dress, drill, and ethos of Frederick the Great, for it was that monarch's philosophy that had guided his Prussian troops to great victories during the Seven Years War. The grenadiers had metal-fronted mitres, twirled moustaches and heavy swords. There were fusiliers too among them, the Erbprinz, Knyphausen or von Lossberg regiments. They wore (slightly smaller) metal-fronted caps, made from cloth of their distinctive colours; carmine, orange or black. They and the British were soon sizing one another up with the pride of military men who each assumed *their* way was better.

Ministers in London had quickly become certain that they could only meet their field commanders' requests for large reinforcements by employing foreign troops. Their arrival in America provided the Whig news-sheets with a rich theme, for the Germans were characterised as brutal automata, brought to ravish the land. Some British officers, particularly those favouring the devastation of the country, concurred. 'The assistance of foreign troops will be highly politick,' one ultra-Tory wrote home, 'they are less likely to be seduced by the artifice and intrigue of these holy hypocrites.'

The Hessian officers themselves were struck by all that was strange about the new land. It began with the non-regulation appearance of Howe's men. 'The English have been clothed according to the hot climate,' one field officer wrote to the Landgrave, 'with very short and light coats, and long linen trousers down to the shoes.' The British, on the other hand, were soon snickering at the perspiring Germans, red-faced and puffing in their heavy woollen coats, obliged by the heat to take off their bayonet belts and slinging them over shoulders on the march so that they could open all the buttons of their waistcoats.

As to what the new arrivals thought of the ordinary redcoat, one acute Bavarian wrote:

the common British soldier is swift, marches easily . . . when they go against an enemy, they are fresh, optimistic, and do not worry about their life . . . the English keep their clothing very clean and have only the vices of cussing, swearing, drinking, whoring, and stealing and these more so than almost all other people.

These then were the qualities, good and bad, of the rankers. General Howe, though, could not get enough such men. Early schemes to expand the establishment of the 23rd and other British regiments up to something over 800 men had proven chimerical.

During the summer of 1776, men were sent to the 23rd Fusiliers in several small detachments. There were some Scottish recruits who thought they were joining another regiment entirely. A further twenty-five men found in England for other regiments were similarly re-routed. Eighteen men had been attracted to volunteer from corps serving in Ireland, and in addition to the German-speakers who served in the Hessian regiments, a few hundred were sent to British ones as reinforcements, the 23rd's quota being thirty-seven privates, a corporal and one serjeant. In sum, the regiment that Lieutenant Williams had thought the previous summer contained rather too many 'young troops' found itself receiving dozens of new men speaking different languages, from widely differing backgrounds.

Dispersing these little parties of arrivals to their different companies fell to the junior officers and serjeants. They would assign the newcomers to a mess, or group of six soldiers, so called because such groups shared a camp kettle for cooking up meals.

The non-commissioned officers knew the newcomers came in two categories: draftees and recruits. Draftees were men from other corps; some, like the volunteers from the regiments based in Ireland, would already have been thoroughly familiar with the Manual Exercise of using their musket. Other drafts came from regiments in America that were broken up to augment the remainder. Nine men, for example, came to the 23rd on Staten Island from the 65th Regiment of Foot, and seven from the 69th.

Recruits on the other hand were men more recently enlisted at the tavern or county fair. Some had arrived in America without even a uniform. They had little or no training and some of them, for example the forty men who came on the Clyde transports, had been sweet-talked by the recruiting serjeant of a different regiment. These greenhorns were often a burden for their non-commissioned officers, since they knew little, and many bitterly regretted joining, sinking into the depths of despair.

Jeffrey Grimes, who had fought at Lexington as a corporal, had by late 1775 been promoted to serjeant, after a service of just five years in the army. To the knot on his shoulder, the serjeant added a sash, coloured scarlet with a stripe of royal blue to tie around his midriff. Grimes was moving up the ranks swiftly for the serjeant's duties were considered onerous.

'A serjeant should . . . be able to instruct', one expert opined, 'and he will not only be required to inform his inferiors alone but sometimes his superiors likewise. He must understand writing and accounts and must be well informed in the whole *routine* of the service and customs of the army.' Another military savant believed it was essential for such non-commissioned officers to display 'honesty, sobriety, and a remarkable attention to every point of duty'.

The burden on serjeants during those weeks on Staten Island was certainly great. Daily, they schooled the new recruits and drafts, getting them to fit into their company, answering words of command as it wheeled about the fields. In many such groups of the 23rd there was only a single lieutenant with any idea of his business, the captains being elsewhere and the 2nd Lieutenants as green as the men.

Those serjeants or corporals who failed to maintain the standards required of them could be broken by regimental court martial. In contrast with the more serious general court martial, this was called for misdemeanours such as spitting, slovenliness or drunkenness. A man would be judged by his own corps, and the proceedings, often held in a tent in the field, dealt with the business in a matter of minutes. They would face the ignominy of having the knot ceremonially cut from their shoulder in front of the regiment, being reduced to the rank of private. It had happened to enough men in the 23rd and it was certainly regarded as a humiliation. It did not happen to Serjeant Grimes.

Throughout July and the early part of August, the regiment bivouacked on the island, living under canvas and marching about between the prosperous farms and orchards. By day there was drill and marching. At night the aroma of cedar and sassafras drifted into the tents.

While the companies went about their business, the regiment itself was almost bereft of leadership. Lieutenant Colonel Bernard had never fully recovered from being shot in the thigh the previous year. He occasionally presented himself for duty, but languished at other times for weeks on his sick bed. One friend of Bernard's noted months previously that 'he is confined and not likely to get better' and upon asking why the colonel did not join all the other wounded officers going home, the old gentleman opined he did 'not think he would be better there than here'.

It may be that Bernard stayed because he hoped for some promotion, or that he wanted to keep a fatherly eye on his boy, who still did duty as a lieutenant in the regiment. Disaster struck in early August though. Benjamin Bernard the younger was laid low on Staten Island by one of those 'camp fevers' that afflicted armies under canvas, and by the 12th had died aged just twenty-two. In such difficult times, the regimental major should have been on hand to command, but Blunt had sold the majority to William Blakeney the previous year and that Irishman chose to remain in England. Blakeney was opposed to the war and, having taken a wound at Bunker Hill, was not going to expose himself to the dangers of another campaign. Instead he resorted to ever more fanciful flights of imagination to explain his refusal to return to the 23rd. This unsatisfactory situation left the regiment under the superintendence of an unsatisfactory officer, that boozy Scot Grey Grove.

There can be little doubt that this combination of Captain Grove's taking charge with Lieutenant Colonel Bernard appearing occasionally from his sick bed would have been felt by all ranks. 'The state of the regiment in every military point of view', noted one serjeant of the Royal Welch, 'depends on the exertion and vigilance of the officer commanding.' In one aspect though they were fortunate, for the strokes being planned by General Howe involved warfare on a huge scale, and the 23rd would at least be ably supported in the battle that was about to come.

In his headquarters, the British commander-in-chief eyed the prize of New York like some rare flower surrounded by beds of thorns. Staten was just one of several outlying islands that separated America's principal trading post from the open sea. The long British build-up had allowed George Washington plenty of time to lay out defences. Cannon were sited on the harbour, denying the Howe brothers any chance of sailing straight up to land their men at the city quays. The approach would have to be indirect, overland, so there were lines on Long Island. Where that land came close to Manhattan at Brooklyn, redoubts had been thrown up to guard the most obvious landward route towards the city. Other forts guarded likely landing places or strong ground both above the city of New York and on the Jersey shore.

Washington was certainly outnumbered, having something like 19,000 men at his disposal, and his predicament was made all the more awkward by the dispersal of troops necessary to cover various possible landing places. He would require immediate word of any British move and excellent staff work to get his men to the threatened sector. His only real advantage lay in occupying a central position from which he might quickly move reserves to where they were needed.

General Howe, though, would have an army at his disposal large enough to stage multiple landings or outflank his enemy. So large was it, the brigades formed in Halifax were grouped together into divisions. The Hessians formed one (with a second on its way at sea), and Earl Charles Cornwallis, a general of undoubted gifts and zeal, was given the plum job of commanding the *corps d'élite* containing the grenadiers and light infantry. Generals Percy and Clinton were also available to lead divisions, but their chief had other ideas. Indeed Howe would keep all of the respected senior officers in the army close to himself, commanding elite forces in the coming battle.

Those who led the brigades made up of marching regiments of foot were of a lower quality altogether. Major General Robertson, at the head of the 1st Brigade, was already acquiring a reputation for corruption on a grand scale. Pigot, who had the 2nd, was competent but uninspired and had at least survived his baptism of fire at Bunker Hill. It was, however, the commander of the 4th Brigade, James Grant, who was destined to lead a division in which the 23rd would be employed.

Grant was, depending upon one's perspective, a canny political operator and generous host or a braying buffoon with little idea of generalship. During the siege of Boston, he had given lavish parties, sustaining many an impoverished officer. Grant himself had grown fat and gouty from overindulgence, savouring the delicacies prepared by Baptiste, his black cook, who accompanied him on campaign. As a veteran of the Seven Years War in America and former governor of Florida he also knew the colonial political scene.

Although Grant's letters revealed a sharp mind, he succumbed easily to hubris and had moments of dreadful judgement. As a Member of Parliament he had made a notorious speech early in 1775 in which he predicted the Americans 'would never dare to face an English army', and that he would be able to march from one end of the continent to the other with 5,000 men. These public utterances were surpassed by blistering private rhetoric, Grant writing to one correspondent as the New York campaign began that 'if a good bleeding can bring those Bible-faced Yankees to their senses – the fever of Independence should soon abate'.

Officers who considered themselves more sane on the subject of dealing with the rebellion bemoaned Grant's influence over General Howe. Earl Percy noted tartly, 'Brigadier General Grant directs our Commander-in-chief in all his operations. Mr Howe is I believe the only man in his army who does not perceive it.' Percy and others thought Grant and one or two other influential Scots such as Captain Nisbet Balfour, one of Howe's aides-de-camp, pushed their chief to take brutal measures against the Americans. Certainly it was clear by mid-August, with 350 ships and tens of thousands of men, that the tables had been turned since the march to Lexington, and that General Howe was ready to bring overwhelming force to bear on the rebellion.

For Major General William Alexander the first real intimation of battle came when he was roused at 3 a.m. on 27 August. Alexander, or Lord Stirling as his men called him, since he had claimed right to an old Scottish earldom, had been placed in charge of the American right at Long Island. Five days earlier, the British had moved over from Staten Island using seventy-five specially built flat-bottomed boats. It was a textbook operation in which 15,000 soldiers were ferried across in a day.

Trouble then was expected, as Alexander issued orders to his battalions and went forward to see what was going on. There was only a faint glimmer of light on the eastern horizon, over to his left, as he met Lieutenant Colonel Samuel Attlee, in command of the Pennsylvania Musket Battalion, a light infantry corps that furnished his outposts. There had already been some scattered firing as British scouts ran into Attlee's outlying men. Alexander and Attlee conferred atop Gowanus Ridge, the feature forming the main American

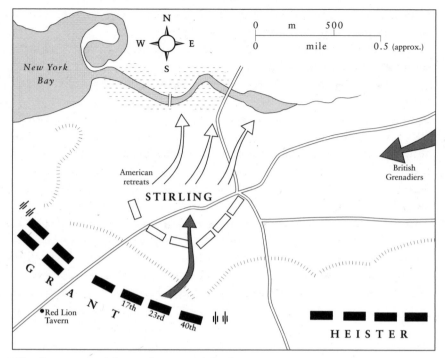

The disposition of the 23rd at Long Island

defensive position on Long Island. It was ground well suited for defence, having the advantage of height, with sea anchoring Alexander's right flank at Gowanus Bay and a thick wood giving some security to his left. The only drawback to this fighting ground was that the bay curved around behind some of it, and a swamp extended a little inland, making it hard for the general's men, particularly on his right, to get away quickly if they had to.

General Alexander was no defeatist however – far from it. He had called up his regiments from their bivouacs and would soon have them deployed. Before the general had finished conferring with the commander of his outposts, he spotted the first redcoats through the murk of the early summer morning, less than half a mile ahead, near the Red Lion Tavern.

A road ran down Alexander's sector of Gowanus Ridge, towards the enemy, and as his troops marched up he directed Attlee to fall back to the left of the road, and re-form in the woods, while his two best regiments, from Delaware and Maryland, got into position, forming a line ready to receive their enemy. At this point, dawn, Alexander's forces in place topped 1,000. Far more redcoats could be seen in front of them, but the American commander could at least reckon on having the best men in the American battle line.

The 'Delaware Blues' were so nicknamed because they were virtually the only American regiment in the battle that were smartly uniformed in blue coats with red cuffs and lapels, as well as domed leather caps shaped a little like those of the Hessian fusiliers. The Maryland soldiers, noted as 'men of honour, family and fortune', wore an item more widespread on the lines that morning, a fringed hunting shirt. These garments were usually made of linen, often in its natural colour, sometimes dyed in some suitable forest colour. Washington had ordered these to be the uniform of the Continental Army, a move that was both practical, given the wide availability of such garments, and from a desire to play on redcoat fears, born of the previous year's events in Boston, of American sharpshooters. 'It is a dress', wrote Washington, 'justly supposed to carry no small terror to the enemy, who thinks every such person a complete marksman.'

Approaching these Americans were General Grant's division, 2,650 men in nine regiments. Grant deployed his men into battle formation. On his left, he went for compactness, grouping four of them, two behind two. To the right, Grant extended his formation, pushing four battalions out in line, one next to the other. The 23rd were in this area, finding the 17th to their left and 40th to their right. Two pieces of field artillery were also unlimbered to the Fusiliers' right (and another pair, far off to the left close to Gowanus Bay). One regiment was held in reserve, guarding the baggage. Grant's cannon began to fire about 5 a.m., and the first hours of the battle consisted of bombardment and clashes of musketry where the British tried to explore or push into the American position.

Grant's men probed first on the American right, then on its left. It was during these latter movements that the 23rd and 40th took position on a knoll close to the extreme inland point on Alexander's line. That general's troops meanwhile took great satisfaction from the results of these contests. Attlee, leading a mixed force of his own battalion with some Delawares and riflemen, went to contest the knoll to his front left. Initially his troops were staggered by the fire they received, but soon damned the British for their poor marksmanship and pushed on. 'The enemy', Attlee reported by letter, 'fled with precipitation, leaving behind them twelve killed upon the spot.'

Alexander's men became exultant. The Delawares, Marylanders and other detachments that had joined them were standing in open battle against professional soldiers. Colours flying, they were enduring the enemy bombardment like veterans, and holding at bay a force several times their number. This happy reverie was broken at 9 a.m. when two distinct thumps of a heavy cannon were heard. What could it mean?

Brigadier Grant and his regiments were but bit-players in that morning's drama. His job, and that of a Hessian division to his right under von Heister, was to keep the enemy engaged, so that the army's elite could march around the end of the American line three miles inland. It had been left dangerously hanging on the Gowanus Ridge. William Howe, accompanied by Major Generals Clinton and Cornwallis had set out in the early hours, marching their troops nine miles to the point where they would begin their attack, a devastating onslaught that would sweep along Gowanus Ridge, behind the American defences, cutting continental regiments to pieces as it went.

Major General Alexander did not know what those two guns announced. The higher command of American troops was poor that day; nobody was sent to tell him about the disaster that began to overtake the army, and, being on the extreme right of the American line, the collapse beginning on the left would reach him last.

Grant began to push his own right forward, so as to keep Alexander engaged and get around his inland flank. The 23rd and 40th marched onwards, entering the wood occupied by Attlee's men and driving them through. They emerged to a hail of fire. Several Fusiliers dropped, as did the commanding officer of the 40th, a lieutenant colonel also named Grant. This caused consternation in that regiment, and it fell for some time into disorder. Bullets claimed quite a few Fusiliers in these moments and it was those in particular that day who moved among the men, urging them on, that were targeted. Captain Grove was tumbled, receiving his death wound, as did that ardent Serjeant, Jeffrey Grimes. Poor Grimes would be buried in a common grave in America, his bright career as a soldier terminated abruptly.

The 23rd pushed on, but since its neighbouring battalion had halted, a flank had been left hanging, a position creating on a small scale the crisis that was now enveloping the Americans on the larger – for a long line of troops could deliver fire very well to its front, but when struck from the side end or rear usually collapsed. The Fusiliers weathered the danger, and a soldier in one of the following regiments extolled them: 'The 23rd Regiment signalised themselves in this action, and shewed such a good example, that undisciplined *recruits* among them, that had not even received their regimentals, fought with great courage.'

Howe's hammer-blow was by this point breaking the enemy army to pieces. Many Americans, realising that there were redcoats behind as well as in front, broke ranks and fled. British soldiers gave chase in places, pursuing with little mercy. Other Americans remained in companies here or there trying to offer resistance. The battle broke down into many small engagements, confusion spreading through the copses and fields along with the smoke and cries of anguish.

When the 2nd British Grenadiers arrived close to Grant's right at about 11 a.m., they were received with a smart volley from the men in front. Assuming them to be Hessians carried away in the general confusion, a party of redcoats went forward to ask them to stop. These men were all felled by the answering fire, for the Delaware Blues were no Hessians. Several officers would accuse Grant afterwards of dawdling and not pushing forward at this time as quickly as he ought.

Alexander tried to conduct an orderly withdrawal, but his men had the creek and swamp behind them, and their way to the bridge across it was blocked by British troops. The Marylanders made several attempts to charge through, but without success. Men began their last desperate bid to escape, throwing away their equipment, wading into the water, trying to swim the 80 yards across the creek.

By early afternoon, large parties of American prisoners were being collected. Major General Alexander was captured by Hessians as was the neighbouring divisional commander. There were various reports of summary executions, the commander of the British grenadiers for example, noting, 'the Hessians gave very little quarter to any'. One Hessian returned the compliment, accusing the British of this crime, but admitting in a letter home that his own men beat some prisoners.

Lieutenant Colonel Attlee whose light infantry had clashed with the 23rd that morning surrendered with two dozen of his men at 5 p.m. He had spent some time looking for redcoats to ask for quarter, assuming they would give better treatment than the Germans. The remnants of Alexander's brigade were marched back under guard, 'receiving, as we passed, the most scurrilous and abusive language, both from the officers, soldiers and camp ladies, everyone at the time turning hangman, and demanding of the guard why we were taken'.

The prisoners, gathering in forlorn clumps, took some comfort at least from the news spreading in whispers between them that the hated Grant had been killed in the fight, for word of his bombastic performance in Parliament had spread through Alexander's brigade. The rotund Scottish general had the pleasure of discussing his demise with one captured rebel and did not disabuse him. It was the commanding officer of the 40th, also named Grant, who had fallen that day, and not the noisy gastronome of Ballindalloch Castle.

The British Grenadiers, exulting at their victory, wanted to move straight into an attack on the Brooklyn lines, those built behind Gowanus Ridge on the feature dominating the ferry to Manhattan. Howe would not allow this, earning the scorn of Henry Clinton and several other senior officers, who felt he had failed to turn his victory into an annihilation. At the start of the day there were 10,000 or so American troops on Long Island – more than half of Washington's army defending the whole of New York. The line on Gowanus Ridge accounted for about one third of those men. Howe's attack captured 1,600 (1,100 on the day and 500 during following days), killed another 300 and drove the remainder either back into the Brooklyn lines or to desertion.

Casualties in General Howe's army totalled 377 killed, wounded and missing. The losses, though, were considered small compared to the gain.

In the days after the battle of Long Island, morale soared. Captain Frederick Mackenzie noted in his journal that 'the troops are all in the highest health and spirits'. No matter that Washington managed to escape from Brooklyn with thousands of Continentals, nor that General Howe moved with ponderous slowness to capitalise on his advantage; the stains of 1775 had been effaced, and the British army recovered considerably in its confidence.

While the British enjoyed the advantage of numbers, the story of numerous engagements had also validated General Howe's orders on tactics. The column that delivered the flanking attack had been under strict orders to receive the enemy's first fire before rushing in while the Americans reloaded. In numerous running engagements fought between fences or in the trees, the mystique of the American marksmen had to a considerable extent been destroyed. 'They were not so dreadful as I expected,' reported the commander of one British light infantry company that fell into an American ambush, 'or they must have destroyed me and my whole company before we were supported by anyone else.' Others wrote that rifles took too long to re-load and that some of the Americans had ended up stuck to trees with bayonets as a result.

The Hessians who had attacked in the centre felt that their casualties had been low because the Americans had all fired too high – a fault typical of green troops on high ground. It is clear, on the other hand, that Attlee's advanced corps had contained some skilled marksmen, for they had claimed Grant at the head of the 40th and Grove of the 23rd. However, these dreadful tokens of skill at arms were generally set aside by British officers considering the victory, for their mood was up, they had overcome the fear of an enemy that had made the previous year's retreat from Lexington and Concord such purgatory.

Those who scrambled over the abandoned enemy works could gaze across the water from Brooklyn heights to the city. With its large waterfront warehouses and five- or six-storey brick-built dwellings it projected an image of Dutch solidity. The gabled roofs were tiled with shingles that were 'varnished and painted in a variety of colours, and, as a result, make a splendid appearance'. These reminders of the city's origins as New Amsterdam were supplemented by fine public buildings – eighteen churches thrust their spires into the summer's sky, with those of Trinity, Saint Paul's and Saint George's vying for supremacy. The Fusilier officers who had spent their first year in America garrisoned in New York could have pointed out other landmarks too; from the Old Ship Inn on the left of their panorama to the elegant cupola atop the jail on their right. It was, in short, a bigger and better city than Boston, a place that appeared to offer a better foundation for the reconstruction of British power in America.

It took weeks for General Howe to push forward again after Long Island. There were numerous military preparations and peace envoys were received on Staten Island. The Patriots having pushed forward America's Declaration of Independence on 4 July, these talks proved fruitless. The thirteen states of the new republic saw themselves engaged in a struggle for survival and were no longer willing to discuss the terms of their subjection to a British King. The Howe brothers pressed on and by a series of landings, the British made ready to enter the city of New York.

In the early evening of 15 September the 5th Brigade received orders to march into New York. By 7 p.m. the 22nd Regiment was posted at the

Bowery. The commander, Brigadier Smith, looked up the road. Might it not be a good idea to deploy the brigade in order to block both roads leading out of the city, in case any American troops were still there, his Major of Brigade respectfully suggested? The Brigadier snapped back at Captain Mackenzie that he would not be hurried and would place the brigade as he thought proper. 'Upon which', noted the old Fusilier, 'I was silent.' Brigadier Smith made his own dispositions and went to bed. During the night, Mackenzie felt sure, many rebels found their way out of the city by the road along the North River, which had been left unguarded despite his pleas. Mackenzie retired, damning Smith in his journal, 'he is slow, and not inclined to attend to whatever may be considered as advice, and . . . intent upon looking for comfortable quarters for himself.'

The following day Smith's Brigade moved into the streets of New York passing abandoned fortifications 'truly astonishing in their numbers and extent'. Inhabitants and redcoats stared suspiciously at one another, Mackenzie believing that quite a few of Washington's soldiers were 'now in the town, and as they have changed their dress it [was] extremely difficult to discover them'.

Washington's army had left behind the usual detritus – cannon, blankets and stores of all kinds. Away from the city, Howe's troops were marching on. The New York campaign had already delivered a battlefield victory to the British army, an important city, and a much-needed lift to the army's spirits, but it would also produce some strange fruit. Among those who emerged in the city a couple of days after Smith's brigade had arrived was Thomas Watson, who had deserted the Royal Welch Fusiliers in March 1775. He would soon be on trial for his life.

The Campaign of 1776 Concluded

In Which Private Thomas Watson Stands Trial

On 21 September, five days after the army entered New York, a corporal of the 43rd had apprehended a suspicious character. He believed he recognised a former member of the 23rd from their time together in Boston. Thomas Watson was taken to the provost, locked up and charged with desertion.

General Howe's army wasted little time bringing to trial the rogues who had disgraced the King's uniform during the operations of the previous weeks. A general court martial was convened in New York late in September, and it began working its way through cases. On 3 October, Watson's turn came.

Some ugly events that summer had put the court in an uncompromising mood. Those who longed for General Howe to make some examples felt that he might be answering their entreaties at last. John Hunter, a deserter, had been hanged three weeks earlier. Another man, Private John Winters of the 59th, having deserted from Boston the previous year and taken up arms with the rebels, was also hanged. Two men of the 57th had been sentenced to death for raping a Long Island girl.

The prisoner Watson was led into a large room where he would be judged by twelve men. This general court martial sat under the presidency of Lieutenant Colonel John Gunning, who would chair proceedings. The other eleven were officers of various regiments (none, it so happened, a 23rd Fusilier) who fitted this duty in with their other responsibilities. Convention dictated they be worldly-wise, experienced men, but in this instance two pipsqueak ensigns had joined the board, such were the exigencies of the campaign.

The man standing before them on 3 October 1776 was on trial for his life, for the legal code they worked by, the Articles of War, stipulated that death or lesser punishments could be imposed for desertion.

Watson heard the charge being read, and then the first witnesses were sworn. Serjeant Robert Laithwait and Corporal Thomas Hunter, both of his former company, testified that Watson had absconded early the previous March in Boston. It was time for the prisoner to speak in his own defence.

Watson stood and told his tale of woe. He had gone off drinking with Jacob Jones, of the same company, and Jones's brother, who was a civilian living near Boston. Having boozed away several hours, they staggered to the quay where Private Jones's brother was going to take a rowing boat back across the bay to Dorchester where he lived. Watson told the court he had been knocked down, tied up in the boat, and his captors, 'clapping a pistol to his head, swore that if he made a noise they would shoot him'.

The story of the following months, as told by Watson, was one of his trying to rejoin his regiment, failing to get through the Boston lines and then, once the city was evacuated, subsisting through a series of jobs while he lamented his fate. Watson had gone to White Plains in Connecticut and worked in his old trade as a miner before finding his way down to New York and trying by various desperate measures, including canoeing out to the fleet off Staten Island, to rejoin the Fusiliers. All the time he had been hidden in the house of one Mr Smith, a true friend to the government.

Mary Smith, the daughter-in-law of that loyal New Yorker, was called into the room. Members of the court began their cross-examination and it was soon apparent that they had not believed Watson's story:

'Do you know him to have been in the rebel army?' asked one of the redcoated officers.

'All I know of that is that the prisoner came one day into my house with Jones, who was a Drum Major in the rebel army,' Mary Smith began her answer. Jacob Jones was the fellow 23rd deserter. Evidently, he had joined the rebels, as had his brother. Miss Smith remembered Watson had cursed Jacob Jones for getting him into his predicament.

'When did you see [Watson] last in the rebel uniform?' she was asked. Why, he had been wearing it until the British arrived in New

York, when Watson had asked her to carry a letter to the royal Governor's house, asking how he might rejoin the King's army. It was afternoon, so the court adjourned for the day.

Watson's meditations that night in jail can only be imagined. The court was clearly examining whether he should be facing the additional capital charge of bearing arms with the enemy. While the redcoats knew of many instances of clemency being shown to deserters, this additional crime was a matter unlikely to be forgiven. The case of Winters of the 59th, hanged just a couple of weeks before, had exhibited almost identical circumstances.

On the morning of 4 October, the court martial resumed its session and Mary Smith was recalled. The officers seated behind their table wasted little time, and immediately began asking her about whether weapons had been in the house with Watson. The charge of 'bearing arms' had to be proven as a fact, for wearing the rebel uniform was not enough to send the defendant to the rope. Watson signalled the president that he wished to ask the witness a question, as was his right.

'Did you not hear me say that I would rather die by [the hands of] my own regiment than stay in the country with the rebels?'

'Indeed,' replied Mrs Smith, and once the British had arrived in New York she heard Watson say that, if he were to be restored to his regiment, he wished immediately 'to be engaged with the rebels that he might have satisfaction of them'.

Another witness was called who had also seen Watson in rebel uniform. Had he been armed? She, like Mrs Smith, could not say that they had ever seen the prisoner carrying a weapon. The witnesses furthermore testified to his desertion from the rebel army when it quit New York and to his attempts to enlist the Governor's help in returning to the army.

The court considered its verdict.

While the general court martial sat, General Howe's army pressed ahead with its campaign against the Continental Army. Inspired by the victory of Long Island and capture of New York, the redcoats yearned to catch up with the rebels and destroy them. This new-found ardour produced frustration both with a commander-in-chief who seemed unable to match this desire for speed and, often, with the local inhabitants upon whom troops cooped up for months on transport ships had been let loose.

On the second day of Watson's trial, Major Kemble, the Deputy Adjutant General, wrote in his journal, 'The ravages committed by the Hessians, and all ranks of the army, on the poor inhabitants of the country make their case deplorable; the Hessians destroy all fruits of the earth without regard to Loyalists or Rebels.' Kemble, American born and connected to a prominent loyalist family, could easily see how counterproductive this might be. It had already become clear that soldiers were allowed by their officers to forage for supplies on lands owned by noted rebels – but how could they tell who owned some stray cow, and did the average soldier even care whose fence he pulled down for firewood?

The entreaties of Kemble and others produced a General Order from Howe. 'The Commander-in-chief is greatly disappointed', it noted, 'that the repeated orders . . . for the suppression of plundering and marauding, have not been attended to by the troops, as he had a right to expect.' Howe, though, was speaking to his men with two voices. He was ready to try soldiers for serious crimes and at the same time hinted to them that rebel lives and property were forfeit.

In September an order from the Commander-in-chief had recorded that, since his assault tactics had won the day at Long Island, 'The general therefore recommends . . . to the troops an entire dependency upon their bayonets, with which they will ever command that success their bravery so well deserves.' Captain Frederick Mackenzie drew the following conclusion in his journal several weeks later: 'In the several attacks lately made on the rebels by the troops under Gen Howe, very few prisoners have been taken. The soldiers generally made use of their bayonets.'

Even some of the more liberal tracts of the time acknowledged that a rebel had lost the right to life and property. Such summary justice had been visited upon the Scots after their rising in 1745 and, a generation before, the Duke of Marlborough's army had used 'devastation' of enemy lands as a deliberate tactic. The Ministerial policy in America, however, was that those who had been seduced into a misguided and unnatural rebellion against their lawful sovereign would be dealt with humanely and allowed every chance to return to their just allegiance.

This desire to communicate a double message – both of mercy and of a desire to crush the rebellion – conditioned Howe's behaviour towards the inhabitants of New York. There would be no executions or repression of Patriot civilians, most of whom had left the city in any case. The general did, however, send to the gallows an American captain who had been captured on 21 September in plain clothes, undertaking a spying mission. He was strung up the following day without the benefit of even a general court martial – evidently Howe wished to send a strong message.

As for the conduct of operations, when the army pushed beyond New York, it may be that having liberated the spirit of the unstoppable charge within his army, Howe did not wish to check it. In a series of amphibious operations beyond New York this aggression had carried the day, even if it looked, at times, that it might get out of hand. The 42nd, the Black Watch, and Light Infantry had suffered a costly rebuff on Harlem Heights, north of New York, on 16 September. At Pell's Point one month later, the defenders exploited British haste to lay a series of ambushes. These actions brought caustic comment from Hessian officers who believed the British emphasis on speed meant formation was often lost and ambushes too easily sprung. They also allowed the Whig news-sheets to find something that might encourage their dispirited partisans.

The overall course of the war in October and November was, though, moving as the King would have wanted. Washington's army was driven away, first to the north, to White Plains, where Howe missed another opportunity to bring him to battle, and then south and west, to the Jerseys.

In this harrying of the Americans, the British general was at least wearing them down through horrendous desertion. Following the humiliations of this campaign, it was the Patriots who began to detect the hostile glances in villages they passed through, wondering whether locals would feed their enemy with intelligence. One general marching through the Jerseys reported to Washington, 'Tories are in my front rear and on my flanks – the mass of the people is strangely contaminated – in short unless something which I do not expect turns up we are lost.'

On 16 November, Fort Washington, which the American commander had unwisely left behind on Manhattan Island, was taken with the loss of more than 2,800 men. The failure of generalship in reinforcing a surrounded post for which there was little hope caused dissension among the Continental Army's senior ranks.

In the coffee houses and across the tables in headquarters, the fall of

Fort Washington prompted a different debate among British officers. Some of the most violent opponents of rebellion argued that the surrender of the doomed garrison should not have been accepted and that, instead, the whole should have been put to the sword. Their argument was that such a massacre would have given the death-blow to the rebellion as a whole. Such views did not hold sway with many though.

The humane treatment of prisoners was well established as a civilised norm for officers like Frederick Mackenzie. 'Many are of the opinion that if Gen Howe had treated the garrison of Fort Washington with the severity which might have been inflicted upon them by the laws of war, it should have struck a panic throughout the Continent,' Mackenzie recorded in his journal, before countering, 'although the humanity hitherto shown to the rebels has not had the desired effect, I hope it may in the end; and I am of the opinion it is right to treat our enemies as of they might one day become our friends.'

Following the fall of that fort, Howe sent Earl Cornwallis with the army's picked troops across the Hudson to New Jersey, where he made an attempt on Fort Lee, which was abandoned by its commander with huge loss of materiel. Cornwallis pursued this retreating garrison west inland and then south, as it struggled to unite with the remnants of the main force under Washington. This swift British advance excited the hope among many redcoats that they might be in Philadelphia, the rebel capital, by Christmas and the campaign finished.

General Howe did not see it that way, though. His concept of strategy was both thorough, in terms of its emphasis on logistic preparation, and plodding, in that he was often able to spot his opening at the scene of a battle but missed every cue on the grand stage of war. Seeing this slowness, some officers began to speculate that Whig sympathies led Howe to let Washington off the hook deliberately, others that their commanders did not want to wind up the war because they were making too much money from it.

By 20 December, Howe's staff issued orders that the army should enter winter quarters – an accepted tradition in European warfare whereby the requirements of staying warm and fed would take over from those of war until the spring came. Several thousand British and Hessian troops were deployed in an arc in New Jersey, in which their scattered outposts enclosed dozens of rural communities, many thousands of citizens that might be reconciled to the restoration of royal rule.

When the court martial delivered its verdict on 4 October, it was brief and to the point. In his copperplate hand, the clerk recorded that Private Watson was guilty and the court 'doth sentence the said Thomas Watson to receive seven hundred lashes on his bare back with a cat of nine tails'.

Members of the court had quickly penetrated Watson's story, about struggling for more than one year to rejoin his regiment, assuming instead that he had joined the rebel army outside Boston with his messmate Jacob Jones and may even have fought the King's troops. There was however no evidence of his bearing arms for the rebels, the particular that saved the Fusilier from a death sentence. It was also evident that Watson regretted his decision to join the American army.

The question of his liaison with a New York woman emerged in court, and may have explained his conduct, but she was not called as a witness, for it was incidental to the matter under examination. Instead the officers sitting under Lieutenant Colonel Gunning's presidency had had to ask themselves to balance the punishment due a deserter with a desire to lure back scores of other men who had done the same thing in the months before war and might be experiencing similar doubts. Suspending Watson from the nearest gallows would simply have sent the message that there was no point trying to return to the King's colours, for the witnesses had been clear on the point that Watson had attempted to arrange his surrender once New York had fallen.

So, the Fusilier had escaped the hanging suffered by Hunter or Winters. The prospect of 700 lashes, delivered by the regiment's drummers, held terror for many men, but it was rare for such large tariffs to be served up in full. What any soldier locked up in the provost could have told Watson was that the British army in America rarely punished its men to the degree it was entitled to.

John Browning, for example, the soldier of the 23rd who had been clapped in irons for striking an officer at Halifax, had stood trial for his life on Staten Island in July. With evidence sketchy to back a lieutenant's claim that he had been hit, Browning was acquitted of the capital charge but found guilty of insulting a serjeant, for which he was ordered to receive 200 lashes. However, General Howe reviewed the case and waived the corporal punishment, arguing that if Browning was acquitted of the more serious offence there was no point in chastising him at all. Despite being found guilty of insulting a serjeant, Browning was therefore allowed to return quietly to the 23rd without sanction. Even when men were tried, awarded the ultimate penalty, and had the sentence confirmed by the commander-in-chief, clemency was usually granted. So, while Howe had proven during his first year as commander-in-chief in America to be a tougher disciplinarian than his predecessor, it was still the case that the majority of men convicted of capital offences, and many of those sentenced to corporal punishment, walked off scot-free.

In the case of the two men of the 57th convicted of rape, and of another soldier later found guilty of that crime, the reprieve followed representations from the victims' families. In noting one of these cases in his journal, one officer pitied 'the fate of many who suffer indiscriminately in a civil war', but also lamented that there had been 'other shocking abuses of this nature that have not come to public notice'. Some others made light of this crime, the young Lord Rawdon writing home facetiously:

The fresh meat our men have got here has made them as riotous as satyrs. A girl cannot step into the bushes to pluck a rose without running the most imminent risk of being ravished, and [the girls] are so little accustomed to these methods that they don't bear them with the proper resignation.

Quite a few officers would have rejected utterly such a frivolous interpretation of the law, considering themselves instead to aspire to a code of chivalry in which they would always take the woman's part or that of the downtrodden. For this reason, they sometimes appealed for clemency when their soldiers explained their desertion for reasons of love. One captain wrote to his mother that he had interceded for his recaptured soldier, because 'for a woman this poor boy ventured his existence'.

The cases tried by general court martial in the second half of 1776 demonstrated that executions were still a rarity. As for the many who were due such punishment for desertion, marauding or striking their officers, there was little to be done with them but to send them back to their regiments, since the army lacked big prisons to accommodate people serving long sentences, particularly after taking thousands of American prisoners.

When it came to those captured in the battles of 1776, some private soldiers had initially been released. For many of those who escaped the bayoneting at Fort Washington that the Tories would have liked, there was the prospect of slow death instead on board one of the prison ships in New York harbour. More than 1,000 men were taken out to the *Jersey*, a rotten old two-decker. Other warships condemned as unseaworthy, called hulks, were used to accommodate the remainder.

It cannot be said that the British had a deliberate policy of starvation on board those ships, rather that the needs of enemy prisoners ranked low, and that the leadership of the two warring parties frittered away years on legalistic bickering about prisoner exchanges while their men rotted in confinement. As 1776 came to an end, though, there was a gross disparity in the numbers of prisoners, for the British held several times as many as the Americans, a happy consequence of their success in battle.

Late that year there was general optimism about the course of the war. 'The destruction of Washington's Army seems extremely possible,' Frederick Mackenzie had written in October, 'the subjugation of the American Colonies, may be said to be nearly effected.' The canny old Fusilier, however, later worried about whether the Americans should be pushed harder in the Jerseys.

With snows falling and the hand of winter gripping the land, British or Hessian sentries gazed across the frigid Jersey country. The 23rd had joined the army's marches north and then south and west, hundreds of miles, without experiencing another battle. Its light infantry and grenadiers, on the other hand, grouped with the battalions of those elite troops had been frequently engaged under the command of Earl Cornwallis.

Some officers worried, as campaigning closed, what the army's indiscipline might do to the possibility of reconciliation with the American people. Major Kemble grumbled about the generals' failure to curb excesses and the wider effect it had. The soldiers involved were, he felt, 'cruel to such a degree as to threaten with death all such as dare obstruct them in their depredations. Violence to officers is frequently used, and every degree of insolence offered.'

Major Charles Stuart, an officer in his mid-twenties and a rising star, was concerned by the political effects of marauding and unpunished army crimes in general. 'Repeated orders was [*sic*] given against this barbarity', Major Stuart wrote home to his father, 'but the punishment annexed to the crime not being put into execution, the soldiers disregarded it.' The consequences of this laxity to the overall struggle for America were clear to this officer as he knew they would be to his father, a former prime minister no less: 'Thus we went on persuading to enmity those minds already undecided, and inducing our friends to fly to the opposite party for protection.'

Late in 1776 Thomas Watson returned to the Royal Welch Fusiliers after an absence of eighteen months. There is no record of whether the lashes awarded by the court martial were ever inflicted, and, by the end of 1776, Watson had the wish he had expressed in front of that tribunal to fight the King's enemies once more. The court martial had given him a second chance.

If British army indiscipline posed risks to the entire enterprise over the long term, then General Howe's enemies had something else in mind that might shift opinion a good deal more quickly. General Washington had no intention of letting the redcoats rest easy that winter.

The 1777 Campaign Opens

Or How Thomas Mecan Fought for the Rest

Colonel Rall's Christmas festivities ended in the most disgraceful manner. Carried to bed after a night's feasting and good cheer, he was roused by the sound of cannon and drumbeats. The British decision to go into winter quarters had been exploited by George Washington to launch a counter-attack. They appeared through the driving snow in the early hours of 26 December, falling on the outposts of Rall's Hessian brigade, which held an exposed position on the Jersey lines.

In the confused melee that followed, Colonel Rall lost 918 of his 1,200 men captured, with a further 105 killed or wounded. Washington had rallied his regiments from the depths of despair and led them to a remarkable success. Certainly it could not have come at a better time for his cause. There was no shortage of explanation or recrimination on the British side: Rall was a drunken fool; the Hessian pickets had not put out proper patrols; General Grant had known about the possibility of American attack but ignored it; the lines were too long, leaving General Howe's troops exposed to being overwhelmed at any point.

Washington's thrusts into the Jerseys forced several British marches or countermarches. Soldiers were snatched from the warmth of their fires, formed into ranks and pushed across the frozen countryside. On 3 January, Washington struck another blow at Princeton, catching the tail-end of a British column and causing them significant casualties. The reputation of Earl Cornwallis was bruised too, since he had left his rear exposed and failed to attack the Americans first.

These events dramatically changed the character of the war in the

Jerseys. Whigs took heart from them, and everywhere became more active. During the early months of 1777 the notion of winter quarters became meaningless because both sides were involved in a rural partisan war, one in which each side vied for information through spies or scouts and attempted to cut off the foraging parties of the other.

'As the rascals are skulking about the whole country,' one British light infantry captain wrote home, 'it is impossible to move with any degree of safety without a pretty large escort, and even then you are exposed to a dirty kind of *tiraillerie*, which is more noisy than dangerous.' The army's extended deployments and lack of supply magazines, noted another, 'made it absolutely necessary for us to enter into a kind of *"petite guerre"* which has kept the army the whole winter in perpetual harassment.'

It was in actions of a hundred men here or a few companies there, encountering similar-sized parties of Americans, that qualities such as alertness, self-reliance, and drive that were little valued in many European armies of the epoch were needed in abundance. Theorists at the time often called this contest of scouting, foraging and outposts *petite guerre* (a French term which in Spanish gave rise to *guerrilla*), denoting a 'small war' in which vital decisions were taken at the lowest level. Those involved understood that such operations suited those with local knowledge and the kind of enthusiasm unleashed by the rebellion.

Faced with this challenge, British generals were tempted to lean once more on those best adapted for *petite guerre*, their own light infantry and the jaegers, German woodsmen dressed in green coats and armed with rifles. Even so, there would never be enough such men – as General Burgoyne had realised when writing one year before about the war – to allow regiments of the line to be excused such duties, so while more specialised troops were raised, the light infantry had a tiresome winter, and officers busied themselves trying to inculcate ordinary regiments with that style of fighting.

It was only due to an uncharacteristic attack of peacetime farsightedness at the War Office back in 1773 that there was any light infantry to be found in General Howe's army. Such troops had been used before, in the Seven Years War, but later dispensed with as an economy measure. When re-introduced two years before the American rebellion, each regiment had been ordered to take one of its ten companies and train it in the necessary tactics. These men, and the grenadiers who formed on parade at the other end of each regiment, had been brigaded into separate battalions since the American war began. Because of their position on the two ends of the regimental battle line they were known as 'flank companies' or indeed 'elite' companies.

Robert Donkin, who had been responsible for training the Welch Fusiliers' reformed Light Company, wrote that an officer leading such troops should be ready to 'harass and ruin the enemy's troops on leaving their quarters; distress them by continual *alertes* . . . [and when a convoy moved] to exert every sort of means to intercept, burn, or destroy it'. This was the philosophy of both sides on the outposts in the Jerseys.

Early in 1777, the 23rd's Light Company was part of the 1st Light Infantry Battalion, occupying quarters quite near those of its parent regiment, the Fusiliers, at New Brunswick. It was under the command of Captain Thomas Mecan (who had led it at Bunker Hill). On paper at least, he commanded two subaltern officers, three serjeants, three corporals, one drummer, and thirty-five privates or 'rank and file'. In practice, some of the men carried on pay lists were always either sick in hospital, missing (prisoners or deserted) or on command somewhere else. The thirst for manpower evident throughout the British army in America was nowhere more insatiable than in the light companies, and in February Mecan was sent another eleven men, transferees from other companies of the Royal Welch Fusiliers.

Of the thirty-five rank and file on his books at the start of the year, only twelve were Light Company veterans who went back to 1773; fifteen had come in after the slaughter of Bunker Hill in June 1775. Robert Mason, the young drummer who had gone out to Lexington at the start of the war, was one of those transferred to the Light Company. Mecan's Lieutenant and 2nd Lieutenant were both new too, being aged in their early twenties and teens.

The element of experience and judgement that cemented these young men together was provided by Mecan himself, his serjeants and corporals. Both serjeants had served in the company since it had been re-named as the light one four years earlier, one of them, Thomas Lightbourn, being promoted from corporal one week after Bunker Hill. Two out of three corporals were also veterans of the original company.

By early 1777, almost everyone in the 23rd Light Company had fought many times. The old sweats had come through Lexington and

Bunker Hill, but most of them had been engaged at Long Island and subsequent affairs the previous year, including Pell's Point in October, when they had fought 'in the hottest part of this action'.

The light infantry was 'the most dangerous and difficult service of this war', according to Captain William Dansey of the 33rd's company, an ambitious officer who believed the risk justified because it was 'a line that must be of infinite service to me hereafter, for the preference in all promotions is given to Light Infantry officers'. Dansey came from Herefordshire and was a little younger than Mecan's thirty-seven years. The 33rd's Light Company commander was the son of an officer and similarly committed to his profession, and would also endure the trials and tribulations of the 1777 campaign working closely with Mecan in the 1st Battalion of Light Infantry.

The business of light companies had become too serious for the gamesters and boozers to be left in command. 'Hamilton was one of the best men that ever was', wrote a captain of the 52nd, 'but drank so hard that it was recommended him to give up the Light Company.' Someone who tumbled insensible into his bed could not be left in charge of the army's outposts, its early warning system.

There was another breed, in addition to the serious professional soldiers, that gravitated towards the light companies, namely adventurers who came out to the army, keen to make a name for themselves in the war. Many of these men had no commissions, and found their services rebuffed. But if equipped with a letter of introduction to General Howe or some other big-wig they would be offered the chance of serving as a 'gentleman volunteer' in the light infantry. If they distinguished themselves serving as an ordinary soldier, a commission might be granted them. If they got killed, *tant pis*.

Two examples of this species that came to the 23rd will suffice. Charles Hastings was a lieutenant in the 12th Regiment who tired of sitting in barracks while his cousin Lord Rawdon made a name for himself. He obtained his colonel's leave and headed to Portsmouth. When the King got wind of it, he sent a messenger ordering Hastings back, for he was anxious to stop dozens of others quitting their regiments to do the same. Hastings remained one step ahead of the messenger, got to America and fought musket in hand with the 23rd Light Infantry at Pell's Point. 'He is much approved of by the officers commanding the battalion', wrote Rawdon with satisfaction.

General Howe, though, evidently divined the King's feelings on the subject of volunteers already possessed of commissions, cold-shouldered Hastings and obliged him to return to his regiment. So while he did duty with the Fusiliers during the first half of 1777, he did not become a permanent fixture. Hastings in any case already possessed certain advantages and volunteering was best left to the truly desperate.

Francis Delaval was the bastard son of a dissolute northern aristocrat. Young Francis's gambling, drinking and general high-living back in England outstripped his slender means. Pleading with an uncle for help when he was £15 in debt, Delaval received £20 and the promise that if he went into the army, his uniform would be paid for and an allowance of one guinea a week made to him. Francis promptly gambled the money away, and found himself in a sponging house or debtors' prison.

When his uncle bailed him out, further escape was impossible and Francis was finally packed on board ship with the requisite letter of introduction to General Howe. Delaval was sent to the light infantry and, his mind being untainted with any previous military experience, a few weeks later in August 1776 he was commissioned a 2nd Lieutenant into the Royal Welch Fusiliers. At least, Mecan might have reasoned, they had got him away from the light company.

Delaval was experienced in gaming anyhow, an asset since in the taverns or backrooms of New Brunswick there was a good deal of gambling that winter. They bet on dice, or with cards at hazard and picquet. To the sober-minded officer who could ill afford it, though, hard service in the Jersey countryside, a continual round of touring sentries, reconnoitring and raiding offered a different life. 'One satisfaction I have in America,' an officer long used to drawing on private means wrote to his mother, 'I save a good deal of money; even some out of my pay.' Many then began to live the life of a professional fighting soldier, and for the light infantry more than any others, there would be no shortage of battle that year.

The march under Colonel Harcourt's command began at 11 p.m. on 12 April. The ground was muddy underfoot, the snows having melted during the previous fortnight. Harcourt, a cavalry officer, had fifty of his own dragoons under command, the army's two battalions of light infantry and one of grenadiers – around 1,200 men. Harcourt had gained great fame in the army by capturing Washington's deputy,

The British attack at Bound Brook

Major General Charles Lee, in a raid near New York four months before. This night, they walked stealthily, following the line of the Raritan River up towards the village of Bound Brook. For months the river had been the front line between British and American forces in that part of Jersey, the soldiers trading shots, shouts and lewd gestures on a daily basis. That night, Harcourt's column was on the American side of the river, where strong outposts had been set up as part of the outer defence of Washington's main encampment nearby at Morristown.

Across the Raritan, on the British-held side, a second column set out under Colonel von Donop, consisting of Hessian grenadiers and some field artillery. They would march towards the main bridge at Bound Brook, on a road where the Americans would have not expected any attack, at dawn.

At 3 a.m., following behind Harcourt's column, a third force began marching towards Bound Brook. Captain Johann Ewald, with thirty of his Hessian jaegers who had volunteered for this special mission, were at its head, followed by two battalions of British Guards. Ewald had earlier conducted reconnaissance of Bound Brook on behalf of Earl Cornwallis, whose plan of attack that night was being put into action.

The plan gave a distinct mission to each column: Harcourt was to move around behind the village, ready to assault it from the rear at dawn but with a strong detachment looking the other way in case American reinforcements were sent from Morristown; Grant was to be in position by the hamlet of Raritan Landing, ready to threaten the village at the same time; von Donop was to attack across the bridge from the British side of the Raritan.

Brigadier Benjamin Lincoln commanded several hundred men in and around Bound Brook. In the village itself there was a redoubt dominating two important crossings over the Raritan and three or four cannon. It was a strong position, where Lincoln might easily have held off hundreds attacking frontally, but Cornwallis's intentions were for a sudden and overwhelming assault.

Most officers engaged in such a complex enterprise, at night, knew that there was much that could go wrong. The firing of a carelessly dropped musket or an escaped sentry could cause the alarm to be raised. With men advancing in darkness through marshy riverside pastures, one column might take longer than expected or get lost. And how would each of the three commanders know that the others were in place before launching his assault?

The first unexpected event was that Harcourt's scouts discovered Brigadier Lincoln was passing the night with a strong guard at Horne's Plantation, a place they would find more than one mile from Bound Brook. The light infantry bayoneted some of his sentries and moved swiftly into the farm. Lincoln and some others escaped from their beds, barely clothed, but the Light Infantry took his papers, a few dozen men and three cannon at the plantation. They pushed through the night to Bound Brook itself.

When Ewald's jaegers bumped into some American sentries close to the village, 'the picket received us spiritedly and withdrew under steady fire'. Ewald pursued the retiring men closely – a sound tactic for rushing a place – until he found himself only 100 yards short of the redoubt, where he stopped. 'The day dawned,' he wrote in his journal, 'and I was exposed to a murderous fire.' In the early light, Ewald made the unpleasant discovery that only ten of his jaegers had followed his earlier rush into the village. They were pinned down.

It was no time before Harcourt and von Donop began their final moves, signalling an all out assault. The Americans abandoned their redoubt, realising they were under fire from all sides, and dozens of Continentals scattered through back gardens or orchards, trying to escape. The British moved into the town and began destroying military stores such as gunpowder. Local homes were not spared either: 'The place was ransacked and plundered because all the inhabitants were rebellious minded.'

As Cornwallis's columns were withdrawn to the British side of the Raritan, they came back leading cows, towing Lincoln's captured artillery and carrying all manner of booty. A light infantry officer summarised the cost to the enemy: 'Three pieces of cannon, a major of artillery and two other officers with upwards of 70 men, and [we] killed and wounded near 100, the loss on our side one man killed and two wounded.'

Captain Ewald, the son of a Kassel bookseller, embodied the chivalrous code of conduct expected of a gentleman of arms with a rigorous attachment to military science, a most unusual combination. To his mind, the raid could have been even more successful but had been marred by Harcourt beginning his assault a little late, allowing many of the Americans around the redoubt to escape, and by Grant not telling him that his own column was only intended to mount a feint or dummy attack.

Ewald certainly had a hard eye – a singular one, since he had lost the other in a duel. It was true that, under slightly different circumstances, several hundred prisoners might have been taken and Harcourt might have added Lincoln to his haul of captured rebel generals, but overall, the army's performance in mounting a difficult night-raid showed a vast improvement over its early fumblings around Boston. This was very different, after all, to the light infantry's flight at Lexington or Lieutenant Lenthall's raid near Penny Ferry in which his Fusiliers had 'run away' in panic.

General Howe was exultant at the results of Bound Brook, for he was evidently anxious for some positive stroke to report to London after the dismal news of December and January. 'It was well conceived and conducted masterly,' Howe wrote home, 'the Light Infantry behaved with *amazing spirit* and with as much cleverness in the night march as possibly could be.' Having lavished such attention on the light corps, Howe was keen to burnish their laurels. Even Ewald agreed that the 'forage war' in the Jerseys had been 'very beneficial for the army, for a renewed spirit entered the hearts of the soldiers, who had been completely disheartened by the disasters of Trenton and Princeton'.

Of course, the action of 13 April was not one that had changed history in any way, and indeed the Americans had also mounted successful raids up to and including Trenton. It had, however, signalled that British soldiers, and particularly the light infantry, were adapted to the American form of war and faced the challenges ahead in high spirits.

The light infantry had mastered skirmishing: moving in small groups and exposing only the minimum necessary to shoot at their targets. Captain Dansey of the 33rd Light Infantry commented after Bound Brook, 'We have learned from the rebels to cover our bodies if there's a rail or a tree near us.' Where circumstances dictated, these two battalions of picked troops could adopt any variety of formation to suit their mission, moving with each pair of men, or file, spaced widely apart or skirmishing through woods. They had definitively dropped the old system of three ranks and only formed with their men shoulder to shoulder at night, when mutual support might be more valuable. If Howe favoured light infantry officers with promotion, it was because he was using those battalions as a school whose graduates would return to their regiments, the lieutenants as captains or the captains as majors, spreading this new doctrine and 'amazing spirit' to the humdrum companies of the line.

In the months between Long Island and Bound Brook a very distinctive ethos had built up in the light infantry, whose men were often called the Light Bobs by brother soldiers. They liked to compare their work to the chase, one writing to his mother that 'a day's Yankie hunting is no more minded than a day's fox hunting'. Moving forward so quickly, and with men spread out, drums were found impractical for signalling. What better to replace them than hunting horns, just like those the Hessian jaegers carried? 'I never felt such a sensation before,' wrote an American officer who, on hearing these sounds, realised he had become the quarry of the British Light Infantry, 'it seemed to crown our disgrace.' Buoyed up by high spirits, Light Bob officers often sought volunteers for dangerous missions, rather than using compulsion with their men.

Light infantry commanders wanted to inspire soldiers, harnessing their enthusiasm, even if that spirit sometimes arose from an expectation that picked troops should have the first right to plunder their enemy. Howe's chosen corps added to their facility at rapid manoeuvre an expertise at stripping American property. Such was the importance of reaping food and forage quickly that the Light Infantry even had their own distinctive language of larceny with 'grabs' and 'lobs'. One young officer who imbibed this culture with alacrity explained:

Grab was a favourite expression among the Light Infantry, and meant any plunder taken by force; a Lob when you got it without any opposition, and I am very certain that there never was a more expert set than the Light Infantry at either grab, lob, or gutting a house.

During raids in the Jerseys, the capture of livestock was often an objective. In these scorched-earth contests to sustain oneself and deny the enemy sustenance, marauding enemy supplies became official policy. One light infantry private responded with the following flippant verse to an appeal by Washington for farmers to fatten up their cattle in preparation for the coming campaign:

> Then honest Whigs, make all your cattle fat
> We, to reward you for all your care and pains,
> Will visit soon your crowded stalls and plains;
> And for your pampered cattle write, at large,
> With bloody bayonets, a full discharge.
> You know that we *light bobs* are tough and hardy,
> And at a push, you'll never find us tardy.
> We have stomach for both *beef* and *battle*;
> So, honest Whigs, once more, feed well your cattle.

One officer, succeeding in his ambition to join the 23rd Light Company, knew its men revelled in a reputation for larceny and was not disappointed on his first mission gathering supplies. When a bystander expressed dismay at redcoats stripping some twenty houses of their doors and window frames, one of the Light Bob Fusiliers shot back saying, 'Damn my eyes, painted wood burns best!'

Donkin, as a former commander of that company of the 23rd, argued that it was best to pay for cows, grain or other food gathered by foraging parties. At times the redcoats did indeed give promissory notes or cash to people they believed to be loyal or neutral, but this did not apply, of course, to rebels. Donkin moreover did not believe in censuring Light Bobs for such behaviour, noting with a certain cynicism that 'as it will not be in [the commander's] power to hinder these excesses . . . it is more prudent to affect an ignorance of them than to be under the necessity of punishing them with severity'.

Hessian officers were sometimes censorious – not of the pillage that was a completely accepted part of European warfare – but of the excess enthusiasm that they believed was being encouraged. It was, in their view, no substitute for proper training and liable to get the Light Bobs into all sorts of scrapes.

Ewald, who co-operated frequently with British light troops, disliked the gentleman amateur approach of many of their officers, 'men who pretend to be acquainted with military matters, and who, while they are ignorant of the method of training light troops, call everything of this nature useless pedantry'. The jaeger captain summed up the mindset of such commanders – and it was very much the 'amazing spirit' fostered by Howe – as being that 'in the presence of the enemy all these school rules fall to the ground . . . light troops must carry everything sword in hand or with charged bayonets'.

Mecan, although comparatively advanced in years, had seen the change in its correct complexion, volunteering even in 1775 to lead the light company, and staying with it despite the obvious dangers, as the surest route to distinction. In this sense his zeal for the service held out longer than that of so many of his companions who had been commanding companies in the Fusiliers as the war started. But the campaign of 1777 was not yet begun and, indeed, half the year would be gone before General Howe launched it in earnest.

Six days after Mecan's excursion to Bound Brook, several of his regimental colleagues found themselves under hot fire hundreds of miles away. An expedition was launched under the command of Major General William Tryon to attack a large American magazine at Danbury in Connecticut. Six regiments, including the 23rd, sent parties of 250 picked men each, removing by this expedient the slow and dubious from their ranks. When they quit the town at 8 a.m. on 27 April they left columns of smoke and widespread destruction behind. Regiments of Connecticut troops under the local firebrand, Brigadier Benedict Arnold, tried to block the redcoats' way back to their ships, but they were bayonet-charged and scattered. The British stayed overnight in a village called Ridgefield before having to mount another charge the following day, dispersing their last opponents and getting back on board their warships.

This excursion into rebel territory was a minor event in the scheme that was unfolding, but it serves as a symptom of the confusion that surrounded the high command of William Howe. There were those who argued that the British war effort should consist entirely of Danbury raids, with some inland devastation carried out by Indian war parties, but Howe was not one of them. After much befuddled communication with London during the winter, he had opted to continue the war against American centres of power, but to do so in several directions at once.

Howe expected John Burgoyne, who was not directly under his command, to continue the work started in 1776 but suspended during the winter, of forcing his way down from Canada towards the Hudson and Albany. There was a plan to send some troops north from New York to assist this movement, a mission that would be entrusted to Lieutenant General Sir Henry Clinton. As if to add to the dispersion of effort, a further expedition of thousands of men had been sent to Rhode Island, which the Navy preferred as an anchorage to New York. Initially Howe had suggested that the Rhode Island force might attack into New England, possibly to draw some enemy away from Burgoyne's push, but early in 1777, after the shock of Trenton, the commander-in-chief had clawed back some of the men sent there, leaving Earl Percy at that base in charge of a few thousand.

Neither Burgoyne, Clinton nor Percy was engaged in the main effort for 1777, though. The commander-in-chief had decided instead to make his decisive push to the south-west, rather than moving north up the Hudson towards Burgoyne. The general and his brother, Admiral Howe, would gather a great fleet and transport 15,000 men by sea up the Delaware River, from where he intended to launch an attack on Philadelphia, the rebel capital. This step ran so clearly counter to the strategic principle of keeping one's forces concentrated that Clinton and Percy, in common with many others, thought it extremely unwise. Howe, though, had made his decision.

On 12 June the regiments on the outpost lines in Jersey received their marching orders. The 23rd was to take part in Howe's expedition, as were his beloved light and grenadier battalions. The wagons were packed, regiments paraded and what could not be carried away was torched. In going, the British army committed its first great betrayal of the war. Thousands of families that had sided with the King in the

Jerseys were simply left behind as Howe's brigades marched down to the waterside.

Major Stuart, son of former prime minister the Earl of Bute and brother-in-law to Earl Percy, thought it both morally dubious and militarily irresponsible to abandon a bridgehead that had cost 2,000 casualties (by his estimate) to maintain during the preceding several months. 'The risk which all armies are liable to was our hindrance here,' he wrote home, reflecting on the strength of opposition in inland areas, 'and has absolutely prevented us from going 15 miles from a navigable river.' Stuart's political instinct was sufficiently good that he smoked out Howe's intention to strike at Philadelphia when most officers would still have been in the dark, and confided to his father that if Burgoyne was not properly supported he would 'tremble for the consequences'.

General Howe wanted, on the other hand, to get two strikes at Washington's army, and the advance on Philadelphia would provide only the second. First he must extricate his redcoats from the Jerseys and get them to the sea, and he hoped that this would tempt the Americans into an attack that might offer a first chance for a major action.

The American supremo was wise to such danger as he escorted the British from New Brunswick, Perth-Amboy and the other centres of New Jersey that they had occupied. Several times during this evacuation, the British rearguard rounded on its pursuers in the hope of bringing on a major engagement. A day-tripper from New York who went to see the fighting on 22 June saw his army's destructive exit from Jersey, recording, shocked, 'All the county houses were in flames as far as we could see.'

In the early hours of 26 June, Howe launched a fully fledged assault, sending several thousand men, one division under Cornwallis and another under Vaughan. Cornwallis's advance of Hessian grenadiers and British guards caught a brigade under Major General Alexander on one steep-sided, wooded hill and managed to deliver a sharp attack. Here they caused several hundred casualties and captured three guns, but it was the closest Howe came to bringing on a major battle with Washington.

Those troops remaining were embarked on boats to Staten Island and by 29 June the Jersey campaign was over. Major Nisbet Balfour, Howe's staff officer, was bewildered that his master's design had not achieved more. 'They will not ever allow us to come near them,'

Balfour wrote to a friend in England, '. . . after attempting to get up with them by every means in our power . . . we chased them from hill to hill.'

The next three weeks were a frenzy of preparation for the expedition to the Delaware. So much time had been lost already that campaigning season that Howe wanted to galvanise his men, to infuse the whole army with some light infantry spirit. There would be no tents, the men would take a blanket each, like the Light Bobs did. All of these company commanders, or majors, lieutenant colonels even, why should they take their riding horses? Had not he, when commanding Wolfe's light infantry at Quebec in 1759, marched the whole campaign on foot? They could sell their nags to the mounted troops for ten guineas each if they liked, but Howe was determined not to have to feed hundreds of officers' horses. By the same logic of hungry mouths, he tried to limit the number of wives embarked.

Howe went aboard the *Eagle*, his brother's flagship, on 17 July. The 23rd would form part of his 1st Brigade. The Fusiliers mustered 416 men when they hitched hammocks on three merchantmen, the *Elenor*, the *Saville Hunstler* and the *Isabella*. Mecan's light company remained in the 1st Light Battalion, which had more than 700 troops. Few of the rank and file had any idea where they were going. Even at this point General Clinton felt sure that Howe was engaged in a clever ruse and would take his men north, up the Hudson to join hands with Burgoyne. This notion, though, vanished when the fleet set sail and headed south, out of New York bay. Burgoyne be buggered, Howe would do things his way.

The March on Philadelphia

In Which Mecan Paid the Price

The procession of warships up the broad Delaware River was an imposing sight. Most redcoats found the business of being at sea oppressive. Their fear of being wrecked, inability to swim and aversion to the sensations of shipboard life often made such voyages frightening and incomprehensible. But they could never fail to be impressed when squadrons came together in their distinctive formations, midshipmen scribbling nervously, signal flags running up lines and tars leaping about the rigging like monkeys, reefing sails. These frenetic sights and sounds brought the army the greatest pleasure when they announced an imminent return to terra firma.

'The sailing up Chesapeak Bay', one Light Bob wrote home, 'was the grandest sight, sure that could be seen, we were upwards of 300 sail, all of which got up safe to the head of the bay. Lord Howe has performed wonders in bringing a fleet here.'

The passage from New York to the Head of Elk, the bay off Delaware that was their destination, had been inordinately long. During an entire month at sea they had been battered by storms and run low on rations – dozens of horses had perished in the dingy holds of their transports. It was an awfully protracted way around for a journey that before the war took three days by the 'Flying Machine', the smartest coach to Philadelphia.

Captain Richard Fitzpatrick of the Guards was among those gazing at the Delaware shore as the wind propelled Howe's fleet up the river. Fitzpatrick was an unusual soldier, a high-living aristocrat, gambling and drinking mate of Charles James Fox, Parliament's most passionate critic of the American war. Fitzpatrick too was a member of that house, and regularly provided Fox with military information so he might better puncture the pomposity of ministers who sought to justify the campaign. Fitzpatrick was so passionate in his anti-ministerial diatribes that Fox had chided him for being 'too violent' a Whig.

Fitzpatrick found the views ravishing as the fleet penetrated deeper into the vast American continent. They could already feel the hot sun on their shoulders, but he did not mind that as much as many did. The clearings among the trees opened up bucolic vistas of peaceful farming communities, a calm which, to his regret, they were about to shatter. Fitzpatrick was an aesthete, who had seen great antiquities in Rome, peppered his conversation with French and found the conflict with the Americans unspeakably sweaty and vulgar, concluding, 'Nothing in the world can be so disagreeable and so odious to me as being obliged to serve in this execrable war, exclusive of the *désagrément* of being banished from society.'

The general understanding had grown during long weeks at sea that their objective was Philadelphia. But why? 'I think it amounts very near to a demonstration,' Fitzpatrick wrote, assuming it some clever blind to draw Washington away from Burgoyne, who was advancing south from Canada. Listening to his Tory messmates, the Guards captain mocked the idea that rebellion could be eradicated, thinking it would mean 'extirpating the whole race'. Fitzpatrick, although aligning himself with the toughest Whig critics of the war, did not, let it be clear, care for Americans any more than the rest of the army, since he thought them 'the most unpleasant, formal, precise, disagreeable people in the world'. For him, as for Fox in the Commons chamber back home, the war was mainly a rod with which to beat the Ministry of the day. They were preoccupied with the wider Whig struggle, and shuddered at the idea that a successful military response to the American colonists' revolt might thwart the cause of liberty in the three home kingdoms, particularly Ireland.

Officers of a more down-to-earth and less Whiggish hue looked forward to the campaign ahead with greater enthusiasm. 'We shall find the rebels enough to do at Philadelphia', wrote William Dansey of the 1st Light Battalion, 'and Burgoyne is playing the Devil with them to the northward.' Howe himself apparently calculated that threatening the rebel capital would have the same effect that landing at New York had had one year before: it would force Washington to give battle.

For the 1st Battalion Light Infantry, action was joined in earnest on 3 September. When scouts detected Washington's advanced guard taking post at Cooch's bridge, it was quickly decided to attack them. There were about 800 enemy soldiers under the command of Major General Maxwell facing 400 Hessians and 1,000 British. General Howe appeared, ordering the Hessians to attack the bridge frontally. They were supported by the 2nd Light Infantry, while the 1st Battalion, containing the company of the 23rd Fusiliers among others, was ordered to move through thick woods to the left, cross the stream being defended by the Americans and attack them from behind.

The plan was pressed with great vigour, the jaegers skirmishing forward until they were near the bridge, and, being armed with rifles that lacked bayonets, drew their swords. The 1st Light Infantry meanwhile hacked its ways through the undergrowth for hours until it finally reached an impassable swamp. Attempts to surround the Americans were thus thwarted by the nature of the country and the enemy withdrew to fight another day. There was a good deal of disappointment in the 1st Light Infantry after this failure, but that just showed the battalion's high morale and their keenness to hit the enemy. The opportunity came one week later at the Brandywine Creek.

At first light on 11 September the light infantry and grenadiers had already been marching for several hours. Two days before, the 1st Light Infantry had taken an American prisoner who confirmed that General Washington had taken post on a river a few dozen miles south of Philadelphia called the Brandywine. William Howe knew that if he was swift, he would catch the rebels and force them to fight a pitched battle. Having gathered intelligence about Washington's position, he had soon detected a weakness, and on that day marched 8,000 men, just over half his army, to take advantage of it.

With Howe were Earl Cornwallis and the picked troops: flank battalions, Guards, Hessian grenadiers and a couple of brigades of British foot. The other arm of his battle, the division under Lieutenant General Knyphausen, would play a role similar to that performed by Grant and von Heister at Long Island, approaching Washington's position frontally and pinning his forces close to three fords over the Brandywine. When Knyphausen heard the battle erupt to his front left, he would know that Cornwallis's attack was going in, and it was time to force the river crossing. Knyphausen too had a couple of British

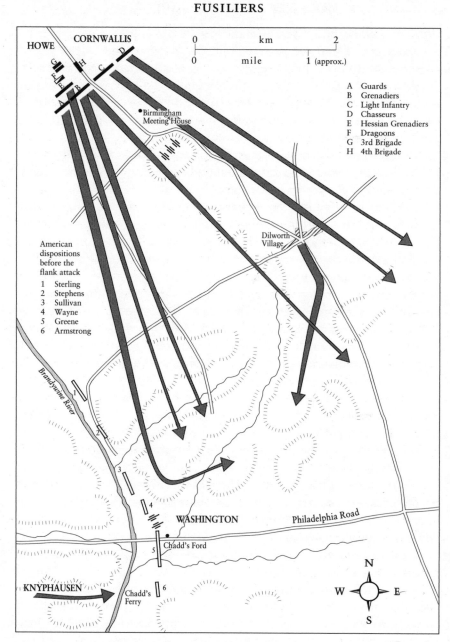

Brandywine, the British flank attack

brigades under his command, one of them including the 23rd Fusiliers.

In order to lead his troops in an arc around Washington's right, Howe had to drive them a very long way, eighteen miles, so that his enemy would not see them coming. While they were marching around, Knyphausen's advanced guard fell in with the Americans on his side of the river, and fought a series of smart skirmishes, driving them from fences and woods as he went. The American light troops were handled skilfully by General Maxwell, making the Hessian general pay for the hillside that would offer his artillery a commanding view of the river fords. In one place they laid a clever ambush for the Queen's Rangers, a light corps raised in America. In another, the 23rd Fusiliers deployed into battle order during running exchanges of fire, taking one wood at the cost of several casualties.

Everything, though, depended on Cornwallis's column. At 3 p.m. they reached Osborne's Hill, the troops stopping hidden from view of the Americans as the rear part of the British column concertinaed. Some jaegers went to the top of the hill where they could see the American lines, with Howe and Cornwallis soon accompanying them, scanning the ridges in front with their telescopes. Even the Light Infantry out of view behind them could see columns of dust being kicked up from Washington's army.

After underestimating the danger to his right for most of the day, and assuming Knyphausen to be the real threat, Washington had been firing off orders to redeploy his army. His line along the Brandywine Creek had to be bent back on its right, so as to construct a new deployment of troops at right angles to the original one.

While the redcoats gnawed on a chunk of meat or a lump of bread plucked from their haversacks, their generals watched the spectacle of their enemy deploying two divisions in their path, some of them just a few hundred yards to their front on Birmingham Hill. Howe was confident that all the sweat and dust being produced across the way were already futile.

The commander-in-chief walked back to a group of light infantry officers and beckoned to his orderlies to bring food. Sitting on the grass, savouring their picnic, the officers of Howe's chosen corps were struck by his composure, one recording, 'Everyone that remembers the anxious moments before an engagement may conceive how animating is the sight of the Commander-in-chief in whose looks nothing but serenity and confidence in his troops is painted.'

So sure was General Howe that things were going his way that he permitted his men a short rest. They were hot with hours of marching, the straps of their cartridge pouches and blankets wrapped around their bodies trapping heat and sweat in their clothes. Many swigged from canteens, knowing battle was imminent. The order to deploy came at 3 p.m. Columns of British troops began moving into the fields on the forward slope of Osborne's Hill, with the companies moving 'without hurry or confusion', out from behind one another into battle order, side by side.

Captain Mecan and the 23rd Light Company were pretty much in the centre of the first line. Looking across his left shoulder he would have seen the 2nd Battalion of light infantry and dozens of green-coated Hessian jaegers trotting into their skirmish line ahead. To his front was a small road that led down the slope of Osborne's Hill, across a stream and up towards a village called Birmingham, several hundred yards to the front. Just to the right of Birmingham was a distinct hill or knoll on which enemy cannon and troops could be seen. Over Mecan's right, across the Birmingham road, were the 2nd Battalion of grenadiers, the 1st Battalion of grenadiers and then two battalions of guards. A second line of troops formed behind, the British 3rd Brigade behind Mecan and the other Light Bobs, the Hessian grenadiers, with their towering brass-plated caps behind their British counterparts. The last brigade of British was formed behind these two, in line with the Birmingham road, a *corps de réserve* should everything go wrong.

When the front battalions were all in line, Lieutenant Colonel William Meadows ordered his grenadiers, 'Put on your caps!' The precious bearskins that had been stowed safely during the morning's long march were placed on the grenadiers' heads as Meadows bellowed out, 'For damned fighting and drinking, I'll match you against the world!'

The bands struck up the grenadier's march and the whole line began to tramp forward. With this stirring theme ringing in their ears, doubts about the purpose of the campaign were banished, officers and men succumbing instead to the intoxicating reverie of power. 'Nothing could be more dreadfully pleasing than the line moving on to the attack,' wrote one captain of the 2nd Grenadiers, who added, 'Believe me I would not exchange those three minutes of rapture to avoid ten thousand times the danger.'

When the grenadiers reached the first American line on Birmingham Hill, there was a spluttering of American musketry, then the grenadiers rushed forward with the bayonet. Most of the defenders did not wait to get acquainted with those blades, running back.

On Mecan's side of the road, things went quite differently. Some Virginia troops and artillery of Major General Adam Stephen's division opened up with musketry and grapeshot. Several light infantry were scythed down in this hail of metal. Captain Mecan was among those hit. The battalion split in that moment of fear; some men rushed into cover behind a wall around the Birmingham Meeting House, others found themselves at the foot of Birmingham Hill, right under the guns. This group of light infantry, gripped by 'the impatient courage of both officers and men', ran up the hill just as the American gunners got their pieces limbered and away.

When the Light Bobs crested Birmingham Hill, they got a shock, for there, just a few score yards in front of them, were revealed new brigades of American troops, moving to the attack. The redcoats, wrote one light company officer, 'had nothing to expect but slaughter', but they pressed on.

Fortunately for the Light Bobs, the flight of the first line of Americans was disordering the new waves sent in by Major General John Sullivan as he struggled to regain control of his flank. Panic was spreading, even among the Marylanders who had shown great courage at Long Island. One of their officers described trying to force his way towards Birmingham Hill:

Of all the Maryland regiments only two ever had an opportunity for form, Gist's and mine, and as soon as they began to fire, those [Americans] who were in our rear could not be prevented from firing also. In a few minutes we were attacked in front and flank and by our people in the rear. Our men ran off in confusion, and were very hard to be rallied.

The British grenadiers worked their way forward in the textbook style, allowing the enemy to fire, returning their own volley, and running in. Some estimated that they repeated this procedure five or six times as their enemies fell back from the line of one fence to another.

When the British got their own field guns on to the hill, they began spewing grapeshot back at the Americans and these showers of lead ripped lumps out of the draught animals pulling back some of General Stephen's guns, cutting them down. Light infantrymen rushed forward claiming five artillery pieces captured, a haul that would be rewarded by their general with a bounty of a hundred dollars per gun.

About one hour into this engagement, the American generals rallied their troops into a second distinct line, in the hope of allowing the soldiers who had been left opposite General Knyphausen to escape. That old German campaigner had however begun his own attack at around 4 p.m. when he heard the action becoming general.

The 4th and 5th Regiments went over first. Knyphausen moved them to Chadd's Ferry, 300 yards to the right of Chadd's Ford, the obvious crossing point on the Philadelphia road, in order to avoid some obstacles the Americans had placed there. Doing so, they also sidestepped the worst of the fire of several cannon covering the ford. British artillery had been firing rapidly from the height overlooking the river in order to ease the assault, but such an operation could be very tricky if the enemy put up a spirited defence, since men crossing a river packed together presented a tempting target. The 23rd waited its turn to cross behind them.

As the first British wave charged across the Creek, they were wading up to their stomachs through the stream, grapeshot smacking into bodies and water as they went. The defenders for the most part, however, were wisely reserving their fire until the British were right in front of them. The two advanced regiments splashed out of the creek, formed and moved forward. The redcoats were growing more tense with each step, knowing that the Americans to their front must let fly any moment with their saved volley. When the explosion of fire came, it 'fortunately being directed too high, did but little execution', the relieved serjeant major of the 5th wrote. The British response, though, did its job; the rippling wave of musketry broke the Americans and sent them running for the hills behind.

Advancing elements on Cornwallis's right, the Guards and some of the grenadiers, could see the effects of Knyphausen's attack as they pushed on. The two halves of General Howe's vice were only a few dozen yards apart and, by 4.30, several of Washington's brigades had already been broken by them. The 23rd, crossing Chadd's Ferry without loss, moved up towards the Guards.

In the woods where Sullivan's flank had formed its second line, there were still heavy exchanges of musketry to be heard, which caused some loss to the British brigade that had moved up through the grenadiers. By 5 p.m., though, the battle was effectively over.

Washington was able to extricate several more brigades in good order, to add to those that had run off in panic and might be rallied during the following days.

Of the human cost, estimates of the American casualties ranged from 400 to 1,200, exact figures being hard to reach due to the numbers that absconded from broken regiments. The British received 315 American deserters in the aftermath of the battle. Howe's own losses had been 577 killed, wounded and missing. Major Andre, of the commander-in-chief's staff, considered that 'the Light Infantry met with the chief resistance' on Birmingham Hill. The 1st Light Infantry had lost that day seven killed and 54 wounded. The casualties, among them Captain Thomas Mecan, were loaded on wagons to be taken to the port of Wilmington.

Mecan had shed blood for his sovereign before. Nearly seventeen years had passed since he was shot during a failed assault on a French-held convent at Campen, during the German campaigns of the Seven Years War. He knew that a saw-bones of an army surgeon or a stinking hospital could send a man to his maker more efficiently than any American sharpshooter. But his wound did not prove this time too serious. The light infantry had begun to quip that their tactic of using trees and other cover made them favourites for bullets in the arms or legs. Mecan would, though, be unable to serve for the remainder of that campaign, a military expedition that was already being picked over by the commander-in-chief's critics and supporters alike.

Brandywine was most certainly a victory. In tactical terms it was Howe's finest battle, but the strategy of going to Philadelphia as Burgoyne got deeper and deeper into trouble further north had not produced a decisive battle. 'The consequences of this victory have been exactly like those of the others,' Fitzpatrick wrote wearily, 'it is really melancholy to see so much misery occasioned and so many troops sacrificed every day to so little purpose.' Those who attacked Howe from the military rather than party-political angle asked why he hadn't started his flank march earlier, since arriving so late in the day had allowed Washington to salvage his broken army by night. The failure to pursue the following day left quite a few wondering again why their commander-in-chief was reluctant to press home his military advantages.

Camping near the field of Brandywine for a couple of days after the battle, the British dealt with some of their usual problems. The march from the Head of Elk had been accompanied by some looting that once again nettled many officers. Earl Cornwallis seems to have been the angriest of all. It had become clear that General Howe would not confirm death sentences awarded by courts martial to soldiers who robbed civilians. Cornwallis could stand this no longer, so took the extraordinary step of summarily judging and hanging two men of his elite corps.

At 11 a.m. on 15 September the 1st Battalion of Grenadiers were ordered on parade. The resulting sentence of death was pronounced on the two miscreants and without further ado they were hanged. Lieutenant John Peebles, a veteran grenadier of the Black Watch, noted approvingly that these two men were 'the first examples made, though often threatened and many deserved it'.

After two and a half years of campaigning, and numerous capital sentences for such crimes, the British army had actually started executing its looters. How far any lesson was learned in the army was open to question.

General Howe still preferred to play the part of merciful father to his army, frequently using the commander-in-chief's prerogative to pardon the condemned. Howe, it appears, also regarded devastation as part of his scheme of operations against the rebels. Three men of the 23rd Fusiliers court-martialled for looting soon after the army landed at the Head of Elk had been awarded 1,000 lashes but orders announced: 'The Commander-in-chief, considering the punishment inadequate to their crimes, is pleased to remit the punishment and to order the prisoners to be released and to join their regiment.' If letting guilty men off because the punishment was not severe enough seemed an odd stance for the general to take, so too was his explanation of the latest stealing. After Brandywine, Howe put at least some of the blame for encouraging marauding on local people since they had gone to impromptu markets to buy back stolen goods. The examples made by Cornwallis on 16 September were not therefore regularly repeated, for quite a few condemned men escaped that fate.

With disciplinary matters attended to, the British army moved towards Philadelphia. On 21 September, General Grey pulled off a daring night raid with some companies of the 2nd Light Infantry and some regular infantry. Creeping through the darkness they had surprised the camp of some Pennsylvania regiments and done terrible slaughter with their bayonets. Around 150 Americans were killed, and seventy-one taken prisoner.

It may come as no surprise that the kind of propagandists who dubbed the killing of five demonstrators in 1770 a 'massacre' would have no trouble making use of the same word to described the events at Paoli. Rumours were spread that the British had refused quarter to wounded men, and such reports may have helped keep up the fighting spirit of demoralised Continental regiments, and no matter that dozens of captives were actually taken alive.

On 26 September, Earl Cornwallis marched at the head of his grenadiers into Philadelphia. Howe had gained his objective, but to little effect.

Brandywine and Paoli had shown the more politically perceptive officers in Howe's army that the effects of military victory on support for the enemy cause would always be limited. How would the King's partisans ever win when victories would be denounced as bloody massacres, and more dubious outcomes hailed as great American victories? Since the British newspapers routinely reprinted American dispatches or reports, the consequences of this battle of words were important in undermining support at home, causing many officers to become increasingly embittered by what they saw as American lies.

Captain Mecan did not share in the triumphal entry to Philadelphia, as he languished on his sick bed. His life was not in danger, but he had left the command of the 23rd Light Company vacant and another officer eyed it jealously.

The Surprise of Germantown

After Which the Honourable Lionel Smythe Appeared Among the Fusiliers

The Americans that morning sounded reveille for the 2nd Light Infantry in dashing style. Creeping towards the forward outposts of William Howe's army they had obtained the element of surprise at Germantown. Running out of the dawn mist, the attackers gave war whoops, shouting that they were there to get revenge for Paoli. The British, who were mainly asleep at this hour, tried to organise their defences but soon found themselves streaming back.

During the hours of darkness some of Howe's commanders had become concerned by intelligence that Washington's army was moving towards them. Several regiments, including the 1st Light Infantry Battalion, which lay to the right and a little closer to headquarters than the 2nd, had put on their cartridge-pouch belts and equipment but had not been 'stood to arms' or paraded formed up and ready for action.

Washington had not obtained, in that sense, complete surprise but he had done well enough to cause the British serious difficulties. On the hill at the northern edge of Germantown where the 2nd L.I. had made their camp, men were hurriedly formed into platoons and companies and thrown forward against the large numbers of Pennsylvanians. The ground was much intersected with fences, buildings and clumps of trees, so the action yawed back and forth as little groups of men gained or lost local advantage. After a couple of attempts to recover the situation, wrote a young officer of the Light Bobs, 'The battalion was so reduced by killed and wounded that the bugle was sounded to retreat.' The rigours of campaigning had cut the number of fit men in the 2nd Battalion to below 400, and in the first hour at Germantown, they took scores of casualties.

Howe's force had divided itself into several elements in and around Philadelphia. Among those detachments were the 23rd, who had gone marching back into the city as an escort for some artillery and missed this battle. The army under his command that morning was only around 7,500. Washington, having excellent intelligence of British dispositions, concerted a plan to bring something like 12,000 of his own troops from different directions to fall upon Germantown. He intended to reap the rewards of sound generalship, concentrating his forces at the very time and place that Howe had dispersed his.

Some time not long after 6 a.m. General Howe, trotting up towards the sound of fighting, saw clumps of men racing back along the road or through gardens. 'For shame! For shame, Light Infantry!' the general shouted at his men. 'I never saw you retreat before.' The 2nd Light Infantry had been placed too far away from the main British encampment to receive rapid support from their comrades who were now under arms and marching up. This separation of two miles from headquarters was also apparently the reason why the troops at the northern edge of Howe's deployment had not received the warnings of imminent attack during the night. As the Light Bobs ran back past their general those left behind in the bivouac, the 40th Foot, were the next to face the torrent rushing towards them.

Washington's plan did not, however, simply involve attack from one direction. The 1st Light Infantry (in which the 23rd's company served without the wounded Mecan) was soon attacked too. They were in battle formation, with the 4th Regiment formed to their left and facing in the right direction, but 'the morning was so foggy that their columns could not be distinguished at twenty paces distance'. With a crash of musketry, an enemy brigade launched itself out of the miasma to their front and fell upon the right wing (or half) of the 4th, next to the 1st Light Infantry, sending them fleeing backwards. With the Americans rushing past their left, the 1st L.I. 'instantly attempted wheeling to the left', to catch them in the flank.

During the confused close-range battle, the 1st Light Infantry broke into two wings, as it had at Brandywine, with their right, formed of nearly five companies, fighting in one direction, while the left (including the 23rd Light Company) continued their attack. In this melee, the 9th Virginia Regiment got between the two wings of the 1st

L.I., and when soldiers of the smaller right wing started trudging back from beating off another enemy force, they saw the Virginians plundering the battalion's encampment, 'upon which the officers with the most determined bravery encouraging their men, . . . charged [the Americans] though very inferior to their numbers and effectually routed them'. The 9th Virginians were caught between two fires, having light infantry to their front and rear, and suffered accordingly.

After three hours of fighting in fenced fields and copses, the tide began to turn. The early morning mist burned off, allowing the British, exploiting their central position, to concert counter-attacks on the different American columns. The 40th Regiment, holding out in the brick-built Cliveden mansion, had occupied hundreds of Continentals, who tried in vain to storm the building supported by artillery, rather than exploiting their initial success and pushing into the heart of the enemy position. Poor co-ordination between Washington's different columns meant that two engaged each other by mistake, and there was little hope of responding to the growing number of counter-attacks.

In these actions redcoat brigades and battalions worked smoothly together, smashing apart Washington's columns and driving them back. The attack cost the Americans more than 1,000 men, of whom 400 were taken prisoner (a significant proportion being from the 9th Virginia after it was surrounded by the Light Infantry) and more than 150 killed. Howe's loss was about half that, but it was nonetheless a significant blow, coming near the end of a long campaign. Washington had in any case ably demonstrated at Germantown that he was still capable of offensive action and retained an effective army in being.

In the days after Germantown, Howe set his men to work reducing American fortifications on the Delaware River that effectively prevented British ships sailing up from the open seas to re-supply him. This was a difficult task, for the defenders of the two main forts proved tenacious and tactics employed by Howe's subordinates rather inefficient.

In late October, nonetheless, Howe and his people pronounced themselves satisfied with the campaign, believing they had discomfited the naysayers. 'The movement of the army', wrote Major Balfour, 'has convinced the Americans of a truth they ever doubted before, that we can penetrate into their country, whenever we please.' Certainly, it was true that plenty had asserted that a British army that went far from the sea would be overwhelmed, but the campaign was not over and the fate of

Burgoyne's force advancing from Canada was, to put it mildly, uncertain.

Writing the following day, a young friend of Earl Percy's alluded to disturbing rumours about the fate of Burgoyne's column. American prisoners and civilians would regularly report with glee news of British reverses elsewhere, but often this was dismissed as wishful thinking or the wilful distortion of the Whig presses. Lieutenant Lionel Smythe, though, was sufficiently worried to repeat the reports, such as that in an American newspaper published nearby in Reading that said, 'The most favourable accounts are that [Burgoyne] has returned to Fort Ticonderoga with the loss of heavy artillery.'

Smythe wrote his letter on 26 October, the same day his name appeared in orders, promoted from his lieutenancy in the 49th to captain in the Royal Welch Fusiliers. The young man's patron, through skilful hints via his proxies at headquarters (for Percy himself was back in England by this time), had obtained a veritable prize, command of the 23rd's Light Company. One of the senior officer's correspondents reported back to Percy that gaining Mecan's crack company for Smythe had 'made him one of the happiest men in the army'.

The twenty-four-year-old officer might have seemed an unlikely subject for the earl's patronage, being the heir to Viscount Strangford, a landowner and clergyman from Ireland. Young Lionel, entering his new regiment, was indeed the only officer of the Welch Fusiliers at that moment with a peerage to looked forward to. The handsome, titled officer had brought some glamour to the Fusiliers *enfin*. The Strangford lands, however, were much diminished and his father's position as Dean of Derry did not give him great wealth either. Smythe, in other words, was a hard-up aristocrat who relied upon Earl Percy paying the entire £550 the cost of his step.

As to why Percy had done it, his motives were neither entirely corrupt nor could they be guaranteed pure. While he had gained a sterling reputation as a soldier, Percy's private life was wreathed in scandalous rumour. Relations with his wife, the countess, had broken down, and they had not slept together for years. The countess's friends put it about that Percy had rendered himself impotent, discharging his lifetime's supply of seed by prodigious masturbation at school and whoring in adulthood. Even if the charge of impotence were false, it was apparent that the earl, who like many of his elevated social stratum had imbibed much about the ancient Greeks, considered the company of beautiful boys to be just as desirable as that of attractive women.

Smythe and other handsome young men sometimes infatuated the noble general. Late in 1777, the paths of this and another Adonis crossed in the 23rd's Light Company. The other was William Russell, who had been through most of the company's fights of 1777 as Mecan's junior lieutenant. Russell was quite unable to afford a commission of any sort, and had first been commissioned in the 5th Regiment at the personal expense of its colonel, Earl Percy. Later he transferred into the 23rd. Russell was known for his looks, but while pretty enough had no real ambition to be a soldier and may in any case have regarded his private financial position as inadequate for such a path. He left the army early in 1778.

Lionel Smythe was a somewhat different case, for at this time certainly he was determined to make a career in the army, and brought a lively intellect as well as a handsome face to the general's table. He served as one of Percy's aides-de-camp through most of the New York campaign, a dutiful young man who repaid the general's generosity with monthly letters from America. Smythe eschewed army politics or gossip in these missives, confining himself to factual accounts of what he had seen. He would thank his patron and flatter him, constantly asking when the general might return to the war and telling him there 'never was a person that had a people's affection and gratitude more strongly than your Lordship'. Whatever the gossips might have thought of it, there was no hint of sexual intimacy in the correspondence between Smythe and Percy. In any case, Smythe was probably anxious to avoid calling on Percy's purse again, for he soon gravitated towards wealthy society in Philadelphia, making connections that would serve him well later.

It is enough to say, then, that the earl assisted the careers of Russell and Smythe because a certain type of gilded youth excited him. His aesthetic sensibilities, sentimentality and love of good company led him to open his purse to Russell or Smythe, and to get desirable postings for those desirable boys, while middle-aged, plain officers of the Fusiliers who claimed his friendship from the time of Boston received a courteous reply to their letters but rarely more.

As the campaign of 1777 came towards its end, Smythe was installed as the commander of the 23rd Light Company and many of its non-commissioned officers were sent to other companies to impart the lessons of their most active campaign. The Light Bobs and grenadiers had been repeatedly engaged since the year began that

January, fighting in raids like Bound Brook or Paoli and major battles such as Brandywine. During the winter of 1777/78 there were many changes, with those who had gained this vital experience transferred to inculcate their parent regiments with the Howe style of fighting. This happened with Thomas Mecan, when he recovered from his wound, and several other officers from the 1st Light Infantry Battalion who had learned such tough lessons during the fights of 1777.

Dansey, commanding the 33rd Light Company, reckoned that the casualties had exceeded the original numbers of the company that had begun campaigning nearly two years previously, with eight other ranks killed, twenty-three wounded and five taken prisoner. 'I cannot easily *express* to you,' Dansey wrote to his mother, 'how thankful we ought to be to heaven that I am still alive and well to write to you at present.' His company, however, had been particularly roughly handled, suffering losses at Long Island, Pell's Point, in the Jerseys and Pennsylvania. By contrast, the 5th Light Company, also in the 1st Light Infantry Battalion, had suffered ten men wounded since landing at the Head of Elk at the start of the Philadelphia campaign, the 23rd fewer than that.

Even so, the army's picked troops had become at last worthy of the name 'elite'. In two years of campaigning they had been galvanised by Howe's tactics and ethos, as well as skilfully led in battle by Cornwallis and some excellent battalion commanders. Their spirit was high at the close of 1777, and a pervasive fear of the enemy that had gripped them in 1775 had evaporated in the rush of a dozen battles. One young grenadier officer summed up in a letter home his feelings about the superiority of British soldiers in those chosen corps:

Light Infantry accustomed to fight from tree to tree, or charge even in woods; and grenadiers who after the first fire lose no time in loading again, but rush on, trusting entirely to that most decisive of weapons the bayonet; will ever be superior to any troops the rebels can bring against them.

As for the parent regiments of the light and grenadier companies, the same officer commented, 'The brigades have been looked upon as nurseries only for the flank corps.' Inevitably when some battalions are called upon to shed their blood regularly and others hardly at all, it can cause resentment and is not good for the efficiency of that wider army. Howe, though, seemed to lack the enthusiasm to give the rest of his army the same attention he had lavished on those chosen corps. He was apparently indifferent to many of the British line regiments and had become contemptuous of the Hessians, believing their movements on the battlefield hopelessly slow and their commanders 'totally unfit for our service'. After 1777, they were largely confined to garrison duties.

When it came to the dozens of regiments of British foot, one or two were allowed to share the laurels of the elite corps, but even Howe's own regiment, the 23rd, had for the most part marched hither and thither in obscurity during the previous two campaigns.

Since its participation at Long Island, the Royal Welch Fusiliers had not come under heavy fire, losing more men to disease and desertion than enemy action. Instead the Fusiliers, like other regiments, simply fed replacements to their detached light or grenadier companies as required, while bit by bit the weak men died off, the unwilling disappeared and the recruits were tempered into something more solid.

Everything was changing, however, as 1777 drew to an end. On 2 November, official reports in the Tory press confirmed what the other side had been saying for days, that General Burgoyne had been forced to surrender his army at Saratoga, having lost in his struggle to fight his way down the Hudson valley. To inveterate Whigs like Captain Fitzpatrick of the Guards, the conclusions to be drawn from this cataclysm were obvious: 'If all reasoning and speculation was not exploded one would conclude that an immediate change of Ministry and peace with the *United States* must be the necessary consequence of it.' But in his desire to pack off the government in London (making way for the letter's reader, his friend Charles Fox), Fitzpatrick had underestimated the King's desire to continue the war. Furthermore Burgoyne's disaster on the Hudson would soon spark intervention by other European powers, changing the complexion of the struggle from an internecine or civil one among English men to a conflict between nations.

All of the variables of the war facing the Fusiliers were thus in a state of flux as 1777 came to a close. Howe's gamble, his hope for a decisive battle in front of Philadelphia, had failed spectacularly. Not only had he contributed to the surrender of 5,000 redcoats at Saratoga by taking himself off to Pennsylvania, but he had failed to cripple Washington's corps of the Continental Army, a reality brought home by the battle of Germantown. A man in such a position could not continue to serve. Howe would be going but might still have time to make some changes to his army and his regiment to ensure that they would be ready to face the next campaign without trepidation.

Winter in Philadelphia

How Nisbet Balfour Won the Prize

By early December 1777, the army was settled in Philadelphia. A line of outposts had been built to prevent any unpleasant surprises. Foraging expeditions were occasionally conducted, but even these were 'very peaceable, quite different from our Jersey excursions last year, where we were generally sure of fighting twice a week'.

The shock of Saratoga created a sense that change was imperative – either a general peace or a new system of war. Months of carefully considered correspondence would be required to arrange this, so in the meantime, why take risks? 'If', reasoned the Whig Captain Richard Fitzpatrick in a letter to his friend Charles Fox, 'General Howe attempts anything but securing his army for the winter I shall consider him, after what has happened in the north, a very rash man. But if he lets himself be governed by General Grant I shall not be surprised if we get into some cursed scrape.'

Howe decided to play it safe, all the more so since he was aware that his own time as commander-in-chief was coming to an end. Thus, General Washington's army was able to spend its winter in cantonments at Valley Forge, just one day's ride from Philadelphia, without the serious possibility of British attack. Soon after hearing of Saratoga, Howe had requested his recall – a new general would have the task of untangling the Gordian Knot of American affairs.

Philadelphia thus provided agreeable winter quarters, with little risk to life and plentiful possibilities for amusement. It had, before the redcoats' arrival, been the most populous city in America. Of its 30,000 inhabitants around 8,000 civilians had left, mainly Whigs or

Patriots, call them what you will, to have their places taken by soldiers. Philadelphia's position on the broad Delaware River had guaranteed its status as a great trading centre. It had also become an important seat of politics and of related trades such as printing. The city's spoils were divided between Quakers and less religious merchants. Sufficient wealthy families remained, though, for elegant society to be maintained as 1777 ebbed into its dying days.

Officers could find plentiful company at the Bunch of Grapes or the Indian Queen. At Smith's City Tavern there were assembly rooms large enough to host regular dances. Captain Hale of the grenadiers described the scene there:

Rooms are opened at the City Tavern by a subscription of two days' pay from each officer, a genteel coffee house where you meet and converse or play from six o'clock to twelve; to prevent any disorders an officer's Guard from the grenadiers mounts there every evening, Sundays excepted, when the rooms are shut. Tea, coffee, lemonade and orgeat are the only licquors allowed, except on ball nights, when negus is permitted.

As for play, there were quite a few opportunities for men to ruin themselves. Captain Wreden of the Hessian jaegers set up a Faro bank at the city tavern, and there were frequent games of cards or dice. For those enjoying more energetic sport, a cock-pit at Moore's Alley was the scene of raucous fights.

There was good game too for the fighting cocks of the army, those dandies who sought to win American beauties. Major Lord Cathcart pursued Miss Eliot relentlessly, a match described by one Tory as uniting 'a fine girl, of good fortune, to a Scottish lord with a moderate one'. Captain Lionel Smythe was on the same social circuit, attending the theatre and dances in the great homes along Water or Market streets. Having been settled with his company of the 23rd, his thoughts were turning to finding a mate, and the principle followed by Cathcart, of uniting American wealth with impoverished title, had much to commend it.

For those who had left their wives in New York or England, or simply wanted some uncomplicated fornication, Philadelphia had possibilities too. Colonel Birch of the light dragoons and Major Williams of the artillery both acquired handsome mistresses during their stay.

General Howe was as fond of the bottle and boudoir as any, but there were some professional matters that would require his attention before he returned home. It was time to give some thought to his responsibilities as colonel of the Royal Welch Fusiliers, for once he was back in England an exchange of letters to settle some delicate matter would take three months at least. The regiment had scarcely been led for two years since neither of the officers who would naturally provide such direction – the lieutenant colonel or major – had been capable of doing so owing to Bernard's incapacity and Blakeney's refusal to leave his parlour in England. It was imperative that the matter be settled before the general left, preferably by installing new men in both posts. General Howe knew by then also that it was the King's desire that preference be given to officers already serving in America, as a reward for the hardships suffered on campaign.

Blakeney's ability to avoid serving two and a half years after his wounding at Bunker Hill said much for how a wily officer could work the system. 'I have lately received a message from Sir William Howe desiring that you may be ordered out to your duty,' Lord Barrington, the Secretary at War, wrote to Blakeney on 9 December 1777. Barrington confessed that he was under the impression the major had returned to America months before, instead of hiding away in Newcastle. Blakeney had no intention of budging.

When he had first gone home, Blakeney had formed part of the recruiting effort, and was evidently fit enough to go looking for fresh cannon fodder. Later, on being promoted major, he had tried to swap commissions with a keener man of the same rank serving in America. Alas, the swap between fireater and firesider was stopped when that man was promoted. Blakeney then requested leave, saying that his Bunker Hill wound was playing up.

By the end of 1777, Lord Barrington was putting matters quite bluntly to him: 'Those who are no longer capable of doing their duty should dispose of their commissions, nor expect to be continued in the army to the detriment of the service, and the prejudice of other officers who are still able and willing to serve.' But Blakeney wanted to stay on the army list, and indeed to advance himself to lieutenant colonel, so that he might then gain further promotions by seniority alone, the better to feather his nest.

When the matter came to the attention of the King himself, Blakeney was told he must sell his majority in the 23rd and leave the army. General Howe sent him the same message. Still, Blakeney ignored the orders of his sovereign and regimental colonel alike. He intended to hang on to his property, for that was what a purchased commission was. Blakeney's skill at fending off these requests even extended to getting his Member of Parliament to take up the cudgels in his defence.

After months of tiresome correspondence, it must have become apparent to Howe that the issue of Blakeney's majority would not be settled before his own departure from Philadelphia. As for the commanding officer, Benjamin Bernard had shown similar tenacity in holding on. In his case, greater sympathy was due since he had remained in America, nursing the wound suffered when the contest began, transferring himself from a succession of sick beds in rented rooms from Boston to Halifax to New York. Nevertheless a suspicious regimental colonel might have asked himself why it was that Bernard, Blakeney and Donkin, three men who were close allies in the 23rd at the outbreak of the war, sharing an Irish gentry background (such folk being among the most sceptical about the justice of Britain's American war), had managed to avoid fighting the rebels for so long. Henry Blunt, the Fusiliers' major until his disgrace in the summer of 1777 alluded to the subtext when pleading with a patron for reinstatement as an officer:

this war . . . is an unpopular war, and perhaps it may be thought I am one of those who disapprove of it. Was that the case, I have honesty enough to have declared my sentiments openly and would have given that as a reason for my retiring, but it is quite the reverse . . . I wish for nothing more than to be employed on it.

Blakeney did not have the honesty to tell his king and minister about his opposition to the war, for he wished to retain the benefits or army pay and pension. Bernard was a trickier case, but Howe had resolved all the same during the latter part of 1777 that he must find a new commanding officer – someone prepared to do the job properly.

Quite a few men had been readying themselves for Bernard to sell out. Robert Donkin was a shrewd fellow whom Bernard himself wanted to ease into the job. Donkin had exposed himself to even less gunfire than Blakeney, but kept safe while serving in America in a succession of staff appointments, insisting all the time to his superiors that he was zealous for the cause. Although still only technically a captain in the 23rd, Donkin had gained two steps of acting rank or brevet promotions, finding himself in temporary charge of the 44th whose commanding officer had been killed at Germantown.

Donkin could not afford the full price to buy his way up to lieutenant colonel. Attempting it would have exposed himself to a fiasco like Henry Blunt's. Donkin, though, had seen enough of these battles to plan his campaign carefully; he had agreed private terms, less expensive of course, with his mentor Bernard for the deal to be done. In this way, let it be clear, Bernard and Donkin had entered into a conspiracy against the other actors in this drama including General William Howe.

Who else was there to beat? Joseph Ferguson had got himself promoted to a majority away from the 23rd, but hankered after the lieutenant colonelcy of the Fusiliers, describing it as 'the corps I love'. Ferguson at least could raise the money, for £900 was normally needed, the difference between the price of a major's commission and a lieutenant colonel's. Both Ferguson and Donkin, however, were thwarted.

By mid-January, the identity of the officer that had gained the prize was being whispered through the coffee houses and taverns of Philadelphia. Bernard was out, and the new lieutenant colonel would be Major Nisbet Balfour of General Howe's staff. One of Earl Percy's correspondents in the city reported with the relish of an inveterate gossip, 'This matter seems to give no *little* offence.'

Ferguson was quick to denounce it, and knew how he had been beaten: 'I offered the sum to purchase, but I have no interest.' Balfour, of course could wield decisive 'interest' or patronage in this matter – he had served Howe as part of his inner circle, but could fully expect to be cast out by the new commander-in-chief. If Howe was to show Balfour gratitude, he must do it before leaving Philadelphia.

When Donkin realised that he had been beaten he was furious, because he had previously gone to Howe to press his case in person. During their interview Howe had insisted, as a means of fobbing off Donkin with his small purse, that Bernard should only sell for the full price. Alas, Howe was a more powerful practitioner of the black arts of promotion. The general's request for payment of the £900 for the lieutenant colonelcy was simply a tactic to get rid of this particular applicant. Donkin's anger was vented on paper when he discovered not only that he had been refused the job, but that his rival could not afford the full price either: 'Balfour with his master's authority snatched the bit out of my mouth, by paying only £400.'

Those who discussed the matter over a bumper of negus at the Indian Queen or Smith's Tavern could have fed Donkin's anger with all sorts of stories about Balfour. Was he not one of the cabal who had urged the commander-in-chief towards the disastrous abandonment of Burgoyne?

Rumours were widespread in Philadelphia that the surprise at Germantown was also the fault of Howe's favourite. Some said that an American deserter had gone in the night before with warning of Washington's attack, but that Balfour had been too lazy to get out of bed and question him. Another account suggested there had been no warning and that Balfour had been so furious about it that after the battle he had bellowed at the locals that he would devastate the country for miles about, blaming them for allowing the rebels to approach the King's army unreported.

Unknown to those officers chewing the fat in Philadelphia, one other protagonist claimed great hurt at Howe's proceedings with Balfour. Blakeney wrote full of grievance to the War Office, wondering how he could have been subject to 'this very great injustice', since – the major insisted – he had been on his way to America when the news of Balfour's appointment arrived. Just a few lines later, he contradicted these assertions of fitness by pleading, 'I hope, as my health still continues in a very precarious state, that His Majesty will not insist on my setting out to join my regiment.' When Blakeney's intervention was reported to Howe, he replied with cold anger to the Secretary at War, 'Had [Blakeney] been present with his regiment after upwards of two years absence, I should not have put any officer over him.'

For all the opprobrium and expressions of wounded honour that greeted Balfour's appointment, Howe had undoubtedly chosen a singularly able officer. Lord Rawdon, for example, had recommended Balfour to his uncle as 'one of my most intimate acquaintances . . . a very worthy man'.

Balfour was desperate for advancement, driven by family circumstances that few of his rivals could have guessed at. Although he had ties of marriage to the aristocracy of Galloway in south-west Scotland, a father who had been laird, and one or two valuable political contacts, none of these acquaintances was willing to buy him up the army or indeed to exert influence in Nisbet's favour.

When General Howe sent the captain home with dispatches announcing the capture of Fort Washington in the autumn of 1776, it opened the way to promotion which might have been effected without purchase, for such was the customary reward for a man bringing good news to his sovereign. Howe, though, insisted Balfour pay full price for his majority. Balfour thus found himself being forced to borrow money at punitive rates in order to take advantage of the 'honour' his patron had given him.

The newly made major had evaded his creditors, and returned to the American war, telling one friend, 'I believe I must keep out of England now, for fear of a confinement a little closer than Boston was.' Being out of the country, in other words, he escaped the spectre of financial ruin and debtors' prison. Howe belatedly realised his error in expecting such a man to pay the regulation price for a second promotion, and tried to make matters right by offering Balfour the lieutenant colonelcy of the 23rd at a knockdown price. 'It will cost me but four hundred,' wrote Balfour, 'which with my last purchase will bring me monstrously in debt, but I must trust to fortune to clear me.'

Selling the command of the Royal Welch Fusiliers at a discount had irked Donkin and Ferguson beyond measure, but it was the only way for Howe to get the man he wanted in the job, since the Balfour family fortunes had been almost ruined by army service and the purchase system.

Balfour's father Henry had died late in 1776 while serving as a major, and two of his three brothers had also died in the army. An ailing officer could sell out, redeeming his investment in commissions; a dead one could not. These three having perished in the service, the family had sunk thousands into military careers with Nisbet's mother Katherine being unable to redeem a single pound. Anxious at her growing impoverishment and lonely existence at the Balfour seat in Dunbog, Nisbet had petitioned the American Secretary, asking him to provide a pension for her. There was no reply. Matters were only made worse by the fact that Henry had never actually married Katherine, and that Nisbet had no wife or heirs himself. The Balfour line thus confronted financial ruin and extinction.

Faced with such dire circumstances, Nisbet Balfour was guided by his own moral code as he piloted his way through the army, dodging death and the cold indifference of officialdom alike. His first rule was to do whatever was necessary to gain the right person's patronage; as he wrote to one friend triumphantly, 'You see what it is, to be *well connected*.' Having succeeded in this aim, Balfour's second rule was not to care too much about upsetting those without similar interest: 'The friend you like, and the woman you love, are the only objects worth giving oneself a moment's trouble about.' Fuelled by ambition, bereft of doubt, Balfour exuded considerable presence.

Balfour's choice of words about the woman one loved rather than married was revealing. Like his father, Nisbet never endured a church wedding, but did not allow this omission to prevent him siring children. Certainly, there was at least one daughter that he provided for.

The qualities that had gained General Howe's notice were: bravery, as Balfour had shown in front of the rail fence at Bunker Hill and on several other occasions; total loyalty to his patron; sound political acumen; an apparently tireless application to official correspondence; and a fine eye for military detail. As a commanding officer of the 23rd, a junior dispenser of patronage in his own right, Balfour also proved to be an advocate of merit, finding innovative ways to advance those without fortune.

As for the man's faults, certainly he had a fearsome temper. Of the two tales told against him about Germantown, that of him threatening to torch the villages for miles around seemed the more believable, the idea that he was too lazy to interview a prisoner less so. Balfour was a big man, broad too, and when in full flow was undoubtedly an intimidating presence. His greatest flaw though was that in playing the game to ensure he was 'well connected', Balfour entered rather too fully into the violent partisanship that characterised high-level army or parliamentary politics. He was ready to consider almost any step in support of his master.

On 31 January 1778 Balfour's appointment was announced in General Orders, and for the first time in years the Fusiliers had an effective commanding officer. He wasted no time in getting to grips with his soldiers, many of whom he already knew, since his old regiment, the King's Own or 4th Foot, had served in the same brigade as the 23rd in Boston. Balfour's proximity to General Howe would have told him that, whatever strategy was resolved in London, the army would have to quit Philadelphia and he must therefore prepare his regiment for the campaign ahead.

Just twenty miles from the British soldiers in Philadelphia, Washington's army occupied its winter quarters at Valley Forge. Arriving there on 17 December, in their tattered campaign clothes, his men had been obliged to construct their own camp on the frozen hillsides. One private from Connecticut wrote:

To build us habitations to *stay* (not to *live*) in such a weak, starved and naked condition was appalling in the highest degree . . . however there was no remedy, no alternative but this or dispersion . . . we had engaged in the defence of our injured country and were determined to persevere as long as such hardships were not altogether intolerable.

Having fortified their camp, and built log cabins – each to accommodate twelve soldiers – the Continentals set about dealing with a complete collapse of their supply system. Washington directed his men to forage the surrounding countryside, taking by force if necessary the food and clothing they needed to survive. 'Such procedures', he warned the President of Congress, 'may give a momentary relief but if repeated will prove of the most pernicious consequence . . . not only ruinous to the inhabitants but in many instances to the armies themselves.'

So great were the hardships of the army's winter at Valley Forge that around one quarter of the 10,000 men billeted there were lost to their regiments. Many died from smallpox and other diseases that ravaged the encampment while others wandered off, unable to bear it any longer.

Although British troops threatened Valley Forge on a couple of occasions, the loss of direction in Howe's army and news of the supercession of that general meant Washington's quarters were never seriously in danger.

As 1778 got under way and weather improved, a thoroughgoing programme of training was instituted: 'it was one constant drill'. With such a large proportion of the Continental Army united in one place, the perfect opportunity presented itself for imposing some standard procedures and manoeuvres. Washington's bitter experiences with the militiamen of New England or New York led him to believe in a professional army, and he strove to make the troops at Valley Forge fully as proficient as the redcoats. He aped some of their practices, too, creating light infantry companies in each regiment that might be banded together into larger corps. In this way Howe's success in creating his light battalions, a step taken in response to American tactics, was itself so successful that it prompted Washington to imitate it.

One of those being marched about the training ground of Valley Forge as the longer days began to ease winter's grip on the land was

William Hewitt who had deserted the 23rd Fusiliers in Boston three years earlier. Hewitt had settled initially in Ipswich, New Hampshire, where he had joined the militia. By early 1778 he had forsaken civilian life and joined the 7th Company of the 1st New Hampshire Regiment. Hewitt undoubtedly felt there was justice in the Patriot cause, but was this all that had caused him to resume the harsh life of a soldier?

For many of the men at Valley Forge, their motives for service were undoubtedly similar to those of British foot-sloggers: the army offered them booze, food and clothing, as well as affording the prospect of adventure. Payment was always a source of difficulty, since the paper money issued by Congress continually depreciated. Some men were lured by the promise of land when the war ended. That perhaps was one of the American army's secrets: it provided its privates with just enough to keep them going, but continually held out the prospect of a brighter future; of a thumping backlog of pay, of land, and of course of 'Liberty'.

The men who were serving at Valley Forge were, therefore, for the most part very different to the yeoman farmers or tradesmen who chased Percy's brigade back to Boston in April 1775. They were closer to the margins of society, more similar to the rank and file of the British army. For this reason, the traffic of deserters became more of a two-way phenomenon. New corps formed from American loyalists began to harvest hundreds of deserters from the Patriot cause.

If the American army became more like those of European powers in its recruitment, so Washington sought to impose discipline in the customary manner. His men became subject more often to the gallows and the lash. The election of officers might still take place in some militia regiments, but in the Continental Army its chief had instilled a system of regular military subordination. This, combined with the intensive tactical training given them during that winter meant that Washington felt confident that his regiments would be ready to attack the British when they quit Philadelphia.

The scene that unfolded on the Delaware on the night of 18 May 1778 proved sensational – Philadelphians would talk about it for decades and it even produced calls for an inquiry in the House of Commons. General Howe was that night brought up the river in an open barge with his suite; Sir Henry Clinton – his successor – was likewise afloat, as were Lieutenant General Knyphausen, the ranking Hessian officer, and numerous other grand personages. The guest of honour was taken from a jetty through a triumphal arch garlanded with flowers and into handsome gardens where a medieval spectacular, called the *Mischianza* or Medley, had been laid out.

Mingling about the gardens were officers dressed as knights, with flowing capes, feathered helms and shields bearing ancient family arms. Local damsels, similarly accoutred in lavish fancy dress, gave tokens to their champions who enacted jousts in front of them. Nothing was stinted in laying on the finest music, wines and food that could be procured.

Captain Smythe, who had been out on a fighting expedition with the light infantry until just a couple of days before, wandered through it all in fancy dress, eyes wide in wonderment. Smythe called it 'a most pompous piece of pageantry and parade, the expense reckoned three thousand guineas'. Four officers, among them two of the Guards and Howe's engineer, Captain Montresor (who would later plead impoverishment), footed most of the bill.

'I do not believe', wrote Major John Andre of Howe's staff, 'there is upon record an instance of a commander-in-chief having so universally endeared himself to those under his command.' Balfour might have agreed, but many would have differed. The fireworks that boomed over America's principal city that night sounded the end of Howe and his misguided idea that threatening Philadelphia would produce a decisive battle or indeed that taking it would provide a mortal blow to the prestige of the revolutionary leaders.

Instead the failure of the 1777 campaign produced a worldwide crisis for the British Empire. It had emboldened France, then Spain and the Netherlands, to join the onslaught against England's colonies and interests. As the army prepared to quit Philadelphia, the wisdom of driving into the continent had been demolished but the strategy that Howe's critics had advocated as an alternative, that of crippling the rebel economy through sea-based raiding, had begun to look dubious too.

Powerful French and Spanish fleets were preparing to contest the high seas. Ministers in London knew that a great portion of the army in America would have to be sent to the Caribbean to protect Britain's spice islands there. This was the dismal strategic panorama opening up for Henry Clinton, the new commander-in-chief, as he downed his wine or chewed over his beef at the *Mischianza*.

Through most of the preceding winter Smythe and others had

regarded imminent peace as 'the constant topick'. It had not come, and with the spring thaw the young Fusilier captain began thinking about the host that 'Mr Washington' had gathered and re-trained at Valley Forge, wondering when and where that general intended to 'collect the formidable army that is to be offensive'. Smythe was right to be concerned.

What the campaign of 1778 promised the British army was a fight against dramatically worse odds. Within months the 23rd would see action both against Washington's army and the French. Under their new commanding officer, the Royal Welch Fusiliers had at least been given someone able to lead, someone able to complete its resurrection as a fighting regiment.

British Grenadiers

Or How Corporal Roger Lamb Declined American Hospitality

Colonel Henley, the American commandant, was known to the inmates of Prospect Hill barracks as a tyrant. True, his job was not the easiest, superintending thousands of British soldiers taken at Saratoga, for they frequently gave little signs of their disdain for the American nation. But Henley returned their contempt with interest, as well as showing himself capable of brutality. One winter's morning, Henley arrived on horseback at the guardhouse.

The inmates of the makeshift brig, one dozen redcoats including two corporals, were lined up for inspection. Colonel Henley approached them while still mounted, and asked one of the guards why the first man, Corporal Reeves, had been locked up. It was for abusing a Continental officer.

'What was the reason of your abuse?' Henley asked.

Reeves replied that he had been in liquor at the time so could hardly remember, was very sorry, and anyway could not recognise the man in question as an officer. Was this a dig at the authority of the man Reeves had sworn at? What followed escalated quickly into a violent confrontation between men speaking the same language but who had grown in a couple of short years to consider themselves utterly different.

COLONEL HENLEY: 'Had it been me [you had abused] I would have run you through the body. I believe you are a rascal.'

CORPORAL REEVES: 'I am no rascal but a true Briton and by God I will stand up for my King and Country until the day I die!'

COLONEL HENLEY: 'You are a good lad for keeping up for your King and Country, I don't blame you, but hold your tongue.'

At this point, the American commandant tried to end this tense confrontation, turning his attention to the next detainee, Corporal Buchanan of the 9th.

> CORPORAL REEVES (to Buchanan): 'Why don't you stand up for your king and your country?'
> COLONEL HENLEY: 'Be still.'
> CORPORAL REEVES: 'God damn them all! I'll stand up for my King and country while I have life; if I had arms and ammunition, I would soon be with General Howe, and be revenged of them.'

At this point, Colonel Henley exploded in anger and ordered one of his guards to run through Reeves with his bayonet. Nobody obeyed this command. Seeing his men struck immobile, Henley leapt from his horse, grabbed one of their muskets and levelled it at Reeves's chest.

> COLONEL HENLEY: 'You rascal, I'll run you through or I'll blow your brains out if you don't hold your tongue!'
> CORPORAL REEVES: 'By God I'll stand up for my King and Country, and if you have a mind to kill me, you may.'

The Colonel lunged forward with the musket, stabbing the bayonet into Reeves's chest. The prisoner started back to save himself, so the blade did not go deep.

> COLONEL HENLEY: 'If you do not hold your tongue, I'll run you through!'

As Reeves repeated his defiance again, Henley tried to make good his threat with a further lunge, but Corporal Buchanan grabbed the weapon and parried it. Thwarted, Henley ordered the prisoners taken back to their cells.

Matters came to a head once more on 8 January 1778. Henley had paraded the guard at Prospect Hill fort. There were about seventy American soldiers lined up. An audience of 300 or so redcoats had watched the proceedings and began as a crowd to move closer to their custodians until they were actually pressing in on them. The incident with Corporal Reeves had evidently gone around the camp and whetted the appetite for confrontation. When the Americans tried to grab one of the Britons from the crowd, the inmates hauled him back, which produced 'a good deal of laughing and jeering'. Henley ordered the guard to load their muskets and level them at the men just a few feet in front. He called out that he would blow out the brains of anyone who attempted another rescue, commanding them to disperse.

The British soldiers began to trudge away from Henley's men but not without some jeering of 'damn Yanks' and other insults. Nettled once more, Henley rushed forward ordering them to move faster. When his command was unheeded by the truculent soldiers he attacked them with his sword, plunging it so hard into the arm of one corporal that he bent the blade. There were further volleys of derision while Henley knelt and, comically, tried to straighten his sword blade over his knee.

These incidents served to show that the Saratoga men were near mutiny by early 1778 but were also evidence of the lively hatred between peoples. Rank and file redcoats did not in these moments of danger adopt the officers' language of Whig and Tory, but instead declared themselves patriots fighting for King and Country. They considered their enemies a different nation.

Following these violent incidents, which shocked even some of the people of Boston, the Americans acceded to British demands that Henley be brought to a court martial for his brutality. However, he was acquitted by his American fellow-officers.

After the capitulation of Saratoga in October 1777, the captured men had been marched 200 miles east to Boston. The Convention under which they had 'piled their arms', not 'surrendered' – the distinction was important given what subsequently happened – stated that once they were in Massachusetts, they would be put on board British ships for home.

Corporal Roger Lamb of the 9th (the same regiment as Reeves and Buchanan) described conditions in the clapboard shacks on Prospect Hill that winter:

It was not infrequent for thirty or forty persons, men women and children, to be indiscriminately crowded together in one small, miserable, open hut; their provisions and fire wood on short allowance; and a scanty portion of straw in their bed, their own blankets their only covering.

Lamb, twenty-two years old at the time, was one of eleven children from Dublin. He left this description of himself:

I was about five feet nine inches. I had a cadaverous countenance full of cavities and projections and a body as thin, and straight as a lath, and in spite of the meekness of my name I was neither gentle by nature nor polished by education, I was rough and active with the voice of a lion, and a long black head of hair tied behind.

This Irish corporal had yearned for a life of adventure at sea, but joined the 9th in 1773. He had lost his money gambling but was too frightened of his father to tell him about it. The breach with his father became one of the defining moments of the young man's life.

As a literate, intelligent fellow, Lamb had been made a corporal by the age of nineteen but had risked his new-found status by the heavy drinking and gambling that preoccupied officers and men of the Irish garrison at that time. Broken back to the ranks once, Lamb suffered the indignity of having his shoulder knot off cut off in front of the regiment. Shamed by the experience, he resolved to reform himself.

Engaged in the game of chance that is war, fighting his way towards Saratoga, Lamb had turned his back on vice. He became instead one of those smart soldiers upon whom captains or colonels of the time relied to do the company accounts or help with other administrative duties. Ambition or yearning for self-improvement had taken hold, for Lamb began assisting the regimental surgeon, a part-time duty that could lead to promotion in the medical line or even an officer's commission.

It might be observed that the hardships Lamb and the others suffered on Prospect Hill were mild compared to those endured by American prisoners on the prison hulks in New York. However the redcoats' privations were lessened once the Americans hit upon the idea of getting the British to be responsible for the welfare of their own prisoners, providing rations for their prisoners, as well as maintaining the men's pay. This allowed the captured redcoats to buy all manner of extras, including drink of course, from the local people. This particular violation of the Saratoga Convention cannot have bothered the British, since the Americans would have experienced all manner of difficulties feeding them, but as the months went on it became clear that there was a more fundamental question playing itself out.

Major General Horatio Gates had negotiated the Convention after fighting Burgoyne's army to a standstill, and surrounding it. Gates's concern about British attempts to link up from New York made him do a deal quickly. After receiving the glorious fillip to the cause of this British capitulation, many politicians in the Continental Congress decided that Gates had been too generous by far. After all, if Burgoyne's regiments were shipped back to England or Ireland, wouldn't that simply free others to replace them in America?

So while the British government was sufficiently convinced by American good faith even to send a fleet of transports to its base at Rhode Island, in readiness to collect the so-called Convention Army, the Americans had changed their mind about letting them go. This, of course, exacerbated the widespread prejudice among British soldiers serving in America that the rebels were untrustworthy – guilty of one lie or hypocrisy after another.

For the brighter men like Lamb, this violation of principle was important. If Burgoyne's regiments had not actually surrendered, would escape constitute desertion from their own army? Initially, British officers had insisted precisely that, but as the spring of 1778 arrived in Boston, American behaviour caused minds to change. 'When I saw', wrote Lamb, 'that the American rulers had no intention of allowing British troops to return to England, I determined on attempting my escape into New York.'

Colonel Henley and men of his ilk had no desire to make such flight any easier and, early in April 1778, the Convention Army was marched more than sixty miles inland to Rutland County, New Hampshire. During the move, Lamb became involved in a confront-ation with local authorities.

Accused by a publican of breaking glasses in a tavern, Lamb denied responsibility and refused to pay. He was ordered to suffer the gauntlet, being whipped with sticks by two lines of men he had to run between. After refusing again to pay, Lamb was forced to submit to the same punishment once more.

On arriving in Rutland, the redcoats were placed in a wooden fenced enclosure, given nails and planks and told to build their own camp. Lamb began to discuss his escape plan with a couple of other soldiers.

Travelling long distances through the American countryside was bound to be difficult. Everywhere there were committees of public safety, patrols and movements of Continental regiments along the roads. A small group of British soldiers wearing their uniforms could only cross such a land with the greatest difficulty. It was, however, not impossible, indeed some men had already achieved it, getting to New York, Rhode Island or Canada with the help of loyal Americans.

Faced with a slowly increasing trickle of British escapees and a constant fear of loyalists holding secret correspondence with the British army, Congress had enacted a new law on collaboration early in 1778, and by the summer there were hangings galore of those accused of diverse offences. An extract from a letter by John Stark, whose success at Bunker Hill had gained him brigadier's rank, will suffice to illustrate. 'They do very well in the hanging way,' he wrote of the Albany courts in June 1778. 'They hanged nine on the 16th of May, and on the 5th June nine; and have 120 in jail of which, I believe, more than one half will go the same way.' Many of these condemned men were ordinary criminals, but Stark was evidently worried about those with loyalist sympathies, saying he had 'the enemy on my front and the devil in my rear'.

In dispensing summary justice, American courts martial or committees of public safety benefited from there being a poorly defined legal hierarchy and right of appeal. One English civilian who found himself accused of spying in Virginia noted that while travelling in the back-country these proceedings were conducted in absentia: 'I was arraigned, tried, condemned, and the sentence nearly put into execution before I knew anything about it.' The court in this case suggested its prisoner would remain in jail until 'convinced of [his] political errors', but he eventually was released on parole. A rapid promenade to the gallows, though, was the fate awaiting many others, and it would not be stating matters too boldly to say that much of the American countryside was in the grip of terror at this time. In planning their escape, Lamb and his friends would therefore need to pool cash for bribes and trust that providence might bring them to some civilians willing to risk all in order to help them. While they made their preparations, the British main army was re-deploying, abandoning Philadelphia.

During early June, General Sir Henry Clinton's army quickened preparations for its departure. Their stay in Philadelphia had lasted barely eight months but even in this short time men who are accustomed to perpetual motion will start to put down roots. Ten Fusiliers deserted in May and June 1778, the worst spate of absconding since the war had begun. A couple of others had gone in March and April, including Thomas Watson, the private court-martialled in New York in October 1776 for his previous desertion. This time, Watson evaded re-capture, and the general presumption was that these men left because of attachments to local women whom they did not wish to abandon when the army marched and who then aided their desertion.

The same was seen in other regiments, amounting to a loss to the army totalling hundreds of men. The tender charms of American womanhood thus cost Britain's commander-in-chief as many men in 1778 as Brandywine and Germantown combined had the previous year. Thomas Sullivan of the 49th was one such, deserting near the end of June. Sullivan wrote that he did it because of 'the ill usage I received . . . and partly on account of my being married to a young woman who was born in America, whom I knew wished me to be clear of the army'.

In other cases, those women who had become tied to the British army left with it. Many families were evacuated along with the wounded by ships that sailed down the Delaware. Most of the merchant families who had entertained young officers at assemblies in their mansions decided to stay, gambling that their status would save them from harsh retribution. Others, such as Joseph Galloway, a prominent loyalist who had become the city's chief of police under William Howe, decamped before the troops marched out.

During the final days in the city, a peace delegation arrived from Britain to see the Americans. Their meetings, like those held on Staten Island two years earlier, did not produce a successful outcome. Although it was rumoured among British officers that the King's commissioners would even offer to recognise American independence, the colonists were expecting the imminent assistance of a powerful French fleet and were inclined to press on with the war.

The failed mission of the peace commissioners and the preparations for departure underlined to the army just how dire was their national emergency. General Clinton knew that anything up to one third of the troops under his command would soon be taken away and sent south to defend British Caribbean possessions from French attack. Clinton, often a morose and lugubrious character, felt that the Ministry's will to prosecute the American war had evaporated, even if the King still wanted it. The General felt helpless at being placed in charge: 'Neither honour nor credit could be expected from it, but on the contrary a considerable portion of the blame . . . seemed to be almost inevitable.' Surveying these gloomy prospects, one grenadier officer in Philadelphia exclaimed, 'Alas Britain how art thou fallen.'

On 18 June the army marched, shedding the odd lovelorn member and pushing towards New York. This journey might be accomplished in as little as one week's march if unopposed, but Clinton had every reason to believe that General Washington would pursue him with the Continental Army, and that the Jersey militia would be alarmed everywhere to his front.

For the soldiers tramping forward with full equipment, overcast weather during the early days of the march gave way to scorching June heat, an additional and quite deadly enemy. In many places it became hard to fill up a canteen because the American militia filled in the wells. They also did their best to help Washington's pursuit. 'The enemy had all along', wrote one of Clinton's officers, 'made some . . . attempts to obstruct or at least retard our march by pulling up the bridges thrown across small creeks and causeways, and felling timber across the roads.'

Ten days after leaving Philadelphia, on Sunday the 28th, with the British troops just a couple of marches from their destination, Washington caught up with them at a place called Monmouth. The American commander-in-chief knew that he would soon lose his chance to engage the British, so, early in the morning, he ordered his advanced guard under Major General Charles Lee to attack the British rear.

It was the middle of the day before Washington, riding forward, saw streams of fleeing men coming past, informing him that the British had counter-attacked and Lee was falling back in all places. Clinton had rounded on his pursuers. Sending one division to keep going towards New York (this included the 23rd under Lieutenant Colonel Balfour), he had rounded with another, under Earl Cornwallis.

Clinton and his divisional commander were concerting a plan when they spotted a group of enemy officers watching them from a hill. This party included Colonel John Laurens, a principal aide to Washington, and Major General Baron von Steuben, a Prussian émigré who, inflating his prior military credentials and social rank, had gained a position of some influence in the American general's camp. Clinton mistook the figure of von Steuben, with his bejewelled star (denoting a European order of distinction), for the Marquis de Lafayette, Washington's young French acolyte, and sent cavalry in pursuit of the enemy staff.

British light dragoons cantered towards the knoll, dividing into two troops so as to encircle the American officers. Had they caught von Steuben it would have been an embarrassment but not a fatal blow to his cause, for in the preceding months at Valley Forge, the German had already made his contribution, imposing uniform drill and inculcating a more soldierly bearing among the ragtag regiments of the Continental Army. But the British were not in luck: Laurens, von Steuben and their comrades outran their pursuers and found their way back to Washington. They reported to their chief that Major General Lee had panicked, ordering a retreat after firing barely a shot. Washington found his advanced guard commander and dismissed him on the spot.

Clinton, seeing an opportunity to strike Washington's main column on its head as it emerged from a series of passes or defiles in the hilly country, sent his grenadiers and Guards to the attack. They went racing forward, but men were soon dropping from the heat. The temperature was such that they could feel the hot sand through their shoes; after a few miles, fainting and expiring soldiers littered the way. One grenadier wrote home of 'the sun beating on our heads with a force to be scarcely conceived in Europe, and not a drop of water to assuage our parching thirst; is it to be wondered that in these circumstances a number of soldiers were unable to support the fatigue and died on the spot.'

As the grenadiers stumbled towards a low ridge Lieutenant Colonel Monkton, the 2nd Battalion commander, squinted at a line of troops forming to the front. When it was suggested that their many different coats made them enemy Monkton insisted they were loyalists but soon paid for his mistake. The Americans gave a first discharge of musketry that felled several men, including Monkton, killed by a bullet through the heart. The grenadiers charged on and drove back the first American line.

It seemed at first like Brandywine all over again, that the grenadiers would chase the enemy from one fence to another, allowing them no time to re-form. But this time it was different. The heat had already accounted for dozens of them during a five-mile race to action. As the younger officers and men rushed forward, 'it was no longer a contest for bringing up our respective companies in the best order, but all officers as well as soldiers strove who could be foremost'. Finding the grenadiers pushing on in ragged formation, Clinton appeared. Far from getting them into some kind of order before the next assault, their general egged them on, shouting, 'Charge Grenadiers, never heed forming!'

They were about to discover another difference from Brandywine. The men facing them, picked Continentals from New Hampshire and New York regiments, were spoiling for action. They had also wheeled several guns into position to support them at the next obstacle they could find to form behind, a hedge separating two farms.

As the British grenadiers rushed up, 1st Battalion (including the 23rd's grenadier company) on the right and 2nd on the left, the Americans let rip a withering volley. Cannon joined in, spewing out grapeshot and case (also called canister, being a tin full of dozens of musket balls). Captain Wills, commanding the grenadiers of the Welch Fusiliers, had a great lump of his thigh ripped off by grapeshot, and went down, blood pouring from the wound. Several Fusiliers carried him off, but he had received his death wound.

British soldiers returned fire, knocking down the men to their front. Going closer to see what was happening through the great clouds of smoke produced by the guns, Colonel Laurens' horse was hit, the animal crumpling to the ground underneath him.

The scene of slaughter then intensified. A further American battery, sited on a hill to the left of the 2nd Grenadiers, opened a withering enfilading fire. Captain Hale of that battalion recorded 'the rebels' cannon playing grape and case upon us at the distance of 40 yards and the small arms within little more than half that space'. In this killing field, with severed limbs yawing through the air and the squelch of blood underfoot, the Continentals halted the grenadiers and resisted their charge. Groups of redcoats hugged the ground, or doubled back to a fold in the land that might offer some cover.

General Clinton brought up some British artillery, producing a roaring exchange of cannon, as both sides extricated their bloodied forward units. All the time, though, the odds were changing for the British as Washington's men debouched into the fields. Under darkness, the British general broke contact with his enemy and turned back towards his destination, New York.

The cost to each side of the battle of Monmouth was similar; around 350 killed, wounded, or missing. Those who died of heat-stroke, contained within those totals, amounted to around sixty to seventy men on each side. Among the British, the loss fell dispro-portionately on the grenadier battalions.

Writing to his father, president of Congress no less, Colonel Laurens was exultant after the battle: 'Our officers and men behaved with that bravery which becomes free men, and have convinced the world that they can beat British grenadiers.'

When the British army resumed its onward march, there was a

problem of what to do with about forty casualties who were too sick to be moved. 'The most mortifying circumstances attending the action', wrote one senior British officer, '. . . we were under the necessity of leaving a great part of our wounded officers and men behind for want of a sufficiency of wagons to bring them off.'

The British army arrived in New York a few days later with a sober appreciation of their enemy. American troops had displayed high qualities in the late battle, and reports were reaching New York of a French squadron appearing any day off the coast.

General Clinton ordered the light and grenadier companies to be returned to their respective regiments. It appeared the elitist system of General Howe was being disbanded, causing alarm among many of those who had spent the previous two years fighting in the flank battalions with their high *esprit de corps*. 'I fear I must descend, painful thought, from the awful sublimity of a Grenadier to the plebeian state of a common battalion officer,' wrote Captain Hale of the 45th Grenadier Company. There were recriminations about why Clinton was doing this. Was it a deliberate attempt to dissolve Howe's picked army within an army?

Officers in these corps had certainly formed a negative view about the new commander-in-chief at Monmouth. An angry Captain Hale wrote,

The general by his rashness in the last action has totally lost the confidence of both officers and soldiers, who were astonished at seeing the commander of an army galloping like a Newmarket jockey at the head of a wing of grenadiers and expressly forbidding all form and order.

The order sending flank-company men back to their regiments was quickly rescinded, the staff insisting that their general had been misunderstood and only envisaged a temporary state of affairs, in which the light infantry and grenadiers would have a short respite before being re-formed. The position of those 'chosen' soldiers had, though, been unmistakably diminished since the departure of William Howe, and the grenadiers knew their reputation had been damaged by impetuosity at Monmouth.

These uncomfortable ruminations were not allowed to go on for long, because on 11 July a French warship was sighted off New York. A powerful squadron under Admiral Count Charles Henri d'Estaing had appeared in American waters and would cause every strategic calculation to be revised.

While British commanders usually assumed naval dominance, it was lost that summer off America. D'Estaing had brought with him twelve line-of-battle ships, whereas the British admiral had only nine with him at New York, and they were mainly old 64s, outgunned by six new 74s and two 80-gun three-deckers of the French squadron.

The set-piece amphibious operations of 1776–77 in which the fraternal collaboration of the Howes had brought hundreds of ships to land thousands of men had disappeared. General William had gone home and would soon be followed by Admiral Lord Richard Howe. Faced with the pressure of potential naval as well as military disaster, deprived too of the Howe double-act, relations between sea and land services became far more difficult.

Whoever cruised on the American station would now have to calculate the effect that a French fleet could have, making it unsafe for any small forces to be sent by sea, and allowing Britain's enemies to land troops of the best quality at times and places of *their* own choosing. This reversal of fortunes may have hung like a black storm-cloud over New York, but it undoubtedly presented a silver lining of sorts, for it pricked the national pride of fleet and army alike.

'A British admiral pent up in harbour,' Captain Dansey of the 1st Light Battalion fumed, as Royal Navy ships came in to shelter from the French squadron beyond Sandy Hook. 'History never furnishes such an instance. How every Englishman's heart felt the indignity of the event.' Matters assumed an even more serious complexion when, after loitering off New York for ten days, the French set sail for a rendez-vous with their American allies further north, with the British base at Rhode Island as their objective.

A relief expedition became imperative, but Lord Howe knew that many of his ships were woefully under-manned. Hundreds of sailors from the transport vessels volunteered, as did redcoats. 'Everybody turned out that were near the fleet, and we were obliged to draw for the honour.'

Lieutenant Colonel Balfour, whose warm partisanship for the late commander-in-chief was well known to General Clinton, could expect little but suspicion from the new man. Clinton was putting his own people in, just as Howe had done when succeeding Gage. The atmosphere was acrimonious. Balfour therefore hit upon a stroke: he volunteered the Royal Welch Fusiliers for service at sea as marines, an offer Admiral Howe was happy to accept. The 23rd were going to fight the French.

With late summer, Britain's Convention prisoners learnt that the Americans intended to march them hundreds of miles southwards to Virginia. This would present Corporal Lamb and his mates with an opportunity to abscond from the march at some point far closer to New York. They formed a plan to escape close to the North or Hudson River, an unmistakable landmark and feature that they could follow south to their destination.

Several days into their march, Lamb conferred with his two comrades about the best time to make a break. The idea of escaping the American regime and finding the British army had possessed him:

I weighed in my mind all the consequences that would probably result, should I be taken by the natives; and the more I thought of the attempt, the more I began to feel a degree of enthusiasm, to which I was before a stranger. I looked forward, not without hope, to the prospects before me and I began already to indulge the exultation of effecting my escape.

One evening when their march had halted for the day, one of Lamb's fellow escapers, a German speaker, got chatting to the guards, who were Americans of that nation. He persuaded the guards to let them go several hundred yards beyond their sentries to a nearby house in search of food. The prisoners 'moved further from the guards, by degrees; until we entirely lost sight of them'. Finding an old woman living in a small farmstead nearby they paid her to hide them, which she did until later that night, when she came to tell them that the column had crossed the Hudson and was on the other side.

It took Lamb and the others six days to work their way down close to Kingsbridge, a town where the British lines extended on the mainland just north of Manhattan. There had been many close shaves and moments of despair on the way. One guide agreed to take them for ten dollars and two new blankets. When they could see American soldiers through the undergrowth, this 'pilot' despaired, saying, 'This is a dangerous troublesome piece of work . . . here is an American encampment within a mile of us; if I should be taken, I shall lose my life.' Another twelve dollars secured his services to their next shelter.

These three escapers were sent along an underground of mercenary Americans or Tory sympathisers that had helped quite a few redcoats before them and would assist scores more afterwards. They risked their lives in this work, and at length got many of their charges to the gates of New York.

When Lamb's moment came to cross no-man's-land and walk towards sentries with their primed muskets, the escaped corporal cried out, 'We are British soldiers who have made good our escape!' With the tension and danger of crossing lines behind them, the three escapees were swiftly conducted through the works to a redoubt. 'We were conducted with joy and wonder to the fort, and received with great kindness by the officers and men,' wrote Lamb.

Once at headquarters, Lamb, as ringleader of the escape, underwent a lengthy interview with Major Andre, a staff officer much involved with intelligence matters who was anxious for every detail that could be remembered. 'The major then, with much feeling and politeness', wrote Lamb, 'informed me that he was authorized by Sir Henry Clinton, to offer me my choice of entering in any regiment, then serving in America. I came to the resolution of serving in the 23rd, or Royal Welch Fuzileers.'

General Clinton received through hundreds of escapers an unexpected reinforcement of high quality for his depleted regiments. In the case of the 23rd, Lamb was one of forty-two men of the Convention Army who became Fusiliers, a significant number for a regiment that rarely put more than 400 men in the field during these campaigns.

The challenge of escape ensured that those who reached General Clinton's regiments were the most resourceful and highly motivated men. Captain Frederick Mackenzie confirmed, 'Many of them are the best soldiers.' The escapers were the very opposite of the boozers and Lotharios responsible for most of the desertion from the Fusiliers in 1775 as the war was about to start. Lamb and men of his type were not only battle-hardened but they had seen how America kept its bargains, observed Colonel Henley's brutality and tasted the 'Liberty and Justice' extolled by the revolution's ideologues.

As the war became strategically far more complicated and dangerous for Britain, the army had been infused with the fighting spirit needed to carry on. The talk of 'civil war' and 'kindred people' that had been common in Boston in 1775 disappeared from officers' letters and journals. As for the rank and file, Corporal Reeves represented many when he spoke of fighting for 'King and Country' and regarded the Americans as an enemy people. Had they not allied themselves with Britain's oldest and most implacable foe, France? In August 1778, it was against this unholy alliance that the Fusiliers were about to enter battle.

The World at War

Or How the Fusiliers Became Sea Dogs

The appearance of two French frigates a little after 5 a.m. on 5 August 1778 was enough to trigger an orgy of self-destruction. The ships stood round the northern tip of Conanicut Island, which lay like a barrier across the water from the British base at Newport on Rhode Island. For several days the defenders had awaited the battle with Admiral d'Estaing's squadron, knowing that the motley collection of little vessels under their own ensign would soon be pounded to matchwood by the enemy's two- and three-deckers.

As the French ships turned south, a British frigate, the *Cerberus*, slipped its cables, made sail and tried to run about four miles down to the safety of Newport harbour. It was a futile attempt. Seeing that the French were gaining on her, and fearing his vessel could soon become their prize, the *Cerberus*'s captain ordered her steered to port and deliberately run aground. Torches were kindled and the frigate fired. At about 8 a.m. it blew up. The masters of some smaller vessels took similar action and one by one the columns of smoke winding up into the Atlantic sky multiplied as the *Juno, Orpheus, Lark* and *Pigot* were all deliberately destroyed.

When the *Lark* went up, with seventy-six barrels of gunpowder on board, the explosion was calamitous. Tons of wood, stores and cordage went up into the air, showering glowing fragments across the western side of Rhode Island. Gunners in the Windmill Hill redoubt quickly smothered the sizzling embers that fell about them, lest they touch off their own powder.

Captain Frederick Mackenzie watched it all, 'a most mortifying sight . . . to see so many fine frigates destroyed in so short a time, without any loss to the enemy'. The morning's events rattled nerves as well as windows, since the inhabitants of Newport had for weeks been dreading the prospect of a siege.

The Island, occupied by the British, was a little under fourteen miles long. Its northern end was separated by narrow channels (plied by ferries in happier times) from Providence, the nearest enemy town, and the backcountry of the province. Conanicut Island, lying parallel with it, sheltered Newport from the full force of ocean storms, but offered a convenient jumping off point to the French, who had brought regiments of troops and siege guns with them too.

Mackenzie, as one of the small staff at headquarters, had an important role concerting the defensive plan for the British garrison, a force of 5,000 troops under Major General Robert Pigot, veteran of Bunker Hill. Since they could not defend the Island in its entirety, they planned to abandon their positions at the northern end, and fall back to defensive fieldworks around Newport itself. Above all, they were anxious that the four British and one Hessian regiment defending against American landings in the north should not be cut off. Mackenzie wrote witheringly of the foreign troops that 'they are not inspired by the high sense of national and personal honour which is characteristic of British troops'.

While preparing for the last stand, Mackenzie and his superiors were sanguine about the possibilities of resistance. Most of the British cannon were field guns, 6- and 12-pounders, unable to dent warships or smash down besieging batteries. The works and redoubts positioned around the town were made of packed earth with a ditch and abatises – tree trunks with sharpened branches – scattered in front. If the French, whose engineers were the masters of siegecraft, brought 24-pounders to bear on such walls they would soon be blown away. Mackenzie reckoned that once such a bombardment started they could not count on holding out for more than twelve days. 'We are all extremely anxious', he wrote, 'for some account from Lord Howe or a sight of his fleet.'

With the prospect of impending disaster, many civilians left Newport. Mrs Mac and George, Mackenzie's three-year-old boy who had been born in Boston, joined this exodus, adopting a life under canvas on a hillside considered safe from bombardment somewhat to the south of town. Some of the married 23rd Fusiliers officers had shipped their wives and children home during the siege of Boston or while the army was at Halifax. Not so Fred Mackenzie, whose desire to keep the family together now produced an anxious reckoning.

The predicament that these people found themselves in arose entirely from France's entry into the war. From the Caribbean to the Channel Islands or Coromandel Coast, French fleets had begun a worldwide onslaught against British interests. The Spanish and Dutch were set to join in too, producing a combination that was simply too much for the Lords of the Admiralty to defend against.

British troops had been at Rhode Island since late 1776. They were sent there by General Howe both because the Navy preferred the look of it, as a base, to New York, and because the commander-in-chief harboured ideas of how troops advancing from such a base might thrust into New England, alarming the enemy or pushing towards Burgoyne's expedition.

At the start of 1777 Lieutenant General Earl Percy found himself in command. It was his sense of the impossibility of plunging into the New England hornet's nest with just a few thousand redcoats that brought a simmering conflict between himself and Howe to the boil. Percy effectively resigned and went back to England, but incurred the King's displeasure for giving up his mission. It blighted Percy's career.

Without a commander willing or able to use Rhode Island as a raiding base, from which to pin down American troops all around, its only purpose was as a naval anchorage and supply centre. Using 5,000 troops to secure such a depot was profligate to say the least. With France's entry into the war, the ease of access from the high seas, the very thing that had appealed to Admiral Howe, turned Rhode Island from an asset into a distinct liability.

This reversal in strategic fortunes was signalled with terrible clarity by Admiral d'Estaing on 8 August. At 3 p.m. the Count ordered eight ships of the line, headed by his flagship *Languedoc*, to head north between Conanicut Island and the mouth of Newport harbour. The *Languedoc* was a monster, bristling with eighty heavy cannon. As these ships ran up the strait between the two islands, all manner of British batteries opened up.

Watchers on shore every now and then saw a great ripple of fire along the *Languedoc*'s two decks, followed moments later by the thundering peal of a broadside. But d'Estaing was less concerned at that moment with doing damage than engaging in reconnaissance, taking a look at his objective, keeping his line close to the Conanicut shore so an hour and a half's burning of gunpowder by the two sides produced little damage. The French admiral had, however, demonstrated the power at his disposal, deepening the despondency among those who remained in town.

D'Estaing's little cruise had another effect: it triggered the pull-back of British troops from the north of the Island into their defensive works and announced the siege was under way in earnest. As soon as the British had gone from their outlying positions, American regiments began to cross.

A joint plan was moving to its decisive phase. There were about 10,000 American troops moving down the island. A further 4,000 French would be employed on land, giving the attackers a near threefold superiority.

Down in Newport, Mackenzie supervised the burning of some houses outside the British works. General Pigot did not want his artillery's fields of fire obstructed. The lone member of the 23rd Fusiliers prepared for a fight at close quarters, little suspecting that the rest of his regiment was on its way to help.

Having awaited the arrival of a reinforcement of several ships under his successor, Lord Howe had sailed from New York on 1 August. His vessels were older and less heavily armed than d'Estaing's, but he felt it vital to draw the French away from Rhode Island and was ready to give battle if he had to.

Howe's flagship, the *Eagle*, was a 64, and among the diverse officers who crowded the admiral's stateroom for dinner each evening was Lieutenant Colonel Nisbet Balfour of the 23rd. The regiment itself had been split into parcels of men aboard each of Howe's larger ships. The largest were aboard the *Cornwall* (under the direction of Thomas Mecan, once more fighting fit), the *Saint Albans* and the *Nonsuch*. They were all two-deckers, but only the *Cornwall* mounted 74 guns in the modern style, the remainder being older vessels like the *Eagle*.

Among the other ships making up Howe's force was the *Isis*, a large frigate or small battleship, according to one's prejudice, of 50 guns under the command of Captain Raynor. Lionel Smythe's light company had piled on board at New York on 29 July and pitched into the cramped quarters below decks.

Isis displaced about 1,000 tons and its hull was 150 feet long. It had sailed with a full complement of 350 men, who squeezed themselves into two gun decks and the orlop. The heady air of patriotic outrage triggered by the appearance of d'Estaing's fleet had brought sailors volunteering from the merchantmen or transports, so the *matelots* who sailed under Captain Raynor included a sizeable reinforcement from the *Philippa, Betsy, Bowman, Thames* and *Echo*. These men had to be melded quickly by the gun captains or bosuns into an effective crew.

Smythe had thirty-five Fusiliers with him, comprising a lieutenant, serjeant, two corporals and thirty-one rank and file. Among the latter was Robert Mason, the company drummer (or bugler). The throwing together of disparate men on Howe's fleet hardly seemed to matter, one Fusilier noting that they were 'in the highest spirits, anxiously wishing for an opportunity to signalise themselves in the service of their country against its ancient and perfidious enemy'.

Sailing towards their rendezvous with the French, the Light Bobs had to practise climbing the shrouds with weapons and ammunition. It was in the tops, the platforms on the frigate's masts, that many of these lubbers would be expected to take their place in battle, ready to act as snipers. Whatever the terrors of racing up, clinging on for grim life as the ship pitched and rolled with the sea, escaping New York had at least removed the soldiers from a stultifying heat.

Even once they were under way, the decks were roasting hot. There was a general expectation that such crazy weather would have to be broken by storms and lightning. Howe's squadron had arrived off Newport on 9 August, forcing d'Estaing to put to sea and prepare for action. It took days of manoeuvre for the fleets to form their battle lines but on 12 August barometers plunged and trouble arrived.

At 4 a.m. the *Isis* was rocked by 'heavy gales and a heavy sea'. Dawn appeared little more than a glimmer of light, since driving rain and driving winds continued unabated for hours. The ships had closed up on the Admiral's orders just before the storm hit, trying to keep their stations in the line of battle. Captain Raynor trimmed his sails to give him control over *Isis* without keeping so much out that the canvas would get ripped to shreds or the masts brought down. Through the driving squall they could see *Raisonnable* about one mile to windward, signalling distress with its flags. It was a matter of clinging on for several hours until the storm abated.

When the gale finally blew itself out, the two sides took stock of the damage. Howe's squadron had escaped in a more or less seaworthy state. But d'Estaing had suffered disaster. Just a few days after weathering the pinpricks of British artillery at Newport, the *Languedoc* had been completely dismasted by the storm. 'It appears', wrote a German private within the British lines at Newport, 'as if the powers of heaven watched over the English.'

The storm damage made it essential for the French to avoid a fleet action. Instead, the British attempted to cut out some of the enemy's choice ships, making prizes of them. The *Renown* attacked the crippled *Languedoc*, tacking back and forth across the enemy's stern, bringing a full broadside to bear, raking the length of the Frenchman's decks. *Languedoc*'s captain had cut clear the fallen rigging, leaving three stumps of masts, and used a yard to jury-rig two small sail so that he might have some sort of control over his wallowing ship. The punishment went on for a couple of hours, with cannon balls smashing through the gilded woodwork of *Languedoc*'s stern. D'Estaing was sufficiently worried at the prospect of being boarded that he started dumping his confidential papers into the sea. Timidity on the part of *Renown*'s captain, and the arrival of French reinforcements, saved the French flagship from capture.

Captain Raynor of the *Isis*, on the other hand, could certainly not be accused of lacking aggression. When one of the enemy's 74s appeared three miles behind him, he declined to take flight, despite the obvious inferiority of his own armament. Allowing the enemy, coming up from astern, to get nearer and nearer, Raynor ordered 'clear for action'. The Fusiliers scampered up to their tops or lined points on the deck where they might pot their Frenchman. If the 74 could be overpowered and taken there would be a vast sum of prize money and the captain's name would be made for life.

By 3 p.m., the Frenchman, César, was one mile to leeward of *Isis*, the French colours were broken out and a gun fired to signal the start of the fight. The two ships manoeuvred an hour longer, before César ran fast towards its enemy. As the French vessel caught up, its crew gave three cheers. The *Isis* turned slightly to face the César's bow and gave its first broadside.

When the French responded, they fired into Isis's rigging. Their captain wanted to cripple his prey before moving in to smash her up with close-range broadsides and take her. Usually the rigging was attacked with chain or bar shot, which used a pair of balls connected together to yaw madly through the air, taking down lines or ripping sails. The masts themselves, though, had to be cut down with round shot.

Many of the Fusiliers therefore soon found themselves in a hell of screaming and whizzing metal as they clung to their posts in the tops. Corporal John Fowler was killed and three light company men wounded.

Isis responded in kind, attacking César's rigging, but increasingly, as the ships drew together, directing fire on to her decks. 'Their musketry', wrote one officer, 'was silenced by that of our marines and a detachment of the Light Company of the 23rd.' Those trying to manage the French warship found themselves under a hail of small arms fire from *Isis*.

Captain Raynor added to the pressure, managing to get his ship around to César's stern and give three broadsides that amounted nearly to rakes along the length of the 74, cutting down many men as they went. This was a very dangerous moment for the Frenchman, for such salvoes could be devastating. One French officer was seen to emerge from below decks to dump papers into the sea, an act that marked him for death at the hands of one of the Fusiliers sniping from the tops.

The slugging match went on for one hour and thirty-five minutes before 'the enemy sheered off and bore away to the south west'. When the Fusiliers realised what was happening they sent up a loud Indian war whoop, that exultant cry that they had heard in the forests of Pennsylvania and Jersey. In addition to the casualties among the Fusiliers, thirteen seamen had been wounded on board the *Isis*. Neither captain had been gratified with a prize, but there was general satisfaction in Howe's fleet with the pluck with which the smaller ship repulsed her assailant.

A triumphant Lionel Smythe wrote to England, estimating the damage done to the French 74:

He has lost his right [yard]arm and his first lieutenant a def[inite] with about 20 killed and 50 wounded. He does Captain Raynor the justice of saying that our ship was so well worked as to prevent his getting any guns to bear whilst he suffered from the quick well directed fire of the *Isis*.

Even that violent Whig, Captain Fitzpatrick of the Guards, got caught up in the anti-French ebullience of the moment, writing enthusiastically about the *Isis*'s action. Unfortunately for the remainder of the 23rd, none of their detachments aboard other vessels experienced a similar fight, so the Light Bobs were lucky enough to hog the action once more.

One week after the storm, d'Estaing returned to Narragansett Bay off Newport with his crippled ships. The Americans were all for pressing on with the attack on Newport immediately, but the French admiral had other ideas. The fleet entrusted to the admiral by his king was a prized asset, the result of a vast investment in the navy in order to try and catch up with the English. D'Estaing did not want to risk the chance of Howe sailing into the bay on some raid to beat up his damaged ships at anchor. Furthermore, he was uncertain how the balance of naval forces might tip against the French. The admiral therefore informed his allies that he would soon sail for Boston where he intended to repair his squadron.

The Americans were furious but could do nothing. In the days that followed, thousands of New England militia decided to go home. There were accusations of French betrayal and a hopelessness about conquering General Pigot's defences. As the Franco-American siege plan disintegrated, the British commander decided to send the Americans at the gates of Newport packing.

On 29 August, the British, seeing the Americans had struck their tents at the siege lines, came out to pursue them off the island. The redcoats raced five miles quickly up to Quaker Hill on the north of the Island, where the enemy had posted troops to cover a withdrawal over the ferries. Here the two armies fought a sharp little battle, as the American rearguard protected their evacuation.

After the events of the 13th, Admiral Howe too had seen to the repair of his ships, taking them to New York, before sailing back to Rhode Island escorting dozens of transports carrying an army under General Clinton. These seventy sail arrived at Rhode Island on 1 September. The relief force, unneeded, returned to New York two days later.

Frederick Mackenzie knew that Clinton had reacted with petulance upon his arrival at Rhode Island, being annoyed that Pigot had driven the Americans back on his own. 'As they did not come in for any share of the credit,' wrote Mackenzie, 'they thought proper to find fault with every thing, and went off in a very ill humour.' The Fusilier captain remembered that he had played a prominent role in convincing Pigot of the value of racing up to Quaker Hill and harassing the Americans and was therefore particularly irked by Clinton's bad grace. While Mackenzie was himself an officer demanding high standards, he could at least grasp the wider picture and see beyond the petty jealousy of his commander-in-chief: the British had beaten off a concerted attack by their allied enemies and thus averted a disaster that might have eclipsed even Saratoga.

Several weeks after their action at sea, the Fusiliers were back in New York. Officers and men got reacquainted with their favourite houses of the coffee, drinking and whoring varieties. There was a general uncertainty about what lay ahead. The government in London had still not recovered from the double shocks of Saratoga and France's entry into the war. Recriminations had to be played out for Burgoyne's disaster and a discussion had about how Britain could possibly prosecute a global war on so many fronts. All of this would take many months, being slowed by the pace of transatlantic letter-writing and the King's need to rally political support at home for the war.

It had been understood for months that Clinton would have to send a large force to the Caribbean – a place regarded by many officers as a disease-ridden hell. Ten British regiments were packed off under James Grant, who, being part of William Howe's inner circle, had nothing to expect but disappointment if he remained close to Clinton. With this detachment, late in 1778, the commander-in-chief had lost a sizeable proportion of his battle-hardened redcoats. These included Earl Percy's pride and joy, the 5th, and other regiments, like the 4th, who had shared the experience of the Fusiliers' campaigning around Boston. There were many farewells to old friends, including Jo Ferguson, the Scottish officer formerly of the 23rd, who went to the Caribbean on Grant's staff.

As to the consequences of losing such a proportion of the army, consideration had already been given to abandoning Rhode Island, bringing as many troops back into play (albeit many of them from the German states) as had just been sent off with Grant. But the weeks following a heroic defence were not the best time to do this, and anyway, there were other options including withdrawing the army from New York. The Ministry would have to make its mind up, and they would have to reconcile the very different demands of King and Parliament, which was anxious to debate these issues.

'The meeting of Parliament will determine the fate of this country and settle the wavering opinion of many here,' wrote Captain Smythe in November. Discussions around the 23rd's mess table or in New

York's better society had convinced the young Irishman that 'the majority think a total evacuation of the frontier colonies (Rhode Island and Halifax excepted) will take place in Spring, while the main army take post in Canada and joining the irregulars and Indians proceed to the destruction of the country'. Such a strategy, exploiting both Danbury-style naval raids and expeditions from Canada into the northern states of a kind that had been started that year by parties of Tories and Iroquois, would aim to force Congress or the states to the expense of garrisoning scores of possible targets while torching many valuable commodities – in sum to destroy the new republic economically.

As he sat reading the *New York Gazette* after his return from sea, Lieutenant Colonel Balfour found his anger getting the better of him. In the extracts of dispatches printed in that paper, he could detect unmistakable signs of the Ministry, in the form of its American Secretary, Lord Germain, seeking to put the blame for Saratoga on his former chief. General Howe's intimates were also angry that Clinton had abandoned Philadelphia, ashamed that the previous year's sacrifice had been thrown away so peremptorily.

Balfour was an astute enough political operator to suspect the *Gazette*'s publisher, James Rivington, of selecting stories and quotations from public dispatches to support Clinton and Germain while blackening Howe's name. In a former time Balfour might have gone to curse such a scoundrel at James Grant's table or jab at the offending newspaper paragraphs in front of Admiral Howe. But Grant was bound for the Caribbean and Lord Howe had turned over his command and set sail for England, penning Balfour a warm letter of thanks for the 23rd's service at sea before he went. In this season of departures, the colonel himself had obtained leave to travel home as well, having urgent public and private business there. He decided to deal in person with Rivington before he left.

Rivington was something of an institution in the city. English born, he had emigrated to America eighteen years before, setting himself up as a printer and bookseller. In the troubled days of 1775 Rivington had endured all manner of insults and threats from the Patriot party for trying to publish both points of view in his paper. Fearing for his life, Rivington fled after the war started, but returned following the capture of New York in 1776 and resumed publication. Late one November's evening in 1778 though, he found Colonel Balfour on his doorstep.

Balfour pointed to some offending paragraphs in the paper and asked Rivington what his motive was for publishing them. Rivington stood his ground, and argued the rights of a free press. Balfour's big physical presence and forceful manner meant he usually got his way, but not this time. Realising that the printer would not budge, the colonel became equally intransigent, and rather more indignant. Rivington wrote, 'This gentleman (disappointed in his expectations of an answer to his requisition) left me suddenly with the following menace: "I am Sir W. H.'s friend and I shall allow it to go no further."'

Rivington realised that Balfour was going back to England and wrote to a confidant in Lord Germain's office telling him to be on the lookout for the lieutenant colonel in order to deny him any favours: 'You are to be apprized how far [Balfour] should be thought deserving of the countenance of the most elegant nobleman in the British realm.' The publisher asked his correspondent to reply swiftly, 'which shall immediately be answered in case Colonel Balfour's bludgeon may not put an end to the existence, dear sir, of your ever faithful and obedient servant'. While delivered in a knowingly melodramatic way, Rivington's final words left little doubt either about the temperature of his conversation or of Balfour's desire to intimidate.

Just a few days later, Balfour too boarded a ship bound for England. He disliked Atlantic crossings but found no reason to stay in America, 'this hated country', while there was no prospect of further campaigning. He had in any case been induced to go by his great patron. General Howe. Nettled by government whispering, Balfour's master was demanding an open examination, in front of Parliament, of his conduct of the war and would need some of his former staff to assist him.

Faced with the King's refusal to accept defeat, the issues of what had gone wrong in America had combined with those about how Britain could carry on fighting, to produce a monumental political crisis. The Lieutenant Colonel of the Royal Welch Fusiliers packed his trunk and endured his crossing, as he prepared to second his regimental master (Howe), in battle at Westminster.

The Divided Nation

Or How Lieutenant Colonel Balfour Fought at Home

By the last day of 1778, Nisbet Balfour was in London; having enjoyed a speedy Atlantic crossing, he came by coach from Portsmouth to the metropolis. He had been invited to spend the following day, the first of 1779, with Admiral Lord Howe.

Balfour, however, was in no mood to celebrate. He was ill: dyspeptic and listless, suffering 'a very violent scorbutic disorder'. There would be no Hogmanay boozing, nor would he partake of the fine feasts on offer at his Lordship's, for a physician had prescribed a strict vegetarian diet and Balfour was a man who knew how to execute orders. The colonel's corporeal concerns gave him, in any case, less anguish than those of his family.

His homecoming brought dread intelligence that the ship on which his brother Walter was travelling back from India was believed lost at sea. This was shocking news indeed, coming after the deaths of two other brothers and his father. The colonel's mother was stricken with grief, and he reflected, 'No family ever experienced so many tragical accidents as ours. Indeed we are well-nigh totally extinct.'

The Balfours of Dunbog were also well-nigh totally broke. Some of their property had been sequestrated after the 1715 Jacobite rising, because of the suspicion of disloyalty. They had been trying to disprove this charge ever since, pawning their few lands buying advancement in the King's service. When that money had gone, Nisbet had run up thousands of pounds of debt buying his majority and lieutenant colonelcy. His early days back in England were therefore punctuated by letter-writing to friends and patrons seeking some sort of pension for his mother. Always a volatile woman, she had been prostrated with sorrow for Walter. Balfour postponed the emotional turmoil of his reunion with her while he attended to military business in London.

In addition to the loss of his last brother, poor health, and even poorer finances, Balfour was required to second the efforts of 'my good and friendly General', his great patron, Sir William Howe, to clear his name. While the colonel was at sea, an acrimonious exchange in Parliament had produced the inquiry that Howe had long believed necessary to defend his reputation.

Sir William had complained that his plans for prosecuting the war 'were frequently thrown by unnoticed, and he was left to proceed at his own risk'. The general said he had no criticism of Lord North, the Prime Minister, but attacked the American Secretary, Lord Germain, arguing that 'the peace of that country will never be restored, while its affairs are suffered to pass through that noble Lord's hands'. Germain was stunned by the attack, but readily agreed to Howe's request for the whole matter of why the British army had failed to defeat the rebellion during 1776 and 1777 to be placed before Parliament.

While the legislative machinery began turning in its intricate way to assemble documents and witnesses, Balfour and his master were due to appear before the King. The colonel had never been to a levee before, and it was at these morning audiences that royal favour was shown. In the very week of hearing further misfortune, Balfour therefore went to reap the reward of his family's sacrifice, presenting himself at the centre of power, in front of the monarch's person.

On 4 January, Balfour and Howe travelled to St James's Palace to receive this mark of favour and condescension on the part of their sovereign King George III of Great Britain and Ireland. The normal form was for the guests to form a circle or arc in the drawing room, bowing or curtseying as the King entered, and affecting polite chatter among themselves as he moved along the line, granting each of them a little conversation.

The man that Balfour clapped eyes on that morning was in his forty-third year of life and nineteenth as king. His usual court dress was a coat of royal blue, waistcoat, breeches, stockings and shoes. These clothes had been let out inch by inch as his bulk expanded, despite his best efforts to defy the family tendency to corpulence with a monastic lifestyle.

George usually rose at around 5 a.m. In town he would ride the short distance from Buckingham House, where he lived, to St James's, where official business was done. He went to chapel every day, usually after a couple of hours with state papers, and often continued working until 6 p.m. The King's personality was marked by emotional and financial parsimony. His intellectual horizons were as narrow as his geographical ones.

Throughout his long reign, George III never travelled to Wales, Scotland or Ireland. He only twice got as far as Portsmouth, his main naval base on the south coast. George confined himself instead to private residences in London and Kew, with corresponding official palaces at St James's and Windsor. He shared almost nothing of official business with his queen, Charlotte, and no courtier was allowed to attain any kind of personal intimacy.

The King kept himself *au fait* with his generals or the commanding officers of his regiments, and insisted on personally approving promotions, transfers or executions. Taking such a keen interest in the administration of his forces, there would have been much to chat about with Howe and Balfour that January morning, without trespassing on the sensitive territory of what could be done to win the war in America.

George III was quite adamant that the American war should go on, and had barely paused to question this assumption after the defeat of Saratoga. He did not attempt to direct military operations, a matter that was left to his Prime Minister, American Secretary and a handful of other senior figures including General Lord Amherst, commander-in-chief of the Army. The conflict between Howe and Lord Germain was not a matter which the King could settle, for he thought both of them broadly on the right side of the argument compared to many politicians and officers whom he despised. General Howe's demand for an inquiry coincided with the acquittal of one of the king's admirals (Augustus Keppel) by court martial. Ministers worried that Howe's desire to clear his name would produce a second pitched battle between those who supported the king's policies, notably in America, and those who sought any chance to discredit them. This opposition ranged from many of the great Whig landed families to the London mob.

During the early spring of 1779 the Ministry stalled for time, trying to slow any public examination of the Howe brothers' war and hoping that everything could be held up until the Parliamentary session ended, when the matter might go away. Balfour, therefore, was kept hanging around in London for weeks while he, and other intimates such as the general's secretary, waited to scrutinise on Howe's behalf the official correspondence produced by ministers.

While Balfour idled, the hurly-burly of life in Georgian England went on about him: Parliament moved a bill to allow Earl Percy to divorce his wife; the mob burnt down a Catholic chapel in Blackfriars, going on to sack the houses of several well-known local Papists; David Garrick, the great Shakespearean actor, died and was buried, his hearse being 'followed by more than 50 coaches of the principal nobility and gentry in and about the metropolies [sic]'; the 'Young Prince of Annamaboe', a 'free black', successfully won £500 damages from a ship's captain who had employed him as a navigator but then, upon their arrival in Jamaica, double-crossed him and sold him as a slave; and the Secretary at War introduced into Parliament a new bill for recruiting soldiers and sailors. It is this last item, gleaned from the newspapers of that spring, apparently the driest and least interesting, that would be of the greatest importance to the Fusiliers, as they fought on at war.

Towards the end of March, Balfour left the febrile political battle-ground of the capital and headed east to Chatham. The army had turned this naval base into its main port of embarkation for recruits heading to America. The lieutenant colonel went to meet the 23rd's latest batch of men, that included thirty-six rank and file, and thirteen pressed men. The latter were being sent under the new legislation that allowed magistrates to send those convicted of minor crimes into the army or navy.

There were three pipsqueak second lieutenants, the senior of whom was sixteen years old, travelling with the forty-nine privates. Seeing the potential for all manner of trouble if these virgin officers were put to sea in charge of a motley crew of recruits and criminals, Balfour intervened, insisting a more senior officer go on the transport, a 270-ton cargo ship called the *Anne*, with them. It was duly done.

On 26 March, the *Anne* left Chatham, much to the excitement of one of those subalterns, the fifteen-year-old Harry Calvert. This young man was one of the first officers of the Royal Welch ever to have benefited from a military education in his own country, having been enrolled the previous year at the Royal Military Academy in

Woolwich. This establishment trained cadets for commissioning in the artillery and engineers – there was no school for infantry officers in Britain at the time – and Calvert had been sent there after sound instruction at Harrow school.

Calvert's father, Peter, was very ambitious on the boy's behalf. After barely half a year at Woolwich, Peter accepted, in the son's words, that 'the advantage of witnessing actual service . . . was esteemed as over-balance to the interruption it would give to my military education'. Calvert bought his boy a second lieutenancy in the 23rd. The father had plenty of money to spend because he and two brothers were partners in a highly successful brewery.

Having been gazetted into the 23rd, Harry Calvert 'very joyfully' removed his trunk from Woolwich, where the rigid curriculum and oppression of senior cadets had made him unhappy. He embarked upon his campaigns with enormous enthusiasm, an excellent education, military diligence and an acceptance of fate born of religious faith. Propelled by the ambition to escape the status of a tradesman's son, Calvert would prove a great catch for the regiment and the army.

While one contingent was packed off to sea on the *Anne*, the regiment's recruiting parties were beginning their campaign of 1779. Ministers hoped that the new Press Act would produce a great harvest of recruits, so parties of redcoats were sent all over the country to shepherd this livestock towards Chatham and America. In the north of England this effort was led by the commander of the Northern District, none other than that veteran of Lexington and recent divorcee, Lieutenant General Earl Percy, whose family estates were in Northumberland. The general had an acting major called Richard Temple in charge of the effort in Lancashire, an officer of the 23rd who was also responsible for running his own regiment's recruiting parties.

Temple had set himself up in Preston, as ordered, in February. Another officer of the Royal Welch Fusiliers, complete with recruiting serjeants and corporals, was in Manchester. Liverpool was the province of the 46th Regiment's parties, Lancaster of the 20th's and so on, with different corps carving up all the counties under Percy's aegis.

Recruiting had become very difficult by the fourth year of the American war. Tens of thousands of men had already been swept up. While the prospect of French and Spanish invasion did lift the country's sagging patriotism somewhat, those who were keen to defend against this threat joined the militia or local defence volunteers.

There were dangers facing a recruiting officer like Temple, and they did not arise from shot or shell. Having been retrieved from half pay at the outset of the American war, he had not even left British shores. Rather Temple and others like him performed a function 'attended with many disagreeable circumstances to the officers employed on it, and very often the cause of their total ruin'. Since these parties often lived at inns and used drink to ply their prospective recruits, it was frequently the case that men forgot to draw the line between imbibing for work and pleasure. One of the 23rd's recruiting serjeants had, for example, left England with the regiment in 1773 pursued by the constable of Yeovil for a great sum in unpaid booze bills, and also owing his captain money. He had been broken to the ranks for this misdemeanour.

As for the 'disagreeable' nature of the work, this often resulted from the parents of the hero who had enlisted when drunk pursuing the recruiting party, trying to persuade their boy to desert or the officer to release him. Sometimes the army would have to do so – if the lad was apprenticed to somebody, too small or too young – but in many cases the unpleasantness often resulted from the man himself realising that he had sold his life for a few guineas of bounty money, the so-called King's shilling, and might never see his loved ones again.

Temple's solution to this problem during 1775 and 1776 had been to maintain the momentum of his party through the countryside. He wrote it was 'absolutely impossible to keep many recruits long together whilst surrounded by their friends and relations who employ every allurement possible to prevail upon them to desert'. The recruit who absconded left Temple three guineas the poorer, since he had to account for the money.

During the first year of the war, Temple's party had tried to work the northern parts of Ireland, but it soon proved to be a fruitless task, and by the latter part of 1776 the recruiting reports for the army as a whole show months going by without the island yielding a single recruit. With the army's recruiting ground of earlier decades proving so barren, efforts were made in Scotland, which proved so successful that several large battalions of highlanders were raised. The Fusiliers could not, however, recruit north of the Tweed, and, abandoning Ireland, they were left to trawl the counties of England and Wales.

Faced with such difficulty in finding enough volunteers the

government sanctioned a series of steps: bounty money had been raised, recruits offered the chance from December 1775 to enlist for the duration of the war only (rather than, as usual, for life), recruiters permitted to take 'rogues and vagabonds' off the hands of magistrates, the height limit had been reduced and the ban on Catholics enlisting relaxed. Finally, many categories of criminal had been added to the first two, and a system put in place whereby magistrates who sent men for foreign service would be paid for each one they delivered.

So, in March 1779, Major Temple turned up at the local sessions and awaited his men. The first difficulty arose when some of the inmates realised that by volunteering before they were convicted, they might still get paid their three guineas bounty. Temple would not have minded personally, but he knew the court officers would soon become disgruntled because they would not get their fee, and could therefore, he wrote, 'no longer be expected to exert themselves on a service attended with danger and possible odium'.

As the major had noticed, once the element of compulsion had been introduced by the Press Act, the emotional temperature had risen considerably. Those whom he collected from the House of Correction in Preston were guilty of such crimes as fathering illegitimate children, poaching or being a runaway servant. William Smith, who came to the 23rd via the Manchester assizes, had stolen two and a half yards of linen from a merchant. Reports of army life were sufficiently alarming for many of these men to be terrified by what awaited them. Smith, it can be recorded, went quietly to the Fusiliers and died of fever two years later in an American hospital. Others did not go willingly.

On 27 March, four pressed men escaped from Preston House of Correction. Temple suggested such felons be gathered in Lancaster Castle instead since it was more secure. When the time came to move them down to Chatham, the 23rd's new recruits were marched under armed guard.

The officer of the Royal Welch who went to collect a party from Manchester House of Correction was shocked to find that two of the inmates had cut off their own thumbs rather than serve in the war. 'Please inform me in what manner I am to deal with these two men,' he asked the War Office. The answer came back that by this act of self-mutilation, they had succeeded in cheating the press.

Once the army began accepting prisoners in large numbers it noted a marked drop in the fitness of its recruits. The officer responsible for running the depot at Chatham complained loudly to his masters, 'The magistrates from several parts had sent in wretched objects totally unfit for service.' Few, though, were discharged for this reason, rather they were marched on to transports – volunteers and pressed men alike.

The scenes at the quay were vividly described by one recruit of the 33rd: 'The cries and lamentations of the poor, raw country soldiers were sufficient to have excited the compassion in the breast of the rudest barbarians; and, as for myself, I thought I was going to the Devil, when they rolled us down the hatchways like so much lumber.'

Packed into their berths, the sick jail-house men often infected the volunteers. Certainly one officer in New York complained of many perishing from 'epidemic distemper' when they arrived later that year. This proved true of the 23rd's recruits – more than half of those recruited in 1779 died of various fevers within two years of arriving in America, a far higher mortality rate than among the veteran soldiers serving there. A further factor in the poor health of those men gathered early in 1779 proved to be the inordinate length of their journey, berthed in fetid transports.

Calvert and his young friends had set off in high spirits at the end of March, but found themselves waiting many weeks at Spithead, the Nore and the Downs. First they were expecting other vessels to join them, then the winds were contrary and finally their naval hosts conceded that the presence of a powerful French fleet in the western approaches made it impossible for a large convoy of transports to sail. They would spend more than four months on board the *Anne* before reaching New York. In that time the Howe brothers inquiry and the future direction of the war would be decided in London.

Parliament's examination of the American war proved a lengthy and involved affair. Beginning in late April 1779, witnesses were called throughout May and the first half of June. They gave statements, were examined by members of both houses and cross-examined by the Howe brothers and John Burgoyne. While the committee conducting this business was destined never to issue a report of findings or come to a verdict about the behaviour of its commanders, the machinery of British democracy did at least rumble into action, allowing a full discussion of why Saratoga had happened and whether the war might be won.

William Howe's first witness, Earl Cornwallis, emphasised the difficulties of military operations in America, particularly with regard to supply and intelligence. In general his evidence underlined the hazards of armchair generalship in London, although when asked whether Howe should have supported Burgoyne instead of going to Philadelphia, Cornwallis stayed on the fence, saying only that this was a matter of opinion. Charles Grey, the general who had defeated the Americans at Paoli, proved a rather more useful witness, stating explicitly his view that Howe could not have supported Burgoyne more effectually than by attacking Philadelphia and praising as masterly dispositions for the battle of Brandywine.

Grey's evidence proved most important, though, in informing future policy, for he stated baldly: 'I think with the present force in America there can be no expectation of ending the war by force of arms.' Whereas those called by the Ministry asserted the loyalty of the great majority of Americans, Grey pointedly noted that the army had behaved with no more lenience than it would have to any 'foreign enemy', and that ideas of using punishment to change minds were futile: 'severity would not now signify'. Major General Grey sketched the difficulties of British troops trying to hold ground any distance from their fleet, and argued that vast numbers of troops would be required to hold ground if spectacles like the evacuation of Philadelphia were to be avoided. Of Washington's troops Grey said that 'the enemy were very far from contemptible', and he pinpointed a key advantage they had enjoyed, that of being able to re-assemble forces after every defeat.

The Ministry used mainly political figures to support its case that the Howe brothers had failed to prosecute the campaigns in America properly. They talked about countless missed opportunities and insisted the majority of Americans were loyal to their King.

Major General James Robertson proved to be the Howes' most significant military critic. He described the difficulties that General Washington had in maintaining the Continental Army, Sir William's failure to stop looting (thus alienating the uncommitted) and the lost strategic possibilities of 1776 to 1777. Howe, having been given 'a force that could beat any the rebels could bring against it', had failed to go to Albany instead of Philadelphia, leading directly to Burgoyne's defeat. A frigate, argued Robertson, could sail up the Hudson to within six miles of Albany in as little as twenty hours.

he opening engagement of the wars in Lexington Green, where poor British troop
scipline may have contributed to the outbreak of hostilities.

THE SOLDIERS: Frederick Mackenzie in later life, when his intelligence and diligence marked him out for work at the new Royal Military College.

George Baynton, painted in the mid-1780 in splendid Fusiliers dress uniform. He was one of the lieutenants selected by lot for captivity after Yorktown.

A VIEW from the PUMP ROOM, BATH.

Thomas Saumarez was one of the longest-serving officers of the 23rd during the American war, and commanded the regiment's captives after Yorktown.

This caricature of Robert Donkin shows him as an aged general enjoying the fashionable scene at Bath. Donkin exemplified the eighteenth-century officer who knew how to play the system.

THE COMMANDERS: Earl Cornwallis was admired by many of his officers for his aggression on the field and his desire to protect the army's honour.

George Washington was not a great battle-field commander but a superior strategist to William Howe during the key campaigns of 1776–7.

Harry Calvert (miniature) painted in his twenties, much as he would have appeared during the 1793 Flanders campaign.

BUNKERS HILL
or America's Head-Dress

The British suffered a disastrous defeat at Bunker Hill in 1775. America's success here wa͏
a gift to George III's enemies, who lampooned Britain's failure.

The opening of the battle of Germantown, with British troops around Cliveden manor. This drawing (detail shown) is one of a small number believed to show British uniforms accurately following Howe's relaxation of dress regulations.

A detail from a Richard Williams sketch of Boston during the siege of 1775, in which at one point around 3,500 British soldiers faced an American force several times larger. The picture shows a soldier of the 23rd leaning against a cannon, apparently wearing his fusilier cap.

British troops seizing Rhode Island in 1776 (detail), drawn by an eyewitness, one of the impressive amphibious operations launched by the Howe brothers. The troops in the rowboats also wear uniforms adapted for the campaign.

With the arrival of Admiral d'Estaing's squadron in American waters in 1778, British nav[al] superiority was lost. Only the storm that dismasted the French flagship, *Languedoc*, and other vessels, leaving them at the mercy of British ships, here the *Renown*, prevented dire consequences.

later view of British soldiers attempting to storm one of Yorktown's outer redoubts. The
mphasis is on the patriotic drama of the moment, rather than accurate depiction.

The taking of the British ship *Romulus* in Chesapeake Bay was one of a series of naval setbacks that announced the arrival of a powerful French squadron off Virginia and sealed the fate of Britain's Yorktown garrison.

The march to Yorktown's surrender field, drawn by an artist who witnessed the scene (detail).

Lord Germain's friends did not put forward a specific military strategy in these sessions. After several weeks of hearings, the inquiry petered out as the parliamentary session ended with Whig and Tory happy to draw their own conclusions. Such was the public interest in these proceedings that printed transcripts of the evidence rapidly sold through several editions.

As for Nisbet Balfour, he was not called upon to provide testimony, but had much time to reflect on the decisions made by Howe during the New York and Philadelphia campaigns, of which the colonel, as a member of his kitchen cabinet, had intimate knowledge. Balfour knew Howe had made mistakes, reminding one friend of an aphorism of Marshal Turenne: 'The General who has taken the field and has not committed faults, has not served his country long.' Overall, though, he considered the brothers 'two great and injured men', and fumed at the politicians – in both camps – who waged their war without regard for the lives of their armies or reputations of the country's generals.

Balfour emerged from proceedings with a distinct bitterness towards Parliament, calling it 'a nest of faction and disingenuity where every liberal, manly, sentiment must sooner or later be tainted'. He shared his master's animus towards Germain and thought that General Grey's evidence about the impossibility of winning must be 'food for opposition and death to the American minister'. This did not prove to be the case, however, for during the very months of April, May and June that the hearings were held, a new strategy for America was evolving.

At the beginning of the year, the only thing that had kept the war going was a general conviction on the part of King and Prime Minister that it could not be allowed to fail. Balfour believed the Ministry had nailed its colours to the American mast, and would inevitably sink if forced to concede defeat. The colonel's personal disdain for Germain had begun with that minister ignoring his plea for a pension for his mother. Germain, equally, was probably aware that Balfour had threatened his friend, the newspaper man, James Rivington, in New York.

As to the war, various secret plans had been travelling about Whitehall: one argued that the army should go back to Philadelphia in order to dominate the central states. Major General Robertson had also pushed a memorandum arguing once more for a war centred on the Hudson axis. Both plans shared an optimistic assessment of the kind of loyalist support that could be expected and in this sense were flawed. Both Germain in London and Clinton in New York, however, knew exactly how little the promises of American Tories had proven to be worth in those very places during the campaigns of 1776 and 1777. The king's desire to continue the war might therefore have failed to find any tangible form but for a series of events that opened a new horizon.

News reached London in February 1779 that a small British expedition had captured Savannah in Georgia in the far south. British forces had also re-taken St Lucia in the Caribbean, and then repulsed a French counter-attack, causing them great losses. The centre of gravity was moving southwards.

Further reports from Georgia showed that many loyalists had presented themselves for duty in a way that had been often promised but scarcely achieved before. Germain began to consider building on this success by moving against South Carolina, the neighbouring state to the north. Clinton had long nurtured a desire to return to Charleston, the great trading centre of the Carolinas, the reduction of which that general failed to achieve with his expedition there in 1776. How, though, could a continued war be sustained?

The imminent French threat to the British Isles, and the failure of ministerial strategy highlighted in the Howe hearings, meant that Parliament would never agree to large reinforcements for America. Germain knew that carrying on depended on getting the American loyalists to form more regiments, fighting increasingly for themselves. General Amherst produced another argument for switching the effort southwards – it would make the most of existing forces in America since many regiments might be shuttled down to the Caribbean or Carolinas in the winter when campaigning was impossible further north and then moved back again when these tropical climes became too unhealthy in the summer months.

George III did not make this new strategy, but he endorsed it enthusiastically. In June 1779, he wrote to Lord North arguing that the war must go on. Those who argued that it was unbearably expensive were 'only weighing such events in the scale of a tradesman behind his counter', whereas the King had a God-given duty to look at the principles at stake and believed the American war 'the most serious in which any country was ever engaged'. George argued that defeat could set a juggernaut of dire consequences rolling: 'Should America succeed . . . the West Indies must follow them . . . Ireland would soon follow the same plan and be a separate state, then this island would be reduced to itself, and would soon be a poor island indeed.'

Germain knew that there were many obstacles to driving through his new plan of war: Rhode Island would have to be abandoned, and its 5,000 troops brought down to New York so that a large expedition could be sent south; somehow he would have to persuade that truculent General Clinton to do it – for he was insisting on resigning unless there was a substantial reinforcement; and there needed to be new leadership to launch the army on its southern campaign.

Late in 1778, one colonel had written from New York, 'There is hardly one general officer who does not declare his intention of going home, the same with officers of all ranks who, if they could procure leave, would be happy to leave.' The experiences of American war from Boston to Saratoga had convinced many that it was a conflict in which reputations could be lost but not gained. Clinton's abrasive and suspicious personality had also alienated many of his senior commanders.

Help came in the form of Earl Cornwallis who had told the King in April 1779 that he was willing to serve again in America. This news produced unbridled joy among ministers, for Clinton might thus be used as a supreme administrative figure and Cornwallis as the principal field commander.

Cornwallis's private views about whether the war could be won, it must be owned, did not differ very much from those of Charles Grey. The earl's wife had died in February, leaving him distraught. He returned to America, in his own words, 'not with views of conquest and ambition, nothing brilliant can be expected in that quarter, but I find this country quite unsupportable to me. I must shift the scene; I have many friends in the American army; I love that army.'

During early 1779 the Whigs had poured scorn upon the Ministry, but as the summer went on, they too had to acknowledge certain realities. The appearance of a powerful Franco-Spanish combined fleet in the Channel made it unpatriotic, treasonable indeed, to carry opposition to the King too far. Those fashionable ladies of the rich Whig families such as Georgiana, Duchess of Devonshire, who had gone to parties dressed as American soldiers during the early years of the revolution, got themselves measured up for British regimentals once France entered the war. They accompanied their husbands to the great militia summer training camps as they awaited invasion of the home islands.

Die-hard opponents of the war could rail at the Ministry's stupidity for carrying on in America when England and Ireland were under threat of invasion, but even they would have acknowledged that the American army could not have been extricated fast enough to have averted the crisis of August 1779, when the enemy fleet appeared off Plymouth and the Royal Navy stayed in port – fearful of defeat, touching off near hysteria.

'How strange must our system of politicks appear in future ages,' wrote Balfour, prevented from getting back to his regiment because of the crisis in the Channel, 'when it appears, that while we were carrying on offensive wars in all quarters of the Globe with vast fleets and armies, that an enemy rode triumphant in our own harbours.' The 23rd's commanding officer had spent most of the year in Britain, but his time there would soon be over.

Balfour had been home to visit his mother Katherine. They had been overjoyed to discover that Walter Balfour had not after all been lost at sea, but she had reacted with horror at the idea that Nisbet must once again return to America, with all the risks that involved. But the colonel himself had grown listless. Just as he had been glad to leave America the previous November, he had found the partisan bear pit of Westminster too disgusting to stomach. He wanted to return to the Fusiliers, writing, 'I hate to remain longer an idle spectator.'

There was little prospect of that, for although the colonel did not know it yet, the new course of the war had been set. The army would be heading for South Carolina, with Cornwallis, Balfour and the 23rd all centre-stage.

SIXTEEN

The War Moves South

In Which 2nd Lieutenant Harry Calvert Makes His Debut

It was already dark when Calvert and the recruits boarded their little sailing ship on the Hudson. Snows, schooners and sloops plied up and down that great waterway, carrying the stuff of war hither and thither. Five months had elapsed since their departure from Chatham, and still these green lads in red coats had not seen their regiment. It had been tedious, to say the least, but spirits had been revived when their convoy had arrived at Sandy Hook, the entrance to New York harbour.

The following day Calvert's journey was near its end. As their vessel got under way that evening of 28 August 1779, they were only a dozen miles from the Royal Welch Fusiliers' bivouac. This excursion from the city had been made necessary by a daring American operation the previous month which had captured the river-side fort at Stoney Point. General Clinton, who suffered the humiliating loss of more than 600 men (killed, wounded and, the great majority, captured) had marched several regiments north to re-take the fort.

The army's situation showed how the combination of political deadlock in London and a timorous commander-in-chief had rebounded on them. One lieutenant colonel who called upon Clinton found him in despair after the Stoney Point debacle. '[He] stated how particularly cruel it was to be served so ill by subordinate officers,' wrote Charles Stuart. 'He told me with tears in his eyes that he was quite an altered man – that business so oppressed him that he felt himself unequal to his station.' Sunk in his pathos, Clinton told his visitor that the army hated him.

Many officers had indeed come to despair the army's inactivity and deride the 'Clintonian expeditions' to burn down American buildings along the coast, missions their commander-in-chief sometimes sent them upon to convince himself he was still actively engaged in operations. The 23rd had been involved in just such an operation in July 1779, falling upon some small towns in Connecticut, burning down anything of value they could find. There was a logic to these grim raids, for they caused many states to remove soldiers from central or Continental command and use them to defend the homes and property of those who had paid to raise them. Although there was some effect, in reducing General Washington's army, the strategy was pursued with half measures while the soldiers themselves had mixed feelings about torching peaceable settlements.

'No doubt in such excursions many scenes occur', Serjeant Roger Lamb wrote of their July expedition, 'at which the feeling heart must revolt; but in war, all that the brave and the humane can do, is to soften and alleviate its horrors; to prevent them entirely is altogether beyond the power of man.'

Calvert arrived at a time when the British army had become a victim of events rather than their master and – the connection might be speculated upon – discipline had hit one of its periodic lows. The 23rd Light Company, no less, had witnessed a grievous case of desertion that July. It involved Robert Mason, who had served since Lexington and been aboard the *Isis* the previous year, James Watson, a draftee from the 65th who had been serving with the Fusiliers for three years and Henry Smith, another veteran of the *Isis* fight who had been transferred into the Light Company late in 1777.

Opinion within the regiment was divided as to why they had done it. Some said it was a drunken lark that got out of hand. Captain Smythe, who knew them all well, thought that Mason had been the ringleader and that he had decided to desert out of fear of two fellow soldiers whose wives he had been pursuing. Whatever the trigger, the men had taken advantage of their proximity to the American outposts near Throg's Neck to steal off on 28 July. Since they were not on duty, they did not carry their muskets, but had each concealed bayonets about their clothing.

Stopping at a house, the three Fusiliers had asked the way to the American lines. Lawrence Tolcot, the householder, was a Tory who instantly suspected desertion. As soon as the redcoats left, he went off in search of some other men, loyalist refugees who had settled the area. When they saw Mason and the others doubling back, Tolcot and a friend, who were both armed, arrested them and took them to the local command. Although the Fusiliers pleaded that they had only been going to wash their clothes, they were ordered to be taken to the provost for detention as deserters.

A small party of refugees under Major Barymore was assigned to escort them. Half a mile into their baleful journey, realising the seriousness of their situation, the Fusiliers tried to escape. Mason leapt on Tolcot and wrestled his musket from him, while Watson disarmed another. Major Barymore, however, proved to be one of those characters capable of resorting instantly to great violence. He drew his sword and ran Smith through the body. As the wounded man crumpled to the ground, the other two faced the choice of surrender or receiving the same treatment.

Mason and Watson gave up, looking on mutely while Smith bled to death. The survivors were brought to a general court martial, receiving their sentence on 16 August, 'to suffer death by being hanged by the neck until they are dead'. Those familiar with the army's disciplinary system would have been unsurprised to learn that Mason and Watson were not frog-marched forthwith to the gallows. Instead clemency was sought and, during the months that this matter took to settle, the two men were locked up in jail. Smythe had regarded Watson in any case as a good soldier led astray, and Mason, who was able to charm officers as well as regimental wives, was a good musician, a rarity prized by many commanding officers on campaign.

After its brief excursion up the Hudson, the army returned to New York. In the August heat, streets packed with redcoats, it was not the season for energetic socialising. Sea-bathing was popular among officers, who slaked their thirsts with bowls of chilled punch. Calvert took his turn with the various duties required to maintain good order on the streets and protect against surprise.

What did the soldiers make of this teenager placed in command of them? Roger Lamb, who had been promoted to serjeant earlier that year, did duty with Calvert on the first night that he was entrusted with guard mounting in New York. Lamb took an instant liking to the young man because he was diligent about his work, exhibiting 'ability and professional knowledge'. Calvert's earnest attitude thus overcame any scepticism that might have been caused by his callow years and appearance, for with his large round eyes and button nose there was something quite boyish in his looks.

In Lieutenant Colonel Balfour's absence, the regiment was commanded by Thomas Mecan. Four years after William Blakeney's wounding at Bunker Hill, that officer remained rooted to his parlour in England. Blakeney was finally elbowed aside when Mecan was appointed as the 23rd's major in April 1779. Balfour and Howe, both in England at the time, appear to have conspired to ignore the fact that Mecan could not afford to buy his way up in order to get the best soldier for the job. In this way, Mecan received for hard service, and his Brandywine wound, his second promotion in four years.

Balfour in particular would try almost anything by way of exploiting the army's arcane promotion system in order to elevate the most able men. Before leaving America he had raised the regimental serjeant major, George Watson, from the ranks to the post of adjutant. This office, like that of quartermaster, could be held by a promoted soldier without his having to buy a commission. However, those who aspired to follow in the footsteps of Richard Baily, the former quartermaster of the Royal Welch who by this year was a captain in the 2nd Foot, or indeed those who simply wanted to ensure a comfortable retirement by selling out of the army, needed to get a fully fledged officer's commission.

While in London, Balfour had brokered a deal whereby Alexander Innes, a Scotsman who held the colonelcy of a loyalist American regiment, would advance Adjutant Watson 180 guineas towards the price of a second lieutenancy. In return, Balfour agreed to put Innes's son James on the list for commissioning into the 23rd, a consideration he might have expected for nothing.

Mecan and Watson between them brought the regiment to a high pitch of discipline. The Irish major in particular proved unforgiving to those who obstructed regimental efficiency, for he was capable of giving those who crossed him or the 23rd a fearful dressing down. One example will suffice. Late in 1779, when the regiment put various items in store, Major Mecan discovered that one of the houses intended for this purpose had already been seized by a functionary from the Barrack Office. Sending soldiers down to re-take his storehouse, Mecan fired off a rocket to the clerk that started, 'How dare you, contrary to a General Order of the Commander-in-chief, let people to be quartered in the house which is the store of the 23rd'! It was this kind of spirit and attention to detail that caused others to treat Mecan with respect. As the summer wore on rumours abounded that the Welch Fusiliers would soon be embarked for Caribbean service, and this may have played in a role in some desertions, when soldiers feared they might be wrenched from a local girl and sent southward to that cockpit of disease and suffering.

These reports may also have prompted Lionel Smythe to declare himself for the heart of Marie Phillips, a young lady 'celebrated for her beauty, wit, and accomplishments; indeed so immensely sensible that it was thought a bold officer who ventured on her'. She was the daughter of Frederick Phillips, a wealthy landowner from West Chester County who rallied early to the royal cause. Young women like Marie were pursued by scores of 'danglers', the single young officers who packed any half-respectable social function in the city, and bombarded young ladies' homes with their cards, pleading for the honour of some little excursion. 'You cannot imagine,' wrote one socialite, 'what a superfluity of danglers there is here; so that a lady has only to look over a list of a dozen or two when she is going to walk.' Smythe had an edge, bringing title as well as good looks, even if he did not bring a fortune. The Fusilier captain succeeded in winning his woman, the two being married in New York on 5 August.

The 23rd and several other regiments marched down to the docks in September, went aboard transports and stayed on board for nine days before being disembarked. In October, with much swearing and hefting of kit the Fusiliers embarked again, enjoying their naval surroundings for two weeks before being taken off. The regiment had already gone into rather shabby winter quarters – huts on Long Island – when the procedure was repeated for the third time in four months that December.

This time, though, something altogether more serious was afoot. After so many months of prevarication, a major expedition was ordered. This was no descent on some sugar island in the Caribbean, nor the beating up of a few wharves in Connecticut, but an assault upon Charleston, one of the greatest ports in America. Months of preparation had finally born fruit; the war was moving south.

The embarkation at New York began on 16 December and was completed by the 21st. It comprised the light infantry, grenadiers (British and Hessian), four British regiments of the line, one Hessian garrison regiment, the British Legion and another loyalist corps, as well as other detachments totalling nearly 8,000 men. Great quantities of stores had to be shipped, for taking Charleston would require regular approaches, siege-craft with heavy battering guns, pontoons and all manner of engineering works.

As the soldiers abandoned their freezing shacks to tramp down to the quays, many of those staying behind said they were well off out of it – heading to the warmer climes down south while their mates weathered winter in New York. Harry Calvert radiated youthful optimism as he stowed his kit aboard the transport, judging that 'no doubt remained, that the inactivity of the summer would be made up by great exertions in the winter'. An older officer of the 23rd wrote home complaining that 'we have had as fine an army as ever went into the field cooped up in this garrison this whole summer'.

On the night before their intended departure, though, Calvert and the occupants of several other transports were woken by panicked shouting above. Ice coming down the Hudson had severed the ships' anchor cables and they were drifting helplessly towards reefs. One of those embarked wrote:

All the sailors had lost their heads . . . the day broke and the ebb tide came, driving us toward the rocky coast of Long Island and running us so hard against a reef that nearly all the people on board were thrown to the floor by the shock.

When the vessel carrying Calvert and his company struck, its bottom was ripped out and the passengers abandoned ship. Fortunately they survived, only to be re-embarked, and on Christmas Day the fleet set sail.

The thirty-eight days at sea would have tried the patience of the most sanguine sailor, but Clinton, wracked with worry in his stateroom, wrote, 'Scarcely a day during the voyage passed without being marked by the foundering of some transport or other or the dispersion of the fleet.' Battered by storms, the convoys were scattered with one dismasted transport blown all the way to Ireland. Eventually, though, the surviving ships were collected and troops began landing on 10 February 1780.

Their objective, Charleston, was a trading powerhouse, packed with vast warehouses, adorned with beautiful mansions and fuelled by a hinterland of plantations growing rice, tobacco or other cash crops. From the military point of view, the approaches to it were even more problematic than those William Howe faced at New York in 1776.

Broad rivers, the Stono, Ashley and Cooper, lay between General Clinton and an effective blockade of the city. From these mighty waterways, dozens of tributaries branched, draining marshes and creating many little islands. The soldiers who began venturing into this tropical country found all manner of strange beasts, highly coloured birds and trees festooned with great beards of moss.

It took weeks for Clinton's army to work its way across this water-logged land, using islets or peninsulas like stepping stones. The 23rd was initially brigaded with the 7th, another Fusilier regiment known as the English or Royals, under their commanding officer Alured Clarke, acting as brigadier. Lieutenant General Cornwallis was put in charge of Clarke and some other brigades moving to invest the city. During its early fights in this strange new environment, the Fusilier Brigade did not always come off best, as the nature of these forests forced them to act in small parties, as light infantry. In Major Mecan though they had a skilled teacher in this new discipline of soldiering.

By 29 March Cornwallis's troops were establishing themselves on the Charleston peninsula itself, having come behind the city to invest it from the north. On 1 April the trenches were opened, the field engineers beginning their approaches and batteries, the vice of earthworks that would be slowly advanced towards the settlement's landward walls, crushing the defence bit by bit.

The British engineers dug their first trench or parallel several hundred yards from the American works. As the siege progressed, and usually working at night, digging parties pushed their excavations forward, connecting these advances with two more parallels. The third parallel, the one from which the city would be stormed, was only 30 to 40 yards from the American guns. During the long hours of hard labour required to progress with pick and shovel, the defenders pelted Clinton's men with cannon, grape and musketry. Work in the trenches was dirty and dangerous, all the more so because the usual rules of siege warfare were being violated – the attackers, with thirty guns, had barely one third of the number of the defenders.

Captain Ewald's jaegers were ordered to work in the siege lines, acting as sharpshooters against the city's defenders. 'Our batteries opened,' he wrote in his journal for 13 April, 'several pieces of the besieged on the bastion on the left were dismounted.' Pushing forward their excavations on the 17th Ewald recorded, 'The besieged fired continuously with grapeshot and musketry, through which five Hessian grenadiers and three Englishmen were killed and 14 wounded.'

By late April the third parallel was being dug and a weary Ewald wrote, 'The dangers and difficult work are the least of the annoyance:

the intolerable heat, lack of good water and the billions of sandflies and mosquitoes made up the worst nuisance.' Scores of sick were treated in tents set back from the trenches, for no building suitable for a hospital could be found.

Clinton's prosecution of the siege was so slow and deliberate as to frustrate many officers, but the defenders did nothing to take advantage of it. In fact day by day they played into his hands. The Continental regiments that had garrisoned the city from the start were reinforced by South Carolina militia, called up from all over the state. The Continental Army also made preparations to send more troops down to help.

Brigadier General Benjamin Lincoln, the American commander, would more wisely have left the city to the militia and kept his picked troops outside it. This, though, proved politically unacceptable to the city's oligarchs, who insisted Lincoln's men stay, and sucked as many troops as they could into Clinton's trap. As the British guns pounded, day after day shattering windows and terrifying civilians, Charleston began to feel the effects of a siege proper – something that had not happened at New York. It became a contest to the finish in which a victorious enemy was expected to sack the town and seize millions in property from those who had resisted.

In addition to wrapping one hand around the neck of South Carolina's great city, Clinton needed to use the other to fend off any attempt to relieve the siege from the inland side. This duty fell to Earl Cornwallis who arrayed troops in an arc up to fifty miles into the country.

Nisbet Balfour rejoined his regiment on 10 March, after a sea journey that had taken months because of the difficulties of bypassing the French fleet and catching the wind. He returned to find the regiment more than 400 strong, although fifty were already in hospital suffering from the southern agues, and several had been taken prisoner while the 23rd fought its way towards the city. After the trenches had been opened, a strong detachment, 120 men under Major Mecan, had been sent to guard a battery at Fort Johnson, an important point on James Island controlling access to the harbour. With little more than half his regiment left, Balfour bivouacked 40 miles up the Cooper River, sending out patrols to warn of any approaching enemy. This was less dangerous than being in the siege lines, but offered no opportunities for distinction that a fire-eater might seek.

Balfour wrote from his camp in some woods to a friend in New York that he was 'in perfect health, except the amusement of a few muskettoes [*sic*] and rattlesnakes to look at in the morning', and predicting that 'this sun of your latitudes will pepper me'. During his long voyage and duty on the lines Balfour had plenty of time to consider his personal position. He had always operated on the principle that it was essential to be well connected, but his great patron remained in England removed from public life. By returning to America he had placed himself once more under Henry Clinton, a man whom he despised. However, the logic of operations and the balance of personalities in the army began to work in Balfour's favour.

With each crash of British shot into the walls of Charleston the defenders' time was reduced, and with each day on outpost duty, Balfour's personal situation became less isolated. For the 23rd's commanding officer was gaining the trust of Earl Cornwallis, and that noble general valued new allies because he was losing the faith of his commander-in-chief.

Clinton had been wary of Cornwallis since the campaign of 1776, when he discovered that a remark he made to the earl, disparaging William Howe, was promptly reported back to that general. In April 1780, with his grip closing on Charleston, Clinton jotted in his diary that Cornwallis was spreading rumours, but that when challenged, 'Lord Cornwallis never writes an answer.' Several days later the commander-in-chief was worried whether he had done the right thing sending Cornwallis to command the inland forces and fretting about the peer's aide-de-camp Charles Ross: 'He [Cornwallis] will play me false, I fear; at least Ross will.' Even so, these suspicions or rivalries were kept in check as long as the army was successful and on 11 May, after four months' campaigning, its operations were crowned with triumph.

By the night of 11 May, Captain Ewald's jaegers were fighting from a storming trench just thirty paces from the enemy defences, enduring a 'horrible' fire that cut many men down and dismounted all of the forward British guns (although the Americans did not realise their success). Clinton forced matters by firing red-hot shot into the city, a grim tactic that, if kept up, would burn down the entire place. 'During this murdering and burning, I heard the sound of a drum,' wrote the Hessian jaeger. An American drummer had been sent up to the walls and was beating out the signal for a parley. Brigadier Lincoln had previously refused to surrender, but with the British ready to storm or incinerate the town, further resistance was futile.

When the defenders marched out, the British realised the scale of defeat they had inflicted. In his dispatch to London, Clinton said he had taken 5,618 enemy troops as well as 1,000 armed sailors. The loss to the attacking forces was 76 killed and 189 wounded. The British were quite unprepared to deal with such a vast number of captives, and in any case it was the 2,600 Continental troops that formed the mainstay of the garrison – most of the remainder had played little active role in the defence, and were soon released on their word, or parole, that they would never bear arms against the King's troops again.

In addition to the loss of these regiments and 400 cannon, the Americans had to surrender a squadron of frigates. The city merchants were further mortified by dozens of trading ships being impounded. There was a vast sum in prize money to be made from the Charleston business, and a tetchy dispute soon started between army and fleet over whether the sailors were entitled to half of the money. Clinton had made himself a fortune.

The fall of Charleston was in many respects worse for the Americans than Saratoga had been for the British. In addition to losing a large army, a city central to the prosperity and livelihoods of the southern states had been seized. Patriot spirits were depressed, and the war party in London received an enormous boost. That ardent Whig, Richard Fitzpatrick of the Guards, wrote to his friend Charles Fox, 'The camps fired a *feu de joie* upon this occasion, because now as you may imagine *the war is finished*.' The prediction proved erroneous, but many of those who had assumed since Burgoyne's surrender that George III's Ministry was simply looking for the right peace terms were disabused. After Charleston it became clear that the British army was fighting again, not for time but to win.

General Clinton quickly began re-embarking his *corps d'élite*, the light infantry and grenadiers, for a voyage back to New York. He intended to leave behind Lord Cornwallis and a small army that included the 23rd Fusiliers. Civil rule would be re-established in South Carolina as it had been in Georgia. Thousands of loyal inhabitants would be armed and formed into militia regiments so that Cornwallis's regulars might move to North Carolina and repeat the process, working their way up the states. Cornwallis was given his orders, and General Clinton even had a task in mind for Lieutenant Colonel Balfour.

As they considered how South Carolina should be garrisoned, British commanders were conditioned by geography. Charleston's immediate hinterland, stretching about 100 miles inland, was a swampy, unhealthy terrain crossed by several major rivers. This lowland was also the most economically productive part of the province, with its large plantations. Beyond the coastal strip, there was a distinct change, a rolling landscape of sand hills, the so-called piedmont, began; and beyond that, a further 100 miles or so from the sea, were the Appalachian mountains. The uplands had been colonised later than the coast, by settlers coming down from the north on the Great Wagon Road from Virginia. As for the mountains, they were home only to a few frontier communities.

Cornwallis soon realised that the piedmont would have to be dominated. There were three reasons for this: Continental Army troops marching down via Virginia and North Carolina along the Great Wagon Road would arrive in those sandy uplands, not on the coast; the main rivers were more easily forded there, so therefore less of a barrier to military operations; and there were some sizeable communities of loyalists among the new inland settlements that would have to be protected. So whereas some of the British generals who had fought in the north four years earlier thought that operations in America any further than 15 miles from their fleet were a dubious proposition, Cornwallis and his people would have to operate ten times that distance from their main base and stores at Charleston.

Although the war had been going on for five years, the army's push deep into South Carolina was its first concerted attempt to establish control over a large inland territory. The few months of fighting in the Jerseys during the first half of 1777 were the only similar experience that Cornwallis, Balfour or Mecan had. Even so, the bases at New York or Rhode Island had been maintained for years with minimal garrisoning of the hinterland. In Georgia, captured the previous year, royal forces were thinly deployed away from the coast.

The task General Clinton had in mind for Balfour was to establish the new order in a far-flung part of the backcountry. On 22 May, he invited the lieutenant colonel to discuss this perilous mission. Clinton was a miserable physical specimen compared to Howe, Balfour's handsome strapping hero of old. The man giving Balfour his orders was short, his few strands of grey hair were scraped across a bulbous pate, his lower set of teeth protruded beyond the upper and he tended

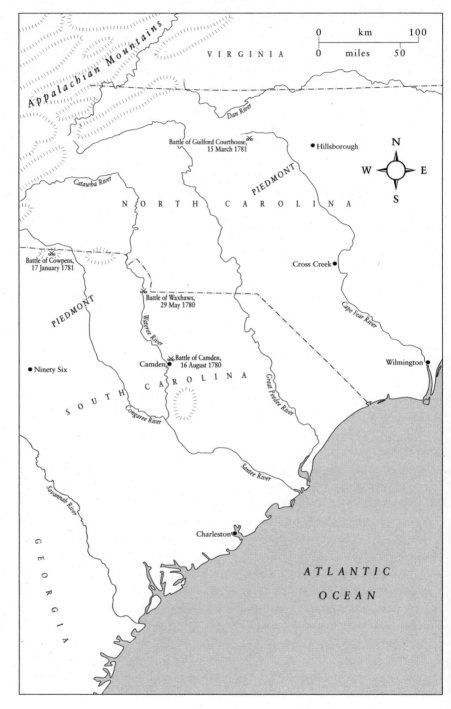

to mumble. Clinton, though, was cleverer and far more intellectually engaged than his predecessor, and as he spoke to the commanding officer of the 23rd the general detected the old prejudices of the 1777 campaign.

Major Patrick Ferguson was to be sent under Balfour's command as inspector of militia. It was to be Ferguson's task to raise several new regiments of Tories in the backcountry. Ferguson, an aggressive and innovative soldier, had fallen foul of Howe during the Philadelphia campaign, when the general had disbanded Ferguson's special corps of sharpshooters equipped with rifles of his own design. Ferguson, though, had retained Clinton's faith, so both Balfour and Cornwallis immediately suspected that Ferguson was being sent upcountry as Clinton's representative.

Balfour wondered aloud to his commander-in-chief whether Ferguson was the right man for the job – it was generally reported that the new inspector of militia was violent-tempered and ill-treated his men. 'I am not interested in "general" reports,' replied Clinton, brushing Balfour aside, but noted to himself, 'I see [the] infernal party still prevails.' The general knew that Balfour was his enemy and yearned for an opportunity to trip him up, writing in his journal, 'I wish this remark of *Balfour's* turns out lucky.' Perhaps Clinton even entertained the hope that Balfour might not return from his grim backcountry mission.

Several days later, Balfour set off with a small brigade of 580 under his command, including some light infantry and loyalists of the American Volunteers and the Prince of Wales's Volunteers. A detachment of the 23rd Fusiliers would also travel inland with their commanding officer but most of the regiment would initially remain in Charleston.

The formation of local regiments was a key part of Balfour's mission. Even by early 1780, the number of these corps and the thousands of troops employed had grown considerably since General Howe had made a tentative start. Clinton proved the more committed and effective recruiter of loyal Americans and by late 1780 there were about 7,500 under arms. These regiments fell roughly into three categories: provincial corps that were well established, such as the British Legion or the Volunteers of Ireland (the latter under the

Principal sites of the southern campaigns

colonelcy of Lord Rawdon, the army's darling from the dark days of Boston); provincial regiments, such as the Prince of Wales's Volunteers that had been recruited in the northern states with the men serving full time for the duration of the war; and local militia units, subject to temporary call-out, much like those serving the Patriot or Whig cause.

From the outset, as Balfour and Cornwallis prepared to lead different columns into the backcountry, they understood that the task of re-imposing royal authority would be difficult and that there would be many restrictions in how they could discharge it. In giving Cornwallis his terms of reference, Clinton had, for example, limited the power of general courts martial, making it impossible for Cornwallis to execute anyone or very hard to dismiss any officer. Those men who were guilty of what were normally capital offences were therefore to be broken from their regiments and sent aboard Royal Navy ships or to regiments serving in pestilential Caribbean garrisons. Denied the ultimate sanction, Cornwallis had to lead his redcoats by positive exhortations and by his own vigorous example. Even more importantly for his mission, the general understood the critical importance of winning over the people of South Carolina, telling his men early on:

The great object of his Majesty's force in this country is to protect and secure His Majesty's faithful and loyal subjects, and to encourage and assist them in arming and opposing the tyranny and oppression of the rebels. His Lordship therefore recommends it to them in the strongest manner to treat with kindness all those who have sought protection in the British army.

Cornwallis knew that leadership would be at a premium in his army, since advancing into the American hinterland held myriad dangers obvious to anyone who had experienced the hornet's nest of a roused American countryside as Mecan had at Lexington, or Lamb at Saratoga. The general knew that he must inspire his officers and none was considered insignificant in this effort. Thus, as he travelled about, the earl jotted a note to himself that one of his correspondents in England 'desired that I should be civil to Lt Calvert of the Welsh Fuzileers. He is from Richmond.' Thus the teenage subaltern would earn an invitation to sup at the general's table one evening or a kind word on the line of march. The young officer would never forget it, and would exert himself prodigiously to please the great man. Of course Calvert's uncle was an MP and his father a rich man, but by making similar examples of his kind condescension, Cornwallis would tie his subordinates to him in the execution of the great enterprise now under way.

Balfour and Ferguson were ordered to head up the Santee River, then about 100 miles inland, to the point where the river forked into several tributaries in the uplands. Here, they were to spread into detachments, with Balfour taking his men furthest to the west, to Ninety Six, less than 20 miles from the Savannah River, which marked the beginning of Georgia. There were several thousand loyalists at Ninety Six (so named because it was supposedly that number of miles from Fort St George, a frontier outpost). Earl Cornwallis, meanwhile, would be heading to Camden, about 100 miles north of Charleston, and almost the same distance east of Ninety Six, in order to establish the fortified supply base necessary for the British army's operations in the backcountry. As the colonel and his general got going, they exchanged in their letters knowing and complicit remarks about Ferguson, their shared suspicion of him increasing their mutual bond. The general displayed his trust in Balfour, giving him carte blanche to act, assuring him, 'I have a thorough confidence in your ability and attention . . . you may depend upon it that every step you take shall meet my hearty approbation.' Cornwallis was already sufficiently impressed with Balfour to urge, 'I beg you to continue to mention your opinions freely to me.'

Cornwallis had sent ahead Lieutenant Colonel Banastre Tarleton with his British Legion to push up to the borders of North Carolina. Tarleton was a twenty-six-year-old cavalry officer who had made a name for himself as one of the officers who had captured Major General Lee near New York in 1776. Stocky, red-haired and utterly aggressive, Tarleton's credo was simply expressed in a letter he sent in 1780: 'The more difficulty, the more glory.' Guided by this idea, he plunged into the backcountry in May 1780 as he would plunge into action many times, apparently oblivious to all that might go wrong. In the absence of the light infantry battalions and main body of the 17th Light Dragoons, who were sent back to New York, Tarleton's Legion combined forty British dragoons of the 17th, 130 loyalist cavalry and about 120 more of them on foot, to become the advanced guard of Cornwallis's army.

Tarleton and his Legion had already distinguished themselves fighting inland of the siege of Charleston and on 29 May approached an enemy force under Colonel Abraham Buford at Waxhaws close to the North Carolina line. Tarleton demanded Buford's surrender, was refused and promptly charged his enemy. The Americans, a Virginia regiment of foot and some troops of horse, were quickly broken and Tarleton's men, who believed for a time that he had been killed by an American abusing a white flag of truce, went on a rampage killing many of their enemies, even when they tried to surrender.

At the end of the battle, Tarleton jotted a note of enemy casualties: there were 113 killed, 150 wounded and left where they were on their word to quit the enemy army, and 53 prisoners marched away. To the experienced reader of such documents these figures are suggestive: the number of killed is higher than the normal ratio of dead to injured, so there must have been some merciless swordplay by the Legion, but the survival of at least 203 Americans (others escaped into the woods) implies that there was no blanket order of 'no quarter'. Tarleton's abandonment of the injured fits in with military doctrines of the time that the commander of an advanced corps could not slow himself down with wounded prisoners.

The episode of Paoli soon after Brandywine in 1777 had already shown the tendency for Britain's enemies to respond to defeat with allegations of massacre, and so it proved again after the Waxhaws. Cries of 'Tarleton's Quarter!' or 'Revenge Buford!' were adopted by American commanders stirring their men following the disaster at Charleston. But even before the news of the 'Waxhaws Massacre' was broadcast about the backcountry, some partisan bands were forming, ready to contest that land.

It was already roastingly hot by the time Balfour got to Ninety Six in mid-June, after an arduous fortnight's march, with sickness beginning to sap his regiments. He had formed an assessment of the rural mood on his way up, and understood that few of the inland settlements shared Ninety Six's loyalism. Many were itching for some activity from their Whig friends while others simply wanted to stay neutral while waiting to see what would happen. Balfour put forward two ideas of how the country might be dominated – one involved marching into disaffected villages, disarming and punishing people, and the other proposal was to 'get the leading men to be answerable for the conduct of their people'.

The British and their loyalist allies set about creating seven militia regiments in that part of the uplands and were soon training 4,000 men. Balfour, from the start, was dubious about the idea of embodying them for any active service, believing most of their officers incapable. He thought that militia might have uses in patrolling the wagon routes, suppressing banditry, and defending their own homes as a last resort. Ferguson, though, was much more ambitious for the new recruits.

Within a couple of weeks of starting, Balfour was already aware of a challenge emerging in the backcountry. He wrote to Cornwallis on 12 July, telling him about Colonel Thomas Sumpter raising a force of militia, with a sprinkling of Continentals, that had launched itself from North Carolina and had already 'made inroads into this province with large plundering parties chasing the loyalists from their plantations'. The uncertainty and poor leadership of Tory militias was exposed in some early skirmishes, where, by contrast, the ardent spirit of their enemies manifested itself too. Balfour warned his general, 'I find the enemy exerting themselves wonderfully and successfully in stirring up the people', and he detected that some of the American militia pardoned and released by the British after the fall of Charleston 'have already joined them and a very great number are ready at the smallest reverse of our fortunes'.

In many of the piedmont settlements, Britain's most hard-bitten adversaries were Irish immigrants or those of so-called Scotch-Irish descent. The latter type came from the ranks of Scottish Presbyterian settlers in Ireland who, having lived one or two generations on that island, had left for America, many after losing their livelihoods when the British raised taxes on imported linen. They were thus embittered against the British Crown. There were more general Irish grievances too, General Clinton noting, 'the emigrants from Ireland were in general to be looked upon as our most serious antagonists. They had fled from the real or imagined oppression of their landlords.' Clinton believed the Irish retained a greater sense of national identity than other immigrant groups and tried to play on this by forming two distinct loyalist regiments, the Volunteers of Ireland and Roman Catholic Volunteers. There was some success, and one British general estimated early in 1779 that half of all Continental deserters received in British lines were Irish.

However, the Hibernian strain that had planted itself in the hills between Camden and the North Carolina border was to prove well-nigh irreconcilable. The meagre existence scraped from the sandy soil of the uplands created a tough, self-reliant patchwork of communities that greatly resented outside interference, be it from redcoats, the Charleston merchant elite, or even tithe-gathering churchmen. One officer of the British Legion called these backcountry settlers 'Crackers', recoiling at both their miserable existence and their lax morals, saying they were 'more savage than the Indians, and possess *every* one of their vices, but *none* of their virtues'.

Settlements of Scots who had not lived in Ireland, by contrast, were often loyalist. The fact that so many of General Cornwallis's commanders were Scots contributed to an easier relationship with them, as did the perception that many prominent Caledonians at home or in America saw in the war a chance for rehabilitation and profit after the Jacobite rebellions of the previous generation.

Balfour, however, was given little time for Old Country reminiscences with the many Scots at Ninety Six. He had only been in place for one month, when his efforts to nurture the shoots of royal authority in the scorching ground of the backcountry were cut short by a dramatic letter from Earl Cornwallis. The commandant of Charleston, Major General Pattinson of the artillery, had quit his post pleading sickness and was to return to New York. Pattinson had a reputation as an inefficient drunk, so this was no great loss. An able man was needed in that city, for it formed the main supply depot for the south as well as being a great trading and political hub. Who to replace Pattinson then? There were no other generals willing to serve in South Carolina, whereas aggressive youngsters like Rawdon or Tarleton were best left on the battlefield. The earl chose Balfour:

I know you will say that you would rather go with your Regiment but they must go where they are most wanted, and it is absolutely necessary for the good of the service, that you should take the management of the town, which will, in fact, be the management of the province. I must insist on hearing no excuses.

So, the lieutenant colonel was ordered to forsake the chance of leading the 23rd in battle, and undertake a complex administrative office instead. Balfour instantly worried about the money – if he was expected to entertain and hold court in Charleston from his existing pay, and with his many debts, he would be ruined. Cornwallis succeeded in getting him brigadier's money. In addition, as commandant, Balfour would have the use of a large public purse, a chance to make sure his pockets were never empty. The post thus offered Balfour the chance to set right his finances but avoid the dangers of the battlefield that might once more bring sorrow to his poor mother's heart.

While Balfour travelled down from Ninety Six to Charleston, Cornwallis was receiving reports that a powerful enemy force – several thousand troops under Major General Gates, the victor of Saratoga – were moving towards Camden. Several British regiments, including the Royal Welch Fusiliers, were concentrated at that place under Lord Rawdon. Earl Cornwallis was in Charleston awaiting Balfour.

On 6 August, Cornwallis handed over business at that headquarters to the new commandant. There were disturbing reports from the inland settlements – one of the newly formed militia battalions had defected in its entirety to Sumpter, having been convinced by a local officer paroled by the British after the fall of Charleston. Reports from Camden meanwhile suggested Gates might have as many as 5,000 troops at his disposal, whereas the King's troops at that post numbered little more than 2,000.

Balfour settled in to his splendid new office. Meanwhile, 100 miles away, the 23rd, under Major Mecan, awaited their general and fate at Camden. Despite the privations of service at that remote post and of the summer heat reaching its boiling peak, morale was good.

With the enemy approaching, Rawdon wrote urgently to Cornwallis on 11 August, 'Gates may attack me tomorrow morning: if he does, I think he will find us in better spirits than he expects.' The general had already left Charleston and was on his way.

The Battle of Camden

In Which the 23rd Cover Themselves With Glory

The scene around the American bivouacs at Rugeley's Mill on 13 August 1780 was one of nervous anticipation. Thousands of troops had marched into that South Carolinian township earlier in the day, scattering the Tory militia, who had kept up some outposts there. Serjeant Major William Seymour, of the Delaware Regiment, summed up the mood of Horatio Gates's army as it anticipated its march on Camden: 'Confident . . . that we should drive the enemy, we being far superior to them in numbers.'

At the core of Gates's army was a division of 1,400 Continental troops, seven regiments from Maryland and one from Delaware. Their campaign had begun four months before at Morristown in Pennsylvania with orders to make haste for Charleston, in order to repel the British. They were seasoned regiments, quite the best division for such a task at General Washington's disposal. It was the Marylanders and Delaware men who had faced the 23rd at Long Island in 1776, or been part of Sullivan's division thrown back at Brandywine in 1777. Hard fighting and hard living had tempered them into something quite impressive. One British officer, a prisoner of the Americans in Pennsylvania, watched one of the Maryland brigades marching by shortly after it set off and recorded, 'They were 450 strong, had good clothing, were well armed, and showed more of the military in their appearance than I had ever conceived American troops had yet obtained.'

Some of the journey down south had been done by ship, but most of it by foot-slogging through baking Virginia and North Carolina's backcountry. Serjeant Major Seymour meticulously noted the marches in his journal: 843 miles to Rugeley's Mill. Towards the end, problems started.

As the Continental troops joined with Virginia men and thousands of militia from the Carolinas, food had run out. Gates blamed the local militia for 'devouring' the little fat of the land and admonished their commander, telling him, 'This is a mode of conducting war I am a stranger to — the whole should support and sustain the whole, or the parts will soon go to decay.' Gates sent off to Virginia, pleading for supplies, setting his sights also on the British magazines at Camden.

Cast in the role of pillagers of meagre Carolinian farms, the American soldiers returned hostile stares from the locals and convinced themselves there were loyalists everywhere. During the first two weeks of August the official ration had amounted to just half a pound of beef per man, 'and that so miserable poor', wrote the Delaware serjeant major, 'that scarce any mortal could make use of it. Living chiefly on green apples and peaches which rendered our situation truly miserable, being in a weak and sickly condition and surrounded on all sides by our enemies the Tories.'

This bad atmosphere helped starve Gates of information as well as rations. Even early in August, his picture of British dispositions was hopelessly wrong, believing that Cornwallis had left the state and forces at Camden were being run down. Gates pushed on, anxious to do battle.

On the same evening that the Americans reached Rugeley's Mill, Cornwallis had arrived in Camden, just eleven miles to the south. There the British had built a base with ample stores, protected by redoubts and a palisade of wooden stakes. The town had been established in 1733 as part of the early upland settlement and many of its citizens were hostile to the Crown forces. Even so, with 3,000 of them present, the locals exploited the opportunity to sell the product of their distillery and other supplies to the army.

When Cornwallis arrived it was the height of summer, a time considered by many as unsuitable for campaigning in those latitudes because of the epidemics it touched off. Some 800 of the troops at Camden were sick, stricken down by fluxes and fevers to which local people were often immune. In the township's military hospital as well as many private houses, soldiers endured their personal hell, festering with fever and flux.

Among those who had fallen ill that August was none other than the

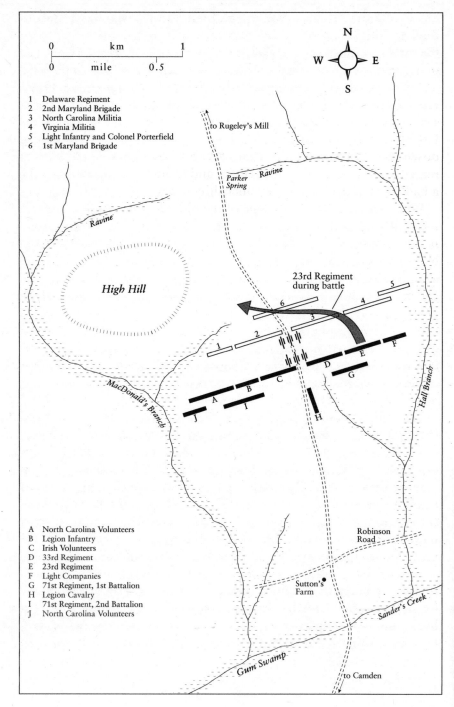

1 Delaware Regiment
2 2nd Maryland Brigade
3 North Carolina Militia
4 Virginia Militia
5 Light Infantry and Colonel Porterfield
6 1st Maryland Brigade

to Rugeley's Mill

Parker
Spring

Ravine

Ravine

High Hill

23rd Regiment
during battle

MacDonald's Branch

Hall Branch

A North Carolina Volunteers
B Legion Infantry
C Irish Volunteers
D 33rd Regiment
E 23rd Regiment
F Light Companies
G 71st Regiment, 1st Battalion
H Legion Cavalry
I 71st Regiment, 2nd Battalion
J North Carolina Volunteers

Robinson
Road

Sutton's
Farm

Sander's Creek

Gum Swamp

to Camden

23rd's major, Thomas Mecan. He had come through Lexington, Bunker Hill, Long Island, Brandywine and a dozen other affairs, but the forty-one-year-old Irishman, a tough customer, was finally faltering in his fight for life on that sweat-drenched bed. In the space of a couple of days Mecan burned up and died. One New York newspaper reported it thus: 'We feel great concern in communicating the death of a brave veteran officer, Major Thomas Mecan, of the Royal Welch Fusiliers; a violent fever carried him off.' Lieutenant Colonel Balfour, down in Charleston, wrote that Mecan's 'loss will be long felt and regretted in the regiment, his activity and exertions were too much for a bad constitution in this very unhealthy climate'.

With Mecan's death, only one of the older generation of officers remained. Frederick Mackenzie was last of the Minden leaders, but was far away in New York where, since the evacuation of Rhode Island, he had found his way on to General Clinton's staff. The command of the 23rd in the field therefore went to a younger generation.

Cornwallis was loath to remove Balfour from that city, regarding his presence there as essential for the efficient administration of army and province. He could not, in any case, travel upcountry before the anticipated engagement. Control in the field of the Royal Welch thus devolved upon a twenty-five-year-old captain named Forbes Champagne. Irish-born of Huguenot descent, Champagne's family was connected by marriage to an aristocrat who was willing to advance the young man's career. Balfour, who knew Champagne well from the time they had both spent in the 4th Foot, would have preferred somebody else, but at that moment, on 15 August, news had not yet reached the lieutenant colonel in Charleston that his major and second in command had died.

On the eve of battle, the 23rd was able to parade thirteen serjeants, eight drummers and 261 rank and file. There were three captains and six subalterns. Those officers combined the physical vigour of youth with considerable battle experience. Champagne's brother captains were both in their early twenties, but had served several campaigns.

Harry Calvert, still only sixteen years old, had acquired promotion to a lieutenancy and acting command of a company. Another lieutenant, Thomas Barretté, having none of Calvert's family money to back him, was older, twenty-four, one of ten children (also of Irish-Huguenot origins); he had been in the forces since the age of fourteen,

The battle of Camden

when he joined the marines. For each of Calvert's lucky turns of fate, Barretté might remember a disaster: his wife had died a few years earlier leaving him to maintain a son at school in England; resigning his commission in the marines for a captaincy in a loyalist regiment, he had been swindled by its colonel and left with no choice but to fight as a volunteer in the Guards light company in 1779, getting shot in the arm for his trouble. Barretté had exploited an old family connection to get recommended for a commission and considered himself deeply indebted to General Clinton for it. Sending money home for his son's upkeep, Barretté was barely able to live on his pay.

What that Irish lieutenant, Calvert and the other subalterns had in common was their willingness to perform their duty in this scorching corner of America, to lead their men from the front. Several of these young Fusilier officers had strong religious feeling, and there were also a few loyalist Americans among them. So the 23rd's cadre of officers serving in the field in their teens and twenties were fortified by strong beliefs. They were quite different from those disappointed middle-aged men who had celebrated St David around a festive board in Boston in March 1775, especially that dismal selection of them who had gone to such lengths to avoid serving in the field.

With such a shortage of officers, arrangements were reached that might have caused George III to splutter into his Bath water if he had ever found out about them. Intelligent young serjeants like Roger Lamb could play the part of officers, so when the 23rd marched out of Camden, he would be taking that honourable but dangerous post as Mecan had done at Minden, carrying one of the regiment's two colours. The wise old head of Adjutant George Watson, in his early forties, was there to maintain discipline and administer the regiment.

Despite the sickness, the temperature and the loss of their major, the Welch Fusiliers were ready to take to the field with alacrity – morale was high. Credit for this belonged to two men outside the regiment, as well as all those active officers and serjeants within it. General Cornwallis, from the moment he arrived in Camden, infused the army with what Lieutenant Calvert called 'that decision and promptitude which marks his military character'. The other vital character was James Webster, lieutenant colonel of Cornwallis's own regiment, the 33rd, and commander of the brigade formed by uniting that corps with the 23rd.

Webster, the son of an influential Edinburgh theologian, an elder in the Church of Scotland, was a professional soldier of unstinting energy and zeal for the service. Many officers had marvelled at Webster's bravery in battle. His religious faith and occasionally maudlin personality left him apparently indifferent to death. After suffering the hardships of campaigning in Germany during the Seven Years War, Webster told his cousin, the diarist James Boswell, 'Men are in that way rendered desperate; and I wished for an action, either to get out of the world altogether or to get a little rest after it.' It can easily be imagined that Webster's 'wish for an action' was just as great that 15 August in Camden.

Cornwallis had invested enormous energy and considerable sums of his own money turning the 33rd into an elite regiment. Years before it was sent to America, he had trained it in light infantry tactics of his own devising. The realisation of Cornwallis's grand designs involved Webster as master builder. The Scotsman's desire to gratify his patron was such that one captain of the 33rd noted bitterly, '[Webster] wishes to make his Lordship believe there is not an officer in the regiment but himself and that he is the only man of merit.'

In America during the campaigns of 1776 and 1777, Cornwallis had employed the 33rd as a full regiment of light infantry, taking them with his flank battalions on numerous operations. Even Henry Clinton had acknowledged admiringly this patronage in command, telling the earl, 'Wherever you are I shall naturally expect to find them [the 33rd].' Cornwallis, then, was the type of committed colonel that the 23rd lacked in William Howe, and Webster the excellent executive officer that circumstances had denied them for so long. Serjeant Roger Lamb had seen the 33rd serving in Ireland and noted a little enviously, 'I never witnessed any regiment that excelled it in discipline and military appearance.'

It might be imagined that finding themselves thrown together with a model regiment such as the 33rd, under the eye of its impassioned leaders, the Welch Fusiliers might resent it, assuming that they would come second in all matters. This did not happen. Quite the contrary, for the spirit of emulation and competition possessed the Fusiliers and, as Serjeant Lamb wrote, 'Both regiments were well united together, and furnished an example for cleanliness, martial spirit, and good behaviour.' So well did they mix that the two understrength corps that formed Webster's 'brigade' might have been assumed to be a single regiment of two wings or halves.

Webster's brigade was guaranteed a key role, as the army prepared to quit Camden, for its 530 troops were the principal redcoat force out of Cornwallis's 2,000 or so troops. Two battalions of the 71st, Fraser's Highlanders, were there too, but their total strength was less than that of the Welch Fusiliers. The British general would have no choice but to put loyalist American regiments into his battle line, namely the Royal North Carolina Regiment, as well as some North Carolina militia, corps made up mainly of Scottish refugees from that state, and the Volunteers of Ireland. As Cornwallis prepared for the fight, these American Tories were brigaded under Lord Rawdon, with Tarleton and his Legion ready to act as advanced guard or, once action was joined, the earl's reserve. They set off on the evening of 15 August.

A few hours before Cornwallis's departure, during the afternoon, Major General Gates had summoned his commanders into the big barn at Rugeley's Mill. They filed in; Brigadier General Stevens, commander of a brigade of Virginia troops that had joined two days before; Major General Caswell, who led the North Carolina militia; Major General Baron Johann de Kalb, commanding the Continental Division (Bavarian-born, he had long service in the French army, joining Washington as a volunteer), and several other officers of note, leaders of various detachments of light troops. The commander of the Southern Department outlined his plans. The army would march at 10 p.m., making its way to a position 5 miles south that had already been reconnoitred. It was a plateau on some sandy uplands, overlooking Sander's Creek. The stream was too deep to be forded, and if the enemy were engaged after they crossed the causeway over the creek (and swamp that surrounded the waterway), they would have to fight with this obstacle to their rear.

Other aspects of Gates's plan also showed that he had considered the forthcoming operation carefully. Detailed orders were given for flanking parties of light troops to be pushed out 200 yards on each side of the main column as it took the road south that night. Gates had also given some thought to the dangers of taking raw militia into battle, and he issued a stern warning that any man who opened fire without orders would be executed on the spot.

There were some shortcomings in Gates's plan, but it is only worth mentioning here the most alimentary. The general had already ordered the men to be served a special meal, rounded off with sweet molasses and dumplings. Even before they marched that night, many men were seized with stomach cramps, dozens falling out of their columns to drop their breeches by the roadside. Troubled by this and countless minor obstacles, the Americans trudged off south into the darkness, little knowing that Cornwallis had departed Camden at almost exactly the same time, heading north up the same route.

It was in the first minutes of 16 August that two forces spotted one another. 'The moon was full and shone beautifully,' wrote an American officer, 'not a breath of air was stirring, nor a cloud to be seen.' The American Scouts were moving down the gentle slope towards Sander's Creek, a party of light infantry on the left of the road, sixty cavalry of Colonel Armand's Legion on the road itself and some Virginian infantry on the right under Colonel Charles Porterfield, an officer who had made his reputation as a commander of light troops and this night was in overall charge of Gates's advance guard.

The British, cavalry and infantry of Tarleton's Legion, were already across the creek and had passed Sutton's House, allowing them to debouch on both sides of the road. The landscape they moved across was a sandy incline dotted with pine trees. Much of the area close to the road had no undergrowth – it had been grazed away by cows – but further out, several hundred yards away, thicker vegetation could be glimpsed.

Colonel Armand's scouts, riding ahead of their troop, were the first to see the British and instantly fired a pistol shot, rending the night air. Moments later, Armand received a verbal report, galloped over to Colonel Porterfield and told him in an audible whisper, 'There is the enemy sir – I must charge him!' Porterfield kept his reply to the point: 'By all means sir.' But during the interval between pistol shot and conversation, Lieutenant Colonel Tarleton had formed his own resolution, ordering his horsemen to charge:

Tarleton . . . and his men came on at the top of his speed, every officer and soldier with the yell of an Indian savage – at every leap their horses took, crying out, 'charge, charge, charge' so that their own voices and the echoes resounded in every direction through the pine forest.

Porterfield, seeing the British horse coming up the road, ordered his infantry to turn to face that route, and as the Legion galloped past, ambushed them with a volley. The Legion went swiftly to the right about, cantering back to their supports. Each side now engaged several hundred men in the contest, with crackling musketry fire from soldiers trotting forward, using the trees for cover. After some minutes of this fusillade, Porterfield was hit in the left leg, shattering the bone, and he slumped forward on his horse. Moments later, another burst of fire, from some British just 30 yards away, brought down Porterfield's mount.

It did not take long for the Legion to send the Americans to flight, the light troops falling back to Gates's main body several hundred yards to the rear. The American general was close to his intended fighting position in any case, but the British, crucially, were across Sander's Creek and deploying their whole army for battle in the moonlight of the early hours. One officer of the Volunteers of Ireland described their situation: 'Day was near three hours off and all the time we remained among the dead and dying, in anxious suspense for the morning.'

When dawn came, it revealed a panorama of military force, the Americans having arrayed their armies in battle order on the grazing lands above Sander's Creek, the British spaced out in front, but their battalions still in column rather than line of battle. 'We saw at a few yards distance our enemy drawn up in very good order,' wrote Serjeant Lamb. There was no question of the British avoiding battle at this stage against Gates's superior numbers; they were too close to break contact and would have to defile along the causeway across Gum Swamp (the soft ground around the creek) to their rear. Cornwallis, an aggressive general in any case, had no such intention.

As for Gates, the shock of finding his intelligence was at fault and a British army in front led him to call a council of war in the early morning. 'Gentlemen, what is to be done?' he asked his disconcerted subordinates. After an awkward silence, Brigadier General Stevens piped up, 'Is it not too late now to do anything but fight?' Of course he was right, because any force that turned its back towards characters like Cornwallis, Webster or Tarleton would simply have invited annihilation.

Major General Gates placed Caswell's great horde of North Carolina militia to the left of the road, Stevens's Virginians out beyond them, with some Virginia light infantry and Armand's horsemen on the far wing. About 350 yards out from the road, the ground dipped down and was obstructed with thick undergrowth. Both sides assumed this to be the start of a swamp, an impassable area that would anchor their flank. On the (American) right of the road, space was more limited for deployment; a thick wood with dense undergrowth and sloping ground also bounded this area. Here, Gates positioned the 2nd Maryland Brigade, with the Delaware Regiment attached. Two other elements of his deployment were worthy of note: a battery of eight artillery pieces (half of them 6-pounders and half lighter pieces) were placed in the centre, across the road itself, on the most obvious route of advance, and behind them, as a reserve, was the 1st Maryland Brigade of Continental troops.

Cornwallis's deployment was quite similar. His right (i.e., opposite the militia) consisted of Webster's brigade, with the 33rd extending from the road, the 23rd to their right and a small corps of about 150 light infantry furthest out, opposite the enemy light troops. The British left was under Rawdon, with the Volunteers of Ireland closest to the road, then Tarleton's Legion infantry and a North Carolina Tory regiment. Cornwallis's reserve, kept on or close to the road, was Tarleton's cavalry and the two battalions of 71st Highlanders.

When the American artillery spotted some redcoated soldiers moving into line about 200 yards in front of them, they shattered the early morning quiet with cannon shot. 'We immediately began the attack with great vigour,' wrote Lamb, 'and in a few minutes the action became general along the whole line.' Webster marched his regiments forward briskly, while the enemy, seeing the attack on this flank, sent some sharp shooters to open up on them.

The 23rd extended 'two deep with open files so as occupy as great a front as possible'. Their enemy, the North Carolina and Virginia militia, by contrast, were, due to their much greater numbers, packed four deep and shoulder to shoulder in the same space. But the militia were full of trepidation, which increased as they saw their first sporadic firing having no effect on the advancing British. Garret Watts, a North Carolina militiaman, later recalled, 'I believe my gun was the first fired, notwithstanding the orders, for we were close to the enemy, who appeared to move in contempt of us.'

As if to emphasise that 'contempt', the Welch Fusiliers gave three cheers as they came on. Militiaman Watts's comrades followed his fire with a spluttering discharge of musketry along the line, although many did not fire at all. It knocked down a handful of Fusiliers, but the regiment kept coming. The opposing forces, just 40 or 50 yards apart, could look into one another's faces. The Fusiliers stopped, presented their loaded muskets and let fly a great crashing volley, 'and immediately rushed in upon them with our bayonets before they could load a second time'. Colonel Otho Williams, one of Gates's staff who had gone to this flank, saw the redcoat attack and paid tribute to its effectiveness: 'The impetuosity with which they advanced, firing and huzzaing, threw the whole body of the militia into such a panic that they in general threw down their loaded arms and fled, in the utmost consternation.'

Watts described it: 'I confess I was amongst the first that fled. The cause of that I cannot tell, except that everyone I saw was about to do the same. It was instantaneous. There was no effort to rally, no encouragement to fight.' Marching deliberately into the ground vacated by this stampede, the Fusiliers saw the backs of their enemy disappearing into the scrub to their right and front, 'lightening themselves with the loss of their arms and packs which they threw away as they ran along'.

To the 23rd's left, the 33rd had encountered something quite different. Their march was taking them, or at least the left wing of their regiment, towards the mouths of the American artillery. The Americans fired salvo after salvo, initially grape shot, but then, as the redcoats got really near, canister or case-shot spewing tins of musket balls in to the 33rd's ranks. These discharges scythed down dozens of men, the hellish scene of wounding and death being completed by great billows of black smoke from the cannon that hung in the still morning air.

The American artillery similarly found the right of Rawdon's Volunteers of Ireland to be within canister range and served them up the same hot stuff, one of their officers recording grimly, 'The enemy surpassed us in artillery, and threw in horrid showers of grape.' Rawdon's Volunteers and the Royal North Carolina Regiment were soon coming under heavy musket fire too, from the 2nd Maryland Brigade to their front. The Continentals advanced, sending the loyalists falling back. Serjeant Major Seymour of the Delawares described how they went on 'with great alacrity and uncommon bravery making great havoc among them insomuch that the enemy gave way'. This setback on the British left, combined with Webster's success on the right, meant the whole line began to pivot.

Cornwallis, seeing the danger, rode into the smoke. One of the Volunteers of Ireland officers spotted him: 'Our regiment was amazingly incited by Lord Cornwallis, who came up to them with great coolness, in the midst of a heavier fire than the oldest soldier remembers and called out "Volunteers of Ireland, you are fine fellows! Charge the rascals – by heaven you behave nobly!" '

With the left stabilised and resuming its advance, Colonel Webster turned his attention to the Continental brigades whose right had been exposed by the militia's flight. He wheeled the 23rd, who initially came up against a remnant of the North Carolina militia under Brigadier General Gregory that had been formed in a last attempt to protect the American's hanging flank. These men were swiftly given a volley and the bayonet, Serjeant Lamb noting that Gregory was captured with two stab wounds, 'and many of his brigade who were made prisoner had no wound except from bayonets'.

The 23rd pushed on, by this point almost at right angles to Rawdon's Brigade; they had become Cornwallis's hammer moving to smash de Kalb's Continentals. Initially, the 1st Maryland Brigade formed to face Webster, at right angles to the 2nd, who were still engaged with Rawdon. But the 1st Brigade gave way after being charged by Webster's men, who were flushed with success. As a result, the 2nd Maryland Brigade were herded back and a little to their right, into thicker woods on somewhat higher than their original position. They were being shot at from the front, then the volleys began from their left, then word began flying that some of Webster's men were getting to their rear. Lieutenant Barretté of the 23rd evaluated the Americans' crisis well enough through the smoke and trees. Knowing that any commander dreaded having an enemy fall on his flank, because an infantry line could not turn quickly enough to face the new threat, the Fusilier officer observed that the Continentals 'finding themselves in a situation ever to be guarded against in any disposition of war . . . readily broke'.

Many of the Marylanders were now running back into the trees, trying to escape the completion of the British encirclement. Cornwallis unleashed Tarleton's cavalry to seal their fate. 'We were obliged to retire,' wrote Serjeant Major Seymour, 'and left the enemy master of the field, the enemy's horse making great slaughter among our men as they retreated.' Some of the Marylanders continued to fight on in groups in the woods, including one that formed around their general, Baron de Kalb. The redcoats put the bayonet to those who would not surrender, and the cornered general received several such thrusts, crumpling to the ground bleeding profusely. He was captured but would die shortly after the battle.

In little more than an hour of fighting, Gates's army, around twice the size of Cornwallis's, had been completely defeated, with its remnants dispersed. Several veteran regiments of Continental infantry were among the broken force. All of the American cannon were taken too. Colonel Williams noted bitterly, 'Not even a company escaped in good order – everyone escaped as he could.'

The 23rd moved that day beyond the abandoned train of enemy wagons. They tramped through the looted American baggage and were placed in a defensive line, sending out their pickets. They bivouacked that night just beyond the battlefield, Fusiliers swapping tales of the extraordinary day they had just survived.

Four years before, at Long Island, the 23rd had been part of Brigadier James Grant's attack, fighting their way with some difficulty through an American force half their size (composed largely of Maryland and Delaware troops); at Camden the equation was reversed. A British army, far inland, had beaten a larger American enemy, a transformation made possible by having experienced troops, new tactics, and, above all, superior leadership. The soldiers at Camden had just given the rebels the drubbing some had longed for years to administer, and were not slow to recognise what had made it possible.

Serjeant Lamb praised Captain Champagne, as acting commanding officer, for 'perfect intrepidity and valour', and Colonel Webster, whose manoeuvre onto the enemy flank had gained the day, was lauded as 'cool, determined, vigilant, and active'. Lieutenant Barretté felt the results showed 'what a British army can do when they undertake [a task] with alacrity and have confidence in their officers'.

As for Major General Gates, his reputation was ruined. The loss of a battle might have been forgiven, but he had quit the field when he saw the militia on his left flank broken, leaving the Continental troops to their fate. He set spurs to horse and did not stop until he reached Charlotte, 60 miles to the north, that evening. 'Was there ever an instance of a general running away as Gates has done from his whole army? And was there ever so precipitous a flight?' asked Alexander Hamilton, one of Washington's inner circle. 'It does admirable credit to the activity of a man at his time of life. But it disgraces the general and the soldier.'

The losses taken by the 23rd on 16 August were mercifully light – just six men killed and eighteen wounded. The 33rd by contrast, standing under withering American fire, had eighteen killed and eighty-one wounded. The casualties for Cornwallis's army as a whole were sixty-eight killed and 238 wounded. This was a significant figure as a proportion of those who took part, but the earl's men were phlegmatic about losses taken when fighting aggressively so it did not dent the general's popularity in the days after the battle. In any case, the accounting for the victory of Camden looked a little better after 18 August, when Tarleton surprised Colonel Sumpter at Fishing Creek, re-capturing a hundred British prisoners who had been taken in an action shortly before the main battle. As for the Americans, 650 Continentals were killed or captured, and about a hundred militia suffered the same fate. One British officer at New York, reading of Camden, enthused that it was 'the handsomest and most complete affair that has been done in this war'. Cornwallis himself, in his victory dispatch to Lord Germain, wrote that 'the behaviour of His Majesty's troops in general was beyond all praise – it did honour to themselves and their country'.

During the dog days of August, Lieutenant Colonel Balfour measured his new responsibilities as Commandant of Charleston, and surveyed the surroundings. Headquarters was on King Street, a fine three-storey building possessed of an attic in which the owner had hidden her daughters during General Clinton's residence there. Being Patriots, they had gone upcountry by the time Balfour was at work. King Street was a couple of blocks removed from the bustle and stink of the port, a comparatively tranquil haven for the merchant elite who had built fabulous mansions on this and several other thoroughfares. For many of these dynasties, the town residences were supplemented by plantation homes on the estates that produced their wealth.

The oligarchs of Charleston had divided when the city fell. Some dozens of Whigs or Patriots had been deported by Cornwallis, sent to a form of open arrest at the British base of St Augustin. Others had disappeared into the backcountry. Many families stayed though, and for them the opulent lifestyle – decadent even – for which the city was known continued. There was still money to be made, even if trade with the Caribbean or England was depressed and interrupted by enemy shipping.

Balfour was briefed about Camden by Captain Ross, Cornwallis's aide-de-camp, who passed through Charleston with the general's dis-patches. Having given Ross this task, the earl would get his favourite to the top of the queue for promotion to major, just as Howe had done with Balfour in 1776. Balfour, seeing his chance to ingratiate himself further with his new patron, suggested to Cornwallis that Mecan's death presented an opportunity to promote Ross to the 23rd's vacant majority. What could be better – this way their fortunes could be bound even more closely? Cornwallis though proved the more subtle player of the army patronage business and politely rejected Balfour's suggestion, saying, 'I don't think it would be right for me to meddle.' The decision would have to be made by the powers in London.

This left Balfour with the task of finding another man to take the Welch Fusiliers' majority, for he had been promised by Cornwallis that he could continue to control promotions in his regiment, even as they marched far from Charleston. Balfour chose that Scottish veteran Frederick Mackenzie. Richard Temple, who had spent the war recruiting at home, complained loudly, but there was nothing he could do, for it was the King's desire that those serving in America take precedence. Mackenzie thus reaped the reward for his long years on that Continent. Somehow he scraped together the money, for he had enjoyed several years on staff pay (roughly doubling his salary) and may, like many of the Scots climbing the ranks, have borrowed from friends and relatives.

Mackenzie, however, was tied to his staff duties in New York, just as Balfour was to Charleston, which meant that the 23rd would have to soldier on with a captain in command. Balfour did not want it to be Champagne, instead summoning Thomas Peter, commander of the 23rd Grenadier Company down from New York. Peter, another zealous officer in his early twenties, a Scot to boot, had been in the 23rd for more than two years but had been present since the beginning of the American war in other regiments. He had seen much hard service in the 2nd Grenadier Battalion during the battles of 1776 and 1777, being wounded at Brandywine. Balfour told General Clinton that Peter was 'an attentive officer'.

In the days and weeks that followed Camden, Balfour was sanguine about whether lasting good would come from the victory. Some of the Continental prisoners were re-taken by Colonel Francis Marion's partisan party even as they were being marched down to Charleston. Marion, who became known as the Swamp Fox, played a similar role disrupting the King's authority on the coastal plain to that Sumpter managed in the piedmont.

After his victory at Camden, Cornwallis harboured ideas of pushing into North Carolina in order to begin the conquest of that state. There were many obstacles to such a step though. As August became September, the illnesses that had afflicted the army at Camden worsened. Cornwallis moved Webster's Brigade and Tarleton's British Legion north, closer to his next target, but explained to Balfour, 'I find the ague and the fever all over this country, full as much as at Camden, they say go 40 or 50 miles farther and you will be healthy. It was the same language before we left Camden, there is no trusting such dangerous experiments.' Among those stricken down by fever was Lieutenant Colonel Tarleton himself, and whatever that officer's lack of caution or compassion, he was essential to the army's advanced guard. Indeed the general reflected that 'the whole of the men are very different when Tarleton is present or absent'.

In addition to the sickness in his army, which tended to make him wait until the cooler winter months, Cornwallis would need to build up supplies before launching his next advance. The existence of enemy partisan bands meanwhile would complicate the sending of recruits and stores upcountry, one of Balfour's principal tasks. The character of clashes between Tory detachments and these Patriot groups became increasingly desperate and brutal, with the latter in particular using murder and intimidation to neutralise their enemies.

Balfour was worried by the growing rural violence, but adjusted his message according to the person with whom he was communicating. Being Commandant at Charleston required him to be in regular contact with General Henry Clinton at New York, an onerous duty given their mutual antipathy, but one which Balfour had to conduct with professional decorum. Out of loyalty to General Cornwallis, furthermore, Balfour had to trumpet the earl's achievements, writing to Clinton some weeks after Camden that it had 'produced a very great change . . . in affairs here'. This chimed with Cornwallis's message to London, in his Camden dispatch, that, as a result of the victory 'the internal commotions and insurrections in the province will now subside'. In fact, Balfour knew exactly what to expect. Reports of raids and Tory setbacks simply confirmed in him the view expressed in a private letter to a friend, that 'the rebels, according to custom, have managed to collect again, and make many very serious incursions into this province'.

Colonel Charles O'Hara, a Guards officer of considerable American experience who by the summer of 1780 was on his way back from

England and would soon be serving under Cornwallis, took an even stronger line. He felt the victories of Charleston and Camden had revived 'the old fatal delusion' among the army's political masters: that giving the enemy one more good hiding would stoke an unstoppable loyalist revival. O'Hara noted that 'whenever a rebel army is said to have been cut to pieces, it would be more consonant with the truth to say that they have been dispersed, determined to join again at the first favourable opportunity'. O'Hara, it must be owned, was one of those officers tied to Whiggish high society in England, who habitually questioned the competence of the King's Ministry. Nevertheless he and Balfour were in possession of the essential truth that the British army's victories in South Carolina were all very well but that the enemy, in the words of the general that Washington would send to replace Gates, would 'fight, get beat, rise, and fight again'.

During September and early October, Balfour had to deal with some fruits of victory, namely what to do with the prisoners taken at Camden and Charleston. He realised that if he took them out of prison camps and sent them aboard ships in the harbour, he could free an entire redcoat regiment for service in the countryside. This he did, following an example of the imprisonment of Tory sympathisers in that city before it fell or of the British practice in New York. Even so, the results, in terms of horrendous sickness and death among the prisoners, might have been predicted.

On 7 October British plans for the subjugation of the Carolinas received their first serious check. It happened to the north, on the borders of the two states at King's Mountain. Major Ferguson had gone into the country, with a force of Tory militia, challenging his enemy to fight. This they did with great vigour, defeating and killing the Scottish officer, capturing most of his 1,000 men and hanging nine of them from trees after summary proceedings. This disaster validated Balfour's earlier gloomy assessments about the quality of Tory militia, and the folly of Ferguson's work. Hearing of the debacle, Balfour did not stoop in his letters, private or public, to a tone of 'I told you so.' Instead the lieutenant colonel sympathised for the loss of a dedicated officer and understood that the event would give fresh vigour to Whigs across the Carolinas, cowing the loyalists correspondingly. He worried too about the wisdom of pressing north.

The defeat caused Cornwallis to abandon his first push into North Carolina. Instead he brought his main army back to Winnsborough, a plantation around twenty-five miles north-west of Camden, in order to rest while he completed the build-up of supplies required for a fresh advance. Whatever was in that Camden dispatch, he had evidently grasped that the enemy would recover and re-organise, bringing fresh pressure to bear as soon as it could. Cornwallis was determined not to be at the mercy of events but to master them. This aggressive spirit earned the general great respect in his army, which was just as well, for as soon as he received the recruits, clothing and supplies that he needed, Cornwallis would call upon them to give their all in the new campaign.

Into North Carolina

Or Balfour Delivers the Goods

The scene about the roadside in Landsford, a small upcountry trading post on the Catawba River, was bustling and purposeful that early morning, 22 October 1780. The army had abandoned its march into North Carolina following Ferguson's defeat at King's Mountain and was trying to find a good place to recover itself. Dozens of sick men were that day draped on to wagons or set off on unsteady feet towards Camden. They were the visible, febrile consequence of weeks of hard marching and scanty diet.

There were intermittent fevers, putrid fevers, fluxes so bad that the men were passing blood, and running sores that would not heal. Even many of those who declared themselves fit to send the Whigs to the devil looked little more than skin and bone.

Cornwallis decided to pack off the sick, but they would need a strong escort if they were to get through, so the 7th, the English Fusiliers, were detached for the purpose. The general had moved back from Charlotte, a town on the North Carolina border where he found the locals 'the most rebellious and inveterate that I have met with in this country'. This hostility had produced real difficulties in feeding the men, notwithstanding that by October all of the corn was usually harvested, and the mills working hard to make grist.

During foraging expeditions about Charlotte small parties of British troops frequently came under attack from the locals. In one action, Lieutenant Stephen Guyon of the 23rd was highly commended for holding out at Polk's Mill, two miles from the town. Guyon and a small party of Fusiliers had thrown themselves into a strong-point, using firing slits to engage scores of enemy militia who tried to storm the place. Guyon was another of the teenage subalterns who had sailed to America in 1779 with Calvert, the two youngsters becoming firm friends on the voyage.

Among the soldiers enfeebled by hunger as well as hard service, the sick rate had climbed. Even Cornwallis fell ill. This had caused anxiety in his army, but by the time the wagons were sent off on the 22nd, the general was recovering. Many of the officers involved in operations felt that service in the Carolinas would prove as deadly to their regiments as the Caribbean, where a couple of seasons' fighting were enough to finish off many a toughened corps, the pallid wrecks being sent home to England to recruit. Lieutenant Colonel Balfour predicted that 'a frontier war such as we have, and must expect to continue, will very soon in these latitudes make white flesh and blood very rare'.

Cornwallis was sufficiently worried by the withering of some of his regiments at a time when more hard fighting was in prospect that he asked for reinforcements. On the evening the sick were packed off, the general told his officers in their encampment that a large corps had been embarked from New York under Major General Alexander Leslie and was on its way to co-operate with them. His initial idea was that Leslie might go to the Cape Fear River, on the North Carolina coast, and from there inland a short way to Cross Creeks, a loyalist settlement. But Cornwallis was uncertain about how his own force might co-operate with Leslie or whether this should involve shifting the war closer to the sea, exposing such places as Camden or Ninety Six to attack if he left. His strategy for carrying the war into North Carolina had not, in late October, crystallised, but beset by so many difficulties, trying to raise his men's morale, he chose to let the cat out of the bag that more redcoats might be on their way.

The army marched almost 50 miles after hearing this news, arriving one week later at the plantation of Winnsborough. Lieutenant Calvert had been wondering, as daydreaming men on the march do, what comforts might lie at the end of their exertions. Getting there, he noted disappointedly in his journal, that this settlement 'consists of two hovels'. Quite quickly, though, the troops found the surrounding lands a more benign environment for their foraging expeditions than had been the case further north. 'We frequently sent out twenty and thirty miles and once upwards of forty for forage', wrote Calvert, 'without any Covering Party and never were the least molested by the enemy.'

Food at least could be found in these quarters, but Cornwallis knew he must try to reduce the sickness, bring up some recruits for his regiments that had arrived in Charleston, get new uniforms (for the seasons were turning, and the men's clothes were tattered), replenish stocks of rum, ammunition and all sorts. In short, the army would need several weeks of rest and attention to matters of supply before it would be fit to campaign again.

These problems were all multiplied by the activities of the Swamp Fox and other partisans of his ilk, particularly on the road from Charleston to Camden. Logistics were a weak suit with Cornwallis, who had come to rely largely on Balfour and the civilian commissaries. The wagons at his disposal that moved the sick down to Camden, for example, were driven by men from Ninety Six pressed into service while Balfour was in charge there. With raiding parties frequently attacking the route up from the coast, it became doubtful whether the small number of vehicles could manage the task or a large escort be assembled to protect them. Balfour, writing to a friend near the end of October, stated, 'I have not heard from Lord Cornwallis indeed the communication is cut off, and in sending a letter safe you must send a packet with five hundred men at least as a guard.' This last was an exaggeration, but the Commandant of Charleston understood the precariousness of this supply chain well enough to do something about it.

Early in November, Balfour directed a series of operations to secure the lower part of the Santee River. He was going to move General Cornwallis's supplies on the first part of their journey upcountry by water. The scarce wagons could then be used to shuttle materiel to the magazines at Camden and to Winnsborough. It was his need to free the 64th Regiment for use in these operations that caused Balfour to move American prisoners on to ships in Charleston harbour. Pushing the 64th inland produced a number of skirmishes with the enemy's raiding parties, but soon also the desired effect in opening communications to Camden.

With supplies rolling in, Cornwallis was effusive in his gratitude, writing to Balfour: 'No sooner do I find myself under difficulties to accomplish any very important object than I am relieved by finding that you have already done it for me. You will spoil me from acting with any other person.' Not only were stocks being replenished by mid-November, but the milder weather and plentiful food were restoring the army: 'Our troops get healthier every day, are in high spirits and as soon as they have got their warm clothing will be fit for any thing.'

Those steeped in the ways of military service will be reassured to learn that the men of the Royal Welch Fusiliers had already reaped dividends from having their commanding officer in charge of the port and supply matters. While the 33rd and 71st moped about in their tattered jackets, the 23rd had received their new uniforms some weeks earlier. Supplies of soap and medicines to the regiment had also been expedited. These contributed to high morale and, even during the bad days of October, the proportion of the 23rd that had fallen sick was notably lower than in other regiments. During these days after Camden, the 23rd's surgeon left to work in the General Hospital in Charleston and Serjeant Lamb did temporary duty in charge of the sick. Even so, the Fusiliers maintained fine morale and turnout.

Watching the 23rd turn out in formation to begin the day, early on 18 November, Cornwallis was deeply impressed. He knew how much Balfour would like to read about it, so set pen to paper, averring, 'I saw this morning the parade of the R[oyal]. W[elch]. Fuziliers and I assure you they are in great order and the most willing and good humoured people in all hardships.'

Balfour, though, was uneasy that when his regiment and the rest at Winnsborough were ready to go, they would be hurled northward once more, while South Carolina sank into complete disorder. Late in October he had still been reluctant to share these thoughts fully with Cornwallis, telling a friend that his views would make 'an unpleasant message, I by no means wish to deliver, as I am not ordered so to do'. But the earl *had* asked Balfour for military advice on previous occasions, and by early in November the number of enemy parties were causing such mayhem across the state that the wily Scot felt he must place the exigencies of the service ahead of his desire to please his great new patron. Balfour wrote to Cornwallis with a lucid *tour d'horizon* of the war in the Carolinas, and urged caution upon the general. The lieutenant colonel began by justifying his own decision not to give such potentially unwelcome advice sooner:

The most earnest desire for a forward movement, and an offensive war, prevented my mentioning any sort of obstructions, being most earnestly anxious that your operations should not be retarded by any objections of mine, unless I saw, and felt, difficulty too obvious to be overlooked for the general safety – and your success. The general appearance of things at present is exactly that . . . a general distrust, and a kind of calm to observe what side is to preponderate, the friends of government, anxious to palliate the faults of the rebels, and willing to make as much of their own equivocal merit, as possible.

The 'desire for forward movement' had already produced the defeat at King's Mountain, so Balfour warned Cornwallis that 'in attempting to gain two provinces, one, if not both, might have been lost'. With the 'friends of the government' increasingly moving to a position of neutrality, any thought the general might have about leaving South Carolina would have to be tempered by the possibility of disaster in that state. It would not be possible to leave the royal militia to defend backcountry, for Balfour judged 'I have now totally given up that they can be of use so far as being in arms for us.' Balfour may have despised General Clinton, but had that general been at Winnsborough instead of New York in mid-November, he would probably have given Cornwallis exactly the same advice. The first imperative was for consolidation in South Carolina. Attempts that autumn to eliminate the partisan bands of Marion and Sumpter had failed.

There was much for Cornwallis to reflect upon in this letter, and he realised that he should have to meet Balfour in order to discuss the forthcoming campaign. The earl's particular friend and usual partner in such discussions, Captain Ross, was not yet returned from presenting the Camden dispatches, so the general would make do with an older Scotsman. Conversations of such a delicate nature were best conducted face to face, but the two men were 130 miles apart, the roads poor and infested with enemy banditti. The general would not be able to travel even to Camden for the meeting, so he suggested Balfour come up to Winnsborough.

During the latter part of November and early December, Balfour expedited the dispatch upcountry of much of what Cornwallis needed to re-fit his army. Some recruits arrived – just twenty for the 23rd but several times this number for the 33rd who needed a large addition after their Camden casualties. New uniforms as well as supplies of food and rum were also sent up. Cornwallis was full of gratitude for these efforts, but even in late November was indicating to Balfour: 'We must begin our operations by driving Gates from the frontier, which the first forward movement will instantly effect.' The general intended to campaign with his customary aggression.

Not long after receiving this letter, Balfour was delighted to report the arrival of a convoy of forty-five sail in Charleston. There had been worries that they had been dispersed or wrecked by storms. On 15 December, several thousand troops started to disembark, including the long promised reinforcement under Leslie: the Brigade of Guards, 700 troops, formed the pick, but there was also a company of Hessian jaegers, a Hessian infantry regiment, two newly raised redcoat regiments and elements of some other corps. Balfour considered the two green British corps unfit for anything but garrison duties. All of the reinforcements had been dispatched with the usual chaotic organisation, arriving without ammunition. Balfour instantly whistled up 20,000 rounds for those troops that would march upcountry.

With the arrival of so many men, Balfour realised that his opportunity had come to travel up to see Cornwallis. While the Guards and others prepared themselves to march, he set out on the journey north with hundreds of recruits and convalescents. Captain Thomas Peter, the officer who would lead the 23rd in 1781, had arrived in Charleston with the convoy, and went up with his commanding officer.

Balfour arrived in Winnsborough on the evening of 20 December, and spent a couple of days there. He dined with the officers of the 23rd and with Lord Cornwallis, briefing the general on Leslie's reinforcement and the plans for their movement from Charleston. Whatever representations the commandant of Charleston may have made about the rural insurrection in South Carolina, it was not ultimately the business of lieutenant colonels to dictate strategy to lieutenant generals. Balfour could not challenge Cornwallis's desire to take the fight to the enemy lurking in North Carolina, but he could ensure that the poorer regiments of redcoats recently arrived could be used to reinforce the battle against enemy partisans in his own province. The lieutenant colonel left Winnsborough satisfied that he had been true to his professional convictions about the situation in South Carolina but had not endangered his relationship with his patron. That noble general, on the contrary, had shown him every mark of favour at his table. Returned to Charleston on 29 December, Balfour wrote to the general, 'I got back last night with my heart so strongly impressed with all your goodness to me that believe me, no time can ever erase [it].'

The army at Winnsborough awaited the arrival of Leslie, while celebrating the New Year in the modest manner that their rude surroundings would allow. The arrival of a new general on the

American side would soon upset Cornwallis's plans. Gates had been replaced as the commander of the Southern Department of the Continental Army. The new man had a better brain and a harder conscience. It would be against him that Earl Cornwallis would have to match wits in the weeks ahead.

Major General Nathaniel Greene took command of the remnants of Gates's army on 2 December 1780. Greene, a strapping Rhode Islander, had many advantages over his predecessor: he was fourteen years younger; he enjoyed the confidence of George Washington; as a self-taught soldier he was both more thorough and creative in his methods. The new commander arrived in Charlotte with a mixed reputation – while nobody could doubt his commitment to the revolutionary cause, some rivals blamed him for complicity in the fall of Fort Washington in 1776 and cupidity during his time as the army's quartermaster general.

Surveying the wrecks of Gates's army, Greene's reports painted a sorry picture. There were about 1,500 Continentals, most of them the remnants of de Kalb's division mauled at Camden. While the Mary-landers and Delawares were excellent soldiers, they were suffering from the same agues and shortages that had so recently debilitated the British army. The North Carolina militia had been picking the land clean once more, and were contemptible in Greene's view: 'Everybody is a general and the powers of the government are so feeble that it is with the greatest difficulty you can restrain them from plundering one another . . . they must go to war their way or not at all.'

Greene had already warned Washington while journeying down to take up the command that he would be hard pressed to stop Cornwallis extending the areas under British control. Seeing all the problems that faced his little army at first hand, Greene noted, 'L[or]d Cornwallis has a much greater force on foot than we have and much better provided.' Whatever British officers like Balfour, O'Hara or Clinton might have felt about the dangers of a thrust into North Carolina, the new commander of the Southern Department saw quite clearly how vulnerable his forces would be if Cornwallis pressed ahead. The English earl and the autodidact Rhode Island soldier were thus thinking along very similar lines, Greene stating baldly: 'If Lord Cornwallis knows his true interest he will pursue our army. If he can disperse that, he completes the reduction of the state.'

The American general set to work immediately to thwart such a disaster, firing off directives in the days after he assumed command: to survey the rivers behind him for a fighting retreat across North Carolina to the borders of Virginia; to build boats so that he might ferry troops or supplies rapidly across these obstacles; to get better intelligence reports from the likes of Marion or Sumpter; and to announce his arrival by gripping the discipline of his ragtag army.

Greene's experience of war and countless Patriot setbacks had imbued him with a violent contempt towards recidivism or indiscipline within the Continental Army. Before leaving the north he had pleaded with Washington that one of his soldiers 'be hung without judge or jury as an example to the rest'. Washington agreed and the man, accused of theft, was summarily executed. The major general wanted to signal his arrival in the southern army in a similar way. Finding that many men were absent without leave (usually foraging for food or getting drunk), Greene waited for one of them, Thomas Anderson, a private in the 1st Maryland Regiment to wander back to camp, brought him to trial and had him shot by firing squad on 4 December.

In order to stymie Cornwallis while he tightened his hold over his soldiers, Greene had the inspired idea of sending a raiding force into the earl's backyard. On 21 December, he dispatched Brigadier Daniel Morgan with 600 picked troops as well as authority to call out the South Carolina militia. Morgan was to march deep into the state, threatening Ninety Six and other backcountry posts. Greene knew that this ought to hamper any British offensive thrust into North Carolina, telling Morgan that if Cornwallis advanced anyway, the raiders should 'fall back upon the flank or into the rear of the enemy as occasion may require'. This diversion worked better than Greene could possibly have expected.

On 8 January, the 23rd Fusiliers struck camp at Winnsborough, along with the 33rd and 2nd Battalion of the 71st, marching off at a blistering pace, covering eighteen miles that day. They were following behind Tarleton who had already left with the British Legion, 7th Fusiliers, and 1st Battalion 71st. Cornwallis had launched his campaign of 1781 on hearing reports of Morgan's presence in the province, but it would develop in ways he had not anticipated at all.

The first battle-stained stragglers came into the encampment in the evening of 17 January. Lieutenant Harry Calvert of the Fusiliers was quick to spot them – troopers of the 17th Light Dragoons, one or two officers of the British Legion, on exhausted horses stumbling into the plantation where Lord Cornwallis's main force had marched 50 miles from Winnsborough. The soldiers spat out their gobbets of bad news through powder-blackened faces. Calvert recorded they 'came in with accounts of having been totally defeated that morning by General Morgan, and most of them affirmed, that Colonel Tarleton was killed'.

The American brigadier, who went by the nickname of 'the Old Waggoner', had drawn Tarleton to a place called Cowpens, close to the North Carolina border, luring him on to a fighting position of his own choosing. As one fugitive after another wandered into the British camp, Calvert pieced together the story of what had gone wrong. Tarleton, as was his custom, had hurled his troops into action before they were all up, and the 71st had advanced towards their enemy, taking significant losses from enemy sharpshooters as they went. The 71st had gone forward just like the 23rd at Camden, two deep and very open (i.e., with a few feet separating each file or pair of men), but the outcome had been very different. Morgan had put his best troops in line behind the militia. Once the redcoats charged and burst through this first line they had gone on to the second. It was at that point, according to Calvert's interpretation of the accounts he heard over the campfire that evening, that things had gone wrong: 'Instead of continuing the charge the infantry halted to load again; the enemy rallied and gave them a very severe fire and the British troops lost the action more by their own misconduct, than by the enemy's bravery.' A prompt charge by William Washington, an American cavalry commander in the same mould as Tarleton himself, had then put the Legion horse to rout. 'The whole of his flying army except the Legion cavalry, who secured themselves by a disgraceful flight', wrote Calvert with some disgust, 'were either killed, wounded, or missing.'

These early reports were, unfortunately for Cornwallis, all too accurate except in one detail. Tarleton himself got into the bivouac early on the morning of the 18th. The majority of the 7th and 71st were lost – the English Fusiliers sustaining the odious distinction of having the Americans relieve them of their colours for a second time (the first had been in Canada five years earlier). Tarleton had lost his cannon and all his Legion infantry too. Cornwallis was beside himself, feeling that all the gains of his recent build-up had been lost.

At the very moment of receiving the dismal news from Cowpens, the

Guards Grenadier Company had been marching into Cornwallis's encampment from the south. Major General Leslie had arrived with 1,200 soldiers, including two battalions of Guards, the Hessian Regiment von Bose, a company of Hessian jaegers and the North Carolina Volunteers loyalists. Any joy at this substantial reinforcement had evaporated due to Tarleton's defeat.

'The late affair has almost broke my heart,' Cornwallis wrote to Lord Rawdon. 'Morgan is at Gilbertown, I shall march tomorrow with 1,200 infantry and the cavalry to attack or follow him to the banks of the Catawba . . . I was never more surrounded with difficulty and distress but practice in the school of adversity has strengthened me.' He launched the army in hot pursuit. Three days of hard marching followed, but without bringing the redcoats up with Morgan. The American ability to move so quickly was a problem that would frustrate Cornwallis throughout the coming weeks.

On 22 January, he ordered the 'bad marchers' and regimental baggage left with the von Bose Regiment and loyalists. He pushed the men on into North Carolina, but still did not succeed in catching up. Four days on, after reaching Ramsour's Mill, Cornwallis took the dramatic step of ordering the army's wagons burnt so that it might travel faster. It should not be imagined that they were moving around with some vast train of wheeled transport. The 23rd, like other regiments, had been given three large wagons, each towed by four horses, during the Camden part of the campaign. This had later been reduced to a single four-wheeled vehicle, 'which is intended for the conveyance of their medicine chest, sick men, forage or any other necessary purpose'. Officers' little luxuries would have to be carried on their own packhorse, with strict limits set on them. As for the men, they had long been equipped in the light infantry style, carrying everything about their person with a blanket, haversack and knapsack.

While Cornwallis consigned all but one of his personal wagons to the bonfire to show that he was sharing in the hardships, there was one aspect of his army's train that he was failing to rein in. Since their arrival in South Carolina, the redcoats had picked up hundreds of black servants. Many of these people were slaves who took advantage of British offers of freedom. Senior officers had at first looked the other way, accepting that a regiment with a retinue of hired officers' servants would be able to return to the battle-line soldiers previously used for the same purpose. However, every quartermaster and many non-commissioned officers had acquired their own negroes and the numbers were getting too large – for they had to be fed and camp followers were felt more likely to loot than soldiers on duty. On the same day that he ordered the wagons burnt, Cornwallis issued a General Order concerning 'negroes and horses', limiting field officers (majors and lieutenant colonels) to two and three of each respectively, captains to one servant and two horses and so on. Like many instructions of this kind, its effects were limited.

Before leaving Ramsour's Mill supplies of leather were handed out so the men could re-sole their shoes and carry a spare pair. On 28 January, Cornwallis launched them forward once more with morning orders warning that 'the supply of rum for a time will be absolutely impossible, and that of meal very uncertain'. They were marching for the Catawba River – Cornwallis and Greene both understood the contest now, it was about whether the British general could smash the Continental troops before they could escape.

When the redcoats came into view early in the morning on 1 February on the far bank of the Catawba, General William Lee Davidson's militia prepared their weapons. There were some 300 ready to contest the McGowan's Ford. The local men had reason to feel confident. The river was broad at that point, nearly half a mile wide. Its waters, swollen by recent rains, ran fast and deep. If the redcoats made it across, they would find the militia posted on parts of the bank that rose several feet above the water. They would watch their enemy splash in – and wait. These militia were not going to run away.

The Guards had gone into the water first, with their Light Bobs and Cornwallis himself, mounted, at their head. Then some horses pulling two little 3-pounders of the Royal Artillery followed, and after them the Royal Welch Fusiliers. The men soon found the water rushing round their legs and as they pressed on it was up to their bellies. They held their muskets, bayonets fixed, above their heads, tying their cartridge boxes to their necks so the precious contents would not get spoiled.

As they got to the middle of the stream the fast torrent was tugging at their clothes, the stones and mud slippery beneath their feet. Few could swim, and they were all heavily laden in any case. Struggling forward, many men were gripped with the fear of drowning, but for one bombardier, or corporal of the artillery, the current proved stronger than his grip on a gun carriage and he was swept off by the waters. Serjeant Lamb of the 23rd, seeing the man's head disappear below the brown foaming waters, 'determined to save his life or perish in the attempt'. Lamb, who was a strong swimmer, dived in, being swept 40 yards downstream holding on to the corporal. Eventually he stopped the man, got him to his feet and heaved him back to the 3-pounder.

Soon, though, Davidson's militia were adding to the redcoats' troubles with a crackling fire. Lord Cornwallis's horse was hit, but struggled across the river, expiring only after it had delivered its noble rider to dry land. Once the British were a few dozen yards from their enemy, the militia's fire began to bite, sending plumes of water into the air and cutting down a soldier of the Guards here and there – about fifteen did not make it across, lost either to bullets or the waters. The rest kept thrashing onward, struggling up the banks. Lieutenant Calvert was struck by the soldiers' composure throughout this ordeal, declaring, 'They gained the opposite shore without returning a single shot, they then formed with the greatest coolness and drove the militia from a post which they might have defended against any body of men.' 'I believe', wrote Lamb, a little more generous to the 23rd's foe, 'not one of them moved from his post till we mounted the hill and used our bayonets; their general was the first man that received us sword in hand and suffered himself to be cut to pieces sooner than retreat.' The Catawba was forced and its defenders dispersed.

Cornwallis was racing after Greene, the two men united in their understanding that the American must retreat to the line of the River Dan, the border between North Carolina and Virginia. Greene had appealed for help and expected reinforcements from that state, but he did not feel himself strong enough in early February to engage Cornwallis in open battle; on the contrary, he felt that such an event might be disastrous. The British general congratulated the Guards on their coolness crossing the Catawba and pressed on.

Moving forward at such a pace, through a land that was often hostile, there was no possibility of maintaining a regular line of communication to the depots at Camden. The soldiers initially were fed from bags of cornmeal prepared to support the expedition. In time, though, this resource began to run low, and in any case the men often found their bivouacs far ahead of the remaining wagons in the army. Unripe ears of maize were frequently taken from the fields, and the men instructed in how to rasp them in order to detach the corn from the cob. Cattle too were run into camp, swiftly slaughtered and divided up between messes of six soldiers each.

One soldier of Webster's brigade described the cooking arrangements on these marches: 'My mess mates and I made two meals a day, which we managed by first boiling the beef, and then taking it out and having mixed our pound of flour with some water, we put it into the kettle in which the beef had been boiled; and when sufficiently heated we took it off the fire . . . This served us for breakfast and the beef we kept for dinner.'

A fellow-soldier in that brigade, Serjeant Lamb, wrote of each evening's smooth routine once they halted. He gives some sense of how the simple comforts of a field camp sustained such hard campaigning:

It is a pleasing sight to see a column arrive at its halting ground. The camp is generally marked out, if circumstances allow of it, on the edge of some wood, and near a river or stream. The troops are halted in open columns and arms piled, pickets and guards paraded and posted, and in two minutes all appear at home. Some fetch large stones to form fire places; others hurry off with canteens and kettles for water while the wood resounds with the blows of the tomahawk. Dispersed under the more distant trees you see the officers, some dressing, some arranging a few boughs to shelter them by night, others kindling their own fires. How often under some spreading pine tree which afforded shade, shelter and fuel have I taken up my lodging for the night. Sitting in the midst of my comrades, men whom I loved and esteemed partaking of a coarse but wholesome meal.

Their journey often resumed in the early hours – 2 a.m., for example, on the day they had forced the Catawba. Once under way, the redcoats had no idea whether they would walk four miles or twenty-four, or what they might get by way of supplies at the end of it. In the week after crossing the Catawba, there were slim pickings and organised foraging degenerated into looting with violence. Cornwallis, though, spared the blame from his fighting soldiers when he issued a General Order on 5 February saying,'Great complaints having been made of negroes straggling from the line of march, plundering and using violence to the inhabitants, it is Lord Cornwallis' positive order that no negro shall be suffered to carry arms on any pretence.' The following day, orders were issued for the formation of a strong rear-guard of redcoats to sweep up the stragglers falling to the back of the marching column.

A man who became lame, or too sick to walk, it should be clear, could not be evacuated back to South Carolina. Four of the ten or so wagons saved from the conflagration at Ramsour's Mill were ear-marked for carrying sick and wounded. Some men, though, could stand this relentless marching no longer, falling deliberately behind, resolved to surrender to their enemies. For the great majority, who remained with the colours, marches sometimes brought pleasant surprises to palliate grinding hardship.

On 10 February, approaching Salem, Cornwallis's column passed through several villages of Moravians – a German-speaking religious sect who had settled the area and remained neutral in the conflict. There they were able to buy good food and puncheons of home-distilled whiskey. One private of the 33rd even suspected the Germans were trying to get them intoxicated so they might be surprised, noting 'their liberality in furnishing us so abundantly with spiritous liquors, as all the world knows that a soldier's chief delight is in drinking'.

The marches continued, twenty-four miles on 13 February, twenty-two on the 14th, bringing them to a place called Dobbin's Plant, just one more gruelling day's hike from the River Dan, and Greene's sanctuary in Virginia. It had been raining hard and many of the roads they slogged along were muddy quagmires – shoes had been sucked off, soles hurriedly stitched at Ramsour's Mill had come apart. Cornwallis wanted to ask his men for one last exertion. Were they willing to make the final effort to reach the Dan? 'The soldiers had the same wish as their general,' wrote Lieutenant Calvert.

During one month's marching this small army had kept up high morale, intoxicated by its own daring hardiness, plunging after Nathaniel Greene's army. Cornwallis led by example, Serjeant Lamb writing, 'He fared like a common soldier . . . he would admit of no distinction.' So when Cornwallis appealed for the good marchers that night of the 14th, they responded. So did those who were not able to press on after their few hours of sleep in sodden blankets. Lieutenant Calvert explained: 'At night the sick and lame received orders to give their shoes to those men who were in health and had none.' Thus those who could march did so, in many cases in the shoes of those who could not.

The Legion cavalry reached the banks of the Dan ahead of the rest of the army on 15 February. There was disappointment, a sense of anti-climax, after all they had endured. Some heard that Greene had crossed six hours earlier, others averred that it was twelve. At times

Cornwallis's intelligence had been poor and many hours had been lost – they had sometimes used the wrong fords or advanced mistakenly up poor roads. He had in any case succeeded in chasing his enemy out of North Carolina. More important than this, however, for the redcoats that had followed him hundreds of miles up muddy roads with execrable rations, was a strong bond of respect as well as loyalty that now existed between the general and his troops.

Months earlier, Brigadier O'Hara of the Guards had been very worried about marching into the Carolinas, believing 'The smallest check to any of his detachments would in all probability end like the unfortunate affair of Saratoga in the total demolition of Lord Cornwallis's corps.' There was truth in this: a defeat would indeed have ruined Cornwallis. But having taken part in the race to the Dan, O'Hara's tone changed. He had never been convinced that the campaign could subjugate North Carolina nor that Britain could win its war in America, but to O'Hara their commander's decision to pursue his enemy 'was taken, and carried into execution in a style that must ever do the greatest honour to Lord Cornwallis's military reputation.' The soldiers would have expressed it differently, but they too respected their leader's yearning for a battle, for it was upon that quality that their self-respect as British fighting men rested. How different it was campaigning under Cornwallis to tramping behind that plodder Howe or sitting cooped up in New York for years with Clinton!

It should not be imagined that Major General Greene's escape was easy. He had made judicious preparations in surveying his route, preparing for the many river crossings. Sick or lame soldiers did not slow him down, they could be left in the care of local people. 'No general could have conducted his Army better that General Greene did his,' Lieutenant Calvert averred, before insisting, 'He had a great advantage in being in a friend's country – without it he could never have escaped.'

For Serjeant Major Seymour, that survivor of Camden from Delaware, the retreat to the Dan had been every bit as gruelling as for his pursuers. He had frequently fought in the rearguard, having been formed with other remnants of his regiment into a special light company under Captain Kirkwood. 'The army', noted Seymour, 'specially the light troops were very much fatigued by the travelling and want of sleep, for you must understand that we marched for the most part both day and night, the main army of the British being close in our rears so we had not scarce time to cook our victuals.' Greene, however, proved adept at motivating his men with both carrot and stick: there were patriotic exhortations and executions. The major general moreover had played time and distance cleverly in his favour, moving closer to reinforcements in Virginia, while calling out thousands of North Carolina militia. He was shifting the balance of forces.

After one day's rest, Cornwallis's army proceeded around 50 miles south, back into the interior of North Carolina. At noon on 25 February the 23rd arrived in a place called Hillsborough, where Lieutenant General Cornwallis went through the formality of 'raising the King's standard' and summoning loyalists to join his army.

O'Hara wrote back to England, 'Greene's march or rather flight from the Catawba over the Dan, closely pursued by our army, had given some *éclat* and credit to our arms, that hour of triumph and exultation was considered favourable for calling upon the many friends government had persuaded themselves that we had in every part of North Carolina.' The Whiggish brigadier was quite cynical about this, believing the government had 'grossly deceived' itself once more about the possibilities of Americans being willing to fight for their King.

In one sense the stop at Hillsborough was even worse than O'Hara thought, for it was there that a few British soldiers chose to desert. The 23rd lost eleven men this way in January and February 1781 (although some of them may have been sick or thieving stragglers seized by their enemy), but the majority of that number went during the days in and around Hillsborough. One, John Bennett, was even a serjeant – desertion at this rank was quite a rarity. Cornwallis put such losses down to 'soldiers being taken by the enemy, in consequence of their straggling out of camp in search of whiskey'. Certainly, it is true that morale remained high overall in the army at this time, but it must be allowed that the weariness at what they had been through must have combined in the minds of deserting soldiers with a dread of what lay ahead.

While Cornwallis paused at Hillsborough everything was changing. Having united with his fresh brigade of Virginia troops, Greene came south of the Dan once more. He was not yet ready to fight Cornwallis but wanted to assemble the North Carolina militia, and, despite Brigadier O'Hara's weary cynicism, thwart the loyalists that the

American commander was sure would join the King's troops.

Greene sent a force of light troops ahead under Colonel Henry Lee, whose Legion played much the same role and wore much the same dress as Tarleton's British Legion. Lee marched close to Hillsborough with orders from Greene to interrupt Cornwallis's communication with the surrounding country 'to repress the meditated rising of the loyalists, and, at all events, to intercept any party of them which might attempt to join the enemy'. The Patriots soon received reports of a large party of loyalist Americans – 400 men under Colonel Joseph Pyle – who had assembled and were moving towards Hillsborough. This was precisely the kind of assembly that his Major General wanted 'repressed', so Lee, a man well suited to the wily stratagems required of a commander of light troops, hit upon a ruse. He would pretend that his troops were Tarleton's in order to lure Pyle's men into a trap. Different participants left various versions of how this stratagem was sprung. According to one, some Tories found Lee's party and he told them to return with their friends.

Lieutenant Manning of Lee's Legion supplied another version, later claiming he was sent into Pyle's camp, pretending to be a deserter seeking to join them. He carried his deception so far as to drink with them, raising a toast: 'Here's confusion to Greene, and success to the King and his friends!' The following day, 25 February, Pyle's men were led to a meeting point where Lee's troopers, pretending to be the British Legion, saluted them. Lee rode the length of Pyle's column 'with a smiling countenance, dropping occasionally expressions complimentary to the good looks and commendable conduct of his loyal friends'. And then the killing began.

Ninety or so of Pyle's loyalists were cut down where they stood. Confused to the end, some of those who fled eventually reached the British camp and complained about the brutality of Tarleton's dragoons. Of those wounded men who surrendered, some were promptly dispatched by Lee's men with cries of 'Remember Buford', a reference to Tarleton's treatment of Virginians who tried to surrender at Waxhaws in May 1780. Lee subsequently said that the killing had been started by the loyalists when they recognised a Patriot neighbour among the Legion. Equally it is clear that Lee's mission included frightening local loyalists into submission. Lieutenant Manning subsequently remarked that the majority of Tories had been allowed to escape, precisely to spread terror among the King's friends. Greene greeted the news by saying, 'It has had a very happy effect on those disaffected persons, of which there are too many in this county.' Since Greene did not hesitate to make examples of his own men, it is hard to imagine that he had ordered Lee to be merciful towards his enemies.

News of these events caused great shock in the British camp. It was denounced as 'Pyle's Massacre', and exaggerated stories about what had happened were added to the grisly reality. One officer of the 23rd Fusiliers wrote to his brother, '300 of our friends . . . were every man scalped, and their leader, Colonel Pyle, hung up by his heels.' For Greene, intimidation worked, and only a handful of loyalists came in to Hillsborough before Cornwallis moved his army off.

Cornwallis had been, until he reached the Dan, the hunter. As March began, Greene assumed that role, and Cornwallis would have to decide whether to retreat or to do as he had done at Camden, and take his chances against a superior foe.

Greene Offers Battle

Or James Webster's Finest Hour

The encounter between Tarleton's Legion and Colonel Lee's American horse was like many affairs of the advanced guards; a brief, frightening scramble in which high spirits and superior tactics vied for superiority. The British Legion cavalry had come forward in a narrow lane, hemmed in with high fences, near New Garden, a backcountry Quaker community. Tarleton's men, seeing cavalry at what they imagined was the tail end of an enemy column just a few yards ahead, fired their pistols, let out a great cry and set spurs to their horses. Colonel Lee, however, had concealed two of his three cavalry troops to the sides of the road, who came charging down on the Tories. The British Legion were rebuffed, having several men dismounted, others receiving cuts from the flashing sabres of their adversaries.

Tarleton's horsemen went to the right about, galloping down the narrow lane, back towards their comrades. The wise commander on the march gave particular attention to the order in which his companies proceeded, for in the fast, furious moments in which combat was joined, this would determine the order in which they could be brought into action. Hearing the commotion ahead of them, the Guards Light Company had deployed its platoons ready to fire. When the British Legion horse came galloping by, they were ready for the pursuing Americans. The Guards let fly a volley. Most aimed too high, showering the American dragoons with leaves and severed twigs as they reined in their mounts. Lee was thrown from his horse but quickly remounted another, then threw his own infantry into play.

A general *tiraillade* began, with the light infantry of both sides using what cover they could, blazing away at one another. 'The action became very sharp,' wrote Lee, 'and was bravely maintained in both sides.' Lieutenant Colonel Tarleton was hit in the hand by one shot. Soon it was the turn of the 23rd Fusiliers to be fed into the battle. Seeing larger numbers of redcoats filing up, Colonel Lee felt that discretion was the better part of valour, retiring his men back towards Greene's position at Guilford Courthouse.

Each side had jockeyed for advantage in that short rencounter with the idea not of extirpating their enemy, but of gaining a feel for whether they were in the presence of one another's main army or just a far-flung scouting party. Lee rode back to Major General Nathaniel Greene with the news that Cornwallis's army was marching towards them, and would soon arrive.

A few days before Tarleton and Lee's affair, Richard Tattersall of the 23rd and John Shaw of the 33rd had 'made a push for the country', moving away from their bivouac after a long day's slog. Were they just looking for food and drink or had they decided to desert? Even they probably weren't sure. The two and a half weeks since the British left Hillsborough in late February had been spent in a fruitless marching and countermarching about the interior of North Carolina. The excitement of daily exertions as they pressed up to the Dan had been followed by an uncertainty about what would become of them.

Tattersall was one of those scooped up in Lancashire the previous year by the army's recruiting dragnet. He had joined the Fusiliers with the party of recruits that arrived in December 1780. The strain of months campaigning had evidently got to him. He and his friend Shaw found a farmhouse in the woods and announced themselves, hoping to find food. Lo and behold, the place was already packed with ravenous redcoats. On they went to another farmstead, where a doughty lady presented herself as the wife of Major Bell in the American service, but nevertheless invited them in for something to eat. Sitting beside the warm hearth, eating Johnny Cakes, the two soldiers soon began eyeing the major's daughters. Why not join our side, asked Mrs Bell, promising them work and the hands of her own daughters. 'Such good fortune was not to be expected,' Shaw wrote later, 'and we had no time to delay, my comrade and I, after we finished our meal, took our leave of the old lady.' They emerged to find themselves surrounded by dragoons.

Guilford
Courthouse •

Naseby
Fields

American
Third Line

N E
W S

American
Second Line

23rd Regiment
during battle

American
First Line

Hoskins
Fields

A B
E

C D
F

A 33rd Regiment
B 23rd Regiment
C 71st Highlanders
D Bose's Hessians
E Guards, 2nd Battalion
F Guards, 1st Battalion

0   m   500
0   yards   500

Thinking them a part of Tarleton's cavalry sent out to find deserters, Tattersall began crying. In fact Mrs Bell had sent word to Colonel Lee's Legion that she had a couple of redcoats that could easily be made prisoner. By her deception, Mrs Bell thus robbed Earl Cornwallis of two more men, and gained information about what was going on in the British camp for her own side.

Cornwallis did not want to stay too long in one place, because thousands of enemy militia were collecting. Many Tories, on the other hand, had decided to wait and see, Colonel Pyle's affair having frightened them into inaction. Uncertain of the best course of action, Cornwallis had begun to worry about re-supply. He was considering heading down to the coast, to Wilmington, where a British force sent from Charleston by Lieutenant Colonel Balfour had seized the port in order to open a new line of communications with the earl's army inland.

Lieutenant General Cornwallis, however, had been receiving reports about General Greene, who was staying close to the British as he received reinforcements. Eight hundred soldiers of the Virginia line under Brigadier General Isaac Huger had joined, followed by nearly 1,500 militia from the same state (many of whom were actually troops seasoned by previous campaigns). While the redcoats marched about, closely observed by Colonel Lee's corps, he and Greene exchanged messages, as the balance of advantage tipped. 'One thing is pretty certain,' Greene told Lee on 9 March, 'which is Lord Cornwallis don't wish a general action.'

Colonel Lee interrogated Tattersall and Shaw after they were brought into his camp on 10 March, and having heard what they had to say, decided it was time to egg on his chief, writing back to Major General Greene the following day, 'It appears to me that his Lordship and army begin to possess disagreeable apprehensions. If you dare, get near him.' The colonel sent the captured pair of redcoats on to Greene's headquarters where the general questioned them himself.

The Americans had detected in the British meanderings of early March an aimlessness or lack of clear purpose. Greene gained a further insight into British morale from Tattersall and Shaw. Acute as the American commander was, he could not know all of the possible courses of action that were playing out in his adversary's mind.

The 23rd's line of action at Guilford Courthouse

Cornwallis had three choices: first, he might march towards another British force that was operating not far to the north, raiding coastal areas in Virginia; second, he could head south to Wilmington, deposit the sick or wounded he was carting about, re-supply and receive dispatches; third, he could give up the game, accepting his failure to prompt a loyalist rising in North Carolina, returning to South Carolina. Whichever of these options he followed, the British commander would worry about moving with a larger American army to his rear. Greene's ability, demonstrated in the race to the Dan, to move a little faster than he could had been frustrating when the British were advancing but it could spell disaster if they tried to retreat. Cornwallis, true to character, decided to fight. In any event, he needed to disperse his enemy and buy some weeks or months of freedom to act. He needed another Camden. Cornwallis's advance guard commander, Lieutenant Colonel Tarleton, would later differ with his chief's judgement, arguing that 'a defeat would have been attended with the total destruction of Earl Cornwallis's infantry, whilst a victory at this juncture could produce no very decisive consequences against the Americans'. Such critics, however, probably understood Greene's calculations less well than Cornwallis did. If the British could temporarily disperse the Continentals then the caution exhibited so far in the campaign by the American commander would probably have dictated he break off any pursuit.

By mid-March Greene also was ready to give battle. He chose a point a little further up the same road from the skirmish of early on the 15th. It was more open, but undulating, ground, covered for the most part by woods of evergreen pine and some deciduous trees that were just coming into leaf. Greene's main, or final, position was just in front of Guilford Courthouse, where he posted 1,400 Continental troops (Marylanders and Virginians). The land dropped quite steeply in front of these men to an area cleared of trees known locally as Naseby Fields. The open nature of this place made it a fine killing-ground, so two 6-pounder cannon were also positioned among the Marylanders, overlooking it. Heading towards the British from Naseby Fields, there was a rise, and here, among trees, Greene posted a line of Virginia militia. Hundreds of yards to the front of them, he drew up the North Carolina militia. They were deployed on either side of the road up to Guilford, along a fence where the woods stopped and another area of open ground, Hoskins' Field, began. This was another ideal place to engage the redcoats at longer range than in woods, so Greene put another two cannon in the centre of this line. Horsemen were posted on each flank – Lee's to the right and Colonel Washington's to the left, and some parties of riflemen assigned to act with them.

The deployment chosen by Greene thus put his 4,400 or so men in three distinct lines, with the British forced to fight their way through the worst troops first, then the Virginia militia in the woods, to the best men posted on the strongest ground. It was an admirable arrangement that married the lie of the land to the distinctive qualities of various contingents.

Most of the Americans were militia called up for limited periods of service. There was nervousness in the American camp about whether the disgraceful stampede of Camden would be repeated, and the North Carolina men once more prove first in flight. Brigadier General Morgan, obliged by sickness to abandon the campaign after his victory at Cowpens, had advised Greene to deploy in lines, and to put steadier militia behind the shakier companies, 'with orders to shoot down the first man that runs'. Morgan clearly possessed a character even harder than that of Greene. At Guilford, Greene hesitated to give general instructions for one body of Americans to shoot down another, but one of his subordinates, Brigadier General Stevens, whose Virginia militia had also fled at Camden, did take picked men to the rear of his brigade, with orders to kill anyone who tried to flee or raise a panic.

Greene, it is clear, had thought of most things in his plan. He also had the advantage of outnumbering Cornwallis by a considerable margin, since the British army marching towards them mustered no more than 1,900 officers and men. Cornwallis knew the ground, for he had stopped in Guilford during the manoeuvring of the previous weeks, but had no idea exactly how his enemy would deploy. He went into battle, however, undaunted, and after a march of near 16 miles, at mid-day on 15 March.

As the leading redcoats crossed a small creek and saw the open ground of Hoskins' Field ahead, they began deploying into their battle formation. Colonel Webster moved to the left of the road, keeping the 23rd next to that axis and pushing the 33rd out to his wing. Major General Leslie formed his brigade on the other side of the road to Guilford, with the 2nd Battalion of the 71st nearest to it (and the

23rd), the von Bose Hessian regiment to the 71st's right. Cornwallis kept certain troops as a second line of his own, ready to plug gaps or rush to a threatened flank; the 2nd Battalion of the Guards was behind Webster, with some jaegers, the Guards Light and Grenadier companies. The 1st Battalion of Guards stood behind Leslie. The army's small battery of guns was in the first line, on the road, commanded by Lieutenant John MacLeod, and Tarleton's cavalry in reserve, in the centre but back beyond the Guards.

As at Camden, the British went forward as soon as they were in line. Captain Peter led the 23rd on as acting commanding officer, with the regiment effectively in two wings under captains Saumarez and Champagne. As they went forward, one of them noticed the 'field lately ploughed, which was wet and muddy from the rains which had recently fallen'. On they trudged towards the fence that marked the end of Hoskins' cornfield and the beginning of the woods to the fore, observing as they grew closer that the rails were lined with men. MacLeod's cannon opened fire, sending their ball whooshing into the American lines.

Colonel Webster, on horseback, trotted to the front of his brigade and called out so that all could hear, 'Charge!' The men began jogging forward, bayonets fixed and muskets levelled towards the enemy. A crackling fire from their left, Kirkwood's riflemen, began knocking down a redcoat here or there, but did nothing to check their impetus. When the British line was little more than 50 yards from the North Carolina militia everything seemed to stop for Serjeant Lamb:

. . . it was perceived the whole of their force had their arms presented, and resting on a rail fence . . . they were taking aim with the nicest precision. At this awful period a general pause took place; both parties surveyed each other for the moment with the most anxious suspense . . .

Colonel Webster spurred his horse to the head of the 23rd and bellowed out, 'Come on my brave Fusiliers!' Some of the Americans started to run, but most held on for a moment; there was a rippling crash of American musketry when the redcoats were at optimum range, 40 to 50 yards away. Dozens of Webster's men went down as the musket balls cut legs from under them or smashed into their chests. Lieutenant Calvert worried for an instant how his men might react to such a heavy fire: 'They instantly returned it and did not give the enemy time to repeat their fire but rushed on them with bayonets.'

Captain Saumarez noted with pride, 'No troops could behave better than the regiment . . . they never returned the enemy's fire but by word of command and marched on with the most undaunted courage.' Most of the Carolinians did not wait longer but broke and ran. Calvert spotted them disappearing into the trees and felt a pang of frustration that they had got away.

About 400 yards further on, behind a low ridge obscuring what had just happened, the Virginia militia waited with some trepidation. Samuel Houston, a man from Rockbridge County, Virginia, had been standing with others in Steven's brigade for more than two hours. They had been told to pick a tree and take firing positions, but there were more men than trees, with the nervous Houston observing, 'The men run to choose their trees, but with difficulty, many crowding to one.' When Webster's brigade hit the friends to Houston's front, the Virginians could hear it all but not see it, adding to their feeling of suspense.

Coming over the ridge that separated the first and second of Greene's defensive lines, Webster's brigade had lost some of its order. The 33rd had moved off to the left somewhat, trying to force back Kirkwood's riflemen. As the 23rd's officers saw the Virginians in front of them they quickly perceived that some of Stevens's militia companies had used their waiting time to advantage, piling up brushwood and branches in front of their position. They wheeled the 23rd slightly to the right to get around this obstruction. As Webster's two regiments came down the gentle slope towards Stevens's men, a considerable gap had opened between them, leaving the right end of the 33rd's line and the left of the 23rd's in the air.

Houston's company 'fired on their flank, and that brought down many of them'. Instinctively the Fusiliers turned around and ran back towards the ridge they had just descended, with the Virginians in pursuit. The fight became one of companies and even smaller groups of men, as the redcoats rallied and came forward. After 'severe firing', the Virginians began to break.

One of the Virginian officers, over to the (American) left of the road where the 71st and von Bose Regiment had gone in, wrote grimly, 'Holcombe's Regiment and ours broke off without firing a single gun and dispersed like a flock of frightened sheep.' When he bellowed at the men, trying to halt their flight, this major received a bayonet wound from one of his own soldiers. As the left part of Greene's second line broke, it ran away from the Guilford road, with Leslie's brigade in pursuit. This movement, along with that by the 33rd to the opposite flank, prompted Cornwallis to push the Guards up in order to plug the gap opening in his centre.

Cornwallis was anxious to ascertain what was happening in the woods, spurring his horse into the trees. There was a crack as his mount was shot, crumpling beneath him. A dragoon's horse was swiftly produced and his lordship remounted, pushing forward towards where he expected to find Webster's men.

Serjeant Lamb was one of many engaged in short range exchanges of fire, as the Fusiliers tried to deal with the last of Stevens's men, approaching all the while the clearing of Naseby Fields. Attempts to rally the 23rd may have been hampered by the fact that their acting commander, Captain Peter, had been shot in the leg early in the engagement. At one point Lamb realised he was just a few yards from several Americans who levelled their weapons at him, and observed, 'In such moments all fears of death are over.' Lamb ducked down, noticing a dead guardsman in front of him, and started to help himself to the man's cartridges. The Americans fired, but missed, the balls whistling over the Fusilier serjeant's head. Lamb doubled back towards friendly troops and then spotted General Cornwallis, alone on his dragoon's horse, disorientated and heading towards the Americans. Lamb explained:

I immediately laid hold of the bridle of his horse, and turned his head. I then mentioned to him that if his lordship had pursued the same direction, he would have been surrounded by the enemy, and, perhaps, cut to pieces or captured. I continued to run along side of the horse, keeping the bridle in my hand, until his lordship gained the 23rd Regiment.

In the confused woodland fighting required to dispatch the more stubborn of Stevens's Virginian militia, the 23rd and companies of the 2nd Guards had become mixed up. Officers and serjeants went about the trees bellowing to get their men back into order. Off to the (British) left Webster managed to keep the 33rd, several dozen jaegers and Guards Light Company together. Nearing the clearing of Naseby Fields, he formed his men into line, ready to press on immediately with an assault on the final American position, the hill to his front held by Continental troops.

It was probably still less than an hour since the action had started, when Webster led his men into Greene's chosen killing ground. From the position where they had emerged from the trees, and perhaps also from Webster's fine tactical eye, they tried not to cross directly in front of the 1st Maryland Regiment and 6-pounders, keeping instead to the left side of the fields, coming up towards Huger's brigade of Virginians on the ridge. The Delaware and Virginian rifle companies that had galled Webster's advance in front of the American first line had by this time raced back to join the third to the (American) right of Huger. As the 33rd, Guards Light Bobs and Jaegers pressed on, Kirkwood's riflemen started to pick them off and the cannon crews heaved their weapons about so they might begin hurling grapeshot into their ranks. Lieutenant Colonel John Howard's 1st Maryland Regiment readied their muskets.

With men falling to left and right, Webster himself was hit and went down. His attack was faltering. Kirkwood's Delawares and some Virginian riflemen charged the 33rd and sent them running back up the hill they had just tramped down. The first men to reach the safety of this position formed up, and received the Americans, 'pouring in a very heavy fire on them'. At this see-saw moment, it was the Americans' turn to run back to safety.

The 2nd Battalion of Guards, 'impatient to signalise themselves', went forward to attack the Americans on the hill. By this time both Maryland regiments and Huger's Virginians were lined up on that eminence, in front of Webster's brigade, events on the other side of the road having separated into a distinct and less pivotal battle. Having formed quite near the road, the 2nd Guards, who were commanded by Lieutenant Colonel Stewart but also had their brigadier (O'Hara) with them, pushed on with levelled muskets towards the 2nd Maryland Regiment, which was posted on the flank of the position, almost at right angles to the 1st Marylanders and parallel to the road.

Lieutenant Colonel Howard (in overall charge of the Maryland contingent) watched as the Guards ran 'at the 2nd Regiment, which immediately gave way . . . The Guards pushed them to our rear where they took two pieces of artillery.' Matters had reached a crisis for Greene, whose third line now stood in a danger very similar to that which had destroyed de Kalb's command at Camden. Greene had Webster and the 33rd to his front and the 2nd Guards breaking his left flank, threatening to get behind his main defensive line. Howard wheeled the veterans of the 1st Maryland Regiment, many of whom had survived that dreadful *debandade* at Camden, and opened a volleying fire on the Guards.

'The conflict between the . . . Guards and the first regiment of Marylanders was most terrific', wrote one watching militiaman, 'for they fired at the same instant, and they appeared so near that the blazes from their guns seemed to meet.' Soon they were fighting hand to hand. It was in these grim moments of frenzied swordplay that Lieutenant Colonel Stewart was killed by a stroke across the head from a captain of the Marylanders. In this desperate struggle, Brigadier O'Hara was bayoneted and at one stage collared by Americans, only to be recovered by his men.

Having cleared the 2nd Marylanders, the Guards were too eager to press on and complete the destruction of their enemy. With the 1st Marylanders opposing their front, the 2nd Guards had left their right flank hanging dangerously, and it was on to this most tempting spot that Colonel William Washington directed several dozen of his horsemen in the attack.

Washington's men 'charged them so furiously that they either killed or wounded almost every man in the regiment, charging through them, breaking their ranks three or four times'. The broken 2nd Guards fled back down the hill towards their redcoat comrades. Rallying his dragoons about him after their dizzying success, Washington looked down from his vantage point, atop the hill of Guilford Courthouse, and saw Lieutenant MacLeod's small battery in the low ground to his front. He ordered a fresh charge and the men came careering down the slope. Cornwallis, who was standing close to the battery, saw the danger, and ordered MacLeod to fire salvoes of grape into the enemy horse. It took no more than a few moments of this punishment to convince Washington's troopers of the futility of going on, and, in Cornwallis's words, 'The enemy's cavalry was soon repulsed by a well-directed fire.'

When the enemy horse were driven off, the way was open for the third and decisive British assault on Greene's last position. The 23rd formed on the edge of Naseby Fields, with several dozen men of the 2nd Guards, bloodied survivors of Colonel Washington's cavalry charge, rallying on their right. The 2nd Battalion of the 71st had been formed close to the road and fell in to the right of the Guards. Up the British line marched into a hail of musketry and grapeshot.

The height, wrote Calvert, was 'defended with great obstinacy', but with the redcoats marching towards the muzzles of the Americans' two 6-pounders, 'They fled on all sides.' Greene ordered a general retreat, anxious to avoid the 71st getting behind them.

'Such men of the Fusiliers and 71st as had strength', wrote Saumarez of the 23rd, 'were ordered to pursue the dispersed enemy.' This they did for two miles, capturing two more American cannon, until, as Calvert put it, 'From the fatigue these troops had sustained during the day it was absolutely impossible to pursue them further.'

By late afternoon the Fusiliers had returned to the battlefield and were helping to separate the wounded from the dead among those carpeting Naseby Fields and suffering on beds of pine needles in the woods. A heavy downpour set in, drenching those who cried out in the trees for deliverance.

Cornwallis's losses had been shockingly high, with the Guards the worst afflicted. Their 216 casualties (of whom thirty-seven were dead) amounted to almost half of them that had gone into battle. The 23rd, which had got off lightly at Camden, was not so lucky this time, suffering thirteen killed and fifty-five wounded. In all, Cornwallis lost 532 men, more than twice as many as Greene.

Greene himself initially evaluated the results of the battle as 'unfortunate', for all three of his lines had been broken. But the American general soon realised how great the loss had been to the British, and the critical situation in which Cornwallis had been left. Greene fulminated about the North Carolina militia, claiming they had 'deserted the most advantageous post I ever saw and without scarcely firing a gun'. He was unfair, without doubt, in suggesting that few of them had fired, for it was in front of these militia on Hoskins' Field that the 23rd had taken their first heavy blow of the day. To the credit of that regiment, however, it had not stalled as the Grenadiers had at Bunker Hill in a similar situation, but pressed on with its attack, forcing the Americans to flee. Later, they had formed the mainstay of the assault that carried Greene's last position. Little wonder that Cornwallis wrote to Balfour after Guilford that 'nothing could behave better than the 23rd'.

The earl, on the day following the battle, wrote an emotional order to be read at the head of each regiment:

Lord Cornwallis desires the officers and Soldiers to accept of his warmest acknowledgements for their very extraordinary valour displayed by them in the action of yesterday; he will endeavour to do justice to their merit in his representation to their Sovereign and the Commander-in-chief and shall consider it the greatest honour of his life to have been placed at the head of so gallant an army.

Several hundred miles marched under the most trying conditions, two major battles and any number of minor skirmishes had produced a powerful bond between the general and his men. There was, inevitably, after 15 March, a sorrow that so many had lost their lives, and that the results had not been more productive. Cornwallis in his dispatch paid tribute in formal style, but perhaps the most remarkable testimony to his small army, its trials and tribulations came in a private letter home from Brigadier O'Hara of the Guards:

No zeal or courage is equal to the constant exertions we are making; tho' you will not find it in the Gazette, every part of our army was beat repeatedly, on 15th March, and were obliged to fall back twice. The rebels were so exceedingly numerous, as to be constantly able to oppose fresh troops to us, and to be in force in our front, flanks, and rear: it is impossible to say too much in praise of our officers and men in a conflict that lasted near two hours, tho' so powerfully out-numbered, their spirit and constancy never forsook them, and at length crowned their manly exertions with victory.

The brigadier survived two wounds sustained in the battle. Webster's case was more doubtful, since one of his legs had been shattered and he was in extreme pain. For many of the soldiers, lying, pleading for help, their misery was just beginning that evening. The downpour that set in lasted the best part of two days, and the army 'remained on the very ground on which it had been fought, covered with dead and dying and with hundreds of wounded, rebels, as well as our own'.

At length, wagons took the survivors back down the road to New Garden, where a makeshift hospital was set up in the New Garden Meeting House.

For Surgeon Hill and his mates tip-toeing between the groaning bodies, each day at New Garden required incredible exertions, for hundreds of wounded – American, Hessian and British – had been placed under the care of half a dozen medics. The good Quakers of that settlement lent a hand, mopping the blood and excrement from the floors of their Meeting House-turned-hospital. Major General Greene had, at British request, sent a couple of his own physicians across the lines to help. Hill had no more than a couple of chests of instruments that had been carried on one of the army's last remaining wagons, and a meagre supply of tinctures or opiates to dull the pain of his patients. He operated long hours, hacking off limbs until his arms were stiff and his saws blunt, probing about in writhing bodies, trying to extract the lumps of metal traded by the two armies on the 15th.

A wound such as Captain Peter's was a relatively straightforward matter for Hill, since the acting commanding officer of the 23rd had been shot through the fleshy part of the leg. It could be cleaned, dressed, and with luck the patient would survive. Colonel Webster on the other hand had his thigh shattered – there were pieces of bone throughout his leg. Amputation high up on the leg under field conditions would probably kill him.

As the pouring rain finally let up, two days after the battle, Lieutenant General Cornwallis added considerably to the stresses facing his surgeon. It was too dangerous for the army to stay where it was, when there was every possibility that Greene might move in for the kill. In 1777, Burgoyne had lingered too long after the first battle of Saratoga, allowing the New England militia to surround him, preventing his escape. Cornwallis did not intend to do the same. Hill was told to select the men who could march and those who would have to be left behind. The latter, of course, would instantly become prisoners, as would Hill and two mates caring for their patients.

On 17 March, Hill therefore conducted a swift and novel form of triage, deciding who could be moved and who could not. As regards the 23rd, there were fifty-five wounded to be considered. Quite a few, who had been patched up quickly and had their wounds staunched, were already regaining their strength. Others were more seriously afflicted.

Thomas Parks, a private from Birmingham, had been hit in the head by an enemy ball. He was, however, conscious, and, once bandaged, started to recover, so he was selected to march. Robert Butler, shot through the knee, evidently could not walk. Hill in any event wanted more time to observe the case; he would stay, and the surgeon amputated the private's leg on 24 March. With Jones, Murphy and Yewell, there was a similar problem, leg wounds, so they would stay at New Garden. Some of the men, like Shakle and Deacon, had abdominal wounds, something considered very dangerous. In Deacon's case, Hill's examination revealed the passage of a bullet through the ileum. Both stayed put, Shakle dying and Deacon, against the odds, pulling through.

The surgeon selected sixty-four serious cases to be left at New Garden Meeting House. Ten were from the 23rd Fusiliers, but the

Guards, unsurprisingly, predominated with twenty-eight patients.

On 18 March the army set off, moving twelve miles, as it headed south. Cornwallis initially took them to Cross Creek, a journey of nearly two weeks. As the crow flies, it was eighty miles, but it proved difficult, with the army having to build its own bridge to cross one major river. The general had hoped to find friends and supplies at Cross Creek, for the settlement had a largely loyalist population of immigrant Scots who had revolted against Congress earlier in the war. These hopes were dashed, though, with the redcoats finding that some stores left in Cross Creek for them had already been destroyed by their enemies. Most local people did not wish to come out in active support. Cornwallis had also entertained hopes, prior to arriving, that he might supply his army by boats on the Cape Fear River, which wound a hundred miles down to the port of Wilmington, in British hands. However he was told in Cross Creek that the inhabitants along much of that waterway were hostile and would attempt to stop such shipments.

All of these disappointments caused Cornwallis to decide to march to Wilmington itself, a momentous resolution as going to the coast meant abandoning the idea of returning overland towards Camden in South Carolina. Once Greene decided not to follow the British to Wilmington but to head instead into the piedmont, to attack the bases from which Cornwallis had launched his assault on North Carolina, it became clear that all of the British gains there since Camden were being given up.

It was therefore a morose British general who ordered his men to resume their march south, towards the sea, on 1 April, because he knew he had failed in his attempt to protect royal gains in South Carolina by invading the north state. This setback would also give ammunition to his critics, most obviously General Henry Clinton, the commander-in-chief at New York. The gloom deepened on 2 April when Webster, who had been taken along on a wagon, finally died of his Guilford wounds after suffering dreadful agonies.

Cornwallis wrote to Lieutenant Colonel Balfour in Charleston, appealing for supplies and explaining his decision to abandon Cross Creek: 'the army was barefooted and in the utmost want of necessaries of every kind, and I was embarrassed with about 400 sick and wounded. These considerations made me determine to march down to Wilmington. Now, my dear Balfour, send me with all possible despatch shoes and necessaries of all kinds.'

On 5 April, the army found some boats on the Cape Fear River that had been sent up from Wilmington with barrels of food and drink. It was the first time since 28 January that Cornwallis's men had been fed by the government, as opposed to their own foraging, living off the land. One week later, they arrived at the port itself.

At Wilmington Cornwallis faced more choices: to go north to Virginia, uniting with an expedition there under Major General Phillips, or to return to South Carolina? And once he resolved that dilemma, another presented itself; to go overland or sail? 'I am quite tired of marching about the country in search of adventures,' Cornwallis wrote to Phillips. He knew that Greene would get to Camden and other inland settlements to the south before his own army could be extracted from Wilmington, making its way back up there. Instinctively, the earl knew that his ideas of making war, far inland, would have to yield to those of General Clinton and Lord Germain, both of whom had been pushing for months to concentrate on campaigning in Virginia, but to do so with raids and expeditions aimed at destroying the enemy economy. 'If our plan is to be defensive, mixed with desultory expeditions,' a weary but unbowed Cornwallis reflected to Phillips, 'let us quit the Carolinas . . . and stick to our salt pork at New York, sending now and then a detachment to steal tobacco etc.'

While Balfour tried to anticipate the army's needs for a return to South Carolina, sending a supply ship to rendezvous with Cornwallis on the coastal route back, the earl's mind was already elsewhere. Inwardly, he had 'quit the Carolinas'. He would go the way he knew best, forward, overland to Phillips. Cornwallis rationalised that heading up to Virginia contained its own risks – 'the attempt is exceedingly hazardous' – but when had that sort of thing worried him? The general would leave Lord Rawdon and Nisbet Balfour to manage the unmanageable in South Carolina and he would take his men to Virginia.

Nathaniel Greene wasted little time moving towards Camden. There was another American army in Virginia to deal with British forces there. The campaign in North Carolina had ground down Earl Cornwallis's army; it entered that state with 2,774 men at the start of February but ended the campaign at Wilmington two and a half months later with 870 fewer soldiers. These men were very hard for the British to replace, so General Clinton would bear a grudge about it. The Fusiliers and other members of that army, by contrast, were sanguine about the loss, rationalising that their general was at least a fighting man, unlike most of those serving in America, and that they had achieved prodigies under him.

The Americans, though, could suffer one reverse after another, shrugging off their losses of manpower by obtaining new levies or raising militia. Greene had campaigned judiciously, for he was a highly intelligent man, delaying a general action until it absolutely suited him. Admirers penned many a panegyric to Greene's abilities, but he summed up best what had just happened. 'Here has been the field for the exercise of genius,' Greene wrote three days after the battle of Guilford Courthouse, 'and an opportunity to practise the great and little arts of war. Fortunately we have blundered through without meeting any capital misfortune.'

A strategy of trying to pacify South Carolina in its entirety had produced the 23rd's marches to Camden, the Dan and Guilford. Cornwallis had refused to wait passively as sickness sapped his army, partisan bands multiplied and the Continental Army marched down to try and recover that province. 'Consolidation' of South Carolina would almost certainly have failed too, but Cornwallis's forward strategy had brought matters to a head more quickly. The appearance of French fleets, and uniting of a large force of Continentals under Washington was about to produce a new crisis for the British. Once more the 23rd were destined to be in the thick of it.

The Beginning of the End

Or How Balfour and his Regiment Endured Adversity

For Nisbet Balfour, sitting at headquarters in King Street, Charleston, in April 1781, each day brought some unwelcome revelation. While maintaining to superiors that his Lordship's action at Guilford was a signal victory, the 23rd's commanding officer understood soon enough both that the heavy losses rendered the army unable to continue its campaign in North Carolina and that Greene would soon move into South Carolina. While Cornwallis stopped at Wilmington, he and Balfour were able to exchange some letters.

The commandant of Charleston, facing rebel insurrection in every corner of the province as well as the imminent arrival of Greene's Continentals, still hoped that Cornwallis would come back to help him. Preparations were set in train to supply the earl on the coastal route from Wilmington to Charleston. Balfour's sense of complicity with the general was such that he told Cornwallis he had only reported the state of affairs in South Carolina to General Clinton, their mutual bugbear in New York, in 'a guarded, cautious, manner'.

Even before news of Guilford, Balfour had been feeling powerless in the face of growing revolt and its tactics. The lieutenant colonel told one friend, 'Universal disaffection must moulder us away, when joined to the millions of advantages those people have over us.' In particular, he felt there was no answer to the increasingly brutal methods being used by the king's enemies to extinguish British power in the countryside.

During the first part of April, Captain Haring, for example, had led some rebel parties into Dorchester on a killing spree. This town was only 40 miles to the north-west of Charleston, but the Tory irregulars there did not prove equal to the enemy challenge, as Balfour explained to Cornwallis: 'They have adopted the system of murdering every militia officer of ours, as well as every man (although unarmed) who is known to be a loyalist. The terror this mode of conduct has struck, you will easily suppose.'

Colonel Marion, the Swamp Fox, was operating close to Monk's Corner, a similar distance from Charleston, and he too used gruesome methods, including impaling the severed heads of suspected spies on stakes. It might have been supposed that these excesses were restricted to some wayward characters in out of the way places, but this was not the case, for when Greene began his advance into the province, the main army too began executing many loyalists.

While Cornwallis was gathering strength at faraway Wilmington, Greene had moved on Camden in the middle of April 1781. Lord Rawdon, who commanded a garrison of provincials and regulars there, decided to confront the invasion close to the site of Cornwallis's victory over Gates the previous August. On 25 April, Rawdon fought and defeated Greene at Hobkirk's Hill, checking his progress for just long enough to evacuate Camden, removing or destroying the magazines there. Greene pressed on to snuff out several minor posts in May. The farthest-flung loyalist settlement, Ninety Six, continued to hold out against the odds; its refusal to surrender to besieging forces probably owed much to their expectation of what they might receive from their captors.

Serjeant Major Seymour of the Delawares kept writing his journal, recording a vivid impression of the progress of Greene's army through the backcountry. On 17 May, 'were executed five of our deserters'; two days later, 'executed three more of our deserters who were taken in the late Fort'; on 21 May, 'took and killed about 12 Tories', and the next day, 'took and killed about eleven of the Tories within encampment'. The order of events – 'took' then 'killed' – leaves little doubt these were summary executions.

Balfour was deeply angered by reports of these killings. He felt he had to do something for the sake of maintaining morale among the King's troops. In May, following reports of brutality towards prisoners by Marion, Balfour ordered more than 130 American militia to be put on board prison ships as 'hostages', in case of further abuses. Balfour's temper sometimes overwhelmed his common sense for this was an arbitrary step that produced howls of outrage from the officers concerned, seconded by Nathaniel Greene himself.

The confinement of these unfortunate men was not in any case of long duration, for in June 1781 there was a general exchange of prisoners that finally allowed those Continentals who had survived the siege of Charleston and one year aboard the hulks to be released; 740 men marched away that month. Of the others, 530 had already escaped their captivity by enlisting with loyalist regiments, and something like 800 had died of various illnesses while prisoners. An American surgeon sent to care for the men aboard the ships in Charleston harbour had reported that 'these vessels were in general infected with small pox', and that this sickness had been complicated by dysentery and putrid fevers, thus carrying off many men. These deaths undoubtedly stained Britain's reputation, poisoning the opinion of many in Charleston. It mattered little in the war for opinion in the Carolinas that Balfour generally tried to help the doctors to stamp out disease, the prisoners received the same rations as British troops, and the death rate, though shockingly high, was comparable to that of some regiments on Caribbean service.

While Balfour tried to deal with the enemy to his front, he was also to discover, during those difficult months of April to June 1781, the risks of being stabbed in the back. When a convoy of supply ships had arrived in Charleston in April, they had been swiftly unloaded, with some sent on to New York and others straight back to Europe. General Clinton, who faced shortages of transports that hampered his operations elsewhere, was livid. The commander-in-chief had long been hoping to catch out Balfour. Clinton started firing off letters about his grievances against the commanding officer of the 23rd and commandant of Charleston. Not only had the ships been stupidly sent back to Europe when they were needed in American waters, but Balfour had used defeatist language to Lord Rawdon about the state of the rebellion in South Carolina, and had done nothing to repair Charleston's defences as Greene marched into the province.

Clinton held forth at his dinner table in New York, Frederick Mackenzie, Major of the 23rd as well as a senior staff officer at head-quarters, noting, 'I find the Commander-in-chief has been a good deal displeased of late by the conduct of Lieut Colonel Balfour.' More dangerously for that officer, Clinton wrote to Lord Germain in London about the matter and to Earl Cornwallis in Wilmington.

Cornwallis, no doubt, understood the personal animus that lay behind the commander-in-chief's sudden assault. He wrote back, swiftly and vigorously backing his man. Cornwallis suggested to Clinton that he must have been misinformed by crooks anxious to make money keeping rotten vessels in government service; Balfour had only sent back those ships that were unfit for further operations. In words that go some way to explaining why Cornwallis inspired such loyalty among his subordinates, the earl told Clinton, 'Whatever was done . . . was with my approbation at the time, appearing evidently for the good of the service, I therefore think it my duty to exculpate Lt Col Balfour, whom I have found on all occasions, a most zealous, intelligent, and deserving officer.'

Clinton would not let the matter lie, for he knew how his enemies combined against him. He instituted an inquiry, taking statements from officers of various branches insisting that the ships were seaworthy and very much needed at New York. Cornwallis's loyal defence of Balfour produced a sheaf of papers in return, in which Clinton told his lieutenant general, 'I can be the only proper judge' of whether that officer had erred. 'I therefore cannot but disapprove of Lt Col Balfour.' But Clinton seemed to sense that he did not have the absolute power to break Balfour, for authority had been migrating steadily towards Cornwallis. Lord Germain, it was clear from their official correspondence, had approved of Cornwallis's vigorous operations in the Carolinas and was fed up with Clinton's inaction. The spat over the transports was therefore symbolic of who was really in charge and who was going to determine the future shape of operations.

Clinton harboured ideas of conquering a peninsula formed by two of America's great rivers, the Chesapeake and Delaware. This land, comprising the state of Delaware and much of Maryland, would provide a substantial agricultural resource, give plentiful anchorages for the navy and would keep Britain's field armies – under Cornwallis, Phillips and Clinton himself in New York – close enough to support one another.

Cornwallis, a lesser strategist it is clear, had persuaded himself that it was pointless to campaign in the Carolinas as the unhealthiest season of the year came on, and that those provinces would never be tranquil for as long as men and supplies could be sent down from Virginia. It was that state's resources, after all, that had allowed Greene, after he crossed the Dan, to turn the tables. Lord Germain, hotfoot from Court, told both Clinton and Cornwallis, 'It is the King's firm purpose to recover these [southern] provinces in preference to all others, and to push the war from south to north, securing what is conquered as we go on.' Official guidance coincided with gut instinct as far as Cornwallis was concerned, for he was interested in fighting with distinction, believing that would be better done in Virginia, with Major General Phillips's division added to his own depleted army.

On 25 April, Cornwallis marched around 1,500 men (including a little over 200 of the 23rd) out of Wilmington and began his journey north. Only the fit ones had gone, hundreds more were left at the port for shipment back to Charleston where they might convalesce. The general covered himself against a sudden recall to Charleston or New York by keeping a squadron of transports in Wilmington. On 12 May dispatches reached him that Rawdon had beaten Greene at Hobkirk's Hill, and Cornwallis marched on into Virginia. By this step he unilaterally determined that Britain's campaign for the summer of 1781 would take place in that province.

'How great was my disappointment and astonishment when', wrote Clinton some years later, 'I found he had come to the fatal resolution of abandoning both Carolinas to their fate and flying into Virginia.' The commander-in-chief, though, might still be able to bring about a change, and determined to write to Cornwallis as soon as he emerged from the interior and united with Phillips.

Given that Balfour had spared his patron no detail about the desperation of affairs in South Carolina, it can be imagined that, sitting in Charleston, he too might have felt 'disappointment and astonishment'. However, Balfour had always harboured doubts about pacifying the province, and these had intensified as he had observed the ruthlessness of the Whigs and relative timidity of the King's friends. The compact between Balfour and Cornwallis moreover had become so strong, that the Scottish colonel tended to blame Clinton for everything, from pardoning too many rebels back in May 1780 to failing to give proper support to operations in the Carolinas.

As Cornwallis ploughed on northward, affairs stabilised somewhat in South Carolina. After giving Greene a costly check at Ninety Six, that last major backcountry settlement was abandoned and British forces set about trying to consolidate their hold on the coastal hinterland. Balfour decided to resettle some of the piedmont loyalist refugees on sequestered properties in this new, smaller, province, a step that had military logic but simply exacerbated the sectarian unpleasantness between Tory and Whig. Greene, for all his grasp of strategy, was, during the summer of 1781, drawn into an attempt to reclaim South Carolina that claimed much of his army and was only partially successful, while Cornwallis led his host into Virginia.

The marches up into Virginia passed virtually without incident. Great rivers were crossed with practised ease, while the redcoats received little more than hostile glares from the townships they passed through. Battle, disease and desertion had honed Cornwallis's troops into a very lean body of men. There was little straggling or trouble on the march up, and on 15 May, they linked up with a party of scouts from under Colonel Simcoe from the Queen's Rangers, a loyalist corps similar to the British Legion. Cornwallis pushed on at great speed, sixteen miles on the 16th, eighteen the next day, then twenty miles and so on until they reached Petersburg on 20 May.

The column acquired a steady routine during those stages, with the men marching from midnight until the early morning. They would eat when they bivouacked; the hot middle hours of the day were spent resting or foraging, with a meal being cooked around dusk. A few hours' sleep would be followed by reveille at 11 p.m., everything being in readiness for marching at midnight. It was a strange itinerary, but it worked well enough to spare Cornwallis's precious remaining men from the fatigues of the sun. While still a couple of days from Petersburg, the Earl had received sad news, that Major General Phillips had died of typhoid. Phillips was an officer of the Royal Artillery who had been allowed to command a brigade of the line; ardent, highly professional, he was a veteran of Minden and had masterminded Burgoyne's capture of Fort Ticonderoga in 1777. With his death, command of the detachment in Virginia went to Brigadier Benedict Arnold, that firebrand from Connecticut who had deserted the Patriot cause the previous year.

Arnold's operations in Virginia had caused many of the British officers to ask themselves uncomfortable questions. As an enemy, they had respected his vigour and military skill, for Arnold had proven a singular figure both in the ill-fated American march on Quebec and the defeat of Burgoyne at Saratoga. Had Henry Clinton succeeded in his aim of capturing the Hudson forts by Arnold's defection, it would have proven a grievous blow to the American cause, but the conspiracy had miscarried, gaining the British only the general's person, at the cost of

Major John Andre, the redcoat who was captured after being sent to meet him.

Andre's trial and execution left a bitter taste, for he was a young man much admired in the army. There were a few in the 23rd who could even remember him, as he had served briefly in the regiment before the American wars. He embodied principle and stoicism in the face of fate. In return for him, the British got Arnold with his turned coat, emblematic of selfish opportunism. The defector got a purse of gold, provincial brigadier's rank, and his career in the King's service was soon provoking further unease. Arnold hit Virginia like a tempest, attacking warehouses and plantations, causing enormous economic damage. In truth, he embarrassed many at headquarters because he showed up the mediocrity and lassitude of those few British officers of rank still on the continent. Phillips's death left without a proper commander a large British force of more than 4,000 troops, including the army's two light infantry battalions and two Scottish regiments. On 20 May, Arnold's few days as acting commander of the British on the Virginia coast ended, for Cornwallis's army marched into his camp.

The arrival of the grizzled warriors of Camden and Guilford provoked a strong reaction from the Virginian detachment. Cornwallis's men had, after all, fought repeatedly against intimidating odds, marched 1,500 miles and had weaned themselves from many comforts that other redcoats took for granted. As the 23rd, 33rd and Guards trooped into camp, they cut quite a figure.

'Words can ill describe the admiration in which this band of heroes was held by the two Scotch regiments, and even by the battalions of light infantry,' wrote Captain Samuel Graham of the 76th. 'The gallant earl and his brave officers who had shared with him in his long and arduous marches, as well as in his laurels, were almost idolised.'

Captain Ewald, he of the single hard eye, was in camp too, leading his company of jaegers. He was struck by something different when he saw Cornwallis's column arrive. For in the wake of Cornwallis's 1,500 marching troops came a larger crowd of runaway slaves and servants:

I can testify that every soldier had his negro, who carried his provisions and bundles. This multitude always hunted at a gallop, and behind all the baggage there followed well over four thousand negroes of both sexes and all ages. Any place this horde approached was eaten clean, like an acre invaded by a swarm of locusts . . . I wondered as much about the indulgent character of Lord Cornwallis as I admired him for his military abilities.

Ewald, taking command of the jaegers that had marched up from Wilmington, turned loose their small portion of this crowd. The presence of so many followers – even allowing for some exaggeration of the numbers – undoubtedly complicated operations in the following months, since this ravenous mob excited the fears of the slave-owning Virginia gentry while complicating Cornwallis's movements. The army grew even larger as Cornwallis arrived, with the docking of transports carrying a further brigade of 1,200 men from New York. This reinforcement, which included the 17th and 43rd (the only two regiments with a similarly extensive record of American service to the 23rd) and two German battalions, had swollen the overall force under the Earl's command to 7,200.

While Cornwallis soon set about launching further raids into the plantations and trying to thwart the operations of a picked division of Continental infantry under the Marquis de Lafayette, the vexed question of what so large an armament was doing in Virginia could not be deferred any longer. During a few weeks in June and July, Cornwallis received a flurry of contradictory orders from Clinton. Initially the emphasis was on halting operations in Virginia and sending as many troops as possible back to New York, which the commander-in-chief was convinced would soon come under a substantial assault from a Franco-American force led by General Washington and Count Rochambeau. Later, Clinton directed Cornwallis to find a base at the mouth of the Chesapeake, as part of his long meditated scheme to take the Delaware peninsula.

These instructions, insofar as any clear meaning could be divined from them, marked the end of Cornwallis's independent 'marching about' the southern states in search of adventure. Clinton's scheme, wrote the earl, was for 'ltory expeditions' only. 'As the General's plan is only defensive in this quarter, then I can be of little use,' Cornwallis told Balfour in mid-July. 'I have offered to return to South Carolina.' The general thus expected for a short time to be reunited with his Scottish factor to the south, a turn of events that would have made quite a difference to Cornwallis's later reputation, but Clinton would not have it, ordering instead Major General Leslie southwards. General Cornwallis was to remain in Virginia while a base was chosen and fortified on the Chesapeake. Cornwallis could divine in these instructions unmistakable signs of Clinton's taste for recrimination, telling Lord Rawdon that the commander-in-chief was 'determined to throw all blame on me and to disapprove of all I have done and that nothing but the consciousness that my going home in apparent disgust would essentially hurt our affairs in this country, could possibly induce me to remain'.

Cornwallis and his army, including the 23rd, found themselves therefore marching down another peninsula, that formed by the James and York rivers, towards Chesapeake Bay with the enemy to their rear. The joint command of Washington and Rochambeau were, meanwhile, setting their sights on the same place.

The Fusiliers were, by June, a little less dispersed than they had been during Cornwallis's march through Virginia, but it was still a case of young men being in command. The regiment had Captain Thomas Peter at its head, for Balfour and Mackenzie were still serving in Charleston and New York respectively. The light company men, who were reunited at Petersburg with their brother Fusiliers for the first time in a year, were soon sent off again, not as part of the 1st Light Battalion, as they had been during the hectic campaign of 1777, but, together with the 82nd's Light Bobs, as mounted infantry serving with Tarleton on his raids. Forbes Champagne was put in charge of this detachment, Captain Lionel Smythe having sailed back to England with his wife some weeks earlier. The 23rd's Grenadiers, meanwhile, continued to serve with the 1st Grenadier Battalion in New York. Another party numbering a few dozen men was in Charleston, where the evacuees from Camden and Wilmington were gathered. When recruiting parties and twenty-seven prisoners taken by the Americans during late campaigns were counted in with these scattered detachments, the number of Fusiliers shrank from over 400 on paper to fewer than 200 tramping along behind Captain Peter and forty-six under Champagne.

Among those heading for Williamsburg, the state capital, were Lieutenant Calvert, Serjeant Lamb and Thomas Barretté. George Watson, the former Serjeant Major who had been serving as adjutant, was with them too. Balfour had tried to get him a second lieutenancy by borrowing money from a loyalist colonel, but the loss of William Robinson, killed in action at Guilford, allowed the matter to be settled without money changing hands. Robinson (another ex-ranker) left a vacant commission, which, after Lord Cornwallis's intervention, was given to Watson. In small ways like this, the privations of the Fusiliers' campaigning in the Carolinas were being recognised, but the regiment would soon face fresh hardships and danger.

The Fusiliers' embarkation on the evening of 12 August came as a relief to many of them. Brigaded with their old comrades of the 33rd, they had several days earlier appeared in Portsmouth. The story of their short stay by that harbour was like so many others during the years of the revolution; the King's troops had arrived, compromised their friends, and then left. 'How will this look to the loyal subjects there?' asked one officer. 'Have we not made enough people unhappy already?'

In the case of Portsmouth, the circumstances had been particularly ghastly. Behind the town was a deep morass and if ever a name could be appropriate it was that of the Great Dismal Swamp. From this mire, toxic vapours and miasmas had very nearly ruined the health of the small British garrison that stayed there briefly during the summer of 1781.

Brigadier O'Hara was commandant of Portsmouth during those few weeks, when epidemics had broken out, particularly among the camp followers and those who had fled their masters seeking British protection. On 5 August O'Hara had asked Cornwallis what to do with 'hundreds of wretched negroes that are dying by the scores every day'. Four days later, O'Hara took it upon himself to break open government stores rather than take them with the evacuation, arguing that the blacks struck down by illness 'above 1,000 in number, they would inevitably perish if our support were withdrawn'. Whites too were stricken; shortly before he finally abandoned Portsmouth, O'Hara told his general that he could barely load up his troops because 'we are become extremely sickly'.

The 23rd had somehow maintained the record of its previous summer in South Carolina, remaining the fittest corps for a complicated task. O'Hara did not have enough ships to take everything from Portsmouth around to where the army had been ordered to concentrate, so he ferried dozens of horse and his heavy cannon across the water to Newport News under the protection of the 23rd. They had orders to march overland the dozen or so miles to where they would meet the general. The remainder of O'Hara's command would await news of their safe arrival before sailing around to the same rendezvous.

On 13 August, the Fusiliers, therefore, began the first of two marches that would bring them across the peninsula from its James River side to the York River. The temperature was devilish hot, discomfiting anyone who might have thought that Virginia would be a healthier place to campaign in August than South Carolina.

'For six weeks the heat has been so unbearable', wrote one officer, 'that many men have been lost by sunstroke or their reason has been impaired. Everything that one has on his body is soaked from constant perspiration. The nights are especially terrible, when there is so little air that one can scarcely breathe.'

By mid-August the swarms of insects had at least abated, but many left their own slow-acting death in the veins of men they had fed off. On the 14th, Cornwallis reported to O'Hara that the 23rd had arrived safely and that he should conclude the evacuation of Portsmouth and the concentration of the army on the York River. The Fusiliers began to take in their surroundings at Yorktown.

The settlement dated from 1691; it had grown quickly, profiting from the tobacco and cotton trades. It had 300 or so dwellings, several of them grand brick-built mansions, with a similarly handsome Custom House. During the years leading up to the revolution, Yorktown had become depressed. A few score soldiers had garrisoned it as part of Virginia's defence against coastal raiding, but there were no formal works when Cornwallis arrived there.

Although the town occupied an excellent position for trade, it was less favourably sited as a place of war. Cornwallis and his (rather junior) engineer only realised this after they had started collecting the whole army in Yorktown. It was built on low sandy hills and vulnerable from every point of the compass.

From the north, Gloucester Point, half a mile across the York River, could be used by any attacker to hurl cannon shot into the centre of town. Cornwallis, therefore, seized Gloucester during the latter part of August, and sent the 23rd and others out to work there erecting defences. To the east of Yorktown, a deep cleft in the sandy soil allowed the defenders to site some defensive works that would make it harder for any attacker to approach in any order. West of town too there was an obstacle, a low swampy creek between the plateau of Yorktown and a higher ridge overlooking the river; here a redoubt would be built (by the 23rd Fusiliers) on that commanding ground. Attack from the south presented the greatest difficulty, for there the ground was open. The great majority of British guns were therefore dug in to defensive batteries in this sector.

The days of late August and early September passed in a kind of torpor at Yorktown. On many, the officers declared it too hot for their men to work, insisting that only negroes could labour under such conditions. Cornwallis was initially confident that most of the men would be lifted off by British transports and taken to New York. Defensive preparations seemed to be carried on sporadically and apparently oblivious to the fact that their defence or deliverance would rely upon the Royal Navy.

Day by day unfavourable reports reached Yorktown. Captain Ewald commented caustically in his diary that each was greeted by the general or his staff with 'That cannot be!' By mid-September two particularly worrying items of news were circulating: that Washington was marching down from near New York and that the Royal Navy had fought an unsuccessful engagement against the French off the Virginia Capes. Washington and his French counterpart had successfully humbugged Clinton, who had been convinced until the last that New York would be attacked and that British naval forces would maintain their superiority in American waters.

During these days, working parties were drawn from the various regiments to toil away with pick and shovel, throwing up earthworks, a backbreaking task as the sick list grew daily. Each new portentous report seemed to prompt some measure here or there on the defences; cannon were taken from the lower decks of two frigates to add to the shore batteries; a system of pickets and patrols to prevent an enemy surprise was set in place; the town was divided into defensive sectors.

On 5 September, the 23rd were given custody of a redoubt to the west of town in the shape of a four-pointed star. This work, which would soon become known as the Fusiliers' Redoubt, had a key role in defending Yorktown from an attack along the cliff overlooking the York River. Behind it, the ground sloped down a couple of hundred yards to the Creek, beyond which was a redan, or small work, and a section of the inner defences that were also the responsibility of the 23rd.

While these preparations were made to defend the fixed points around Yorktown, Earl Cornwallis abandoned the mobile, aggressive warfare that had typified his progress through the Carolinas. Why?

'I am now busy fortifying a harbour for line of battle ships,' Cornwallis wrote to a friend from Yorktown during the third week of August. 'Please to observe that it is no plan of mine, and I take no merit in it.' This attitude, whether it arose from pride, petulance, or a belated spirit of subordination to his commander-in-chief, showed how Cornwallis allowed his formidable drive to become disconnected for a few vital weeks in Virginia. It also indicated an over-confidence in the

British ability to beat the French in a stand-up fight, since the Comte d'Estaing was disposed of a powerful naval squadron, siege artillery and excellent engineers.

From the moment on 30 August that large numbers of French ships were sighted off the coast, it must have become apparent to the earl that evacuation by sea or the succour promised by General Clinton from the same quarter might prove impossible. After several reconnaissance missions towards Williamsburg, Lieutenant Colonel Tarleton believed that a breakout and march back towards the Carolinas might be attempted. Cornwallis, though, had received General Clinton's definite orders to make a base on the Chesapeake. He hoped still to give battle in front of the lines in any case. Tarleton felt his reluctance to attempt a breakout 'proceeded from the noble Earl's misconception, or from the suggestions of confidential attendants, who construed the Commander-in-chief's letters into a definite promise of relief'.

As September wore on, however, the concentration of American and French forces proceeded apace. Matters at Yorktown assumed the form of crisis.

Far to the south, Lieutenant Colonel Balfour could only follow reports of events in Virginia with perplexed concern. There had been a time, five or six years before, when he had believed the war could be won with just a few thousand more men. Even as Cornwallis had set off into North Carolina at the beginning of 1781, Balfour had told one friend that he still hoped for 'some better prospects than have of late presented'. But the failure to raise the North Carolina loyalists, followed by the eruption of Greene's army into the south, had ground down any optimism that might have remained.

During the sultry days of July and August, Charleston's high-living society had dwindled to nothing. It was a season when the rich would traditionally retire to their plantations or further north for relief, but at this stage of the war, with the city almost cut from the backcountry by enemy patrols, the boarded-up mansions or quiet streets communicated a quite different message to the commandant. Even among the people of Charleston, there was growing defection to the enemy cause.

Balfour retained the company of Fusiliers whom he had co-opted into the administration of his dwindling fief, but in general he found himself with much work and few reliable collaborators. As the enemy had disposed of countryside loyalists by simple murder or summary execution, Balfour was hamstrung from responding in kind. The commander-in-chief had specifically withheld powers of capital punishment from courts martial sitting there, so Balfour had been forced to back down swiftly when he tried to make some captured militia officers 'hostage', insisting on humane treatment of their British or loyalist counterparts. In the commandant's eyes there was a complete inequality between the methods he was allowed to use and those adopted by his enemies. This was particularly noticeable with those American officers who had been captured when Charleston fell. Once freed and given British 'protections' from further punishment, many had joined the enemy side. In May 1781, Balfour told Clinton that he yearned to 'make the most striking example of such, as having taken protection, snatch every occasion to rise in arms against us'. In July Balfour got his chance.

During one of the innumerable skirmishes of that summer Colonel Isaac Hayne, a one-time horse breeder of York County, South Carolina, was taken. Previously captured in May 1780, Hayne had been given a certificate of protection before being allowed home to his farm. When summoned months later to join the royal militia, he had opted to join the Patriots instead, trying to lead across men of the loyalist militia with him. Balfour locked Hayne up in the provost, the dank cellar beneath Charleston's Exchange, while he considered how this rebel might be dealt with. A civilian trial was out of the question, for the prospect of acquittal by a local jury was too damaging to ponder; likewise, the Commandant did not have the power to bring his prisoner before a general court martial on capital charges.

Balfour decided to invent his own tribunal, which he termed a 'court of inquiry'. This dubious legal expedient had already been followed by the Patriots on several occasions, including the trial of Major John Andre. Knowing that he was treading on potentially dangerous ground, also that he served a commander-in-chief who longed to break him, Balfour sought support, writing to Colonel Lord Rawdon who was fighting in the backcountry, seeking his approval. Once again the commandant argued for 'making an example'.

Rawdon had already shown a taste for summary punishments. He had hanged five Americans in Camden for violating their promise not to join the rebellion. In October 1780, he had executed a deserter from his own regiment, the Volunteers of Ireland, after he was captured in arms with the enemy. Even so, when Rawdon arrived in Charleston in

July 1781, he had, despite such instincts, agreed to look into the Hayne case, after appeals from several female relatives. Rawdon soon satisfied himself that, to use his own pungent phraseology, 'By all the recognised laws of war, nothing was requisite in the case of Hayne, but to identify his person previous to hanging him from the next tree.' On 4 August, that punishment was duly effected, Hayne being taken from the Exchange in a wagon to a place of execution just beyond the city limits.

Hayne was the only person executed while Balfour was commandant of Charleston, but he and Rawdon were excoriated for it by the Whigs who lauded Hayne as a martyr. Certainly the enemy's partisans ensured through their hue and cry that Hayne's execution served as the opposite kind of example to the one Balfour wanted. Compared to the dozens of loyalists hanged or shot after summary proceedings, for example following King's Mountain and during Greene's march through the backcountry in May 1781, Balfour was responsible for this solitary entry on the balance of executions in the battle for South Carolina. The noisy reaction to it helps explain why British officers were so often angered or bemused by the hypocrisy they saw on the other side of the divide. But their enemy was possessed of determination for a cause, as well as a belief in ends justifying means, that they could not match. With Cornwallis's removal from South Carolina, there were some instances of British military executions carried out after summary proceedings. Interestingly, though, the prime offenders in dispensing this type of execution were loyalist Americans. Cornwallis or Balfour embodied, on the other hand, the professional restraint of men who apparently decided that even if they could not win the war, they could at least fight it honourably. Even Rawdon, when criticised later for his role in the Hayne affair, angrily defended himself, arguing, 'Humanity . . . ought to be as dear in a soldier's estimation as valour itself.'

When Greene suffered a defeat near Charleston several weeks after Colonel Hayne's death, Major Frederick Mackenzie marvelled at that general's perseverance: 'The more he is beaten, the farther he advances in the end. He has been indefatigable in collecting troops, and leading them to be defeated.' That Fusilier officer had understood a vital truth as six years of war for America neared their climax: the enemy could withstand any number of drubbings, whereas Britain's resolve to carry on would crumble in the face of one more major setback.

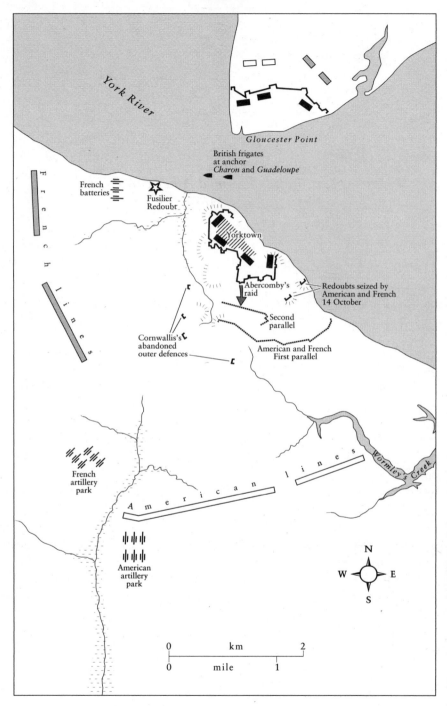

York River

Gloucester Point

British frigates
at anchor
Charon and *Guadeloupe*

French
batteries

French lines

Fusilier
Redoubt

Yorktown

Abercomby's
raid

Redoubts seized by
American and French
14 October

Second
parallel

Cornwallis's
abandoned
outer defences

American and French
First parallel

French
artillery
park

American lines

Wormley's Creek

American
artillery
park

N
W — E
S

0   km   2
0   mile   1

TWENTY-ONE

Yorktown

When Serjeant Lamb Shunned American Hospitality
Once More

The French infantry's white uniforms made them eminently visible at night, so, on the evening of 30 September, some Fusiliers posted as pickets in front of their redoubt, to the west of town, easily spotted their enemy through the murk, coming through the trees. There was a brief exchange of musketry, and the redcoat lookouts took to their heels.

The French troops pushed on up a wooded slope to open, flat ground in front of the Fusiliers' Redoubt. Inside the work, its defenders, roused by the exchange of musketry, leapt to their firing positions. There were about 130 Fusiliers, thirty marines and some gunners who manned two 12-pounder cannon and some small mortars called coehorns. Serjeant Lamb, like many of the men in that small fort, was sick, but had not yet weakened to the point that he had been carried off to one of the many houses being used as makeshift hospitals. Captain Peter had gone down with fever, so the redoubt was under the command of Captain Apthorpe, the New Englander – and the only Fusilier officer still serving with the regiment at Yorktown who had been present at that St David's Day dinner in Boston six and a half years previously.

The defenders waited until the French had trotted to just a few dozen yards from the redoubt before opening fire. Their assailants beat a rapid retreat across the open ground.

When morning came there were unmistakable signs of the French establishing works just 450 paces to the front of the Fusiliers' Redoubt.

The troop dispositions at Yorktown

Elsewhere, at the town's southern defences, the pick-and-shovel work began in earnest too, Earl Cornwallis having given up two redoubts which he felt were too exposed to be defended. Conceding these outlying posts caused much muttering in the British camp, and one French officer noted, 'This . . . gave us the greatest possible advantage.' The move against the Fusiliers' Redoubt on 30 September may have been no more than a reconnaissance in force to see whether it too had been abandoned.

Certainly, the small fort on a cliff overlooking the York River would have been quite a prize for the French. If they could capture it, thus controlling the ridge upon which it stood, they would be able to fire their cannon into the heart of Yorktown, on lower ground to the rear of the redoubt. The game would be up if that happened. The place defended by the Fusiliers, though, was quite strong – a ditch 6 feet deep had been dug in front, its ramparts rose 6 feet above ground level, and sharpened tree trunks had been driven into the ground to thwart anybody climbing the steep walls. Inside this little world, just a hundred feet across, was the sheltered interior with its gun platforms, and firing steps. At quiet times, Fusiliers dozed on their blankets or used small fires to cook. When the alarm was sounded they would grab their muskets and step up to the firing positions.

On the morning of 1 October there was a sense in both camps that the siege was getting under way in earnest. French officers super-intended the unloading of their heavy guns at a landing point on the James River six miles to the south. Once these 24-pounders and heavy mortars were in place, the real smashing of Cornwallis's defences could begin. The Allies divided their line, as they sunk their first parallel, Americans on the right or east, French on the left or south and west. Across the water, at Gloucester, a combined Franco-American force also began its investment. In all the two nations would commit 20,000 troops to the land battle (about 9,000 of them French), while Cornwallis's army of about 7,500 was swollen by about 2,000 men as sailors and others disembarked to join the defence.

In Yorktown itself, the selection of hungry mouths, that ruthless expedient necessary to withstand a siege, had begun. By orders the previous day, all horses except those belonging to the cavalry were to be turned over to the quartermaster general. The lame or sick animals were quickly killed on the beach, some being shot or bled to death, others led out into the surf and drowned by their drivers. It would not be long before the eyes of those directing the defence would fix upon the hundreds of negroes crammed into the town.

As the sick multiplied, medicines began to run out. 'We have already resorted to using earth mixed with sugar to deceive the poor invalids, which is used as an emetic,' wrote Captain Ewald. 'When they are bled, the blood of everyone is vermilion, and it does not take long before the land fever turns into putrid fever.' Officers did not fare particularly well, with Ewald himself resorting to 'the most dreadful remedy in the world', mixing his rum with China powder – the composition of which is uncertain, but it was probably an opiate.

With the siege lines opened, firing into the town began in earnest. American sharpshooters used their long rifles to pick off British gunners or sentries. Field guns were used to annoy one another's forward positions – but the real bombardment would only start when the French assembled the heavy artillery being brought across the peninsula. There were some skirmishes too, particularly on the Gloucester side, where Charles Mair, an officer serving with the 23rd's light company, reinforcing Tarleton, was killed on 3 October.

Three days later, just after dark, the French decided to push their advance once more against Apthorpe's redoubt. This time they were trying to construct a battery, a little forward of their trench, in order to receive the heavy guns. The working party, which consisted of members of the Touraine infantry and Auxonne artillery regiments was met with a hail of fire. 'A rocket rose from the redoubt at once,' wrote a German officer in the British lines, 'whereupon the cannon fire from all our positions in the line began and continued throughout the night.' Six of the Touraine regiment's grenadiers were hurt, as were two artillerymen, one, a young officer, having his leg shot off, later dying from his wounds.

The contest between Apthorpe and the regiments in front of him went on much as the wider struggle, a battle of wits between gunners and engineers as they jockeyed for the best firing points, offering the angles and ranges that would allow them to start blowing holes in Yorktown's earthworks. Unfortunately for the British, the French were much better at this technical business, which meant day by day they advanced their plans despite the defenders' best efforts. Apthorpe's battery could fire 12-pound shot or coehorn shells, exploding grenades the size of pineapples, into the battery being built in front of him. Once the French filled their gabions, big wickerwork baskets full of stones and soil, piling up earth on the enemy side of them, the 12-pound balls had little effect. The coehorn shells shot high into the air over such obstacles, but getting them to fall exactly where the French were working was a tricky feat of marksmanship.

Lieutenant Louis de Clermont-Crevecoeur of the Auxonne Regiment was directing the working parties under fire from the Fusiliers' Redoubt that night of the 6th. A keen officer from an impoverished aristocratic line of Lorraine, he lamented the fatal wounding of his brother officer, but noted phlegmatically, 'The English gave us quite a pounding but did us little harm.' As his men consolidated their earthen walls, they became safer still, and the lieutenant found that one of his principal problems was digging in soil so full of tree roots.

The men of Auxonne and Touraine toiled away day after day building platforms for their guns: four 12-pounders, two 24-pounders, six howitzers and one heavy mortar. This was the battery that opposed the two 12-pounders and coehorns in the Fusilier Redoubt. It is true that Clermont-Crevecoeur's mission was to hit the frigates in the York River just to his left, as well as batter the redoubt, but the imbalance in firepower will give some idea of the situation that the Fusiliers in particular, or British defenders in general, found themselves in.

Clermont-Crevecoeur had spent three of his twenty-nine years at the Metz artillery school, widely admired as the world's finest academy of its kind. Apthorpe, that loyalist Yankee, by contrast possessed plenty of tactical sense about how to handle infantry, developed in countless affairs or skirmishes, but he was no master of field engineering. What he could give his men was dauntless leadership under fire. But what value were heroics in the face of science? The French lieutenant knew that he would soon be bringing a vastly greater weight of shot to bear on the redoubt in front of him than it could possibly return. Its defeat would simply be a matter of time.

At headquarters in New York, unwelcome reports from Virginia had been received in tandem with those of the naval gentlemen filing in from the dockyards. A fleet under that plodder, Admiral Graves, that had been roughly handled off the Virginia Capes early in September had returned to New York to repair and refit. Major Frederick Mackenzie observed the comings and goings at headquarters, growing steadily more angry. He knew that the fate of far more than his regiment was at stake, writing, 'We are certainly now at the most critical period of the war.' As a veteran of the defence of Newport in Rhode Island three years earlier, Mackenzie knew that decisive action could still turn the situation to Britain's favour

Faced with looming crisis, Clinton held meetings. Boards of generals decided that something must be done to relieve Cornwallis. Mackenzie had managed to rub along with his querulous commander-in-chief by working diligently and keeping certain opinions to himself. Privately, he was cynical about how far Clinton really wanted to extract Cornwallis from his predicament, believing that 'should [Clinton] remain . . . without undertaking something, he will be blamed by everyone, let the matter end as it may; and it will be said that he remained an unconcerned spectator of the fate of that Army'.

Henry Clinton made his decisions in committee so that responsibility could be shared. As one meeting of grave-faced officers followed another, he started to insist that everything would depend on the navy. Troops who had been embarked for a cherished scheme of Clinton's to attack Rhode Island were given new orders to be in readiness to sail south.

When could they set off? An initial estimate of 5 October was given. On 28 September Admiral Graves, however, told the commander-in-chief that this must be revised to 8 October. Just two days later, the admiral opined that 12 October might be more a manageable departure date. As one excuse about hemp, cordage or yards followed another, relations between the services became strained. 'If the Navy are not a little more active,' Mackenzie observed bitterly, 'then it will be too late. They do not seem to be hearty in their business or to think that the Army is an object of such material consequence.'

On 6 October, the same day that Lieutenant Clermont-Crevecoeur threw up his battery opposite the Fusiliers' Redoubt, Major Charles Cochrane, one of Cornwallis's ADCs who had come to New York, was sent back with a message for his master. Cochrane would take the risky passage south in a vessel so small that it might run the French blockade of the Virginia capes without arousing suspicion. He was carrying dispatches from the commander-in-chief, telling Lieutenant General Cornwallis what might be done to save his army.

The Fusiliers in the redoubt received their rude awakening around 3 p.m. on 9 October. The great battery in front opened up for the first time, not on them but at the *Guadeloupe*, a Royal Navy frigate anchored a few hundred yards to their right and rear. The army's optimists had been asserting for weeks that the French had no siege guns, but soon enough those who peered over the parapet of their redoubt watched the *Guadeloupe* getting peppered by big-hitting cannon.

Once the Auxonne regiment's gunners had the measure of their targets, they stepped up their bombardment briskly. They poured fire on the *Guadeloupe*, ripping through sails and rigging, smashing into its hull. The captain soon had enough, cutting his cable and steering his vessel into a safer place. The Fusiliers' Redoubt had lost its naval support just as the army had. Having driven off that first vessel, the French gunners moved on to more advanced stuff, heating shot in great braziers, puffing away with bellows until they glowed red hot. The balls were then gingerly placed in cannon (charged with powder behind some particularly thick wadding) before being fired at the *Charon*, a larger frigate of 44 guns that stood off York itself. The heated shot soon succeeded in setting the ship alight; billowing smoke rose from the stricken vessel. The army watched dejectedly as flames consumed the largest naval ship that was supporting them

The opening of the enemy's heavy batteries caused frantic scuttling about in the besieged town. Many places previously thought safe proved to be far from it. Great lumps of metal came smashing into the upper storeys of brick-built houses, showering the sick below with dust and masonry. Mortar bombs held even greater terror. A flat crump announced the launch of a metal sphere of 100 or 150 pounds packed with explosives. The trajectory was high, and these globes could be seen by the naked eye arcing over the town before dropping down into its streets. The fuse, measured by the experienced eye of the master gunner, would be cut to a length that would burn down, ideally, just before the end of its trajectory, exploding over the heads of its victims, showering them with metal casing. At night those manning the British lines could even see the fuses fizzing away on the mortar bombs that flew over their heads.

This danger sent many people scurrying for cover in any place they could find it. Some regiments moved tents into their trenches. Among the few civilians remaining in the town, and the army's frightened servants, refuges were hewn in the sandy cliffs along the river shore. It soon became clear that these caves were the best place to treat casualties too.

On 11 October alone, the besieging French and American guns fired

3,600 shot into Yorktown. 'People were to be seen lying everywhere, fatally wounded', wrote Private Johann Dohla, 'with heads, arms, and legs shot off . . . cannonballs of 24 and more pounds flew over our entire line, and over the city into the river.' When the enemy gunners cut their mortar fuses too long, bombs that dropped in the river went off, sending great plumes of water into the sky.

For the Fusiliers in their redoubt, the dispatch of British vessels supporting their right made them inevitably the target for the full weight of enemy fire from the battery in front. Apthorpe's two 12-pounders were the first target. 'I maintained a barrage that never let up for an instant,' wrote Lieutenant Clermont-Crevecoeur on the 10th. 'I quickly put out of action the enemy batteries on which mine was trained.' Inside the redoubt, the enemy's balls smashed away at the gun positions and the cannon themselves. So incessant was the firing that soon no man wanted to invite death by trying to repair the damage. The following day, the French lieutenant noted with grim satisfaction that 'the enemy fire has slackened to such a degree that it is not really dangerous'. Second Lieutenant Guyon, Calvert's particular friend, was killed at some point in the bombardment.

Even if the guns had been dismounted, the 23rd were far from beaten. The regiment, wrote Serjeant Lamb, 'were greatly exposed to the fire of a battery of nine guns . . . it was reduced to about 120, who had to maintain their post on this galling occasion, as they did with great gallantry, until we were entirely exhausted'. Lamb was so worn out that he was unable to stand. He asked another non-commissioned officer to relieve him at his post, close to the parapet, and sank to the to the ground. Moments later, Lamb's relief became a cloud of blood and bone as a cannon ball ripped him apart. Lamb put his survival down to divine providence.

After just a couple of days of this treatment, Cornwallis's confidence was ebbing away. He wrote to Clinton, 'With such works on disadvantageous ground, against so powerful an attack, we cannot hope to make a long resistance.'

Major Cochrane arrived in Yorktown, having sailed through the French fleet, the day after that urgent appeal was sent at midday on 12 October, and presented the dispatches from New York. 'I am doing everything in my power to relieve you by a direct move,' wrote Clinton, suggesting he would sail from New York on the very day his letter reached Cornwallis. But, Clinton being Clinton, there were the caveats, the promise might be 'subject to disappointment', and the commander-in-chief suggested that by his arrival in the area '[I] may possibly give you an opportunity of doing something to save your army.' The onus was thus placed back on the besieged commander. Cornwallis's ADC, Cochrane, was killed on the lines shortly after bringing this ominous message to Yorktown.

Cornwallis began to measure how many days he might hold out. Some desperate strokes were called for. A sally to destroy the enemy batteries might buy him a little more time. Honour in any case called for a more active defence than he had hitherto put up. What chance did he have of breaking out of Washington's trap? If there was one, it was to the north, from Gloucester Point, not charging out of Yorktown into the mouths of dozens of cannon. He would need his veteran troops for such an attempt. So, on the evening of 12 October, the 23rd were ordered out of the Fusiliers' Redoubt and relieved by the 17th Foot.

Under cover of darkness, the bloodied survivors of Apthorpe's command walked back down the slope towards Yorktown, re-entering the lines just beyond the creek. Their next few days would be spent at that comparatively sheltered point they held at the west of the defences. Although plunging mortar bombs could still hit them there, they were out of the line of direct fire from the besiegers' cannon. Their enemies meanwhile had been advancing a second parallel on the south-eastern part of the town, the place where the fate of the garrison would be decided.

As they got nearer, the French received heavier British fire, dozens of their men being killed or wounded on the night of 13 October. But the weight of shot was on their and the American side. With their batteries pounding the British defensive line from barely 300 yards, the hastily built defences began to disintegrate. Cornwallis's engineers had piled sand or soil into defensive ramparts, placing tree trunks on the outside face to give them greater strength. These methods were satisfactory enough for an upcountry stockade and would have resisted field artillery fire for any amount of time, but 24-pound shot smashed the protective wood out of the way, and heavy howitzers then blew away the foundations or cut down men trying to make repairs. One officer reported that from 10 October onwards 'scarcely a gun could be fired from our works, fascines, stockade, platforms, and earth, with guns and gun-carriages, being all pounded together in a mass'.

With matters assuming a desperate aspect and enemy shot raking the streets every moment, Cornwallis decided to expel the black servants who had been cowering in caves and houses for days. 'We had used them to good advantage and set them free,' wrote Captain Ewald of the former slaves, 'and now, with fear and trembling, they had to face the reward of their cruel masters.' Hundreds of men, women and children, some of whom had been serving the redcoats since their march through the Carolinas, were driven by soldiers into no-man's-land.

Not long after sunset on 14 October, the Allied batteries began a heavy fire on two outlying redoubts on the southern defences. A feint was made to draw British attention towards the work formerly occupied by the Fusiliers, but the main attack went in on the southerly forts. Storming parties – one French, the other American – ran up to them, under heavy fire from the British defenders, and scaled the walls, seizing two key places. From these vantage points, their batteries could flatten what remained of the defences and storming parties would have a short run into the town itself. The end was approaching.

Throughout the following day, the cacophony of cannon continued uninterrupted. Billowing eddies of smoke rolling across the land were reflected above by banks of cloud scudding across the sky. The wind was changing. By sunset, it was completely overcast and a dark night ushered in stiff breezes. Lieutenant Colonel Abercromby, commander of the light infantry during five campaigns, led 350 picked men into the enemy's forward trenches. They bayoneted the sentries and with a blood-curdling cry of 'Skin the bastards!' from Abercromby stormed in, sending the gunners to flight.

A well-planned sally of this sort could change the course of a siege, for the intention was to silence the enemy guns, hammering metal spikes into the cannon's touchholes, making it impossible to fire them. Having gained the battery, Abercromby's Light Bobs attacked eleven guns. Like many aspects of the British defence of Yorktown, this task was poorly carried out. Clermont-Crevecoeur would later comment derisively that the stormers must have been drunk. In fact they did not have the right implements to break the guns and had instead stuck bayonets into the touchholes and broken them off.

When the light infantry returned to British lines they were elated. 'This stroke will save us,' a British officer told Ewald. 'Eleven cannons is a fine thing!' Cornwallis did not intend to gamble, though, on how long the enemy batteries would remain quiet. At 9 p.m., after they had returned from their raid, the light infantry were loaded into dozens of long boats on the York River. As the oarsmen pulled away, with a strong wind making the job harder, other redcoats filed down to the beach. The 23rd, or those of them who could fight in any case, and the Guards were collected as the second wave. Cornwallis was sending his veteran troops over to Gloucester; he intended to attack the enemy there and break out, saving as much of his army as he could. The general, at last, had stirred from his uncharacteristic passivity of previous weeks and was going to fight for it.

It took a couple of hours for the first wave to cross the York River and the boatmen to return to the beach at Yorktown. They came with bad news. The wind had got up to such a pitch that the channel had become very choppy as they rowed. Further crossings would have to be abandoned or the boats might be swamped with the loss of all on board.

On the afternoon of 17 October, a drummer was sent to British ramparts to beat out a parley. Cornwallis requested a ceasefire so that he might discuss terms for the surrender of Yorktown. By 4 p.m. the guns were silent, and the garrison enjoyed their first rest from shelling in many days.

The road south was just two miles, but for many of the 23rd it marked the culmination of more than six years' hard fighting. By the agreement reached between the two armies, the defenders were to march out and surrender their weapons and colours. Cornwallis had tried to obtain terms similar to those at Saratoga, but Washington would have none of it, insisting instead on those imposed on the American defenders of Charleston the previous year.

French and American troops lined each side of the road, as the British and German regiments filed out, drums beating, in order of seniority, the 23rd coming behind the Guards and 17th. 'The British paid the Americans seemingly but little attention as they passed them,' recalled one of Washington's soldiers, 'but they eyed the French with considerable malice.' One soldier of the 1st New Hampshire standing at the fence watched the 23rd pass with particular interest. It was William Hewitt, who had deserted the regiment at Boston in March 1775. As the Fusiliers passed, he recognised quite a few faces. It was, however, a sadly depleted party, for just a few dozen men of the Royal Welch emerged from the besieged town. The regiment returned just sixty-seven rank and file fit at York (plus fewer than two dozen with Champagne's light company across the river) – around 120 men lay sick or wounded in the makeshift hospitals within the lines. So small indeed was the contingent of those able to march that the victors did not notice the absence of colours at the head of the Fusiliers' column.

On the right of the marching column were French regiments in smart white uniforms with white gaiters, their senior officers encrusted with bejewelled stars and sashes denoting ranks or nobility or awards. The Americans by contrast 'made a poor appearance, ragged and tattered'.

The column was led by Brigadier O'Hara (Cornwallis pleading sickness), who was directed into an open field by Brigadier General Lincoln, the loser at Charleston. There a bank of French and American senior officers watched as the regiments were called forward one by one to lay their muskets as well as colours on the ground, turn, and form up ready for the return to Yorktown. One corporal of the 76th threw his weapon down so hard that it broke, exclaiming, 'May you never get so good a master!' When the turn came for the Ansbach-Bayreuth troops to do the same, their colonel was in tears as he gave the order.

O'Hara discharged his melancholy duty that afternoon with his characteristic *sang froid*. He had been convinced for years that the Americans could not be beaten back into a state of loyalty to the Crown but had, on the contrary, become Britain's most inveterate enemies. The brigadier had fought like a tiger at Guilford Courthouse, when the army's honour and self-respect demanded it, but now circumstances dictated a different course. After surrendering the garrison, O'Hara wrote home, 'Our ministers will I hope be now persuaded that America is irretrievably lost.'

Nearly 4,000 men grounded their arms in the surrender field. A similar ceremony took place on the Gloucester side, but 3,000 soldiers were too sick to put in an appearance. Cornwallis had given up 7,668 troops, more than 1,000 sailors and several hundred loyalists and servants; it was disaster on such a scale that it must produce peace.

The British and Hessian regiments marched back in silence, disarmed, into town, enduring some catcalls and insults from the American regiments as they passed. Reunited in their lines, the officers and men of the 23rd made their preparations for departure.

The night before the surrender ceremony, officers throughout Cornwallis's army had drawn lots to see who would march into captivity and who would be free to leave with their general. Slips of paper with words denoting whether they would stay or go were screwed up and placed in a hat or bucket. Given the years of enforced idleness experienced by the Saratoga captives, there was trepidation as each man picked his slip. One captain was needed to command the regiment's party, the duty for the 23rd falling to Thomas Saumarez. The subalterns then chose. 'It was my lot to be on this service,' wrote Lieutenant Calvert, who was joined by a couple of fellow subalterns.

Those officers who had better luck with the draw were free to go. Captain Peter, who had been sick through most of the siege, was well enough to travel. As acting commanding officer, he was determined to deny the enemy one particular triumph over the Fusiliers. Peter detached the 23rd's two colours from their staffs, those flags that symbolised the regiment and the royal cause for which it had fought so earnestly those six and a half years. He and another officer each wrapped a flag around his body, concealed beneath their uniforms, before boarding a transport, the *Earl of Mulgrave*, that was destined for Charleston and New York. It was to prove a stormy and difficult journey, so there must have been times when Peter envied Apthorpe and Champagne, who chose to travel overland to New York.

The walking remains of the regiment left Yorktown on 21 October, under the escort of the Virginia militia. Serjeant Lamb was not with them. The Irishman had every reason to fear captivity, for he had escaped from it before and there might be consequences if he was recognised. He volunteered to do duty at the hospital, putting his skills as an occasional surgeon's mate to good use.

One month later, Lamb went to the head of the British hospital to resign, saying he intended to try and catch up the prisoners' column. He took some pay he was owed and donned a private's uniform, before slipping out of Yorktown while the American guard was changing. During the days that followed, he made his way north.

It was late November so the seasons were changing; somehow he would have to steer clear of American patrols and find his way hundreds of miles back to New York, crossing several great rivers on his way.

During his trek, Lamb came across several American farmers who were prepared to shelter him at night – more through a sense of Christian pity than sympathy for the British. Several of these good Samaritans had other thoughts in mind too, for the economy of rural Virginia, battered by years of war, had a dire shortage of labour. Every kind of inducement was held out to Lamb and other stragglers or escapees to desert the King's service, making a new life. One American offered Lamb a partnership: he would build a school house in his township and the literate Fusilier serjeant would become schoolmaster. Another offered Lamb a grant of 300 acres to farm in the new Kentucky settlements. 'I was determined to die rather than serve any state hostile to Great Britain,' wrote Lamb, explaining his rejection of these proposals. 'Indeed I could not even patiently support the idea of remaining a prisoner among them.'

Lamb's liberty was curtailed after just a few days. He and two other British escapers were arrested in Fredericktown in Maryland, less than halfway to New York. His fears of being recognised as a previously escaped prisoner from Burgoyne's army were realised, and the serjeant passed many cold nights in dark cells before being reunited with his colleagues from the 23rd whom he joined in Winchester, Virginia, during the dying days of 1781.

The mood of the Yorktown prisoners was little improved by the fact that some of their guards were recognised as former British soldiers. The serjeant major of the 33rd spotted John Shaw, the man who had fallen into American hands with Tattersall of the 23rd just before the battle of Guilford Courthouse, in American uniform and denounced Shaw as a damned rebel. Dozens – although still a small minority – had made accommodations like Shaw's, succumbing to the same blandishments that Lamb resisted so indignantly. In Shaw's case, meeting and marrying an Irish Catholic had spurred him to discard the red coat, serving in a Virginia regiment before settling in the country.

In January 1782, the 23rd were moved to a large detention compound near Lancaster in Pennsylvania. It was a gruelling winter's march for many of the men, but from Lamb's point of view, at least, it got them closer still to New York. Arriving in their new surroundings, the Fusiliers were ordered to build their own stockade, the pen of wooden posts that would serve for their confinement. Not far away, what remained of the regiments of Burgoyne's Convention Army had settled themselves rather more comfortably, with wooden huts sleeping six men each, vegetable plots and a church. The Yorktown prisoners soon nicknamed their quarters 'Camp Security' and those of the Saratoga men 'Camp Indulgence'. For Lamb, the early joy at meeting some old comrades from the 9th, in which he formerly served, soon gave way to a sort of contempt for those who had passed four and a half years in captivity. The proud, motivated men, like Lamb himself, had long since escaped, leaving the feckless or those who dared not abandon the local girls they lay with.

Many of the Saratoga prisoners had found themselves jobs with Pennsylvania farmers. Americans seeking some hired help were required to deposit a bond with the authorities and could then take their new man 25 or even 30 miles away to work. Quite a few redcoats were happy enough to pocket two or three dollars each month hunting wolves or mucking out stables while clocking up British pay all the while. Those officers like Saumarez or Calvert of the 23rd, who had accompanied the soldiers into captivity, were there in large part to prevent the soldiers succumbing to offers of permanent local employment. So while they could do nothing to stop men taking jobs, they held back their soldiers' pay in the hope that many would remain loyal, dreaming of the large sum due to them when their confinement ended.

For the officers themselves, captivity was crushingly tedious. Since they had given their parole to remain there, escape would have violated their sense of personal honour. Attempts to do so were extremely rare, although officers of the 23rd might have recalled that one of their number had done so in 1778. Thomas Eyre was an American-born subaltern who, captured during the skirmishing in the Jerseys early in 1777, said he was horribly mistreated, prompting his flight to British lines in Philadelphia. Eyre's escape embarrassed General Howe, and he was soon sent to another regiment. The great majority of officers knew that it was best not even to attempt to flee.

Officers, similarly, could not take work, for it would be ungentlemanly to do so. Some tried to use the time profitably to improve their French or German, but there was a shortage of suitable books. While British or Hessian officers were free to live outside the prison camps, they had to pay rent and for all of the other necessaries of life. Many soon found their pay could barely meet these expenses. The feeling of being hard-up for months at a time added to the general misery conveyed by one captive officer:

Of all the situations of life, that of having no pursuit is the worst . . . time hangs heavy and I scarcely know how to spin out the day. I generally lay til ten, go to breakfast and then down to the town to play billiards or pick up the news. Here I find a number of stupid beings as dull as myself – yawning and sauntering from room to room and cursing their ill stars for keeping them in such a vile hole.

Better-connected Yorktown officers, like those of Saratoga before, soon started writing plaintive letters to their friends or patrons, trying to escape this confinement. The best hope was that the commander-in-chief in New York might include them in an exchange of officers, swapping them for a captured American of similar rank.

For Serjeant Lamb and the rankers there were no such hopes of exchange, so after a couple of months recruiting his strength and waiting for the weather to improve, he was meditating another escape. Lamb, the organiser, soon found several others who wanted to join – among them Serjeant Charles Collins, a veteran of nearly ten years in the regiment and of many of its battles from Lexington onwards. Lamb told Captain Saumarez, the acting commanding officer, of their intentions and, by way of support, that officer advanced them some pay.

On 1 March 1782, the group of eight Fusiliers left their camp at Lancaster. They had availed themselves of a pass from their American commandant that entitled them to seek farm work anywhere within ten miles of the camp, but they soon passed this point of no return, pressing on towards New York. The journey took them three weeks, during which time they picked up another man who had previously deserted the 23rd but wanted to return and seek his pardon. There were numerous close shaves with American patrols and quite a few locals who shunned their appeals for food or shelter. But Lamb and his comrades eventually found their way to the loyalist underground, one farmer near Philadelphia furnishing them with a list of the 'King's Friends' who would help them. Many other escaped redcoats had passed that way before, no doubt, so once in New Jersey, close to their destination, they found men willing to risk death in order to pilot them into British lines. During the last stage of the journey, the Fusiliers divided into two parties, Lamb leading one and Collins the other, in order to reduce their chances of capture.

On the evening of 22 March, a rowing boat pushed off the Jersey shore, heading towards Staten Island. In it were Lamb, two loyalists, and three other escaped Fusiliers. After days of hardships, one of Lamb's party had dropped by the wayside, pleading he could not go on. His fate along with that of Serjeant Collins' party were unknown as the oarsmen began battling against an increasingly strong wind. A storm was blowing up in the channel; the American boatmen feared that their little craft would be swamped. Lamb and the other redcoats left their loyalist friends in no doubt of their determination to persist or perish in the attempt. With driving rain soaking them to the skin, they battled the elements for two hours until they spotted a sloop through the murk. The boatmen felt sure she must be an American privateer, but Lamb ordered them to row on. Water was sloshing about in the bottom of the boat. 'To our unspeakable joy,' he later wrote, 'we saw British soldiers standing on the deck.'

The escapers were conveyed across Staten Island to New York where they were warmly received by Major Frederick Mackenzie. Lamb had succeeded in his second escape. In the days that followed Serjeant Collins and all the remaining Fusiliers came in too. By his initiative and determination, Lamb had reached that level where his superiors began wondering how they might gain him an officer's commission. Mackenzie used his powers of patronage, first to line Lamb's pockets with the allowances of secretary to the Commandant of New York and later to get him appointed adjutant to a loyalist corps in the city.

In early 1782, the 23rd was scattered across the continent. So it would remain until the peace universally expected by those in command of the army. Active operations had all but ceased. The Fusiliers' main body, nearly 200 men under Captain Saumarez, languished in captivity in Pennsylvania; in New York the Grenadier Company remained with the 1st Battalion of those troops, but another company's worth of recruits or escapees was soon formed under Captain Peter; and, to the south, in Charleston, a couple of dozen men recovered from the hospitals of Camden or elsewhere did duty under Captain Blucke, while Lieutenant Colonel Balfour remained as commandant.

During the same month that Lamb arrived in New York, William Dansey, the officer of the 33rd who had commanded its light company during the 1777 campaign, returned to the continent having married in England and been promoted to major. Appearing in Charleston he was placed in command of a battalion scraped together from waifs and strays of the 23rd, 33rd and Guards. His description of their situation provides a telling insight into the mood of those who had survived the epic campaigns of Camden and Guilford. 'As to the situation of affairs here they are as bad as can be,' Dansey wrote home from South Carolina. 'A broken army of all manner of corps, of which the debris of Lord Cornwallis's army are the most respectable amounting to about 300 wounded men and recruits that never joined. We are all much hurt at the seeming indifference at home concerning the fall of Yorktown. Great Britain will not see such an officer or such an army again soon.'

Going Home

Or How the 23rd Left America

The Fusiliers' imprisonment ended at 8 a.m. on the bright morning of 9 May 1783. Nearly three weeks had passed since they had learned of the conclusion of a peace treaty between Great Britain and the American states. 'The joyful news', wrote one private, soon brought 'the long wished for and passionately awaited order, to begin our departure march.'

Captain Saumarez was to receive the honour of leading the first detachment of British prisoners back to New York. The column would be headed by several dozen men of the Royal Artillery, the Light Infantry, then the remnants of the 17th, followed by the 23rd. Some 500 marched behind the young captain, travelling initially to Philadelphia, 125 of them from the 23rd Fusiliers.

There were not many other captains left to dispute the honour of leading this division back, indeed only four others remained in the whole of the Yorktown army. None would have wanted to elbow Saumarez out of the way in any case, since he had emerged as an articulate and forceful spokesman for the prisoners, taking up the cudgels both with their captors as well as British headquarters in New York, ensuring that the men were properly provided for.

During their nineteen months of captivity, a great many officers had looked after themselves rather than their men, using their connections to escape the tedium of Lancaster and the other posts where prisoners had been confined. When the turn of the Guards came to march, around 260 soldiers and non-commissioned officers formed up without a single officer to command them.

News of the peace treaty negotiated by emissaries in Paris had brought all manner of celebrations: bonfires were lit, *feux de joie* echoed across the landscape, festive dances were held, and many a dram drunk. In some places alcohol had worked its malign way on the soldiers, with American cheers of 'Hurrah for Washington!' or 'Hurrah for Congress!', soon answered by cries of 'Hurrah for King George!' Ill-will between prisoners and captors had then shown itself with some brawls, attacks on British or Hessian prisoners as well as absurd orders to the detainees not to sing their national anthem. On the whole though, a spirit of bonhomie was preserved; many local people who came to see the columns tramping off did so with wishes of 'God's speed', cries of farewell and tears in their eyes. The soldiers had consorted with locals around Lancaster just as they had everywhere else when the army stopped for long enough. Transactions – commercial, convivial and carnal – had flourished. Each regiment under orders to march to New York, and via there to return to Europe, faced a reckoning that May, since there were many who did not want to go back.

The German regiments, held near Fredericktown in Virginia, were hard hit by desertion, many men choosing to settle with countrymen or local girls in the New World. As for the 23rd, it had marched around 200 men into captivity at Yorktown, taking 125 back to New York. Of the missing, thirty-three deserted, twenty-four died of natural causes while prisoners, and perhaps fifteen had escaped back to British lines, like Roger Lamb.

By late May, around 4,900 former prisoners of the Americans had come in to New York, the commander-in-chief reporting to his masters in London, 'Much civility has been shewn them on their march through the country.' The returnees included even a few hundred remnants of Burgoyne's Convention Army who had been prisoners for nearly six years. Once back within the British lines, the Fusiliers and other regiments were issued with new muskets, an important moment in their rehabilitation as soldiers.

Britain's disengagement from the thirteen provinces was being conducted by a different set of leaders to those that had prosecuted the war. After Yorktown, the ministry of Lord North had collapsed and Lord Germain had been removed from the American department. General Clinton, after years of attempted resignation, finally shuffled off the duties of commander-in-chief in America. In their place had come a Whiggish bunch that the King could hardly bear to be civil to, including that fiery orator Charles Fox as Foreign Secretary. General Sir Guy Carleton took the reins in New York.

It was to Carleton, during the summer months of 1783, that the huge labour of uprooting the British army from America would fall. In this he was seconded by Major Frederick Mackenzie of the Fusiliers, and many other staff officers. Carleton, like his predecessor, was not an inspiring leader of men. He had a prickly manner and, such were the dynamics of army politics, his actions aroused the scorn of the customary pack of critics. Carleton was, though, the right commander for the moment because he had finely tuned political instincts, a sense of fairness, and was a stickler for keeping track of every farthing of the public money he disbursed. These qualities were required because Britain's war for America had been fought on promises: to loyalist Americans raising troops; to merchants owed thousands of pounds; or to men who had joined the army 'for the duration' of the war only. Now that it was clear that the war was lost, New York was crammed with those who feared that every pledge made by the previous government in London would be liquidated as British power in America ebbed away.

Every sultry morning during the summer of 1783 brought a different procession of petitioners to headquarters. The common sort were sometimes treated with cold indifference, sometimes propelled towards the lower grade of staff officer, men empowered to dispense a few pounds for a home lost or years spent soldiering in some southern swamp. Many of the blacks, former slaves desperate to evade the vengeance of masters they had escaped, found a sympathetic ear at the house of New York's commandant, Colonel Birch, where Serjeant Lamb worked as a secretary. Others, given the runaround by some assistant to the quartermaster general or minor barrack master, criss-crossed the city clutching their memorials, records of service, or title deeds, well-worn papers, unfolded before the weary eyes of each new official that would receive them.

A higher class of desperation could be found in the anteroom to General Carleton's office. It was there that the once-powerful merchants, men of property, or provincial colonels might have their grievances heard by the commander-in-chief in person. In the case of Frederick Phillips, father-in-law of Captain Smythe of the 23rd, these supplications produced a letter from Carleton to a minister in London. The claimant, wrote the general, was 'a gentleman of character and the head of a respectable family, lately possessed of one of the greatest estates in America . . . the circumstances of his being compelled to take refuge in England for personal safety, at an advanced time of life and in a very bad state of health, gives him additional claim to consideration.'

The compensation in store for Frederick Phillips would be a small proportion of what he claimed to have lost. The same principle was applied to the more lowly petitioners, too. Often they got one tenth of the value of their property. Nevertheless, hundreds if not thousands of claims were paid out that summer, many of them coming across Major Frederick Mackenzie's desk. There were 'pilots', farmers who had guided British escapees across the Jerseys, people claiming large unpaid bills for supplies, or widows of men who had died fighting for their king. Those incapable of writing employed scribes to add some copperplate dignity to their pathetic narratives.

Once the question of compensation was settled, many wasted little time escaping the city. The peace treaty between Britain and her enemies (France, Spain and the Netherlands had joined in the global free-for-all against the King's interests) had produced a state of non-belligerence, but the business of extracting garrisons from America would require months. During this ill-defined time, people who had taken different sides began to mix together once again, something that caused particular angst to the Tories. 'Those who would dare to remain in New York look desperate with fear of dark prospects,' wrote one Hessian. 'Rebel sympathisers arrive in the city from all directions by land and water. With a triumphant air they take possession of their dwellings, on which they had turned their backs eight year ago.' With victory in sight, many Patriots began to walk the streets of New York again, sometimes muttering insults at the redcoats or loyalists they passed, producing brawls or even duels in the streets.

Although the city's commerce had largely dried up, the quayside was a place of constant activity during these days. Hundreds of ships were sailing every month. Early in the year, evacuees from Georgia and Charleston, including the one-time commandant Lieutenant Colonel Nisbet Balfour, had arrived in New York. These southern provinces had been given up now the end was in sight. From the harbour thousands of loyalists set sail for the West Indies, Canada or Europe. They wanted a new life, away from their self-righteous former neighbours, smug with triumph. Between 26 May and 17 June, for example, a little over three weeks, 7,556 people applied for passage out of New York. Most were heading north, taking advantage of new land grants in Canada: 3,656 wanted to go to the colonies on River St Johns, 681 to Halifax and 1,218 to the Canadian mainland.

Many soldiers enlisted during the war had been wooed with offers of land, an incentive copied from the rebels. Although they knew that Newfoundland or Nova Scotia were barren forested wastes in which it would be hard to scrape a living, more of the discharged men chose to go to these provinces rather than to the slave economies of the West Indies, or back to Britain or Ireland with a few pounds in their pockets. General Carleton understood the danger that these shiploads of settlers would starve or fall into a desperate situation, arriving too late to clear their land and grow crops before winter. He wrote to the governor in Halifax outlining plans to help the demobilised soldiers: 'Each man has received two pair of stockings, two pair of mitts, and one pair of shoes, extra clothing, also an axe and a spade.' They would also be eligible to draw rations for a full year after they arrived.

Dozens of the Welch Fusiliers took advantage of the offer of free land in Nova Scotia, turning their backs on former lives across the Atlantic. Carleton's staff, meanwhile, planned the evacuation of those that remained with the colours, an enormous undertaking requiring the transport of 3,436 people to Nova Scotia (including six regiments to garrison the place, families and some dischargees), and 11,276 back to Europe.

With the return of the main body of the 23rd from captivity, the regiment had found itself more or less together again, and there were many reunions at Herricks on Long Island, where they were camped the summer of 1783. Lieutenant Colonel Balfour had in March heard that years of assiduous cultivation of his patrons, Sir William Howe and Earl Cornwallis, had paid off, with his appointment as an aide-de-camp to the King. This honorary post promised elevation to the rank of full colonel, ascension beyond regimental service to the general staff; future promotions would then come by seniority alone (so Balfour would not have to purchase). Plums such as regimental colonelcies might be expected and, if he lived long enough, a general's rank. Frederick Mackenzie, meanwhile, enjoyed the fruits of long service and patronage at a proportionately lower scale, banking his ten shillings per diem staff pay and getting his son James, who had been commissioned into the 23rd two years earlier, elevated to the rank of lieutenant while he studied in England.

Serjeant Lamb was sent to take command of the regiment's latest batch of recruits. Robert Mason, the one-time light company bugler, had restored himself to favour following the unpleasant business of his attempted desertion and court martial of four years earlier. A lengthy period in jail, more than one year while he awaited reprieve from his death sentence, had saved Mason from the hardships of the southern campaigns. Since the regiment always needed talented musicians and Mason was a charmer, he had managed not only to rehabilitate himself but to gain promotion to corporal.

During the daily parades and drills, the officers and serjeants tried to get the regiment back into some sort of order. The grenadier company was a pool of veteran soldiers, including several escaped Convention Army men, and it was the one part of the regiment not to have suffered the indignity of capture. The other companies combined soldiers who had shared in Cornwallis's heroic epic in the Carolinas with complete novices or skulkers who had sidestepped service. Major Dansey, drilling the 33rd – brother regiment to the Fusiliers in Webster's brigade at Camden and Guilford – noted in July of 1783, 'I am pleased to find that our groundwork is not quite gone and that Lord Cornwallis and Webster are not wore out of the 33rd.'

The Fusiliers passed the summer months with sea-bathing trips, occasional turns on guard, and preparations for their return to Europe. In contrast to the anguished loyalists, it was a happy time for the regiment, one in which the veterans of many years' hard fighting began to disregard rumours of a posting to Nova Scotia or the Caribbean and imagine a homecoming with families whose faces they struggled to remember. Those who had joined for 'the duration' could prepare for their discharge too. There were few discipline problems, so the Welch Fusiliers lived in near complete harmony with the Long Island farmers around their encampment. So pleasant were these relations that the people of Herricks petitioned General Carleton in July, following a rumour that the regiment was to be re-deployed, noting:

. . . having for sometime past had the 23rd Regiment of troops quartered amongst us, and finding the behaviour of both officers and men to be such as affords the greatest satisfaction from their civil deportment, and carriage, the good order of the troops, and their peaceable behaviour towards the inhabitants in general, [we] cannot but regret their departure from this place' .

So much for the rapacious redcoat of the Whig pamphleteers. Some of the Long Islanders were undoubtedly loyalists fearful of encroachments by rebel patrols from Connecticut, for as the British garrison around New York was wound down and the first regiments shipped home, such incursions increased, but the Fusiliers had found peace during their final months in America.

The mood of the Fusiliers' encampment was most probably lightened by the fact that the majority of soldiers at Long Island were eligible for discharge. Many of them would choose to take it back in Britain, leaving the King the expense of shipping them, their wives and children back across the Atlantic. In early October, however, those wishing to settle in Nova Scotia boarded the suitably named transport *Hopewell* for the journey to that frigid colony. They were formally discharged a couple of weeks later on 24 October, four corporals and fifty privates. These men were paid off-pay and would remain in the Americas, having achieved honourably what dozens had deserted the 23rd to find: a new life, often with an American wife.

On 25 November, the last British regiments, including the 23rd, were ferried off Manhattan to Staten Island, from where they would be embarked home. Washington and his staff rode into the city hot on their heels; New York was taken over by the victors, there were noisy celebrations, and the flag of the United States flew over its streets. British soldiers, always game for some amusement at the expense of the locals, left the Union flag nailed to the flag-post at Fort George on the southern tip of Manhattan. In order to make it even harder for the victors to hoist the thirteen-striped flag of their new republic, the redcoats had removed the rope from its pulley and greased the pole.

That night of the 25th the British could have watched and heard the noisy celebrations on the waterfront, since many royal ships were still anchored in the harbour. A few days later, the Fusiliers embarked, and the transports sailed for England on 5 December; their odyssey of service that had begun more than a decade earlier was over.

From its arrival in America in the summer of 1773 to its departure in November 1783 around 1,250 men had served in the 23rd – the confusions of army bookkeepers make it impossible to give an exact figure.

The number of other ranks (serjeants, drummers, rank and file) going home, though, was 247. About sixty of these survivors were men who, like Robert Mason, had served in the 23rd throughout its decade in America; the remainder were later additions. But if only about one fifth of the total number who had served in America boarded the ships home in 1783, what had happened to the rest? There were seventy-two men still in the recruiting pipeline (back in Britain, and a detachment stranded in Halifax). During the regiment's years in America it had discharged more than 130 men, usually because they were unfit for further service, most of these invalids taking a free passage home. Another forty-four had transferred into other regiments. A total of 493 Fusiliers therefore left the regiment legitimately during the war or were still serving at its end.

One stark fact is clear: the majority of soldiers who joined the 23rd during the preceding decade never left America. There were 193 deserters, around 15 per cent of those who had served. Some had disappeared into the oblivion of forests and swamps, but many like William Hewitt settled, raising children in America. To these men who absconded can be added the fifty-four or so who availed themselves of an official discharge in New York after peace had been declared. Removing the surviving regiment, its dischargees, deserters and invalids from the equation, this leaves around 475 men of the 23rd who died in America. Losses in battle amounted to around seventy-five men (and five officers too), the remaining 400 or so succumbed to illness. The unhealthy winter of 1775–6 in Boston saw dozens claimed by smallpox, consumption and the flux. It was the period of 1780–81, though, that had been particularly disastrous for sickness. The regiment lost 164 soldiers during these two campaigns, and only around one quarter of that number fell in battle. The unhealthy climate of the Carolinas with its swamps, insects and miasmas had played havoc with the 23rd, as Lieutenant Colonel Balfour and Earl Cornwallis knew it would. Keeping them marching and fighting through the Carolinas may have ground down enfeebled soldiers faster or, by contrast, preserved them from the ravages of epidemics that afflicted static garrisons in the backcountry. Cornwallis and Clinton would doubtless have argued opposite views.

In all of this accounting of lives, some salient conclusions emerge. The first is that poor procedures for camp hygiene, an often wretched diet and the lamentable quackery of the few surgeons willing to serve dispatched far more redcoats than any number of actions by the Continental Army. The second is that America's daughters, through the sweet oblivion of the conjugal bed, most likely cost King George more men than America's sons with their noisier manoeuvres. Those deserting Welch Fusiliers who resisted the allure of local women often fell for siren songs of a different kind – the promise of land on the Kentucky frontier or the offers of being set up in business as a teacher, smith or well-digger. The appeal of life in the New World, and its contrast with the hardships of a soldier's lot, proved to be one of the Patriots' best weapons.

The grim reality of campaigning in America, that sickness would claim far more men than enemy fire, would have been apparent among the 23rd's officers too. Some eighty-eight served there during the war, although the time spent on the continent by most officers was considerably shorter than the time served by the men. Those like Charles Apthorpe or Thomas Saumarez who began their campaigns as lowly subalterns, and stayed with the Fusiliers for several years as they rose to captain, were rarities. Far more officers spent one or two campaigns in that regiment before purchasing or transferring into another, or indeed selling out. Five officers of the 23rd were killed in action or died soon afterwards from wounds. Eight received injuries in combat that were serious enough to be recorded, but perhaps twice that number received some sort of non-fatal wound in battle. The number who perished through sickness, by contrast, was thirteen.

Several officers of the regiment undoubtedly profited greatly from their time in America. Happily, none of the 23rd stood accused of fraud on a vast scale, as some men who had run the army's wagon train or arranged its quarters did. Both Balfour and Mackenzie, though, obtained a couple of steps of rank, as well as using the additional pay they were granted to restore their financial health. Others such as Apthorpe or Peter advanced themselves by years of hard fighting. Perhaps the most canny of all the officers who started the war in the 23rd proved to be Robert Donkin. His disappointment at being denied the lieutenant colonelcy of the Royal Welch Fusiliers early in 1778 did not last long, since General Clinton soon established a new post for Donkin with the same rank. Not only did the founding commanding officer of the Royal Garrison Battalion, Donkin, get his step for free, but he also maintained his record of serving in the American theatre without suffering the risks of going into battle. Donkin's battalion was soon dispatched to serve in the balmy safety of the Bahamas. When the war ended he was able to work the army system sufficiently well to ensure that the battalion, along with his job, were transferred to the British establishment. Donkin became a familiar figure in his later years at the spa in Bath, living out his twilight years comfortably on general's pay.

What were the reflections of the army that had lost the war in America? A great many, it is clear, did not accept that the British army had been beaten. Serjeant Lamb, a veteran of both the Saratoga and Yorktown capitulations, wrote: 'It was never said of Burgoyne's army that they ran away, but that they were slain. Nor of Cornwallis' army that they were vanquished but that they were taken.' Many other British veterans felt the same way; their country may have lost the war, but their army had not been defeated on the battlefield. They were sure that they were better soldiers, until the end, than the Americans. It was undoubtedly this pride in country, red coat and regiment that kept many of them fighting. It made them all the more angry with those at home whom they considered to have squandered the overall result of the war.

Balfour articulated the thoughts of many when pouring his vituperation on the heads of those parliamentarians who had put personal or factional interest ahead of any consideration for the soldiers bleeding and dying thousands of miles away. He had written of the army's duty in America to one politician friend, 'We must not only move as machines, but be as insensible too.' Major Dansey too could not contain his bitterness towards those who had recently come to power in London, Whigs who had for years trumpeted every reverse suffered by the British army, such was their contempt for the King's war, and who proudly sported the American cockade on their hats. America, wrote the major, had been 'bartered away by turbulence and faction to the most ignoble of these wretches . . . now the sword is sheathed persecutions are begun more inquisitous and horrid than the Inquisitions.'

For many, the abandonment of the American loyalists was an affront to their feelings of soldierly propriety. 'The desertion of the loyalists is looked upon by all of us as the most dishonourable act that was ever done by a nation,' wrote one officer. 'Faction has done what the sword could not accomplish.' In the 23rd's mess, with four Americans among its depleted corps of officers, the defeat of loyalism must have been particularly hard to stomach. Charles Apthorpe's family in particular stood to lose a fortune, with its estates in New

York and Massachusetts, leaving his captaincy in the Fusiliers one of the few remaining marks of his gentility.

Many British officers believed until the end that most Americans would prefer to remain subjects of King George and that the revolution would prove one in the true sense of the word, taking the settlers through anarchy back around to where they had started off. 'Men of all parties consider another revolution as inevitable and at no great distance,' General Carleton wrote to London just a few weeks before he quit New York, arguing, 'Many [Americans] look back with regard on the tranquillity and happiness of former times and are persuaded that neither peace nor safety can be procured but under their former government.'

Some of the more astute officers who had faced the American army in several campaigns had come to respect their perseverance and to understand that it was buttressed by ideological grit. American soldiers did not have to believe that 'Liberty' would be attained in its most perfect form, only that the cause was worth fighting for. 'Although I shuddered at the distress of these men,' wrote the Hessian Jaeger Captain Ewald after watching a parade of Continentals in ragged uniforms, 'it filled me with awe for them, for I did not think there was an army in the world which could be maintained as cheaply as the American army . . . to what cannot enthusiasm lead a people!'

In addition to inspiring messages from their leaders, the Continental Army more often motivated its men through coercion. Washington executed more of his soldiers than the British did theirs. Throughout these years there was evidence of American commanders being willing to issue orders to shoot their own fleeing troops, whereas the only similar example recorded on the British side was at Lexington. The British also proved less willing to intimidate the general population through capital punishment. Although they did hang spies and several of those who had broken their paroles not to serve against the king in the south, they never put in place that system of 'Committees of Public Safety' that the revolutionaries used to crack down on loyalists or other dissenting opinion across the thirteen provinces.

As for their military strategy, Ewald, that veteran jaeger, and Mackenzie, the long-serving Welch Fusilier, shared many views about why the British had lost. 'One capital error in the conduct of the war in this Country,' wrote Mackenzie, was 'that under the idea of having numerous friends in every Province . . . we have extended our operations throughout most of them; by which we have not been in sufficient strength in any one, and have found those to oppose us in all.' Mackenzie, like his Hessian colleague, felt that strategic vision had been lacking and that too many British generals had proven ineffective placemen more concerned with lining their pockets than defeating their enemy. Mackenzie was disgusted too with the faction prevailing among generals and admirals, but this was a reflection of the bitter struggle between political interests at home.

Those who had felt since the outset that victory was impossible, because you could not shoot or bayonet a civilian population back to their 'true allegiance', tended to be tied to the Whig cause back in Britain. Some, like Fitzpatrick of the Guards, had gone to some trouble to avoid serving in America again, whereas others of the same political cast who could not avoid it, like O'Hara – also a Guards officer – had been pessimists who carried on fighting out of a sense of professional duty. Frederick Mackenzie, by contrast, had believed until the defeat at Yorktown that a victory was possible. This would have taken the form of a loose federation under the sovereignty of King George III (an idea very similar in fact to that Mackenzie heard being preached by that revolutionary agitator Dr Warren from the pulpit of the South Meeting House in Boston in 1775) rather than the re-imposition of full colonial status with its dreaded taxes and the like. Some, like Colonel Balfour, might have shared the view that such an accommodation was possible during earlier years but by 1781 he despaired of the outcome and fought on for professional advancement alone. Cornwallis too, appears to have campaigned for his reputation while trying to exorcise the personal demons unleashed by his wife's death.

A sense of bitterness towards those at home who had attacked the army because of their opposition to the cause it was engaged in extended even to the ranks. Serjeant Lamb, unusual no doubt because of his literacy and general intelligence, was angered by 'virulent party writers' in Britain who picked up American claims of redcoat brutality uncritically. He was convinced that he and his comrades had generally behaved with humanity and professionalism. Lamb the returning veteran felt very differently about himself and war to the headstrong youngster who had taken the king's shilling. His survival through several battles, two escapes, and many fevers convinced him of 'an higher direction, an arm omnipotent, which has been my safeguard'. Lamb realised full well that most redcoats would scorn a man showing religious feelings. Indeed his sense that he had outgrown barrack room vice simply added to the serjeant's conviction that he must seek his discharge as soon as possible.

Since many did not consider themselves to have been broken on the field of battle, those officers who had fostered the 'American style' of fighting, notably Earl Cornwallis, were determined to spread its lessons through the wider army. They favoured rapid manoeuvre, swift bayonet charges, two-deep lines of infantry with the men widely spaced, and set great store by the operations of advance guards or light troops. In time, their struggle to propagate the tactical lessons of the American war would stimulate powerful forces of reaction in the army, but as they sailed home in the short murky days at the end of that year, the guns had fallen silent and the battle of military ideas had not yet begun.

TWENTY-THREE

Home Service

When Lieutenant Colonel Balfour and Serjeant Lamb Parted Company

The sight greeting Lieutenant General James Johnston at the parade ground near Doncaster, Yorkshire, was that of a veteran regiment, proud in its bearing but much reduced in numbers. Undertaking the usual duties of a general commanding a British district, Johnston gave the 23rd its first formal inspection for eleven years. There were 137 Fusiliers drawn up in parade order, with a handful of officers at their head, including Lieutenant Colonel Balfour.

It was the reviewing officer's job, that 14 May 1784, to record what was good and what was bad. His practised eye soon spotted that many of the men had battered belts and pouches or had not been issued with them at all. Their muskets were in a poor state too, many having been lugged about America for years prior to the long sea journey home. In general they were tired men with equipment to match.

Somebody, perhaps Balfour or Adjutant Watson, had hit upon a clever idea though. The regiment's black felt hats sported a festive decoration. Three white feathers had been fixed to each, splaying out from the cockade to make the Prince of Wales's symbol. When the Fusiliers raised their right hands to the brim of their hats and doffed them in honour of the inspecting general, the swish of plumage made 'a very pretty effect when saluting'. General Johnston was not just impressed with this little touch of showmanship, he could see, in the way the 23rd performed its evolutions and in the battle-hardened countenances of its men, all the signs of a veteran corps. He concluded his official report by pronouncing them 'a very remarkable fine battalion'.

The Fusiliers parading that morning in Doncaster were, however, already reduced to the rump, or to put it more kindly, a cadre, of that regiment that had campaigned throughout the American war. They had landed in Portsmouth four months earlier, a chilly homecoming for men who had endured so much. Serjeant Roger Lamb had wasted little time seeking his discharge, applying in person to Colonel Balfour a few days later, while the regiment was halted temporarily in Winchester.

Lamb had been haunted by the circumstances of his leaving home and enlistment more than eleven years previously. He was determined to get back to Ireland as soon as possible, but he knew that the simple pleasure of homecoming would be complicated by sadness at turning his back on his army mentor. Lamb could not heal the rupture with his real father, since he had died years earlier. On the other hand, the man who 'always behaved like a father to me' was very much alive, for Lamb used those words about Nisbet Balfour. That tall, driven Scot had transformed his own life during eight years of the American War. Having begun it as a captain commanding a light company at Bunker Hill, he served as a major on General Howe's staff before reaching the position of commanding officer of the Royal Welch Fusiliers, gaining with it the power to alter Lamb's life.

Balfour knew that the future efficiency of the 23rd depended on retaining men like that Irish serjeant, a veteran of so much fighting, from Saratoga to Camden and Guilford. Balfour, wrote Lamb, 'kindly and humanely reasoned with me, in order to prevail on me to remain in the army'. When flattery and persuasion failed, the commanding officer suggested that there were ways that it could be made financially worthwhile. Lamb had already seen how commanding officers could line his pockets by letting him act as a surgeon's mate, a secretary to the commandant of New York or adjutant of loyalist corps. If he would only stay in the Fusiliers, Lamb had the stuff of which an adjutant or quartermaster were made.

Alas, those arguments in the barracks in Winchester were not sufficiently compelling, so Balfour was disappointed. Lamb loved the family of his regiment, but felt that his affections had not been returned. Shortly before the 23rd had sailed from America, another man had been appointed serjeant major of the Fusiliers. If all of the fine words that Balfour used towards Serjeant Lamb were true, then why had someone else been given the post? Balfour, who had sailed for

England before the unfortunate appointment was made, had evidently erred in this matter. Nettled by the failure of his new family, Lamb sealed his determination to return and make his peace with his old one.

The serjeant was insistent on taking his discharge forthwith. Officers of the 23rd arranged for him to go before the board at the Royal Hospital in Chelsea in the hope that Lamb might begin his new life with a pension of a few pennies each day. The board, though, did not see any obvious injury to the proud man standing before them, nor did they think him old enough to merit a stipend. Lieutenant Calvert and others remonstrated with Lamb to go back before the board, but his impatience to get home had by that time possessed him.

'I left London on the 15th March', wrote Lamb, 'and landed in Dublin on the 19th, to the inexpressible joy of an aged mother, two sisters and other relations who had long given up every hope that I was alive.' Lamb surely grieved that his father, with whom he had argued to the point he left home, did not survive to witness the homecoming.

Lamb's discharge went through the regiment's books officially on 24 February 1784, the same day that a great slew of Fusiliers – half of those who had come back from America – were lost to the army. In all 142 men of the 23rd were discharged that year. Among the other trusted non-commissioned officers that left the regiment before the review at Doncaster in May was Charles Collins, another of the serjeants who had escaped with Lamb after Yorktown.

Of the 137 men standing in front of General Johnston in May 1784, about 115 were veterans, twenty being new recruits. Paradoxically, those who had enlisted before 16 December 1775 and were therefore not eligible for discharge formed a substantial proportion of the soldiers on parade. Men like Corporal Robert Mason, who had been a drummer at Lexington, were still young enough to have some useful service in them. Mason, having survived his court martial for desertion as well as the entire American campaign, proved to one of those soldiers who thrived in a peacetime army. Within a couple of years of the 23rd's return he secured the post of drum major. Marching at the head of the regiment like some strutting peacock was perhaps a fitting destiny for a soldier regarded at the time of that 1779 court martial as a womaniser. As for the other survivors, seventy-three of those still in the 23rd at the time of the Doncaster review were more than thirty years old. Most of them were too aged and worn out for further service and would be discharged within the year. The army's leaders had, by their rule of December 1775, produced the worst of both worlds: scores of men who had valuable battle experience but were still in their twenties grabbed the discharges available to them, disappearing; but those who had enlisted before that date had done so for life and many were, by 1784, too old to offer much further service.

By its ill-considered regulations, Horse Guards thus lost the services of a great many men who had taken part in the victorious charge at Camden or counted the cost of inadequate siege preparations at Yorktown. With officers, though, things were different. Even before the regiment reached its station at Doncaster, Lieutenant Colonel Balfour had scattered notes conferring six months' leave among many of those who performed hard service in the last years of the war.

Lieutenant Calvert had been reunited with his family in London, but had soon set off on a voyage of pleasure around France. Major Mackenzie went off to Scotland for reunions with various branches of his family. Captain Apthorpe meanwhile joined in efforts to re-build the regiment with a new recruiting drive, under guidance of that skilled old man-catcher Richard Temple.

Few of the 23rd's officers sold out during the years that followed the regiment's return. The bargain between them and their sovereign was quite different, after all, to that of the rank and file. The officers would enjoy a genteel life, the happy society of social advantage, while all the time receiving pay – often for doing very little. They remained, though, along with the officers of regiments like the 33rd who had endured the Philadelphia campaigns or those in the Carolinas, a vital fund of experience, men able to contradict with all the authority of veterans the parade-ground pedants who insisted on the formalism of the drill manual. It was to be this fight, the argument about the tactical or disciplinary lessons of America, that would be the battleground of argument in the coming years.

The scene on the pastures of Silesia on the morning of 19 August 1785 was one calculated to impress the visitor. Thousands of troops, clad in the dark blue coats distinctive of the Prussian service, filed out of their bivouacs and arrayed themselves in a single vast battle line, stretching across the gently undulating land. When the signal to begin was given these thousands of souls began moving as if animated by a single intelligence. 'The 29 battalions', wrote Colonel David Dundas, 'were formed with correctness in one line of above 2½ miles in extent, immediately began to fire, each battalion by platoons.' They came forward, a great wall of disciplined manpower, ready to sweep away anyone who stood before them, alternately marching and firing, being put through their paces. The army of Frederick the Great was engaged in its autumn manoeuvres.

The Prussians were showing off for their distinguished guests, displaying to British officers who might struggle to keep three or four battalions wheeling or marching in a compact line that they could do it with ten times that number, and barely a goose-stepped foot put wrong. Colonel Dundas's head told him that there was rarely a place or a situation where 18,000 infantry could be used in this way. But his heart flew when he saw such precision, and he compared it to the absurd heterogeneity that had taken over his own army, where every lieutenant colonel seemed to think he knew best. Beyond his giddy love for things Prussian, Dundas felt something more visceral: envy witnessing the Prussian system that had defeated the French decades before during the Seven Years War. He also harboured a determination to try and raise his own army to an equal footing, for without this, they would stand no chance on the battlefields of Europe. In his official report to George III, Dundas wrote, 'The facility with which these troops manoeuvre and bring superior numbers to a point of attack, must in general be decisive against an enemy not equally expert in movement.'

Dundas attended the Silesian exercises as part of the suite of the King's second son, whom 'Farmer George' had named Frederick, after the Prussian monarch, launching him on the career of a soldier. Prince Frederick, who had taken the title Duke of York, had already been abroad for nearly five years when he attended the Silesian review. He celebrated his 22nd birthday during the trip to Prussia. The strapping young duke had been packed off to the Continent by his father in the hope of learning military science while keeping him clear of the clinches, card tables and capers that had marked his adolescence in England. As he nurtured his military prodigy, George III had already conferred upon the young man the command of a regiment of Guards and the rank of major general.

The duke's party made its way from Berlin to Potsdam and Magdeburg that autumn, along the way being joined by Lieutenant General Earl Cornwallis. They watched one display of Prussian might after another, with great phalanxes of cuirassiers or hussars cantering about with an animation Frederick's infantry could never show, artillery firing off hundreds of shot and household troops all being put through their paces.

Cornwallis had turned his veteran eye first upon the young prince, and he had not been impressed, recording, 'his military ideas are those of a wild boy of the Guards'. The general had seen where the youthful impetuosity of that type had got them at Guilford Courthouse, where the headlong advance of the 2nd Guards Battalion had almost cost him the battle. As an officer who had led a small army through the Carolinas just a few years before, Cornwallis could not quite believe what he was witnessing in Prussia. It was a travesty of military exercise, the product of a force that had not done battle for a quarter of a century boiled down, distilled, into a bizarre tactical caricature.

'The manoeuvres', wrote Cornwallis, 'were such as the worst General in England would be hooted at for practising; two lines coming up within six yards of one another, and firing in one another's faces until they had no ammunition left: nothing could be more ridiculous.'

Prussian drill required the soldiers to be packed shoulder to shoulder, usually in three ranks, to march more slowly than redcoats, and to execute their changes of formation by breaking the regiment down into smaller bodies, each with their own 'pivots' or points of alignment. In short, any adoption of such tactics by the British Army would require term to unlearn every bitter lesson of America. Yet as the Duke of York's Prussian progress of 1785 proceeded, Cornwallis realised this was precisely what was at stake. Dundas was infecting the king's son with his enthusiasm for Frederick the Great's army.

The duke's letters home to George III became increasingly breathless with their expressions of Prussophilia. The experiment of the twenty-nine battalions in line 'never was attempted before . . . it succeeded surprisingly well'; a similarly gargantuan manoeuvre of thirty-five squadrons of cavalry produced a declaration that 'their cavalry is infinitely superior to anything I ever saw . . . there was not a single horse out of place'. The Duke of York faithfully echoed Dundas rather than Cornwallis in accepting that such vast movements were impracticable in battle, but were enormously impressive, a pattern for all of Europe.

Cornwallis, however, had already spotted that the Prussian infantry were 'much slower in their movements' than the similarly trained Hessians used in America and he knew well enough that even those troops had been regarded as quite leaden in battle. Dundas himself conceded that 19 August's great advance of twenty-nine battalions had been preceded by one hour and twenty minutes of forming up. What exactly did Dundas or the Prussian king expect any vaguely enterprising enemy to do during all this dressing of ranks and correcting of lines? They would either strike first or leave the field if they wished to avoid an engagement (as Washington had done during the early years of the American war).

With the conclusion of the 1785 Prussian manoeuvres it was clear to Cornwallis and others that they were losing the argument about the future training of the British army. The Duke of York had spent five years being schooled in the European art of war, taking lessons at the feet of the Duke of Brunswick and 'Old Fritz', Frederick the Great. If his Germanophilia was natural under these circumstances, Colonel Dundas exhibited something altogether less pleasant. He had been quartermaster general in Ireland since 1779, and had grown increasingly contemptuous of officers coming back from America or the Caribbean thinking they had discovered some great new secret of war. Dundas could not accept that the trend, begun by General William Howe in 1776, to get the whole of his army to adopt light infantry tactics had produced an army capable of fast, fluid movement.

The bitterness of Dundas towards officers returning from America, where he never served, could be gauged in the following passage that he wrote about light infantry: 'Instead of being considered as an accessory to the battalion, they have become almost the principal feature of our army, and have almost put grenadiers out of fashion. The showy exercise, the airy dress, the independent modes they have adopted have caught the minds of young officers, and made them imagine that they ought to be general and exclusive.'

Dundas had turned the Irish garrison into a bastion of reaction against the 'American style' of fighting. He organised drills of his own at Phoenix Park in the early 1780s to demonstrate that buttoning up, in dress, movement or attitude, was the key to success. The emergence of the German or Continental school was a turning back of the clock which naturally upset those officers whose hard-earned experience convinced them that the 1781 army in America was infinitely more effective than the one that had opened the campaigns at Boston. One veteran of Burgoyne's Saratoga army, serving in Canada in the summer of 1785, seeing a regiment just arrived from Dundas's Irish establishment, wrote sadly that the fresh corps were 'all young men, great martinets, but so completely Germanised both in dress and manoeuvres that it was some time before we could think them our brother soldiers'.

In the months and years that followed the Duke of York's trip to Prussia, Dundas won the battle to define the army's future drill and tactics. In 1788 he published *Principles of Military Movements, Chiefly Applied to Infantry*, a blueprint for the Prussification of the British army. The following year a modified version was issued in Dublin as official regulations for the army, and in 1791 a London edition completed the process. Dundas insisted that the Prussian system had allowed Frederick to achieve 'actions not to be paralleled in antiquity'. The American war, he maintained, had been a one-off due to its lack of heavy cavalry and wooded terrain. Burying the experience of the American veterans was actually a matter of life and death for Dundas, as he wrote: 'There is a great danger in an *irregular* system becoming the *established* one of a British army; and the most fatal consequences may one day ensue.'

Earl Cornwallis was removed from the scene of these debates to the chief command of British forces in India. As he departed, even some of those who had fought under him were converted to the new orthodoxies. Colonel Banastre Tarleton, for example, in publishing his history of the southern campaigns several years before, had already suggested that his defeat at Cowpens cold be partially blamed on 'the loose manner of forming which had always been practised by the King's troops in America'. General Henry Clinton had always had his doubts, too, that such tactics would work on European battlefields with their abundant cavalry. There was also a feeling that what might vanquish a bunch of half-trained rebels could hardly deliver results against the European masters of war. Had not Yorktown demonstrated the superiority of French arms?

There was, though, a secret of the American and West Indies campaigns that those around the Duke of York simply did not understand. Colonel Dundas might have grasped it, had he wanted to, since there were officers on the Irish establishment who were witness to the one or two occasions where formed bodies of French infantry (as opposed to the proficient engineers and gunners who had won Yorktown) had tested themselves against the redcoats. In these rare moments, the 'flimsy' British line had caused the French horrendous casualties. The French had been beaten back from the British defences at Savannah in October 1779. Before that, in December 1778, French troops had suffered an even worse defeat on the Caribbean island of St Lucia. Advancing on the peninsula of La Vigie, they had been engaged by the 5th Foot and some British light infantry. The British 'gave their fire and retired', wrote the Serjeant Major of the 5th, 'but doing it quite in a light infantry style, dispersing, forming again in small parties according to the advantages of trees or ground, a style which [the French] since confessed they were perfectly unacquainted with.' After this initial blooding, the disordered French threw themselves into disastrously unsuccessful assaults on a British fieldwork.

When using old tactics, quite similar to those being reintroduced by David Dundas in 1788, the 5th had suffered more heavily than any other regiment at Bunker Hill. Adopting the 'light infantry style', they had humbled the French three years later. Opening up formations, using cover, retiring at the run, had all given the redcoats the ability to pour fire on the packed French ranks without allowing them much of a chance to hit back. Serving later in Ireland, the 5th were expected to return to the formalism of a Prussian system. The American tragedy was complete, for no matter whether it was the veterans of St Lucia or men of the 23rd who had smashed the rebels at Camden by using light infantry tactics, they were told that none of this really mattered. As Dundas's new regulations circulated in the army, events in France were taking a course that would ultimately prove just how mistaken the Duke of York and those around him had been. What was more, it would take a veteran of the 23rd's American campaigns to show them.

The Army Re-Born

Or How Harry Calvert Made a Difference

The final days of June 1794 were fraught with a kind of crazy energy for the British army campaigning in the Low Countries. They marched each day in a scorching heat, their parched, dust-choked odyssey ending on many evenings with thunder, lightning and cloudbursts. The trajectory of this army was from west to east, away from the borders of Revolutionary France, towards Holland, where their commanders determined to make a stand on the far side of the River Scheldt.

This army of twenty-three British battalions under the command of the Duke of York was part of a larger coalition assembled to restore Europe to some kind of order after the French had overthrown and executed their king. But the campaign was not going well, for the combined armies had suffered a heavy defeat at Tourcoing in May. Following this setback, the Austrians, who had the chief command of the allied armies, had decided to abandon Flanders, their sovereign's possession on France's borders. A retreat by forces on each side of the Duke of York's contingent made it impossible for the British to stand alone, so by a series of forced marches they were flying in front of the French, passing signposts to places like Mons and Waterloo. These were frenetic, suspicious days in British headquarters, for the duke and his staff felt that every gain their soldiers had made during more than one year's campaigning was being thrown away by Austrian cowardice. Some found the abandonment of Flanders so perplexing that they suspected some kind of treason in the Habsburg court.

British headquarters lodged itself for several nights in the village of Renaix, a weaving town nestled in the rolling country of that region.

The main square that normally thronged with cloth merchants and those who sold the fruit of that fertile land was, on the evening of 1 July, a scene of military comings and goings. Staff officers cantered to and fro, columns of marching troops passed through, generals with staff in tow made their dignified entrance.

The Duke of York returned that evening from a conference at Braine l'Alleud with the Austrian commanders, who signalled their intent to make further retreats. At their quarters, they found that Earl Cornwallis had just arrived. He had lately commanded British troops in India but been called back to Europe by a government nervous that reverses in the Low Countries were exposing the king's son at the head of the British corps to public ridicule.

More than twelve years had passed since Yorktown, and Cornwallis's reputation within the British army was high. The King had made it clear upon the general's return from America that he did not hold the earl to blame for the defeat in Virginia. In 1782 George wrote to Cornwallis noting his faith that 'attachment to my person, to your country and to the military profession are the motives of your actions'. In order to defend his wider reputation, Cornwallis presented his side of the Yorktown story to various friends, prompting a public exchange of self-justificatory pamphlets with General Sir Henry Clinton. Cornwallis, above all, was a fighter, and it was his 'zeal and activity' that caused his stock to remain sound both at court and at the army's headquarters at Horse Guards. During campaigns in India, their faith had been validated, since Cornwallis had won some important victories and extended British control.

When the earl arrived at Renaix, it was therefore as a commander of considerable reputation who might see how the situation could be rescued. Few people were more pleased to see him than Harry Calvert, who as a teenage subaltern in the 23rd had benefited from the general's kind condescension during the Carolina campaigns. The young officer, indeed, almost idolised his former commander, remembering how well their little army had endured every hardship. Calvert had written to his sister that Cornwallis was ' born to be the honour and salvation of the country he belongs to'. The general's arrival in Flanders was 'the only good news I can send you'. Calvert knew that his old chief had been sent because of the Ministry's lack of faith in his new one, the Duke of York. The young staff officer felt that public criticism of the duke had been unfair, for Calvert opined, 'I had rather that [York] should have the approbation of that great and good man [ie Cornwallis] than of any other on this side of the grave.'

During the retrograde marches of the summer of 1794, a depressed Calvert had written: 'I found myself in a situation which it has been my good fortune never to have been in before – namely in a beaten army.' This, if any further proof were needed of Calvert's reverence for the army that marched through the Carolinas in 1780–81 and the man who led it, showed that he never considered his former regiment to have been 'beaten' in America. The defeat at Yorktown was one thing, but the Americans had not broken them on the battlefield or ever driven them across the country in the way the French had in 1794. It was this officer's view indeed, that the Low Countries campaign marked a low ebb for the British army, for he considered numerous problems of recruiting, administration and tactics to have produced an army worse than the one in America. In the view of many officers Cornwallis might be the saviour of the Low Countries army.

The Harry Calvert of the Flanders campaign was a more formidable figure than the callow subaltern who had joined his regiment in New York in 1779. In 1794 he was thirty-one years old, and his father, always anxious to buy his boy past any obstacle that might be created by the brewer's trade, had in 1790 purchased Harry a commission in the Coldstream Guards. Under their curious system of seniority, Calvert's Guards' captaincy ranked him as the equivalent of a lieutenant colonel in the rest of the army. The one-time Fusilier enjoyed other advantages too: his uncle was a Member of Parliament, part of the political class. Calvert's intelligence and fluent grasp of French had marked him out in 1793 for secondment to the Duke of York's staff. Once there, he had soon impressed his royal patron and was entrusted with ever more sensitive and important missions.

As for this coming man's former regiment, it did not participate in the Low Countries campaign, but was fighting the French on the far side of the world in Martinique. The name of Mackenzie remained on the Fusiliers' rolls, but it was Frederick's son James rather than the American veteran himself. George, the boy that Mrs Mac had been carrying when Frederick Mackenzie marched to Lexington in 1775, was promoted into the 23rd as a captain in 1796. Of those zealous young captains that had led the 23rd in its Carolina campaigns, only the American, Charles Apthorpe, was still with the regiment as it fought in the Caribbean. Forbes Champagne and Thomas Peter had both taken advantage of the expansion of the army that accompanied the new war with the French to gain promotion into newly raised corps.

When it came to the serjeants and rankers that had come through Camden or Yorktown, almost none remained with the 23rd. Roger Lamb, having taken his discharge and returned to Dublin, had become a master at the Free School in Whitefriars Lane. Lamb had a weakness for father-figures, and after returning to Dublin he had discovered the prayer meetings organised by Joseph Burgess, the charismatic quarter-master of a cavalry regiment stationed in the city. These sessions, conducted in the language of the ordinary labourer or soldier, had a powerful effect on many who attended. They urged congregants to reject vice. The path to salvation that they appeared to offer seemed altogether more attractive than any preaching in pulpits of the established church. As he attended one meeting after another, Lamb became a very religious man, imbibing the doctrine of the Methodists, while contemplating the folly of his early years. 'He found me out,' Lamb said later of Burgess. 'He bore with my pride, my impertinence, my ignorance, with so much tenderness and love, that at last he entirely won me.'

In a time of social ferment, some at the top of society began to worry about this new sect and its effects on the lower orders. Some generals even believed the Methodists should be repressed in the army, banned from holding meetings. Faced with such hostility, the preachers of this new message became adept at looking after their own, so it was Quartermaster Burgess who fixed Lamb up with his teacher's job at Whitefriars Lane, for that school was a bastion of the new sects struggle to raise the poor through education. It had been established indeed by John Wesley, the sect's founder.

Among the other old campaigners, some went to the opposite extreme, sinking into a life of drink and casual work. The army, though, was able to look after some of the 23rd's American veterans. George Watson, the serjeant major who had later become adjutant to the Fusiliers, had played the military system skilfully in order to ensure a comfortable old age. Watson had been given a captain's commission in 1790, and the superintendence of a Company of Invalids, those worn-out old redcoats still capable of mounting guard at a fortress. Thomas Parks, a private who came through the triage after the bloody battle of Guilford Courthouse, surviving a shot in the head, was discharged from the regiment in 1792, suffering from chronic rheumatism, with a recommendation that he be admitted to the Royal Hospital at Kilmainham near Dublin.

Even if the Royal Welch Fusiliers was absent from Flanders as a regiment, Calvert frequently saw familiar faces from the old American army. Cornwallis's former executives in South Carolina, Francis Rawdon and Nisbet Balfour, were both there. Rawdon, who had by this point inherited the title Earl of Moira, commanded one wing of the army and Balfour, whose connections had always been of a more modest variety, was given the lesser role of commanding a brigade. Through relentless politicking, as well as use of his Scottish family connections, Balfour, who by this point held the rank of major general, had become a Member of Parliament and colonel of a regiment newly raised in Edinburgh. Balfour's quest to reap rewards from the state for his family's heavy sacrifice in its service had resulted at last in success. The former commanding officer of the Fusiliers thus became a minor patron in his own right, giving fellow Scot Thomas Peter day-to-day command of his new regiment, just as he had sent him up to run the 23rd after Thomas Mecan had died in 1780 near Camden. So busy was Balfour with his new career as a man of influence, and so poor were the prospects of the army in Flanders that, after just a few weeks in command of his brigade, Balfour soon pleaded pressure of business and returned to Britain.

It cannot be said that General Cornwallis relished the idea of command in the Low Countries either, for, having discussed the gloomy prognosis for the campaign, he headed off to London after little more than one week in the field in order to brief his masters there. Whatever reports he may have given about the difficulty of the Duke of York's situation, as a supporting member of an Austrian-led army, it did not ultimately save the prince from being recalled. York's army had enjoyed some moments of success, but it was the reports of its setbacks and of the commander-in-chief's own foibles that flew about London, creating the demand for change. The violent partisanship of 1775 lived on in some political circles. Whigs in 1794 also relished spreading accounts about the army's reverses or the drinking and whoring of the King's second son.

In the field the redcoats, bound by David Dundas's clunking system of packed ranks and pivots, had been outmanoeuvred by the more nimble French, who performed their infantry evolutions more quickly, sending throngs of skirmishing light infantry to torment their enemies.

The orchards, hedges and rolling hillsides in which they had to fight bore little resemblance to the open Prussian drill grounds where Dundas and York nine years earlier had lost their hearts to Frederick the Great's system of manoeuvre. As for Old Fritz's progeny, neither the Prussian army nor the Austrians found satisfactory tactical answers to dealing with the French in Flanders. The tragic irony for Cornwallis and his comrades who had campaigned on the other side of the Atlantic was that the system of swift, open movement that had over-whelmed American light troops at Brandywine or Camden might just as easily be used against the French who capered about the woods of Flanders or lined its fences when firing at the redcoats.

The dead hand of Dundas, also present during the Flanders campaign, had not entirely throttled the initiative of those officers who could detect the difference between those tactics that looked good on Wimbledon Common and those which suit the real battlefield with all its natural or man-made obstacles. Equally, Dundas was an awkward opponent for the American veterans, for he continued to rise in the army. He was one representative of a political family that effectively turned Scotland from a rebellious backwater into a bastion of loyalism that had become highly productive – both economically and in terms of recruits – for the King.

During the latter part of 1794, the army kept trudging eastwards. Once in Holland morale sank even lower, for the people, while superficially polite, nurtured a hatred of the European *ancien regime* armies that resulted in many stragglers being picked off and murdered.

In October 1794, Calvert wrote home to an army friend in England, trying to digest the 'dear-bought experience' of the preceding campaign. The army had lacked artillery, skilled engineers, major generals capable of commanding infantry brigades, and its hospitals were sad charnel houses. Calvert's despair of Britain's allies led him to believe that the country could not place the same reliance on them in future campaigns and had to develop a force capable of meeting the French independently. He also felt that the system where powerful men could 'recruit for rank', raising regiments for the King in return for colonelcies and commissions for their cronies, was a complete anachronism that produced third rate bodies of men. In summary, Calvert longed to 'restore to the army those independent disinterested feelings, and those high principles that should actuate a soldier and form the basis of the military discipline of a free country'.

It was in April 1796 that Calvert exploited his hold over the Duke of York to set his trajectory to the top of the army. Since being recalled from the Low Countries the duke had been appointed commander-in-chief of the army as a whole – a post that carried with it the duties of inspecting its forces, regulating its recruitment and training, as well as liaising with ministers. The Cabinet that sent York to his new office at the Horse Guards felt it was the one post where a young prince with the rank of field marshal might be removed without shame from the command of a field army. The duke, however, was to prove an enthusiastic reformer, quickly setting about using the considerable influence that being the king's favourite son gave him in order to change the army. But he was no details man, and, in order to keep track of the many schemes he set in train, he decided he would need Calvert.

The tradesman's son had become an accomplished player of the power game. Tasked by his master in Flanders to keep ministers informed about the progress of the campaign, the lieutenant colonel had begun corresponding directly with men of influence. He had even been sent by the duke on a diplomatic mission to the King of Prussia. Such was Calvert's confidence in the position he was building, that when the duke offered him the position of private secretary upon their return to London, Calvert graciously declined. He wanted something better.

Late in 1795, York asked the young colonel whether he would become deputy quartermaster general to the army. Calvert said no once more, nobly reminding his great patron that the post had been promised to another officer. It was only in April 1796 that Calvert agreed to take the post of deputy adjutant general. In fact, the absence of the deputy quartermaster general, and the fact that the chiefs of both of these divisions of the staff were aged generals with limited commitment to running their departments, meant that, at the age of thirty-three, Calvert was playing a considerable role in managing the entire army. The duke, indeed, laid upon his shoulders the additional and critical burden of surveying southern England in order to plan its defence against a French invasion.

During the young colonel's many rides across the South Downs or along the approaches to London, he observed a countryside full of enclosed fields, copses and farmsteads, a battleground even less well suited to phalanxes of infantry or lines of cavalry than the scene of their late battles on the Continent. And while he made his observations, his masters, the commander-in-chief and Secretary at

War, were petitioned by one senior officer after another who urged the creation of large bodies of men capable of waging irregular warfare in the Kentish hopfields or Essex hedgerows. Earl Cornwallis noted, 'The system of David Dundas, and the total want of light infantry, sit heavy on my mind.' The earl would make his contributions to the debate about re-shaping the army from the margins, since he was later assigned to the chief command in Ireland, where social tensions would produce upheaval in 1798. However, his interventions about the army's structure and tactics played an important part in undermining the Dundas doctrine.

The army hierarchy was slowly but surely adopting the advice of its American veterans or others who could see the folly of its 'Prussian' system. The formation of several companies of volunteer sharp-shooters was authorised as a defence against invasion and a battalion of foreign riflemen entered service in 1798. The influence of that cerebral veteran of the Hessian Jaeger Corps, Johann Ewald was clear in the training given to these new corps, and his texts on irregular warfare appeared in English translation.

To Cornwallis and quite a few other senior officers, the formation of rifle-armed companies was a side issue. He was more concerned with the infantry of the line, urging Horse Guards to adopt 'means of rendering the movements of the regiments more simple, and a little more active'. He wanted the redcoated regiments to repeat the process undergone by General Howe's army in 1776 and 1777 when it adopted light infantry tactics.

Early in 1798 Calvert gained the Duke of York's backing for a plan to reintroduce light infantry battalions. Many officers had reflected on the necessity of this step since the Flanders campaign but nothing had been done. 'I am indeed to flatter myself that some steps will *speedily* be taken to place us in this respect on a footing with our enemy and by that means give full scope to the native gallantry of our troops,' wrote Calvert. He proposed the formation of two battalions on the American war pattern, being the combined light companies of sixteen regiments (including the Royal Welch Fusiliers). General Howe, now approaching seventy years old, stepped forward with an offer to perform the same service he had a quarter of a century before, running a special camp to bring the army's light infantry up to scratch. The wheel was at last being re-invented.

In his private representations, Calvert cited the example of French tactics in Flanders as the reason why British troops must adapt or die. His logic was therefore the same as that deployed by Dundas in 1785 – that success on the Continent required Britain to copy the greatest army of the day. Other senior officers insisted that the prospect of invasion meant things must change quickly. But as the War Office and Cabinet displayed their uncanny ability to shelve one scheme after another, it fell to a general called John Money to ram home publicly what every veteran of an earlier conflict knew: that the lessons required to beat the French had been previously learned and implemented in America. Money had served with Burgoyne's Saratoga expedition, drawing on this experience in an open letter to the Secretary at War published in 1799. Money stressed the similarity of French skirmishing tactics to those practised by the Americans at Saratoga, and warned that if the army did not form light regiments capable of contesting the enclosed fields of southern England, it risked suffering 'another Bunker Hill'.

Money's long missive was unusually well argued for its time, scientific in its assembly of observations, deductions and proposed remedies. It even provided some cover under which the Prussophiles might conduct a dignified retreat, pointing out that land use in Europe had changed markedly since the times of Frederick the Great, for a process of enclosure had divided up many tracts of countryside that had been open decades earlier. Money argued that the defence of southern England would require one fifth of the regular infantry and one quarter of the militia to be converted into *chasseurs* or light infantry.

Despite the urgency of this public advocacy or the Deputy Adjutant General's private entreaties it would take years for the formation of proper light infantry corps and the 'revision' of Dundas's old regulations to the point that they became a dead letter. During the time the Duke of York occupied himself with myriad schemes for improving the efficiency of the army. Military education was to be put on a proper footing, recruiting standards raised and the soldier's lot improved. The climate for this work improved immeasurably as the threat of French invasion produced a national consensus about strengthening the army. The old partisanship of Whig and Tory began to wither. With greater unity in Parliament, York was able to carry his reforms into sensitive areas such as preventing abuses of the commissions system, for many of the maladies that Horse Guards sought to treat (such as commissioning boys or allowing them promotion without any military experience) were ploys favoured by wealthy landowners to buy their sons status.

Fear of Bonaparte's legions was to have a more powerful effect on the landowners than their desire to protect their army privileges. However the yeoman Briton's dread of social upheaval following the French revolution would also see some of the more benign or enlightened customs of the eighteenth-century army swept away. It became far harder to obtain a commission from the ranks, as those sterling serjeants of the 23rd, Richard Baily, William Robinson (killed at Guilford) and George Watson, had done. As the wars against France progressed, it even became unofficial policy to post such men away from the regiments where they had hitherto served, lest their elevation to a gentleman's rank cause too much embarrassment for all concerned. The application of the lash or capital punishment also become more systematic as the officer class sought to crush any unrest.

In the mid-1790s Britain sized up the French revolutionaries and decided it despised them. During the late 1790s, Calvert and the others who ran the army from Horse Guards were engaged in a dizzying wave of reforms necessary to raise the redcoat's game so that it could confront them.

Early in 1799, Calvert was made Adjutant General of the army. In June of the same year he married Caroline Hammersley – a love match, albeit to a banker's daughter, and a family connection that would eventually allow Calvert's first-born to inherit a baronetcy. His social credentials had been vouchsafed at last. With Calvert matured into a man of substance in the world of army politics, the boy whom Fusiliers spotted disembarking in New York two decades before was quite different in appearance. Frequent attendance at the Duke of York's lavsh table had helped him pile on pounds, his complexion was often florid and the recession of his hairline, something that had begun in his twenties, left him with a bald pate. Calvert's bright eyes, though, still radiated their strong intelligence, and his manner reinforced the impression.Not long after his appointment to the head of one of the main branches of the staff, General David Dundas was appointed to the other. Although it is clear that Calvert's friends and mentors were doing their best to subvert Dundas's tactical ideas, the Adjutant General maintained a professional working relationship with the older man.

As Calvert received one promotion after another from his patron he became a valuable ally to some of the old Fusiliers he had known decades before in America. Frederick Mackenzie benefited handsomely, for the veteran of Lexington had reached an age too advanced for active soldiering. Calvert had Mackenzie appointed as secretary to the Royal Military College, the new institute of military learning created under the Duke of York's aegis. The College, which started its work in a tavern but soon moved to more salubrious surroundings, was just one symptom of the great change brought about in the last years of the eighteenth century. A more professional army was taking shape.

It was late in 1808 when Roger Lamb finally bowed to the entreaties of his friends and family. Lamb's meagre pay as schoolmaster had provided but a poor living to his wife and six children. If he had started his family so late in life, was it not due to his service to the Crown? And might not that beneficent Sovereign see fit to grant the former serjeant of Fusiliers a pension? Lamb's relatives urged him to petition the commander-in-chief of Ireland, for was that not the same noble personage who owed his life to Lamb's quick thinking at the battle of Guilford Courthouse when Serjeant Lamb had seized the bridle of the general's horse and guided him back to British lines? The ageing schoolmaster had rejected such suggestions for many years.

In September 1808, however, Lamb finally relented. He had been reading the newspaper, when he noticed an announcement signed by 'Harry Calvert, Adjutant General'. Lamb was by this time fifty-two and feeling the effects of his advancing years. 'It immediately occurred to me', Lamb reflected, 'that this officer served in the 23rd and had always shewed himself my friend.' The teacher's family urged him to write immediately. Lamb petitioned the adjutant general, describing his 'humble confidence' that Calvert would answer his plea.

Calvert replied, recommending Lamb to the quartermaster general in Dublin. When the ageing teacher went to that man's offices, Lamb realised that something stood in the way of his employment. The officer implied that a job could come the way of a non-Methodist, and Lamb realised that his new-found faith was objectionable to these men.

So on 7 January 1809, Lamb wrote once more to his old comrade, stating his 'very great reluctance in giving you so much trouble'. Lamb did not mention the colonel's attempts to stifle his Methodism, rather he asked the general in London to pass an enclosed memorial of his services to the Duke of York, in the hope that he might receive a pension.

At the time Lamb's second letter arrived on Calvert's desk in Horse Guards, fifteen years of hard work by the Duke of York and his staff was bearing fruit in astonishing ways. Lieutenant General Arthur Wellesley, later Duke of Wellington, had defeated the French in Portugal the previous summer. General Sir John Moore had beaten them again at the gates of Corunna, early in 1809, losing his life at the moment of victory. Regiments of riflemen and light infantry were taking to the field, outshooting and outsmarting the French *tirailleurs*. The Frederickian dogmas of the Prussian service, meanwhile, had crumbled with Napoleon's smashing of their armies in 1806. The 23rd Fusiliers was destined to return from the Caribbean, sharing in the armies' epic campaigns in the Iberian peninsula and fighting at Waterloo.

In the hour of excitement of early 1809, the Corunna expedition had no sooner landed than preparations were under way to undertake another major expedition to the Iberian peninsula. Despite the work deluging Horse Guards, General Calvert recommended Lamb's case to the Duke of York, and fulfilled the promise he had made to that Irish serjeant in 1784 upon their return from America. On 25 January, little more than one week after receiving the former serjeant's plea, a reply was fired off from Calvert's office, informing Lamb that he would receive his pension.

Lamb, cannily enough, did not put his entire dependence on this patronage. He also set pen to paper, writing two memoirs of his army service that were published in 1809 and 1811. In one of these works he reflected upon his long relationship with Calvert, and noted undying gratitude for the bond created between them so many years before in the Royal Welch Fusiliers:

Attachments of persons in the army to each other terminate but with life, the friendship of the officer continues with the man who has fought under his command, to the remotest period of declining years, and the old soldier venerates the aged officer far more perhaps he did in his youthful days: it is like friendship between school-boys, which increases in manhood and ripens in old age.

The Royal Welch Fusiliers went into battle at Lexington in 1775 as a typical example of the eighteenth-century British military machine. That army quickly showed itself to be a creaky old device, an assembly of people ill-suited to the task at hand where the time-servers, boozers or shirkers got in the way of those who were trying to do their duty. The regiment evolved through years of difficult service into a pattern for the whole army – employing novel tactics to devastating effect at Camden, while being led by zealous young officers as well as bright, motivated serjeants.

The cause on which the Fusiliers were engaged was unpopular with many at home but the army in America was inspired by men like Cornwallis to fight for is own self-respect, for the love of comrades, for pride in the red coat. In this way, it was the very effrontery of the American rebels or the malign enthusiasm of British Whigs that prompted that army to set aside ideology and evolve into a modern, professional force. It is, after all, the prosecution with honour of an unwanted war that places the hardest demands upon a soldier.

Such was the *esprit de corps* fostered by Cornwallis in particular that regiments that had stumbled in 1775 or 1776, even when out-numbering their enemy, charged headlong into the Carolina backcountry in 1781 despite knowing how badly stacked against them the odds were. Even ten years after the event, the men who could speak of this epic with the authority of veterans were a very small band indeed. Cornwallis had so few regiments of redcoats to start with – the 71st had been disbanded after the war, leaving only the 23rd, 33rd and Guards.

Had the War Office wanted to scatter this precious cadre to the winds they could not have gone about it more thoroughly: so many of the experienced rank and file were discharged during 1783–5; lots of the young officers were encouraged by the promotion system to head off to other regiments; and the tactics evolved at such cost were suppressed by Dundas and his ilk.

The knowledge of what a couple of thousand British soldiers had achieved in some far off pastures above Camden or on the hills of Guilford did not, however, die out. Cornwallis used his great authority in the army to undermine Dundas continually. Eventually that angry Scot lost the battle for the Duke of York's ear to young Harry Calvert. It fell in the end to that man who had been taken into the Royal Welch Fusiliers as a boy, someone forged among its characters and system of fighting to recognise the precious experience he had enjoyed, and using the bitter lessons of America, to educate an army that one day would defeat Napoleon.

Notes on Sources

Abbreviations Used for Manuscript Sources

BL   British Library, London
CHT   Claydon House Trust (the Verney Papers)
DLAR   David Library of the American Revolution, Pennsylvania
DoN   Duke of Northumberland's papers, Alnwick Castle
HMC   *Historical Manuscripts Commission*
HSD   Historical Society of Delaware
LBRO   Luton and Bedfordshire Record Office
LRO   Lancashire Record Office
LoC   Library of Congress, Washington DC
NAS   National Archive of Scotland, Edinburgh
NYPL   New York Public Library
RWF   Royal Welch Fusiliers Archive, Caernarfon, Wales
SRO   Staffordshire Record Office
TNA   The National Archive, Kew, England
UNB   University of New Brunswick, Canada
WLCL   William L. Clements Library, Ann Arbor Michigan

ONE The March From Boston, 19 April 1775

1   *'It was around 9 a.m.'*: Frederick Mackenzie's journal, published as *A British Fusilier in Revolutionary Boston*, edited by Allen French, Boston 1926.
     — *'After him tramped two regiments of foot'*: the 4th and 47th. Since most British regiments fighting in American deployed a single battalion, the terms regiment and battalion are used interchangeably in this narrative. The British Marines, at this time, had not yet become 'Royal'.
     — *'The eight companies of Fusiliers'*: the figures are approximate because Mackenzie gives a figure for rank and file (314) but not one for officers, musicians or serjeants.

2   *'few or no people were to be seen'*: Mackenzie, *British Fusilier*.

— *'It has everywhere the appearance of a park'*: Percy's letter of 18 August 1774, printed in *Letters of Hugh Earl Percy from Boston and New York 1774–1776*, edited by Charles Knowles Bolton, Boston 1902.

3   *'Never did any nation so much deserve to be made an example of'*: this was a letter of 6 December 1774, in *Memoirs and Letters of Captain W. Glanville Evelyn*, edited by G. D. Scull, Oxford 1879.

4   *'This country is now in as open a state of rebellion'*: Percy's letter of 12 September 1774, printed in Bolton's edition.

— *'so they pressed on proudly to the tune of "Yankee Doodle"'*: see the account of William Gordon, 'Letter Written by an American Clergyman', article in *Journal of American History*, vol. 4, January–March 1910.

— *'Captain-Lieutenant Thomas Mecan'*: details of his service from TNA: PRO WO 27 files at the British National Archives (inspection returns of regiments of foot) and Mecan's memorandum of service dated 25 June 1775, Gage Papers, WLCL.

5   *'Robert Mason'*: details of his service from TNA: PRO WO 12 files (muster rolls) and WO 71 (Judge Advocate) at Kew. Grimes' details, WO 12.

— *'From this casualty, the brigadier learnt'*: Mackenzie.

TWO The Royal Welch Fusiliers on the Eve of Revolution

7   *'The delights awaiting'*: this dinner is described in Mackenzie's journal, and Robert Donkin's *Military Collections and Remarks*, New York 1777.

— *'As respectable a corps of gentlemen'*: this letter was from James Rivington, the New York publisher and loyalist, to Henry Knox, Boston bookseller and later commander of George Washington's artillery; it is cited in *Historic Mansions and Highways Around Boston*, by Samuel Adams Drake, Cambridge MA. 1899.

8   *'His father John has been wounded'*: an interesting detail from *Officers of the Royal Welch Fusiliers (23rd Regiment of Foot) 16 March 1689 to 4 August 1914*, compiled by Major E. L. Kirby MC TD FMA DL, privately published for the regiment in the 1990s.

— *'Old Mindonians'*: this term is used in a letter of 26 August 1780 from Lieutenant Thomas Barretté to General Henry Clinton, in the Clinton Papers, WLCL. Barretté was a latecomer to the 23rd, having joined in 1778.

— *'A couple still bore the scars'*: Grey Grove and David Ferguson were among those wounded. Details of Minden in this passage were taken mainly from *Regimental Records of the Royal Welch Fusiliers*, compiled by A. D. L. Cary and Stouppe McCance, vol. I, 1689–1815, London 1921.

— *'Such ease and expertise these Fusileers shew'*: the poem was printed in the *New York Gazette and Weekly Mercury*, no. 1149, 1 November 1773. It is attributed to 'J. H.'.

9   *'nothing should induce him to go to America'*: this was Horsfall quoted in a letter from Mackenzie to his father in *A British Fusilier*.

— *'The captain commanding the regiment's grenadiers'*: William Blakeney's attitudes will be described later and his reluctance to serve will be seen in letters in TNA: PRO WO 1.

9   '*quite reverses our characters*': Williams' journal was published as *Discord and Civil Wars, being a Journal Kept by Lieutenant Williams*, edited by Walter S. Merwin, Buffalo NY 1954.

10   '*Though I must confess I should like to try what stuff I am made of*': letter of 5 December 1774 by George Harris of 5th Regiment in *The Life and Service of General, Lord Harris*, by Stephen R. Lushington, London 1840.

— '*These people, most of them originally Scotch or Irish*': Blunt's letter to Sir Thomas Wilson, 6 July 1774 BL ADD MS 49607A. It also contains an early reference to the rebels calling themselves 'Patriots'.

— '*Grey Grove, who had a reputation*': Mackenzie describes him as a drunk, saying that Grove often needed his 'dose' twice a day during the passage from England; his bitterness about being passed over is shown in a letter of 4 March 1775 in TNA: PRO WO 1/2.

— '*had been petitioning unsuccessfully for removal to a staff job*': a letter from the Secretary at War to Captain Joseph Ferguson of the 23rd, 9 November 1775, alludes to his earlier requests. In TNA: PRO WO 4/95. Ferguson's younger brother David was also anxious to get promoted out of the regiment. Donkin was also trying to get a staff job.

11   '*Robert Donkin, the regimental savant*': his knowledge of these subjects is shown in the book *Military Collections*; the Secretary at War's response to his requests for removal to the staff, dated 18 July 1772, is in TNA: PRO WO 4/90.

— '*only the youngest ... cheerful about his duty*': Captain Edward Evans, according to Mackenzie.

— '*Bernard and Grove were well into their forties*': the ages of many of these officers can be found in TNA: PRO WO 27 files, Inspection Returns. Some other details from Kirby and the 'Army List' annually published by the War Office.

— '*One or two ... could call on considerable reserves of family cash*': I am referring here particularly to the Ferguson brothers. Mackenzie refers to Ferguson's wealth, and a later letter from Joseph Ferguson to Earl Percy (in DON) indicates his willingness and ability to buy the lieutenant colonelcy of the 23rd – it will be dealt with in a later chapter.

— '*Donkin, on the other hand, had some powerful friends*': his letters and *Military Collections* show he enjoyed Earl Granard's patronage early in his career, then Gage's and later Henry Clinton's. Donkin also tried to forge connections with Earl Percy, and it seems from his papers that a letter cited later shows Donkin's inability to buy his promotion.

— '*he had shown himself to have limited influence*': see Bernard's letter to the Secretary at War, 1 February 1775, in TNA: PRO WO 1/2, about an unsuccessful attempt to get a relative commissioned into the regiment.

12   '*just three days later captains Grove and Blakeney joined*': letter of 4 March 1775 in TNA: PRO WO 1/2.

— '*nothing is more mortifying to an old soldier*': letter from Captain Mackintosh, 10th Regiment, to the Secretary at War, 8 January 1776, in TNA: PRO WO 1/992. It alludes to an earlier appeal to Gage.

13   *'the animal gave such a spring from the floor'*: Donkin.

  — *'Our fathers having nobly resolved'*: the text of Warren's address can be found in *American Archives, Containing a Documentary History of The English Colonies in North America*, 4th series, vol. 2, by Peter Force, Washington 1839.

14   *'several British officers signalled their disgust'*: this sequence of events is agreed both by a British report, Mackenzie, and an American one quoted in Force.

  — *'You and I must settle it first'*: Force. The officer's uniform is described in this account as having blue facings and gold lace – the same distinctions as the 23rd's. Was this angry officer Mackenzie, perhaps?

15   *'The people here are a set of sly, artful, hypocritical'*: letter to his second cousin 8 August 1774, Bolton.

16   *'Few were Welsh'*: the Inspection Returns, TNA: PRO WO 27, give national breakdowns for 1770 and 1771 that suggest 80 per cent of soldiers were English. However, while Irish and Scots are separately defined in these records, Welsh are not, being lumped in with English. Even so, analysis both of where the regiment recruited, and the men's surnames in WO 12, Muster Rolls, confirms that the proportion of Welsh would be no higher than one would expect nationally. WO 27 records also give the length of service of soldiers in the regiment, their heights and other interesting details.

  — *'My chief intention'*: *From Redcoat to Rebel: The Thomas Sullivan Journal*, edited by Joseph Lee Boyle, Westminster MD, 2004.

  — *'afraid to return and tell my father'*: this is Roger Lamb, who originally enlisted in the 9th but from whom we will hear much later. He wrote two memoirs, *An Original and Authentic Journal of Occurences during the Late American War*, Dublin 1809, and *Memoir of His Own Life*, 1811. A redacted version of these two texts by Don Hagist was published in Baraboo WI, in 2004, as *A British Soldier's Story*.

  — *'some tried… leapt to their deaths in the sea'*: Lamb.

17   *'two dozen soldiers of the Royal Welch had absconded'*: desertions are recorded in TNA: PRO WO 12/3960, the 23rd's Muster Rolls for 1774–85.

  — *'Watson was a ladies' man'*: his courtship of a New York woman is revealed in TNA: PRO WO 71/83, the record of his court martial (after he was arrested in that city).

  — *'William Hewitt, who deserted the Fusiliers'*: TNA: PRO WO 12/3960; Hewitt's story is also the subject of a family memoir: details are given in James Hewitt's research on his ancestor on the web at www.thehewitt.net.

  — *'finding they were striving to throw off the yoke'*: Sullivan journal.

18   *'General Gage rarely allowed executions'*: for evidence of one hanging that did go ahead in September 1774, witnessed by John Andrews, see *Massachusetts Historical Society Proceedings*, 8 (1864–65), p. 367.

  — *'harsh punishment was out of fashion in the British army'*: quite a few historians have made the mistake of assuming that the death sentences and large tariffs of lashes ordered by courts martial were always, or indeed often, carried out. Research on the Muster Rolls, TNA: PRO WO 12/3960 shows that no man of the 23rd sentenced to death during the American war was actually executed. Furthermore the comments of Adye, Mackenzie, Peebles, Barker and other officers explicitly refer to the policy of pardons and lenient treatment of offenders.

18 *'I disapprove of making capital punishments too familiar'*: A Treatise on Courts Martial, by Stephen Payne Adye, London 1778.

— *'Lieutenant Colonel Bernard's instincts'*: at the court martial of John Jermon, Bernard's lenity was noted. The record is in TNA: PRO WO 71/79.

THREE The Fight at Lexington and Concord

19 *'redcoats of Major John Pitcairn's battalion'*: the early Lexington section of this narrative is based on *The British in Boston, Being the Diary of Lieutenant John Barker of the King's Own Regiment*, edited by Elizabeth Ellery Dana, Cambridge MA 1924; *Transactions of the British Troops previous to, and at the Battle of Lexington* [of Captain Brown, 52nd, and Ensign de Berniere, 10th], *Massachusetts Historical Society Collections*, series 2, vol. 4, 1816; 'Statement of Lt Edward Thoroton Gould, 4th Regiment', in *The Public Advertiser*, Lexington, 25 April 1775; *Concord Fight*, Ensign Jeremy Lister, Cambridge Mass 1931 (Lister was another officer of the 10th, he was wounded); Lieutenant Colonel Francis Smith, letter to Major Robert Donkin, 8 October 1775, in Thomas Gage papers, WLCL.

— *'Disperse! Disperse you damned rebels!'*: variations on these words appear in numerous accounts, including de Berniere. Allen French, *The Day of Lexington and Concord*, Boston 1925, is a rounded account based on many sources, but a particularly useful compilation of the American ones, which agree that Parker's company had begun to disperse when trouble started.

20 *'many redcoats started shouting and cheering'*: the circumstances of how the 'Shot Heard Around the World' came to be fired were the subject of intense debate at the time and subsequently. Many statements were taken by American observers with the intention of proving that the British fired first. The idea that a rush forward by shouting British troops may have triggered a panic response by one or more militia seems the most convincing to me, and is supported by Gould, Barker and de Berniere's accounts. No British officer accepted that the redcoats fired first at Lexington and since observers like Barker were quite happy to concede, for example, that the British fired first at Concord's north bridge, triggering the battle to get under way in earnest, I am inclined to believe them.

— *'Finding the Rebels scamping off'*: Smith's letter to Donkin, above.

— *'the men were so wild they could hear no orders'*: Barker.

21 *'Three companies from Pitcairn's battalion'*: details of the arrangements in Concord come from Barker, de Berniere, French and the account of 'an officer of one of the flank companies' appended to Mackenzie's *British Fusilier*. It is likely that these notes saved by Mackenzie belonged to an officer of one of the grenadier companies. An anonymous account of events in Concord, to be assumed by another officer of Smith's force, was published in *Scots Magazine*, June 1775 issue, and contains much interesting

detail, including some about the later discovery of the scalped soldier.

23 *'they had taken up some of the planks of the bridge'*: de Berniere, who was an officer in the 10th Regiment light company with Parsons's column.

24 *'They hardly ever fired but under cover'*: Mackenzie, describing, presumably the later sniping on the road back to Boston, but a concise description equally applicable here.

— *'We at first kept our order'*: de Berniere.

— *'We had been flattered ever since the morning'*: Barker.

— *'We began to run rather than retreat in order'*: de Berniere.

— *'critical situation'*: Barker.

— *'if they advanced they should die'*: a hair-raising moment from de Berniere's narrative, not explicitly endorsed by others, but with various writers describing the panic and lack of order.

25 *'we were ordered to form the line'*: Mackenzie, *British Fusilier*.

— *'saving them from inevitable destruction'*: Percy's description is in Bolton.

27 *'We were now obliged to force almost every house'*: Barker. Other officers such as Mackenzie and de Berniere also describe the breaking into houses and theft.

— *'issued with only thirty-six rounds each'*: Percy mentions the number of musket rounds per man; the number of artillery rounds is mentioned in a letter of Lord Rawdon's of 3 August 1775, found in *HMC, Report on the Manuscripts of the late Reginald Rawdon Hastings*, edited by Francis Bickley, HMSO 1934.

— *'In the village of Menotomy'*: several diarists mention fighting in Menotomy and several list the wounded, but only de Berniere among those I consulted helpfully notes where during the fighting each officer was wounded.

28 *'they did everything possible to help them back across the bay'*: de Berniere.

— *'As for British losses overall'*: I have used Mackenzie's figures although there are some discrepancies and his were higher than those in the official account. French is the best guide to American casualties.

29 *'William Gordon, minister of the Congregational Church'*: his account in the *Journal of American History*, vol. 4, January–March 1910.

— *'They pillaged almost every house'*: the *Essex Gazette* account was reprinted in *Scots Magazine*, May 1775 issue.

— *'as ill planned and as ill executed'*: Barker.

31 *'taking post at Boston'*: *The Journal of Captain John Montresor*, New-York Historical Society Collections, 1881.

— *'men still lost in a sort of stupefaction'*: Burgoyne's letter of 25 May 1775 printed in *Political and Military Episodes in the Latter Half of the Eighteenth Century Derived from the Life and Correspondence of The Right Hon. John Burgoyne, General, Statesman, Dramatist* by Edward Barrington De Fonblanque, Macmillan and Co., London 1876.

32 *'when troops see others advance'*: *A Treatise of Military Discipline: In which is Laid down and Explained The Duty of the Officer and Soldier, Through the several Branches of the Service*, Humphrey Bland, Lieutenant General, London 1762 edition. With regard to Bland's influence, a letter by

Evelyn notes an earnest young officer in Boston being teased as 'Humphrey Bland' and some of William Howe's orders about attacking and using the bayonet.

33 'instantly determined': Howe in a letter of 22 June 1775, assumed to be to the Adjutant General, in *The Correspondence of King George the Third, From 1760 to 1783*, arranged and edited by the Hon. Sir John Fortescue, 6 vols, London 1928. This work also contains a memorandum of 12 June that sets out the strategy to be followed in attacking the Americans and Gage's prior fears that his troops might be massacred by the inhabitants.

FOUR Bunker Hill

34 'Thomas Mecan joined the boats in command': this is revealed in his memorial to Gage of 19 June 1775 in the Gage Papers, WLCL. The other officers' names all appear on the casualty returns in TNA: PRO CO 5 papers and an interest handwritten note of the 23rd's casualties that day is found on the War Office copy of the Army List at TNA.

— 'It certainly occurred to some': Henry Clinton for example, in a handwritten note in his papers, claimed to have suggested it at the meeting and is cited by Allen French in *The First Years of the American Revolution*, New York 1934. William B. Willcox, editor of Clinton's private memoir, *The American Rebellion*, Hamden CT 1971, takes issue with some of French's interpretations of Clinton's difficult handwriting.

35 'flower of the army': the phrase is used in a letter of 27 June 1775 by Charles Stuart (then a captain commanding the grenadiers of the 37th) to his father in *A Prime Minister and His Son From the Correspondence of the 3rd Earl of Bute and of Lt General The Hon. Sir Charles Bute*, edited by the Hon Mrs E. Stuart Wortley, London 1925.

— 'a strike force under the hand of Major General William Howe': many of the details in this narrative, for example of the 2 p.m. landing or the number of troops in the first wave of boats, or the distances used in Howe's appreciation of the ground, come from two private letters written by Howe after the battle, one on 22 June to his brother Admiral Lord Howe, which is in *HMC, Reports on the Manuscripts of Mrs Stopford-Sackville of Drayton House Northamptonshire*, vol. II (London 1910). Howe's other letter, in Fortescue, was written on the same date and is thought to have been sent to the Adjutant General in London.

37 'When we saw our danger': Brown's letter to his mother is dated 25 June and has been reproduced in various publications of the Massachusetts Historical Society.

— 'The veteran and gallant Stark': this comes from Henry Dearborn's account in *History of the Battle of Breed's Hill, by Major Generals William Heath, Henry Lee, James Wilkinson and Henry Dearborn*, compiled by Charles Coffin, Portland 1835.

38 'take them in the flank': Howe's letter to his brother.

— 'Push on! Push on!': this detail comes from Rawdon's letter of 20 June to his uncle, in Bickley.

38 'his men were directed to reserve their fires': James Wilkinson in Coffin.
— 'began firing, and by crowding fell into disorder': Howe's letter in Fortescue.
— 'received a volley which mowed down the whole front ranks': Wilkinson in
    Coffin.
39 'a moment that I never felt before': (emphasis in original) Howe in Fortescue.
— 'The officer commanding the grenadier battalion and many of its men were
    thus killed by British fire': Rawdon talks about redcoats being killed by their
    own side in his account, but the key source is Brigadier James Grant (who
    arrived in Boston after the battle); he reported to General Harvey in a letter
    of 10 August 1775 that 'poor Abercrombie was killed by our own men, and
    many of the grenadiers under his command fell by the fire of the light
    infantry', NAS GD 494/1/29.
— 'Our men were intent on cutting down every officer': Dearborn in Coffin.
— 'Around two-thirds of the Welch Fusiliers engaged': the casualty figures are
    taken from the annotated Army List at TNA; the figure of five grenadiers being
    fit at the end comes from Historical Record of the Twenty Third Regiment,
    or Royal Welch Fusiliers, compiled by Richard Cannon, London 1850.
— 'The fire of the enemy was so badly directed': Dearborn in Coffin.
40 'prospect of the neighbouring hills': Burgoyne's letter to Lord Stanley, in De
    Fonblanque.
41 'Brown wanted court martial and the death sentence': in fact a letter of
    George Washington's of 20 July 1775 suggested that the artillery officer
    concerned, Captain Callender, be cashiered. It is in vol. 3 of The Writings of
    George Washington (39 vols, ed. by John C. Fitzpatrick, Washington,
    1931–34).
— 'retreating, seemingly without any excuse': Chester's account is in French's
    book of 1934.
— 'Finding our ammunition was almost spent': Prescott's letter to John Adams,
    25 August 1775 is in various Massachusets Historical Society publications,
    as is Lieutenant Waller's.
42 'One officer of the 52nd explained': Martin Hunter of the grenadier
    company in The Journal of Gen. Sir Martin Hunter by Miss A. Hunter (The
    Edinburgh Press, Edinburgh 1894). He also described the mixed-up units in
    front of the rail fence and Rawdon's bravery in front of the breastwork.
— 'Captain Harris of the 5th': Harris letter in Lushington.
43 'to let those damned rascals see that the Yankees will fight': Warren's words
    were reported by Wilkinson (as he heard it from Prescott) in Coffin.
— 'this unhappy day': Howe in Fortescue.
— 'All was in confusion': Clinton's note as quoted by French, The First Years
    of the American Revolution.
44 'As I am certain that every letter from America': Rawdon's letter of 3 August
    1775 to his uncle, full of wise reflections for a man of 21, also in Bickley.
— 'The zeal and intrepidity of the officers': great wisdom from Burgoyne too in
    this letter of late June to the Secretary of State for the Colonies, in De
    Fonblanque.
45 'the Americans, if they are equally well commanded': an interesting letter

from an anonymous officer reproduced in *The Services of Lieutenant Colonel Francis Downman, RA*, edited by Colonel F. A. Whinyates, printed by Royal Artillery Institution 1898.

45 *'The Welch Fuzileers were nearly all cut off'*: I have found this dispatch in a few newspapers including the *Boston Gazette* of 26 June and *Massachusetts Spy* of the same date.

46 *'The events of that day made several vacant companies'*: Mecan's memo of 19 June to Gage, WLCL.

— *'do everything that he can to contribute to the happiness of deserving officers'*: General Amherst to Mecan, 13 October 1775, TNA: PRO WO 3/23.

— *'Lord Rawdon behaved to a charm'*: the full Burgoyne letter to his wife is in De Fonblanque, but sections were published, for example in *Scots Magazine*, August 1775.

— *'Mecan was given several assignments by the general'*: see Howe's Orderly Book, TNA: PRO 30/55/106.

47 *'been entirely set aside'*: Howe in Fortescue.

FIVE Boston Besieged

48 *'the rascals called out to us several times to surrender'*: a letter from Lenthall to Lt Col James of the artillery, dated 15 August 1775. It is reproduced in Downman. This letter is the prime source for the description of this action but it is referred to in Williams and a letter home from Stuart in Wortley.

49 *'We burnt Penny Ferry House'*: Lenthall in Downman.

50 *'gave a general fire of small arms'*: Williams's journal.

51 *'sentenced to receive 500 lashes'*: details of the court martial of Husthwaite (of the 4th) are in a General Order of 26 July 1775 in *General Sir William Howe's Orderly Book 1775–1776*, collected and edited by Benjamin Franklin Stevens, London 1890.

— *'rumours about poor Lieutenant Hull'*: referred to in Williams's journal.

— *'the detachment I was with succeeded'*: Clinton, *American Rebellion*.

— *'had forgot to bring any combustibles'*: letter of Major Francis Hutcheson to Major General Haldimand, in the general's papers, BL ADD MS 21680. The Hutcheson letters are a full and extremely useful account of life in Boston under siege (and beyond).

52 *'The entrance to the harbour'*: Harris in Lushington.

— *'Dozens of redcoats' wives had been pressed into service'*: General Orders, Stevens.

53 *'every inhabitant that can get away is going'*: Hutcheson letters.

— *'If you will quit the service'*: the seditious pamphlet was reprinted in the July 1775 edition of *Scots Magazine*.

— *'Machin, a soldier of Blunt's company'*: details from TNA: PRO WO 12/3960 and Williams.

— *'This fellow will give them good intelligence'*: Williams.

54 *'The next campaign will be be carried on'*: Rawdon's letter of 13 December 1775 in Bickley.

— *'an Ugly Club at the Bunch of Grapes'*: details from the court martial of one of those officers in TNA: PRO WO 71/80.

54 'most scandalous drunkenness at this critical time': General Order quoted by
Barker.

— 'There was an order of this kind': Barker.

55 'The principal failure that day, was in the officers': Washington's letter to
the President of Congress of 20 July 1775 in vol. 3 of Fitzpatrick.

— 'an unaccountable kind of stupidity': Washington to Richard Lee,
29 August, in vol. 3 of Fitzpatrick.

56 'it took more than one year for a proper scheme of punishments': the issue is
discussed in detail in The Morale of the American Revolutionary Army, by
Allen Bowman, Washington 1943.

— 'the enemy, by their not coming out, are, I suppose afraid of us':
Washington to his brother, 13 October 1775, vol. 4 of Fitzpatrick.

— 'far more wealth to their name': New York officers like Philip Schuyler and
Peter Gansevoort belonged to Dutch families with huge estates, similarly
many regimental officers in the Maryland and Virginia forces were reckoned
wealthy.

57 'the dependents on the present commander': Hutcheson letters.

— 'In November 1775': these changes were announced in General Orders,
Stevens.

— 'an establishment of more than 850 men': the establishment was first set out
in a letter of 31st August from Lord Barrington to General Gage, in TNA:
PRO 30/55/1.

58 'one, worthy but penniless old officer': this was Robert Douglas, details in
TNA: PRO WO 4/273.

— 'the second recruiting captain's job': went to Thomas Gibbings, TNA: PRO
WO 12.

— 'pleases them not a little': Hutcheson.

— 'the price of a chicken': from a letter of Captain Evelyn's.

— 'pay the unfortunate fellow': Hutcheson letter of 14 December. The broken
officer was called William Haughton.

59 'He had been commissioned from the ranks': details in TNA: PRO WO 27 and
WO 12. Many letters from him in Portsmouth are in WO 1 files.

60 'permitted to sell out extra quick': a sad letter concerning Williams by the
regimental agent is in TNA: PRO WO 1/994 and a letter allowing his selling
out in WO 4/273.

61 'necessary he should live with the corps': Hutcheson.

— 'Late in November, he sold out': this is announced in a General Order in
Stevens, and its date, 23 November, the same as that of Haldimand's
transfer into the 23rd, linking the two events.

SIX Escape from Boston

62 'The explosions in the night': these descriptions of events during 5–24 March
are based on the Hutcheson letters, Barker and the journal of Captain
William Bamford, 'Bamford's Diary', in Maryland Historical Magazine, vols
27 and 28, 1932 and 1933.

63 'A drill book... 1764': *A New Manual and the Platoon Exercise: With an Explanation*, by Edward Harvey, Adjutant General, London 1764.

64 'Orders were given on 5 March... not to load their weapons': Barker.

— 'had done its best to form three deep': the best evidence of this is actually the sketches of Amos Doolittle, an American soldier at the battle who subsequently sold prints of what he had seen, and the fact that the formation in two ranks on 17 June was a subject of comment.

— 'there would be 18-inch gaps between each "file"': Howe's General Order of 29 February 1776, in the *Journal of Stephen Kemble, 1773–1789; and British Army Orders*, New-York Historical Society Collections for 1884.

— 'Rumours ran around the men': best recorded by Bamford.

65 'I am not one of those bloody-minded people': Harris (evidently quite a moderate) in Lushington.

— 'Britain's best option lay in a war of naval raiding': both Harris and Hutcheson fall into this category.

66 'I confess I should have thought it': Percy's letter of 28 July 1775 to General Harvey, in Bolton.

— 'At dawn on 3 April': many details in this passage drawn from Bamford and Hutcheson's letters.

67 'This winter will improve them much': a letter of 13 January 1776 to his Uncle, in Bickley.

— 'On 14 April the Light Infantry': these details from General Orders kept by Kemble.

— 'provide Frederick Mackenzie with his path out of regimental service': Brigade Majors were appointed by General Order of 17 May 1776, in Kemble.

68 'Every private man will in action be his own general': Burgoyne's memo is undated but reckoned to have been penned early in 1776, in De Fonblanque.

— '18-inch separation between files was just a start': British troops on the Plain of Abraham in 1759 were said to have formed with three feet between files; see, for example, *Historical Journal of the Campaigns in North America*, Captain John Knox, Toronto 1914.

— 'General Howe believed that starting all the changes from the centre': this is clear from his 1774 'Instructions to Light Companies', included for example in *The Elements of Military Arrangement; Comprehending the Tactick, Exercises, Manoeuvres, and Discipline of the British Infantry*, by John Williamson, London 1781.

69 'training them all to perform their manoeuvres at the double': the breathless British exercises are described with horror by Captain George Pausch, of the Hesse Hanau Artillery, *Journal of Captain George Pausch*, New York 1971.

— 'He also used a couple of picked regiments': these were usually the 33rd or 42nd, brigaded with the Light Infantry and Grenadiers.

— 'Bennett Cuthbertson's work was particularly influential': *System for the Compleat Interior Management and Oeconomy of a Battalion of Infantry*, Dublin 1768. Cuthbertson was a former captain of the 5th.

— 'the distinction of wearing bearskin caps': the issue of whether the 23rd actually wore these fancy hats on service is complex. The only evidence of the regiment as a whole parading in them during the 1770s was carried by a newspaper, *The Gazetteer*, reporting a review by the King on Blackheath Common on 5 August 1771 (cited by Cary and McCance), yet even when being given their annual review during the same week, the 23rd were wearing cocked hats (TNA: PRO WO 27/18). In a letter of 12 December 1775, Hutcheson talks about Lieutenant Baily giving young Haldimand his 'cap', sword and sash, noting he will buy replacements in London. 'Cap' in this context can reasonably be inferred to be fur fusilier variety since Baily served on the regimental staff, not the light company which had leather caps. Doolittle's drawings of Lexington and Concord show the British troops in cocked hats, and he was an eyewitness to these events.

70 *'One general, writing two years earlier'*: this book was published anonymously but was widely regarded as being by Major General Richard Lambart, *A New System of Military Discipline, Founded Upon Principle*, by A General Officer, London 1773.

— *'The results, as they moved away from regulation appearance'*: the most complete picture of Howe's new-look British soldier comes from the anonymous 'Letter of a Hessian Officer to the Landgrave of Hesse-Kassel' reproduced in *Militair-Wochenblatt*, 18, Berlin 1833. He reports home that 'the English have been clothed according to the hot climate, with very short and light coats, and long linen trousers down to the shoes'. He also notices the officers changing uniform; see also *The Diary of Lieutenant Bardleben and other von Donop Regiment Documents*, translated by Bruce E. Burgoyne, Bowie MD 1998. The 'jettisoned adornment' included button lace, officers' gorgets (metal plates that were a sign of rank), and halberds.

71 *'the former major of the 23rd was close to Gage'*: in Hutcheson's letters.

— 'from a knowledge of the inextricable difficulties in [Blunt's] private affairs': this comes from a letter of the Secretary at War to Howe, 15 August 1775, in TNA: PRO 30/55/3. Other letters related to the Blunt affair can be found in WO 4/97, 98 and 99.

— 'despotic power of Commanders in Chief abroad': Montresor.

72 *'When presented with the colonelcy of the Royal Welch, Howe had let it be known that he didn't want it'*: Grant to General Harvey, 5 October 1775, NAS GD 494/1/29. It is clear Grant hankered after the 23rd himself, but, as a friend and confidant of Howe's, I find his remarks credible on this subject.

— *'Howe then got into an argument with the widow'*: the correspondence related to Mrs Boscawen and the 1776 uniform issue can be found in TNA: PRO WO 4/95, and 96.

— *'I serve only for credit and not for profit'*: Percy to Northumberland, 12th February 1777, in the DON, the duke's private papers at Alnwick Castle. These are, of course, the best source of information about how Percy ran the 5th, for dozens of letters touch on this theme. More accessible, though, is the appendix on Percy in the back of Evelyn's memoir edited by Scull.

— *'Though his regiment is distinguished for its admirable discipline'*: anonymous soldier's letter in the *London Chronicle*, 7–10 September 1775, cited in Scull's edition of Evelyn's memoir. Burgoyne in his letter home after Bunker Hill, opined that the 5th was the best regiment in action that day (De Fonblanque).

73 *'some of the 23rd's older officers gravitated towards Earl Percy'*: interesting letters from Ferguson and Donkin can be found in the DON.

— *'the heir of that illustrious family'*: Donkin, *Military Collections*.

— *'illiterate and indolent to the last degree'*: this was the captured rebel Major General Charles Lee, in a letter to Benjamin Rush, 4 June 1778, *The Lee Papers*, Collections of the New-York Historical Society, 1872.

— *'the soldiers that served last campaign at Boston'*: Bamford.

74 *'Officers went on trips ashore, hunting wildfowl and fishing'*: Bamford.

— *'John Browning, a rogue in Evans's company'*: General Order of 6 June 1776 and TNA: PRO WO 12.

— *'Three young officers caught gambling'*: Hunter reports this.

SEVEN The Battle for New York

75 *'The Halifax armament, 9,300 men borne in 130 ships'*: the details of these movements can be found in CO 5 files at TNA, however Piers Mackesy in his *War For America 1775–1783*, London 1964 does a masterful job of pulling it all together.

— *'For a major of brigade like Mackenzie'*: in *The Diary of Frederick Mackenzie*, 2 vols, Cambridge MA 1930, there are various tables and returns as well as his pithy observations about Smith and others.

76 *'The assistance of foreign troops will be highly politick'*: Evelyn of the 4th.

— *'The English have been clothed according to the hot climate'*: Anon. 'Letter of a Hessian Officer' cited above.

77 *'the common British soldier is swift, marches easily'*: *A Hessian Diary of the American Revolution*, by Johann Conrad Dohla, translated and edited by Bruce E. Burgoyne, Norman OK 1990.

— *'some Scottish recruits'*: destined originally for the 26th, they were waylaid by the Secretary at War, Howe notified in PRO 30/55/2, arriving with the 42nd at Staten Island, i.e., before Long Island.

— *'A further twenty-five men'*: letter in TNA: PRO WO 4/98.

— *'Eighteen men had been attracted'*: TNA: PRO WO 4/93.

— *'in addition to the German-speakers'*: details of their embarkation in PRO 30/55/2 in a letter of 27 May 1776, a party that seem likely to have arrived before Long Island.

— *'Nine men, for example, came to the 23rd'*: the 65th men are listed as joining on 25 June 1776 in TNA: PRO WO 12, and the 69th on 10 June.

78 *'the forty men who came on the Clyde transports'*: the number is given in a General Order of 6 August 1776. I found it in RWF 8187, a copy of Howe's Orderly Book for the summer of 1776. No published, complete set of General Orders for 1775–7 exists. Instead I have pieced together the whole from Stevens, Kemble, the record mentioned here and TNA: PRO 30/55/106 and 107.

— *'A serjeant should...be able to instruct'*: Williamson. Details of Grimes' promotion from TNA: PRO WO 12.

78 *'honesty, sobriety, and a remarkable attention to every point of duty'*:
   Cuthbertson.

— *'the ignominy of having the knot ceremonially cut'*: this ceremony is
   described by Roger Lamb in his unpublished scrapbook, and was
   communicated to me by Don Hagist. Lamb evidently considered his own
   breaking from the rank of corporal in Ireland to be deeply humiliating.

79 *'he is confined and not likely to get better'*: Hutcheson letter of 23 December
   1775. TNA: PRO WO 12 records list Barnard sick throughout this period, and
   relevant returns in CO 5 generally leave blank the 'lieutenant colonel' box
   for the 23rd, showing he was not serving with his regiment.

— *'by the 12th had died aged just 22'*: TNA: PRO WO 12/3960 for death, TNA:
   PRO WO 27 for his age.

— *'that Irishman chose to remain in England'*: Blakeney was elected to the Irish
   parliament in 1779, sitting with an anti-war faction, he also had his MP,
   who voted against the Ministry on American matters, make representations
   on his behalf. The story of how Blakeney shirked his duty and of Howe's
   annoyance is found mainly in TNA: PRO WO 1 and WO 4 files and will be
   told later.

— *'The state of the regiment in every military point of view'*: Roger Lamb (ed.
   Hagist). Lamb states authoritatively that the regiment improved under its
   next lieutenant colonel, but these must have been the opinions of old sweats
   because Lamb himself did not arrive until after that new CO was installed in
   1778.

80 *'a reputation for corruption on a grand scale'*: exposed early in Hutcheson's
   letters from Boston but also referred to by Mackenzie.

— *'he had given lavish parties'*: Hutcheson, who also mentions Baptiste the
   cook.

81 *'would never dare to face an English army'*: Gentleman's Magazine, vol. 45,
   1775.

— *'if a good bleeding can bring those Bible-faced Yankees'*: Grant's letter of 2
   September 1776 in *General James Grant of Ballindalloch*, by Alistair
   Macpherson Grant, privately published 1930.

— *'Brigadier General Grant directs our Commander-in-chief'*: Percy's letter of
   7 January 1776.

— *'For Major General William Alexander'*: details from his letter of 29 August
   to Washington in *The Life of William Alexander, Earl of Stirling*, by
   William Alexander Duer, New York 1847.

83 *'Alexander's forces in place topped 1,000'*: a difficult thing to calculate, but
   this is based on figures in *The Delaware Continentals 1776–1783*, by
   Christopher L. Ward, Wilmington 1941. This is also the source for
   'Delaware Blues'.

— *'men of honour, family and fortune'*: Mordecai Gist quoted in Ward.

— *'justly supposed to carry no small terror to the enemy'*: Washington used
   these words in a General Order of 24 July 1776. A letter of 27 January 1776
   from Col. Smallwood of the Maryland Regiment advocates hunting shirts

for practical reasons, and can be found in Peter Force, 5th series, vol. 4.

83 *'General Grant's division, 2,650 men'*: An embarkation return of 22 August puts the 4th Brigade at 1,087 men, and the 6th at 1,166. To this I have added the 49th Regiment, 320 and a suitable number of men for the four artillery pieces. The return is in DoN. Contrast the 2,500–2,600 Grant had with him at the outset of this battle, to the 5,000 given to him by American historians (e.g., Christopher Ward, *The War of the Revolution*, 2 vols, New York 1952, a standard work) who evidently want to make much of Alexander's resistance.

— *'Grant deployed his men into battle formation'*: British sources drawn upon include Grant's letter of 2 September, Private Sullivan, Captain Bamford, Major General Vaughan (see below) and 'Letter from an officer of the 17th Foot' in the September 1776 issue of *Scots Magazine*.

— *'The enemy'*: Attlee's journal dated 27 August, reprinted in Thomas W. Field, *The Battle of Long Island*, Brooklyn 1869, which is in general an excellent fusion of various, principally American, sources.

85 *'the 23rd Regiment signalised themselves'*: Sullivan who, being with the 49th, the baggage guard, may not have observed this in person.

— *'the Hessians gave very little quarter to any'*: Vaughan's journal is in BL EGERTON MS 2135.

— *'One Hessian returned the compliment'*: Anon. 'Letter from a Hessian Officer'.

— *'receiving, as we passed'*: Attlee's journal.

86 *'Howe would not allow this'*: Howe's refusal to press on with the attack is notably referred to in Clinton's *American Rebellion*, but is also in several letters written shortly after the battle, for example by Captain Harris of the 5th Grenadiers (in Lushington).

— *'They were not so dreadful as I expected'*: a letter from Captain William Dansey of the 33rd to his mother, 3 September 1776. The Dansey letters are now in the possession of the Delaware Historical Society, but this passage and many others quoted subsequently can be found in old copies of *Iron Duke*, the regimental journal of the Duke of Wellington's Regiment, which printed extracts in issues 79–88.

— *'under strict orders to receive the enemy's first fire before rushing in'*: Percy in a letter home, 1 September 1776.

87 *'the Americans had all fired too high'*: Anon. 'Letter from a Hessian Officer'.

— *'With its large waterfront warehouses'*: my description of New York is based on an engraved panorama *A View of the City of New York from Brooklyn Heights foot of Pierrepoint Street 1798*. The quotation about the roofs comes from Dohla.

— 'In the early evening of 15 September': this passage relies on Mackenzie's diary.

EIGHT The Campaign of 1776 Concluded

89 *'Thomas Watson was taken to the provost'*: the details making up his narrative come from TNA: PRO WO 71/83, court martial records.

89   'John Hunter, a deserter': General Orders (RWF 8187) suggest that a soldier
     of the 42nd named Hunter was hung on 12 August, on which date his
     regimental Muster Rolls mark him as 'deceased'.
 —   'Another man, Private John Winters': Mackenzie's diary, 11 September
     1776. He also records the men of the 57th charged with rape.
92   'the ravages committed by the Hessians': Kemble's journal, 4 October.
 —   'The Commander-in-chief is greatly disappointed': General Order
     19 October 1776.
 —   'The general therefore recommends . . . to the troops': General Order
     13 September 1776, RWF 8187.
93   'an American captain who had been captured on 21 September': this was
     Captain Nathan Hale, see Walter Harold Wilkin, Some British Soldiers in
     America, London 1914.
 —   'caustic comment from Hessian officers': Anon. 'Letter from a Hessian
     Officer' again, also Johann Ewald, Diary of the American War, translated
     and edited by Joseph P. Tustin, New Haven and London 1979.
 —   'Tories are in my front rear and on my flanks': Lee to Gates, 13 December
     1776, Lee Papers.
94   'the whole should have been put to the sword': this issue was discussed, for
     example, at breakfast in England on 13 January 1777 by Major Nisbet
     Balfour (Howe's ADC at the time) and Lord Polwarth. The peer's note of
     the conversation suggests Balfour had been told by ministers that they ought
     to have stormed the place. Polwarth Papers, LBRO L29/214.
 —   'Whig sympathies led Howe to let Washington off the hook': such views get
     repeated airing in Ewald's journal.
 —   'they were making too much money from it': see Bamford for example.
95   'Browning was acquitted of the capital charge': General Order of 14 July
     1776, RWF 8187. By coincidence, the officer he was alleged to have struck,
     Lt Wragg of the Marines Grenadiers, was the one killed by the Maryland
     Blues when he mistook them for Hessians at Long Island. Browning's return
     to the 23rd, TNA: PRO WO 12/3960.
96   'the reprieve followed representations from the victims' families': the
     outcome of these two cases is referred to by John Peebles, an officer of the
     42nd, in his journal, 24 December 1776, John Peebles' American War
     1776–1782, edited by Ira D. Gruber, Stroud 1998.
 —   'the fate of many who suffer indiscriminately': Peebles.
 —   'The fresh meat our men have got here': Lord Rawdon's letter of 5 August
     1776 in Bickley.
 —   'for a woman this poor boy ventured his existence': Harris in Lushington.
97   'cruel to such a degree as to threaten with death': Kemble's journal for
     7 November 1776.
 —   'Repeated orders was given against this barbarity': Stuart's letter of
     4 February 1777 (in Wortley).
98   'There is no record of whether the lashes . . . were ever inflicted': I have not
     found, in all the letters, records, and journals used for this book any first-
     hand account of a British army flogging in America during these campaigns.

It must be possible therefore that these punishments were simply never carried out. Corporal punishment of Hessians, on the other hand, is recorded in several places.

NINE The 1777 Campaign Opens

100 'As the rascals are skulking about the whole country': an epistle of Captain James Murray, 57th, of 25 February 1777, in *Letters From America 1773 to 1780, Being the Letters of a Scots Officer, Sir James Murray, to his home during the War of American Independence*, edited by Eric Robson, Manchester 1951.

— 'made it absolutely necessary for us to enter into a kind of "petite guerre"': Stuart letter of 29 March (in Wortley).

101 'Robert Donkin, who had been responsible': according to Cary and McCance.

— 'harass and ruin the enemy's troops': these quotes on petite guerre come from an essay he wrote in late 1776 or early 1777 and printed at the back of his book *Military Collections*.

— 'It was under the command of Captain Thomas Mecan': the establishment given here applied was stipulated in a General Order of May 1776, except that the order stipulated thirty-nine rank and file whereas Muster Rolls, TNA: PRO WO 12/3960, suggest that at the beginning of 1777 Mecan's company was short of four or two rank and file.

— 'only 12 were Light Company veterans who went back to 1773': TNA: PRO WO 12/3960.

102 'in the hottest part of this action': Lord Rawdon put them there in a letter of 3 November 1776 (in Bickley).

— 'the most dangerous and difficult service of this war': Dansey letter of 15 March 1777, HSD.

— 'Hamilton was one of the best men that ever was': Hunter.

— 'the chance of serving as a "gentleman volunteer" in the light infantry': this seems to have been the general rule although Richard Veale served with the battalion companies of the 23rd.

— 'Charles Hastings was a lieutenant in the 12th Regiment': Hastings's story is pieced together from Rawdon's letter of 3 November 1776, Lord Barrington's letter to William Howe of 24 June 1777 in TNA: PRO WO 4/273, Hastings's letters to Earl Percy of 17 April 1777 and 16 May 1778 in DoN.

103 'Francis Delaval was the bastard son': see *Those Gay Delavals*, by Francis Askham, London 1955.

— 'One satisfaction I have in America': Dansey, 17 February 1777, HSD.

— 'The march under Colonel Harcourt's command began at 11 p.m.': this account is pieced together from Ewald's diary, Peebles's journal and Dansey's letter of 20 April, HSD.

106 'The place was ransacked and plundered': Ewald.

— 'three pieces of cannon, a major of artillery': Dansey, 20 April letter, HSD.

— 'It was well conceived and conducted masterly': Howe's letter of 25 April. It is not clear to whom it was sent, but the fact that the extract from which this paper was taken is in Fortescue's royal papers suggests it was read by the King.

107 *'We have learned from the rebels'*: Dansey letter of 20 April, HSD, one of several in which he offers insights into light infantry or skirmishing tactics.

— *'a day's Yankie hunting is no more minded than a day's fox hunting'*: Dansey of 15 March 1777, HSD.

— *'They had definitively dropped the old system'*: an interesting guide to the tactics of the 1st Battalion Light Infantry can be found in the notes of an anonymous officer, item no. 111 in Sol Feinstone Collection, DLAR.

— *'Light Bob officers often sought volunteers'*: the calling forward of volunteers while under fire is described in one of Dansey's letters, HSD.

108 *'Grab was a favourite expression'*: Hunter.

— *'Then honest Whigs, make all your cattle fat'*: I have produced half of the poem which I found in the DON. It is on a scrap of newsprint and although it is not clear exactly when it was published, I surmise it to have been prior to the 1778 campaign, and quite possibly sent by Lionel Smythe who wrote many letters to Percy at this period.

— *'Damn my eyes, painted wood burns best'*: Lionel Smythe to Earl Percy, 21 January 1778, DON.

— *'as it will not be in [the commander's] power'*: Donkin's *Military Collections*.

109 *'men who pretend to be acquainted with military matters'*: this is from *Treatise of the Duties of Light Troops*, by Colonel Ehwald, published in English in 1803. This is, of course, the same jaeger officer as the diary-writing Ewald above, but I will cite 'Ehwald' to denote quotations from that specific work.

— *'to attack a large American magazine at Danbury in Connecticut'*: the main sources for this are *Archibald Robertson, His Diaries and Sketches in America 1762–1780*, edited by Henry Miller Lydenberg, New York 1930, and the report in *Scots Magazine*, June 1777.

110 *'of the confusion that surrounded the high command of William Howe'*: the best description of Howe's woeful inability to decide on a strategy is in Mackesy.

— *'Clinton and Percy, in common with many others, thought it extremely unwise'*: Clinton's views were recorded in *American Rebellion*, Percy's letter (above) of 28 July 1775 extolled the Hudson strategy and a letter after Saratoga from Francis Hutcheson to the earl (in DON) credits him with always believing Howe should link up with Burgoyne.

111 *'The risk which all armies are liable to was our hindrance'*: Stuart letter of 10 July 1777 (in Wortley), a very prescient text.

— *'General Howe wanted...to get two strikes'*: this is certainly the implication of Nisbet Balfour's letter of 13 July 1777, LBRO L30/12/3/2.

— *'All the county houses were in flames'*: *The Journal of Nicholas Cresswell 1774–1777*, Nicholas Cresswell, New York 1924.

— *'In the early hours of 26 June'*: Ewald's diary is a good source on this.

111 'They will not ever allow us to come near them': Balfour cited above.
112 'There would be no tents': the light infantry were ordered to give up their tents by a General Order of 24 August 1776 (RWF 8187); Ewald says the policy was extended to the rest of the army.
— 'marched the whole campaign on foot': Ehwald says Howe often used to talk about this during these later campaigns.
— 'sell their nags to the mounted troops for ten guineas each': Ewald.
— 'Howe went aboard the Eagle': details of embarkation from Andre's journal. An authentic record of the movements and engagements of the British Army in America from June 1777 to November 1778 as recorded from day to day by Major John Andre, edited by Henry Cabot Lodge, published Boston MA 1903.

TEN The March on Philadelphia

113 'The sailing up Chesapeak Bay': Dansey letter 30 August 1777, HSD.
114 'Fox had chided him for being "too violent" a Whig': Fox letter to Fitzpatrick of 3 February 1777, in BL, ADD MS 47580.
— 'Nothing in the world can be so disagreeable': this is one of five Fitzpatrick letters from America printed in vol. VII of The Letters of Horace Walpole, edited by Peter Cunningham, London 1891.
— 'I think it amounts very near to a demonstration': ibid., letter of 1 September 1777.
— 'extirpating the whole race': ibid., letter of 2 June 1777.
— 'the most unpleasant, formal, precise, disagreeable people': ibid.
— 'We shall find the rebels enough to do at Philadelphia': Dansey, as above.
115 'taking post at Cooch's bridge': this passage is based on Ewald's diary and the journal of 1st L.I. Officer Sol Feinstone, Collection no. 409, DLAR, and Dansey's letters, HSD.
— 'the 1st Light Infantry had taken an American prisoner': Feinstone no. 409, DLAR.
117 'In one place they laid a clever ambush for the Queen's Rangers': in Ehwald.
— 'Everyone that remembers the anxious moments': Feinstone no. 409, DLAR.
118 'without hurry or confusion': ibid.
— 'For damned fighting and drinking': Meadows's words were recorded by Hunter of the 52nd L.I.
— 'Nothing could be more dreadfully pleasing': Captain Hale's letter to his parents of 21 October 1777 (in Wilkin), a startling passage that says much about why British soldiers or officers fought.
119 'the impatient courage of both officers and men': Feinstone no. 409, DLAR.
— 'had nothing to expect but slaughter': ibid.
— 'Of all the Maryland regiments only two': letter of Major Stone in Chronicles of Baltimore, by J. Thomas Scharf, Baltimore 1874.
— 'The British grenadiers worked their way forward in the textbook style': reported by Hale and Captain Friedrich von Muenchausen in At General Howe's Side, journal translated by Ernst Kipping, Monmouth Beach N.J. 1974.

120 *'a bounty of a hundred dollars per gun'*: this nice detail comes from Henry Stirke (a lieutenant in the 10th Light Company serving with 1st L.I. Battalion), 'A British Officer's Revolutionary War Journal 1776–1778', edited by S. Sydney Bradford, *Maryland Historical Magazine*, no. 56, June 1961.

— *'The 4th and 5th Regiments went over first'*: Knyphausen's report to Howe is in TNA: PRO CO 5/94.

— *'fortunately being directed too high'*: letter of Serjeant Major Thorne to Earl Percy, 29 September 1777, in DoN.

121 *'the Light Infantry met with the chief resistance'*: Andre.

— *'Nearly seventeen years had passed since he was shot'*: Mecan's memo of 5 July 1775, Gage Papers, WLCL.

— *'favourites for bullets in the arms or legs'*: this idea appears in a couple of Dansey letters, HSD.

— *'The consequences of this victory'*: Fitzpatrick 26 October 1777 (in Cunningham).

122 *'Cornwallis could stand this no longer'*: unfortunately I have not found any letter of Cornwallis's in which he describes this dramatic and extraordinary act, but it is clear, since the death sentences carried out on 15 September do not appear in General Orders or the TNA: PRO WO 71 Court Martial series that it was a summary process. Peebles's approving tone suggests also that the event needs to be seen in the context of the continuing tensions between lenient commanders-in-chief and more junior officers who felt discipline was being neglected.

— *'the Commander-in-chief, considering the punishment'*: General Order of 2 September 1777, in Kemble.

ELEVEN The Surprise of Germantown

124 *'had put on their cartridge-pouch belts'*: Feinstone no. 409, DLAR.

— *'The battalion was so reduced by killed and wounded'*: Hunter.

125 *'For Shame! For Shame, Light Infantry!'*: ibid. Howe had of course seen the Light Infantry retreat before, in front of the rail fence at Bunker Hill.

— *'the morning was so foggy'*: Stirke.

— *'instantly attempted wheeling'*: Feinstone no. 409, DLAR.

126 *'upon which the officers'*: ibid.

— *'a significant proportion being from the 9th Virginia'*: Peebles suggests the whole regiment laid down its arms.

— *'The movement of the army'*: Balfour's letter of 25 October 1777, Polwarth Papers, LBRO L30/12/3/3.

127 *'The most favourable accounts are that [Burgoyne]'*: Smythe's letter of 26 October 1777 is in DoN, Peebles alludes to the Reading newspaper.

— *'made him one of the happiest men in the army'*: this was Francis Hutcheson to Earl Percy, 30 January 1778, DoN.

— *'Percy paying the entire £550 cost of his step'*: this is in Hutcheson's letter above. This sum was the difference between the cost of Smythe's captaincy and the captain-lieutenancy he sold in the 49th. This officer had played a similar factor's role for General Haldimand. Interestingly, Percy's cash for Smythe's purchase was initially put up by Henry Clinton, and Percy repaid him, an interesting token of the intimacy between the two men.

127 *'Percy had rendered himself impotent'*: so argued an article in *Town and Country Magazine* in 1772. A résumé of these matters may be found in his entry in the 2005 edition of the *Dictionary of National Biography* but the charge is a calumny since the earl fathered children when he subsequently remarried.

128 *'Russell was quite unable to afford a commission'*: his details come from Kirby.

— *'never was a person that had a people's affection'*: Smythe to Percy 21 January 1778, DON.

— *'plain officers of the Fusiliers...received a courteous reply to their letters but rarely more'*: examples are Jo Ferguson, Henry Blunt and Robert Donkin, all of whose letters are in the DON archive. Donkin accounts for the 'rarely' since Clinton invented a lieutenant colonel's job for him in 1779 and may have done so partly through Percy's representations, although I have not seen evidence of it.

129 *'I cannot easily express to you'*: Dansey letter of 4 October 1777, HSD.

— *'Light Infantry accustomed to fight from tree to tree'*: Hale in Wilkin.

— *'The brigades have been looked upon as nurseries'*: ibid.

130 *'totally unfit for our service'*: Howe's letter to Lord Germain, 20 January 1777, TNA: PRO CO 5/94.

— *'If all reasoning and speculation was not exploded'*: Fitzpatrick letter to Fox of 5 November 1777, in BL, ADD MS 47580.

TWELVE Winter in Philadelphia

131 *'very peaceable, quite different from our Jersey excursions'*: Captain Hale's letter of 23 March 1778 in Wilkin.

— *'Captain Richard Fitzpatrick in a letter to his friend'*: dated 5 November 1777, in BL, ADD MS 47580.

132 *'Rooms are opened at the City Tavern'*: Hale's letter as above.

— *'a fine girl, of good fortune'*: this 'Loyalist manuscript' is a long letter describing the American dating scene contained in *The Life and Career of Major John Andre*, by Winthrop Sargent, Boston 1861.

— *'Colonel Birch of the light dragoons and Major Williams'*: in Sargent.

133 *'I have lately received a message from Sir William Howe'*: Barrington's letter of 9 December 1777 is in TNA: PRO 30/55/7.

— *'Blakeney had formed part of the recruiting effort'*: see, for example, Blakeney's letter to Barrington of 16 February 1776 in TNA: PRO WO 4/94, in which the captain has been busy recruiting in Watford.

— *'he had tried to swap commissions'*: Blakeney suggested it on 13 December 1777 (in TNA: PRO 30/55/7); by a letter of 21 January 1778 in TNA: PRO WO 1/1002 Barrington told Blakeney such an exchange was hopeless.

— *'Those who are no longer capable'*: Barrington TNA: PRO 30/55/7.

134 *'Blakeney's skill at fending off these requests'*: Barrington's letter of 9 March

1778 to the MP, Thomas Clavering, is in TNA: PRO WO 4/102.

134 *'this war ... is an unpopular war'*: Blunt to Percy, 24 September 1777, DON.

135 *'Donkin ... had seen enough of these battles'*: these details come from a letter Donkin wrote to Percy on 17 April 1778, in DON.

— *'the corps I love'*: Ferguson's letter to Percy, 2 February 1778, DON.

— *'this matter seems to give no little offence'*: Francis Hutcheson to Percy, 30 January 1778, DON.

— *'I offered the sum to purchase, but I have no interest'*: letter to Percy, above.

— *'Balfour with his master's authority snatched the bit'*: Donkin, as above.

136 *'Balfour had been too lazy to get out of bed'*: related by Hunter, who being in the 2nd Battalion of LI, that bore the brunt at Germantown, had every right to feel aggrieved.

— *'he had bellowed at the locals that he would devastate the country'*: this version is found in 'Diary of Robert Morton', by Robert Morton, *Pennsylvania Magazine of History and Biography*, vol. I 1877.

— *'this very great injustice'*: Blakeney's letter to the War Office comes quite a bit later on 10 February 1779 and is in TNA: PRO WO 1/1002. I could not resist the temptation to use it here in the narrative, since it is the most remarkable example of the self-pitying whining of an eighteenth-century 'gentleman' that I have come across.

— *'Had [Blakeney] been present'*: Howe's letter is dated 19 February 1779, by which time he was back in London and is also in TNA: PRO WO 1/1002.

— *'one of my most intimate acquaintances'*: Rawdon's letter is in Bickley.

137 *'I believe I must keep out of England now'*: Balfour, 5 June 1777, LBRO L29/215.

— *'It will cost me but four hundred'*: Balfour, 5 February 1778, LBRO L30/12/3/4.

— *'Balfour family fortunes had been almost ruined'*: following details gleaned from various letters in LBRO, and the Army Lists various years 1760–79.

— *'you see what it is, to be well connected'*: both quotations in this paragraph come from a letter to a friend, 'Lewis', of 15 May 1780, in Balfour Papers (actually comprising three letters from Nisbet and one from Katherine to said Lewis) in LOC.

138 *'Certainly, there was at least one daughter'*: Balfour makes reference to 'my natural daughter Euphemia' in his will in TNA: PROB 11/1671.

— *'Balfour also proved to be a tireless advocate of merit'*: we will see this with Peter, Blucke, Apthorpe and others mentioned later.

— *'wasted no time in getting to grips with his soldiers'*: Lamb (ed. Hagist) lauds Balfour's leadership in turning around the regiment.

139 *'To build us habitations to stay (not to live) in'*: [original emphasis] J. P. Martin, *Private Yankee Doodle*, New York 1962.

— *'around one quarter of the 10,000 men'*: this estimate by Mark M. Boatner III in *Encyclopedia of the American Revolution*, Mechanicsburg PA 1994.

— *'it was one constant drill'*: Martin.

— *'One of those being marched about ... was William Hewitt'*: Hewitt enlisted in this company on 1 February 1778, according to the muster list in

Revolutionary Muster Rolls, 2 vols, New-York Historical Society Collections, 1914. His view of the justice of the Patriot cause comes from the family memoir alluded to earlier.

140 'His men became subject more often to the gallows': see, for example, Bowman. He charts the gradual ratcheting up of punitive powers in Washington's army.

— 'The scene that unfolded on the Delaware': one of the best sources on the *Mischianza* is a letter from Andre, reprinted in Sargent.

141 'a most pompous piece of pageantry and parade': Smythe to Earl Percy, 23 May 1778, DON.

— 'I do not believe': Andre's letter, in Sargent.

142 'collect the formidable army that is to be offensive': Smythe to Percy, 25 March 1778, DON.

THIRTEEN British Grenadiers

143 'What followed escalated quickly': my dialogue is a composite of many witnesses at the court martial. There are some minor differences between American and British versions but they are not that great, and, in order to be fair, most of the words in my exchange are taken from the evidence of Captain Wild of the American militia. The transcript of these proceedings was published by David Henley as *Proceedings of a Court Martial Held at Cambridge by Order of Major General Heath, Commanding the American Troops for the Northern District, for the Trial of Colonel David Henley, Accused by General Burgoyne of Ill Treatment of the British Soldiers &c'*, taken in shorthand by an officer who was present, London 1778.

145 'it was not infrequent for thirty or forty persons': this chapter relies, unsurprisingly, quite heavily on Lamb's two books, in their combined version edited by Don Hagist.

— 'I was about five feet nine inches': this comes from Lamb's scrapbook, kept in his family and copied by Hagist for his article (forthcoming) in the *Journal for the Society of Army Historical Research*. This account also contains Lamb's account of losing his corporal's knot, an experience so shaming he did not discuss it in his published memoirs.

148 'there were hangings galore of those accused of diverse offences': for an excellent modern study of the Convention Army issue, see *Escape in America, The British Convention Prisoners 1777–1783*, by Richard Sampson, Chippenham, 1995. He cites several examples of hangings of 'collaborators' in 1778.

— 'They do very well in the hanging way': Stark's letter is cited by Sampson.

— 'I was arraigned, tried, condemned': Cresswell's journal.

— 'Ten Fusiliers deserted in May and June 1778': Muster Rolls TNA: PRO WO 12/3960.

149 'the ill usage I received': Sullivan's journal.

— 'a peace delegation arrived from Britain': they got to Philadelphia on 6 June according to Peebles.

— 'Neither honour nor credit could be expected': Clinton, *American Rebellion*.

149 'Alas Britain how art thou fallen': Peebles.
150 'The enemy had all along': this journal is attributed to Brigadier Pattison, commander of British artillery, published as 'A New York Diary of the Revolutionary War', edited by Carson I. A. Ritchie, in *Narratives of the Revolution in New York*, New-York Historical Society, 1975.
— 'they spotted a group of enemy officers watching them from a hill': the Lee Papers are a key source for the primary documents used in my account of Monmouth, including a letter from Laurens in which he describes the reconnaissance party, and Clinton's dispatch to Lord Germain of 5 July 1778 in which he asserts that Lafayette was in the group.
151 'the sun beating on our heads with a force': Hale (in Wilkin). I make no apology for relying quite a bit on Hale in this narrative, his letters about Monmouth and Brandywine in particular are superb reportage.
— 'it was no longer a contest': ibid.
— 'Charge Grenadiers, never heed forming!': ibid.
152 'Captain Wills, commanding the grenadiers of the Welch Fusiliers': Cannon's *Historical Record*, citing a journal by Thomas Saumarez of the 23rd that has sadly eluded subsequent historians.
— 'Our officers and men behaved with that bravery': Laurens letter of 30 June 1778, in the Lee Papers.
153 'The most mortifying circumstances attending the action': Pattison.
— 'I fear I must descend, painful thought': Hale. Peebles also recorded his unhappiness.
154 'Everybody turned out that were near the fleet': Dansey letter of 28 July 1778, HSD.
— 'The atmosphere was acrimonious': this will emerge in Balfour's altercation with Rivington, in the next chapter.
155 'With late summer, Britain's Convention prisoners': readers will forgive, I hope, my taking a chronological liberty here. These events on the Convention Army's march did not happen until October 1778, after most of those episodes described in the next chapter. TNA: PRO WO 12/3960 shows that Lamb and his mates from the 9th were not formally enrolled in the 23rd until 21 December 1778.
156 'Lamb was one of forty-two men of the Convention Army': TNA: PRO WO 12/3960. Brendan Morrissey's excellent work on my behalf on the 23rd Muster Rolls suggests that Sampson is at error in his otherwise very good book on the Convention Army in underestimating the numbers that escaped and re-enlisted. Many of the forty-two Fusiliers found by Brendan are not in the lists of escaped prisoners in Sampson.

FOURTEEN The World at War

157 'The appearance of two French frigates': Mackenzie's diary is the principal source of detail in these sections on Rhode Island, although other journals have been used too, most interestingly, Dohla's.
— 'As the French ships turned south': The ships' names are of interest. From Classical mythology came *Juno* (the Roman queen of the gods), *Orpheus*

(the musical hero) and *Cerberus* (the three-headed dog who guarded the gates of the Underworld). The *Pigot* was named after the commander after the battle of Rhode Island. It was also the same vessel that had brought Howe, Burgoyne and Clinton to Boston in 1775.

159 *'Percy effectively resigned and went back to England'*: there are interesting documents on this in the family archives, DON, of course, but more accessibly in Clinton's *American Rebellion*, and the biographical sketch on Percy in Scull's book of Evelyn's letters.

— *'The* Languedoc *was a monster bristling with eighty heavy cannon'*: much interesting primary material and commentary on the naval aspects of the war can be found in *Navies and the American Revolution 1775–1783*, edited by Robert Gardiner, London 1996.

160 *'The regiment itself had been split into parcels'*: a return of 23rd men, naming their ships, is in Cary and McCance.

161 *'a sizeable reinforcement from the* Philippa, Betsy*'*: the *Isis*'s pay lists are in TNA: PRO ADM 36/7913, and they itemise where all the men had come from.

— *'in the highest spirits, anxiously wishing for an opportunity'*: this is actually Mackenzie, paraphrasing someone who told him the 23rd had arrived with Howe.

— *'heavy gales and a heavy sea'*: Captain Raynor's log book TNA: PRO ADM 51/484, a key source for the subsequent narrative.

162 *'*Languedoc *had been completely dismasted'*: Gardiner, above, contains, for example, a beautiful drawing of the ship, jury-rigged after the storm, by an officer who was there.

163 *'Their musketry'*: this is Hale, a remarkable letter writer who appears to have known Smythe and was on his way home from America.

— *'the enemy sheered off and bore away to the south west'*: TNA: PRO ADM 51/484.

— *'He has lost his right [yard]arm'*: Smythe's account of the engagement, in a letter to Earl Percy, 11 September 1778, DON.

165 *'The meeting of Parliament will determine'*: Smythe's letter to Earl Percy, 23 November 1778, DON.

166 *'As he sat reading the* New York Gazette*'*: Balfour's objections were spelt out in detail by Rivington in a letter of 23 November 1778 to Richard Cumberland at the Board of Trade, in TNA: PRO CO 5/155. This letter is the source of Rivington's quotes too.

167 *'this hated country'*: Balfour letter of 5 June 1777 (on completing his last Atlantic crossing from east to west), Polwarth Papers, LBRO L29/215.

FIFTEEN The Divided Nation

168 *'a very violent scorbutic disorder'*: Balfour letter of 6 January, 1779, LBRO L30/12/3/6.

— *'No family ever experienced so many tragical accidents'*: Balfour 31 December 1778, LBRO L30/12/3/5.

169 *'Always a volatile woman'*: Balfour's fear of her emotional state emerges from his letters at this time. Katherine Balfour's own letter in the Balfour

Papers, LOC, confirms the impression of someone barely in control of herself – unsurprisingly, perhaps, given her unfortunate life.

169 'my good and friendly General': Balfour letter of 5 June 1777, LBRO L29/215.

— 'were frequently thrown by unnoticed': Howe's speech of 4 December 1778 reported in Gentleman's Magazine, April 1779.

170 'George usually rose at around 5 a.m.': details of court life are from Farmer George, 2 vols, by Lewis Melville, London 1907.

171 'the hurly burly of life in Georgian England': these stories are all taken from issues of the Gentleman's Magazine, vol. 49, 1779 – they are not necessarily accurate in all respects.

— 'thirty-six rank and file, and thirteen pressed men': Cary and McCance.

— 'Balfour intervened': according to Calvert in his unpublished autobiography, 9/111 in CHT.

172 'the advantage of witnessing actual service': a direct quotation from 9/111.

— 'Temple had set himself up in Preston': there are many papers relating to the 1779 recruiting drive in the DON.

173 'attended with many disagreeable circumstances': Cuthbertson.

— 'One of the 23rd's recruiting serjeants... left England with the regiment': the story of Serjeant Fleck emerges from letters in TNA: PRO WO 4/90 and WO 1/991, his demotion is noted in WO 12/3960.

— 'absolutely impossible to keep many recruits long': Temple's letter to War Office, 26 December 1775, TNA: PRO WO 1/994. There are several more letters from him in the WO 1 series describing his activities.

174 'no longer be expected to exert themselves on a service': letter from Temple to Percy, 5 March 1779, DON. As above, Temple wrote frequently to Percy too.

— 'William Smith, who came to the 23rd': details of Smith's case and of the offences committed by those in the House of Corrections can be found in LRO QRB 1.

— 'four pressed men escaped from Preston House of Correction': this is the date given in the QRB 1 records, but Temple suggests the escape has already happened in a letter of 24 March to Percy.

— 'Please inform me in what manner': Captain Cochran went to the Manchester House of Corrections and this letter of 5 May 1779 to the War Office is in TNA: PRO WO 1/1002.

175 'The magistrates from several parts had sent in wretched objects': General Calcraft writing to the War Office, 8 July 1780, TNA: PRO WO 1/1007.

— 'The cries and lamentations of the poor, raw country soldiers': John Robert Shaw, an Autobiography of Thirty Years 1777–1807', edited by Oressa M. Teagarden, Athens Ohio 1992.

— 'epidemic distemper': this is Charles Stuart writing on 25 August 1779 (in Wortley) and refers, apparently, to the same convoy that Calvert arrived with.

— 'more than half of those recruited in 1779 died of various fevers': analysis of TNA: PRO WO 12/3960.

176 'William Howe's first witness, Earl Cornwallis': this was before the days of

reliable Hansard reporting. The fullest version of who said what is [Anon.] *The Detail and Conduct of the American War Under Generals Gage, Howe and Burgoyne and Vice Admiral Lord Howe*, London 1780.

177 *'the General who has taken the field and has not committed faults'*: Balfour, March 1779, LBRO L30/12/3/9.

— *'a nest of faction and disingenuity'*: Balfour 2 May 1779, LBRO L30/12/3/10.

— *'food for opposition and death to the American minister'*: Balfour 23 May 1779, LBRO L30/12/3/11.

— *'Balfour believed the Ministry had nailed its colours'*: a sentiment expressed in his letter of 2 May 1779.

— *'various secret plans had been pushed forward'*: those plans are in vol. IV of Fortescue.

178 *'General Amherst produced another argument'*: this memo of 15 September 1779 (in Fortescue) is most interesting in providing an insight into the making of grand strategy.

— *'only weighing such events in the scale of a tradesman behind his counter'*: letter to North of 11 June 1779, in Fortescue.

179 *'There is hardly one general officer who does not declare his intention'*: Stuart letter of 7 October 1778 (in Wortley).

— *'not with views of conquest and ambition'*: Cornwallis's letter to his brother, cited in *Cornwallis and the War of Independence*, by Franklin and Mary Wickwire, London 1970.

— *'Those fashionable ladies of the great Whig families'*: *Georgiana, Duchess of Devonshire*, by Amanda Foreman, London 1998, gives a good insight into this.

180 *'How strange must our system of politicks appear'*: Balfour, 27 August 1779, LBRO L30/12/3/13.

— *'she had reacted with horror at the idea that Nisbet'*: Balfour, 17 August 1779, LBRO L30/12/3/12. Katherine Balfour's letter in the LOC shows how right Nisbet was in his reading of her mood.

SIXTEEN The War Moves South

181 *'It was already dark'*: Calvert's memoir CHT, 9/111.

— *'[He] stated how particularly cruel it was'*: Stuart's letter of August 1779 (in Wortley).

182 *'No doubt in such excursions many scenes occur'*: Lamb's 1809 *Journal of Occurences*.

— *'a grievous case of desertion that July'*: the facts of the Mason/Watson/ Smith desertion come from TNA: PRO WO 71/83; Smythe's opinion, for example, is revealed in his testimony.

184 *'While in London, Balfour had brokered a deal'*: the Innes and Watson deal is revealed in a letter from Balfour to Clinton, 4 September 1780, Clinton Papers, WLCL.

— *'The Irish major in particular proved unforgiving'*: see, for example, Mecan's letter of 21 December 1779 to 'Mr White of the Barrack Office', flaying him for sending soldiers to stay in a store belonging to the 23rd. In Clinton Papers, WLCL.

185 *'celebrated for her beauty, wit, and accomplishments'*: these quotations about Marie Phillips come from the 'Loyalist manuscript' printed in Sargent. The Smythe/Phillips wedding was recorded in the *New York Gazette*, 8 September 1779.

186 *'many of those staying behind said they were well off out of it'*: Ewald.
— *'no doubt remained, that the inactivity of the summer'*: Calvert, CHT 9/111.
— *'An older officer of the 23rd wrote home'*: this was Lieutenant Thomas Barretté, to Lord Dartmouth, 16 December 1779, Dartmouth Papers, SRO D (W) 1778/11/1900.
— *'All the sailors had lost their heads'*: Ewald.
— *'Scarcely a day during the voyage passed'*: Clinton, *American Rebellion*.

187 *'the Fusilier Brigade did not always come off best'*: Ewald suggests a party of twenty or so men of the 7th and 23rd was virtually wiped out during one of these combats, but the official casualty return shows only four Welch Fusiliers wounded and none killed during the entire siege.
— *'Our batteries opened'*: Ewald.

188 *'the regiment more than 400 strong'*: return of 8 March 1780 in TNA: PRO CO 5/99.
— *'120 men under Major Mecan'*: they were detached on 17 March according to the journal of Archibald Robertson.

189 *'in perfect health, except the amusement of a few muskettoes'*: letter to Lewis of 15 May 1780, LOC, which is also the source of the date that Balfour resumed command of the 23rd, and location of its inland bivouac.
— *'a remark he made to the earl, disparaging William Howe'*: Clinton himself reveals this in *American Rebellion*.
— *'Lord Cornwallis never writes an answer'*: from 'Sir Henry Clinton's Journal of the Siege of Charleston 1780', edited by William Bulger, *South Carolina Historical Magazine*, vol. 66, no. 3 July 1965.

190 *'the camps fired a* feu de joie *upon this occasion'*: I should point out that the firing was taking place at camps in Dublin, where Fitzpatrick was serving by that time; his letter to Fox, 8 June 1780, BL ADD MS 47579, Fox Papers.

191 *'On 22 May, he invited the lieutenant colonel to discuss this perilous mission'*: from Clinton's journal of the siege.

193 *'I see [the] infernal party still prevails'*: ibid.
— *'small brigade of 580 under his command'*: Balfour talks about the composition of this force in his letter to Cornwallis, 20 May 1780, TNA: PRO 30/11/2.
— *'by late 1780 there were about 7,500 under arms'*: this figure is based on a return of loyalist corps of 15 December 1780, Clinton Papers, WLCL. I have included officers and men on command, but excluded prisoners and sick.

194 *'Clinton had, for example, limited the power of general courts martial'*: Clinton to Cornwallis, 1 June 1780, TNA: PRO 30/55/24, 'I do hereby approve of the sentences of such courts in all cases not capital, if in your judgement the case should require it; excepting only the reduction of commissioned officers except under very singular circumstances'.
— *'Those men who were guilty of what were normally capital offences'*:

Cornwallis to Balfour 7 January 1781 in TNA: PRO 30/11/84 sets out these punishments for prisoners under capital charges. Clinton's ban on capital punishment was respected within the army – although there were of course cases of locals who broke their parole being executed, as we shall see later. However, there are two key lessons, first that Cornwallis achieved his great prodigies of marching and fighting without the threat of capital punishment and second that the rule of the British army was not quite as brutal as some Patriots liked to claim. I have found only one example of a British military execution in the Carolinas in 1780–81, although Clinton later gave Major General Leslie power to execute men in Charleston, and there is evidence that this may have happened in 1782.

194 *'The great object of his Majesty's force in this country'*: from a General Order of 5 October 1780 in 'A British Orderly Book 1780–1781', A. R. Newsome, *The North Carolina Historical Review*, vol. IX, 1932, nos 1,2 and 3.

— *'desired that I should be civil to Lt Calvert'*: Cornwallis's note is undated but was probably written early in 1781. It is in TNA: PRO 30/11/5.

195 *'they exchanged in their letters knowing and complicit remarks about Ferguson'*: revealed by some letters in TNA: PRO 30/11/2, for example, Balfour to Cornwallis 24 June, where he describes Ferguson's behaviour as 'ridiculous', or Balfour's letter of 6 June which suggested Ferguson had been cowed by a letter from Cornwallis reminding him Balfour was in charge.

— *'I have a thorough confidence in your ability'*: Cornwallis to Balfour of 13 June 1780 in TNA: PRO 30/11/77.

— *'I beg you to continue to mention your opinions freely to me'*: Cornwallis to Balfour, 11 June, TNA: PRO 30/11/5.

— *'The more difficulty, the more glory'*: Tarleton to Lt Haldane (one of Cornwallis's ADCs) 24 December 1780, TNA: PRO 30/11/4.

196 *'Tarleton jotted a note of enemy casualties'*: it remains in his handwriting, dated 29 May 1780 in PRO TNA: CO 5/99.

— *'get the leading men to be answerable'*: Balfour to Cornwallis, 24 June 1780, TNA: PRO 30/11/2.

197 *'Balfour, from the start, was dubious about the idea of embodying them'*: Balfour to Cornwallis 20 May 1780, TNA: PRO 30/11/3; Balfour writes, 'the idea of getting a militia to take arms and join &c &c immediately is to me a very extraordinary one'.

— *'made inroads into this province with large plundering parties'*: Balfour to Cornwallis, 12 July 1780, TNA: PRO 30/11/1.

— *'I find the enemy exerting themselves wonderfully'*: Balfour to Cornwallis, not dated, but marked 'between the Enoree and Tyger rivers' suggests early June 1780, a very early and astute diagnosis of the rural insurgency; no wonder Cornwallis urged Balfour to offer advice just after this. In TNA: PRO 30/11/2.

— *'the emigrants from Ireland were in general'*: Clinton to Germain, 23 October 1778, TNA: PRO 30/55/13.

198 *'more savage than the Indians, and possess every one of their vices'*: George

Hanger, *The Life, Adventures and Opinions of Col George Hanger, written by Himself*, 2 vols, London 1801.

198 *'many prominent Caledonians… saw in the war a chance for rehabilitation'*: the most striking example of this was Simon Fraser. His father, Lord Lovat, had been executed for his part in the 1745 Rebellion, yet Simon restored the family fortunes by serving the King, raising the 71st for service in the American Revolution.

— *'Pattinson had a reputation as an inefficient drunk'*: Mackenzie, diary.

— *'I know you will say that you would rather go'*: Cornwallis to Balfour, 17 July 1780, TNA: PRO 30/11/78.

199 *'one of the newly formed militia battalions had defected'*: Cornwallis to Clinton, 6 August, TNA: PRO 30/55/26. The Patriot officer, Lt Col Lisle, was one of those who had been pardoned at Clinton's behest. Cornwallis and Balfour agreed their commander-in-chief had been quite mistaken in this policy, and this letter from Cornwallis put the matter quite aggressively directly before Clinton.

— *'Gates may attack me tomorrow morning'*: Rawdon to Cornwallis, 11 August 1780, TNA: PRO 30/11/63

SEVENTEEN The Battle of Camden

200 *'Confident… that we should drive the enemy'*: Seymour's journal is in the Peter Force Papers, LOC.

— *'They were 450 strong, had good clothing'*: Thomas Hughes, a prisoner of the 53rd saw them near Lancaster, Pennsylvania, in *A Journal by Thos Hughes, For his Amusement, and Designed only for his Perusal by the time he attains the Age of 50 if he lives so long*, introduction by E. A. Benians, Cambridge 1947.

201 *'This is a mode of conducting war I am a stranger to'*: Gates to Major General Caswell, 3 August 1780. Gates's papers reside at the NYPL.

— 'his picture of British dispositions was hopelessly wrong': Gates, NYPL, reveals these mistakes in a letter to Governor Nash of 3 August 1780.

203 *'We feel great concern in communicating the death… Mecan'*: *Royal Gazette*, New York, 20 September 1780.

— *'loss will be long felt and regretted in the regiment'*: Balfour to Clinton, 4 September 1780, Clinton Papers, WLCL.

— *'Champagne's family was connected by marriage to an aristocrat'*: his sister Jane Champagne was married to Lord Paget, who put up money for one of Forbes's promotions. On background, see Kirby.

— *'thirteen serjeants, eight drummers and 261 rank and file'*: Return of 15 August 1780, PRO TNA: CO 5/100.

— *'Harry Calvert, still only sixteen'*: it emerges from his papers, CHT 9/102, that it was Peter's company.

— *'Another lieutenant, Thomas Barretté'*: Barretté, unsurprisingly perhaps, was a great writer of begging letters or testimonials; details of his circumstances emerge in one of 16 December 1779 to Lord Dartmouth, SRO D (W) 1778/11/1900 and one of 18 December 1779 to Clinton, Clinton Papers, WLCL.

204 'Several of these young Fusilier officers had strong religious feeling': Champagne was the son of a clergyman, as was Captain Smythe (serving in New York at that moment) who indeed was later to become a cleric. Calvert was known in family correspondence (Verney Papers in CHT) to have a strong faith. It can also be assumed that Champagne, Barretté and another subaltern serving at Camden, Stephen Guyon, all shared a strong Protestant identity as Huguenots who had grown up in a predominantly Catholic Ireland.

— 'and there were also a few loyalist Americans': Charles Apthorpe, a New Englander and captain in the 23rd at this time during the later years of the war, Leverett Saltonstall (another New Englander), Philip Skinner (born in New Jersey), John McEvers and in the last months of the conflict Joshua Winslow.

— 'might have caused George III to splutter': the King was very pedantic about army promotion and precedence matters, for example he usually refused to let officers from the artillery or engineers (such as Lieutenant Haldane, one of Cornwallis's ADCs) transfer into line infantry regiments. His adherence to the same policy vis à vis the Marines, was responsible in part for Barretté's predicament, forcing him to resign his lieutenancy in that corps in order to serve in America.

205 'Years before it was sent to America, he had trained it in light infantry tactics': this is referred to by Lamb, but also the 33rd's Inspection Return for 1773, TNA: PRO WO 27/27, gives interesting details of the regiment's tactical drills displayed at Plymouth.

— '[Webster] wishes to make his Lordship believe there is not an officer': William Dansey letter of 16 May 1773, HSD.

— 'had employed the 33rd as a full regiment of light infantry': Peebles and Ewald, for example, both refer to the 33rd being used in that role.

206 'Major General Gates had summoned his commanders': Otho Williams's journal is the source of these details, 'A Narrative of the Campaign of 1780' in Sketches in the Life and Correspondence of General Nathaniel Greene, 2 vols, edited by William Johnson, Charleston SC 1822.

207 'The moon was full and shone beautifully': Guilford Dudley, a volunteer with the North Carolina militia, was with Porterfield and provides much detail in the narrative of the night action. His account has been reproduced in An Officer of Very Extraordinary Merit, a useful biography of Porterfield by Michael Cecere, Westminster MD, 2004.

208 'day was near three hours off': the letter of an [un-named] officer of the Volunteers of Ireland to his friend in Glasgow, dated 25 August 1780, is reproduced in Scots Magazine, October 1780.

— 'Gentlemen, what is to be done?': this exchange is in Williams's journal.

— 'Both sides assumed this to be the start of a swamp': during a visit to the battlefield Charles Baxley, one of those leading the conservation efforts there, showed me clearly that there were no swamps on either side of the road. Participants from both armies nevertheless refer to the swamps on their flanks. The mistake may have occurred because these were areas marking the limit of cattle grazing where the vegetation suddenly became much more dense and the soldiers assumed that something squelchy must lie underfoot.

209 *'two deep with open files so as occupy as great a front as possible'*: Barretté's letter to Clinton of 26 August 1780, contains much interesting detail. It also refers to a journal of the campaign being kept by that lieutenant, but which has not been found to date. Clinton Papers, WLCL.

— *'I believe my gun was the first fired'*: Garret Watts's pension application. It can be found with many others in *The Revolution Remembered, Eyewitness Accounts of the War for Independence*, edited by John C. Dann, London 1980.

— *'and immediately rushed in upon them'*: Barretté, Clinton Papers, WLCL. American witnesses such as Williams emphasises that the militia did not manage a single volley, Barretté is doubtless making the most of his story, but it is evident from Watts and Williams that some of the North Carolinians and Virginians did fire.

210 *'lightening themselves with the loss of their arms'*: Barretté, Clinton Papers, WLCL.

— *'The enemy surpassed us in artillery'*: letter in *Scots Magazine*, above.

— *'Our regiment was amazingly incited by Lord Cornwallis'*: ibid.

211 *'finding themselves in a situation ever to be guarded against'*: Barretté, Clinton Papers, WLCL.

212 *'Was there ever an instance'*: Hamilton to Duane, 6 September 1780, the Hamilton Papers, vol. II.

— *'The losses taken by the 23rd on 16 August'*: casualty return in TNA: PRO 30/55/26.

213 *'the handsomest and most complete affair'*: Peebles.

— *'the behaviour of His Majesty's troops'*: Cornwallis to Germain, 21 August 1780, in Charles Derek Ross (ed.), *The Correspondence of Charles, First Marquess of Cornwallis*, London 1859.

— *'Headquarters was on King Street'*: the building is still there, no. 27.

214 *'I don't think it would be right for me to meddle'*: Cornwallis to Balfour, 24 August 1780, which reveals Balfour's attempt to get Ross appointed to the 23rd, TNA: PRO 30/11/79.

— *'Balfour chose that Scottish veteran Frederick Mackenzie'*: Balfour to Clinton, 4 September 1780, in WLCL.

— *'Richard Temple, who had spent the war recruiting at home, complained loudly'*: Temple's complaint and the adherence to the rule promoting officers in America are noted in Clinton to Secretary at War, 20 September 1781, TNA: PRO 30/55/32.

— *'Balfour did not want it to be Champagne'*: Balfour to Clinton, 9 December 1780, TNA: PRO 30/11/4.

215 *'I find the ague and the fever all over this country'*: Cornwallis to Balfour, 13 September 1780, TNA: PRO 30/11/80.

— *'the whole of the men are very different when Tarleton is present or absent'*: Cornwallis to Balfour, 1 October 1780, TNA: PRO 30/11/81.

215 'produced a very great change... in affairs here': Balfour to Clinton,
4 September 1780, in WLCL.
216 'the old fatal delusion': O'Hara's letter of 1 November 1780 in 'Letters of
Charles O'Hara to the Duke of Grafton', edited by George C. Rogers Jr,
South Carolina Historical Magazine, vol. 65, no. 3 July 1964.
— 'O'Hara... was one of those officers tied to Whiggish high society': in a
letter from Major General Lee to Richard Fitzpatrick of 4 April 1778, Lee
refers approvingly to O'Hara's 'liberal way of thinking' about the American
issue, BL, FOX PAPERS, ADD MS 47,582. O'Hara's hostility to the Tory
Ministry is also evident from his fascinating letters to Grafton, above.
'fight, get beat, rise, and fight again': Greene to Luzerne, 22 June 1781 in
The Papers of Nathaniel Greene, editor Richard K. Showman, 7 vols,
Chapel Hill NC 1976–1994.
— 'He realised that if he took them out of prison camps': papers in TNA: PRO
30/11/82 show that Balfour released the 64th for service in November by
this expedient.

EIGHTEEN Into North Carolina

218 'Dozens of sick men were that day draped on to wagons': the dispatch of the
sick is mentioned by Calvert's journal, CHT, 9/102.
— 'the most rebellious and inveterate that I have met': Cornwallis to Balfour, 3
October 1780, TNA: PRO 30/11/81.
— 'Stephen Guyon of the 23rd was highly commended': some details are in
Banastre Tarleton, *A History of the Campaigns of 1780 and 1781 in the
Southern Provinces of North America*, London 1781, others from Calvert.
219 'a frontier war such as we have': Balfour to Lewis, 17 January 1781, LOC.
— 'the general told his officers... that a large corps had been embarked':
Calvert.
220 'you must send a packet with five hundred men': Balfour to Lewis,
24 October note, LOC.
— 'a series of operations to secure the lower part of the Santee River': details of
the supply problems and Balfour's measures can be found in files TNA: PRO
30/11/81–83.
— 'No sooner do I find myself under difficulties': Cornwallis to Balfour,
17 November 1780, TNA: PRO 30/11/82.
— 'Our troops get healthier every day': ibid.
221 'the 23rd had received their new uniforms some weeks earlier': Calvert's
journal, CHT, 9/102, has details of the new clothing he received for his
company on 28 September 1780.
— 'I saw this morning the parade': Cornwallis to Balfour, 18 November 1780,
in TNA: PRO 30/11/82. The passage gives an interesting indicator of how
highly Cornwallis rated the 23rd, despite his *amour propre* for the 33rd.
— 'an unpleasant message, I by no means wish to deliver': Balfour to Lewis,
the 24 October note on the 15 October letter (LOC).
— 'The most earnest desire for a forward movement': Balfour to Cornwallis, 5
November 1780. This is quite the best among Balfour's many reports to

Cornwallis, including strategic insights and rapier-like dissection of the loyalist militia's weaknesses. It is in TNA: PRO 30/11/4.

222 *'Some recruits arrived – just twenty for the 23rd'*: 2,372 recruits reached New York according to a letter of 30 October 1780 in PRO TNA: CO 5/100. It appears that all of the 23rd's quota and most of the 33rd's were sent down to Charleston, arriving with the main convoy on 13 December.

— *'We must begin our operations by driving Gates'*: Cornwallis to Balfour, 30 November 1780, TNA: PRO 30/11/82.

— *'Balfour was delighted to report the arrival of a convoy'*: Balfour to Cornwallis, 14 December 1780, TNA: PRO 30/11/4.

223 *'I got back last night with my heart so strongly impressed'*: Balfour to Cornwallis, 29 December 1780, TNA: PRO 30/11/4.

224 *'Everybody is a general'*: Gates to Henry Knox, 7 December 1780, in Greene (ed. Showman: the events of late 1780 are dealt with in vol. VI and early 1781 in vol. VII).

— *'L[or]d Cornwallis has a much greater force'*: ibid. Greene's cautious letters, and gloomy assessments, offer a valuable lesson in the dangers of abusing historical hindsight about Cornwallis's decision to fight in North Carolina.

— *'If Lord Cornwallis knows his true interest he will pursue our army'*: this revealing statement came a little later, on 5 February in a letter to Isaac Huger (in Greene, ed. Showman), but is relevant enough in considering the start of the campaign.

225 *'be hung without judge or jury as an example to the rest'*: Greene, to Major Lee, 27 August 1780 (ed. Showman).

— *'Greene waited for one of them, Thomas Anderson'*: details of this case in a paper dated 4 January 1781 (in vol. VII of Showman).

— *'fall back upon the flank or into the rear of the enemy'*: Greene's orders (ed. Showman).

— *'On 8 January, the 23rd Fusiliers struck camp ... marched off at a blistering pace'*: details of the regiment's marches in this campaign from Calvert's journal.

226 *'came in with accounts of having been totally defeated'*: ibid.

227 *'Tarleton's defeat'*: Tarleton's own *History* attempted to place blame for the defeat on others. So disgusted were the officers of the 71st by being blamed, that one of their officer, Roderick Mackenzie published a counterblast, *Strictures of Lieut. Colonel Tarleton's History*, London 1787. Mackenzie makes the valid point that if the 71st were advancing in too thin a formation Tarleton ought to have closed them up.

— *'The late affair has almost broke my heart'*: Cornwallis to Rawdon, 21 January 1781, TNA: PRO 30/11/84.

— *'which is intended for the conveyance of their medicine chest'*: General Order of 2 January 1781. The GOs for the Carolina campaign can be found in A. R. Newsome's article.

228 *'negroes and horses'*: General Order of 26 January 1781.

— *'When the redcoats came into view, early in the morning on 1 February'*: this account is based mainly on those of three Welch Fusiliers: Calvert's journal, Lamb, and a journal by Thomas Saumarez, quoted in Cannon's history of the Royal Welch Fusiliers. Unfortunately, Cannon appears to have lost the original of this valuable document, since the later history by Cary and McCance quotes the same passages of Saumarez and subsequent enquiries have failed to trace the journal. Tarleton, in his *History,* erroneously places the 23rd at another crossing point of the Catawba, under Colonel Webster. Probably Tarleton was referring to the 33rd but was confused.

228 *'Its waters, swollen by recent rains'*: Saumarez journal (Cannon).

229 *'The soldiers initially were fed from bags of cornmeal'*: the preparation of the meal was described by Charles Stedman, Cornwallis's commissary, who later wrote *History of the Origin, Progress and Termination of the American War,* 2 vols, London 1794. The rasping of corn is mentioned in General Orders and by Lamb.

230 *'My mess mates and I made two meals a day'*: Shaw of the 33rd.

— *'It is a pleasing sight to see a column arrive at its halting ground'*: Lamb, quoted by Hagist in *Journal of the Society for Army Historical Research* (forthcoming).

231 *'their liberality in furnishing us so abundantly'*: Shaw.

232 *'The smallest check to any of his detachments'*: O'Hara to Grafton, 1 November 1780.

— *'a style that must ever do the greatest honour to Lord Cornwallis's military reputation'*: O'Hara to Grafton, 20 April 1781, as above.

— *'we marched for the most part both day and night'*: Seymour journal, Force Papers, LOC.

233 *'patriotic exhortations and executions'*: Seymour gives a very good idea of this, noting the execution of a deserter hung from a tree on 1 January and one of William Washington's dragoons shot for desertion on 4 January 1781. Greene's entry into South Carolina later in 1781 was marked by large numbers of executions, but this will be dealt with in its proper place.

— *'Greene's march or rather flight from the Catawba'*: O'Hara to Grafton. O'Hara is so disillusioned by the loyalists that he does not even mention the Pyle disaster described later in this chapter, a measure of the Guards officer's prejudices in this matter.

— *'soldiers being taken by the enemy'*: General Order 22 February 1781 in Newsome.

234 *'to repress the meditated rising of the loyalists'*: *The Revolutionary War Memoirs of General Henry Lee,* edited by Robert E. Lee, 1869.

— *'Lieutenant Manning of Lee's Legion supplied another version'*: Manning's version is recounted in *Anecdotes of the Revolutionary War in America,* by Alexander Garden, Charleston 1822. Garden interviewed Manning in later life. This version avoids Lee's self serving claims about Pyle's men starting the fight and suggests that Greene sent them there to prevent the loyalists rising and that murdering them was, in any case, justified as retaliation for Tarleton's actions at Waxhaws.

— *'Ninety or so of Pyle's loyalists were cut down'*: a modern calculation by

John Buchanan in his *The Road to Guilford Courthouse*, New York 1997.

235 *'It has had a very happy effect'*: Greene to Thomas Jefferson, 29 February 1781 (ed. Showman).

— *'300 of our friends…were every man scalped'*: 'letter from Capt C[hampagne] of the 23rd Regiment, now serving under Lord Cornwallis to his relation Lieutenant C[hampagne] on the recruiting service at Doncaster, dated Wilmington April 17, 1781', printed in *The Leeds Intelligencer*, 26 June 1781. Champagne's excessive Tory language in this letter suggests to me that it may have been written for publication. Unfortunately for us, I have not been able to find other letters from him to his brother or the original of this one.

NINETEEN Greene Offers Battle

236 *'The encounter between Tarleton's Legion'*: this is described by Lee in his *Memoirs*, Tarleton ditto and Cornwallis in his dispatch (in Ross).

237 *'made a push for the country'*: Shaw's memoir. He calls his friend Tattesdell, but it is clearly Tattersall, in TNA: PRO WO 12/3296 although those rolls have him desert later. This may simply have resulted from confusion as to whether Tattersall should be returned as a prisoner (and therefore eligble to continue receiving pay) or not.

239 *'One thing is pretty certain'*: Greene to Lee, 9 March 1781 (ed. Showman).

— *'It appears to me that his Lordship and army begin to possess disagreeable apprehensions'*: while it is impossible to prove with forensic accuracy that Lee formed these views after talking to Shaw and Tattersall, the circumstances fit exactly, for in this letter to Greene (11 March, ed. Showman) he refers to sending two prisoners to the general on the 10th. In Shaw's memoir, he says that he and Tattersall were examined by Greene on 11 March, having been sent to headquarters by Lee.

240 *'a defeat would have been attended with the total destruction'*, Tarleton's *History*.

— *'The ground dropped quite steeply'*: many details of the field of Guilford come from personal observation. I am grateful to Nancy Stewart and John Durham for guidance during my visit to the National Battlefield Park there. I am grateful to them too for providing copies of many accounts relative to the battle, notably Houston, Tucker, Howard and Slade referred to below.

241 *'Colonel Webster moved to the left of the road'*: battle deployments are fully explained in Stedman's *History*.

242 *'field lately ploughed'*: Saumarez journal, in Cannon.

— *'Come on my brave Fusiliers!'*: Lamb.

— *'They instantly returned it and did not give the enemy time'*: Calvert's journal, CHT, 9/102.

243 *'The men run to choose their trees'*: the accounts of Houston, Marshal and Slade are all contained in a digest of American primary accounts collated from various sources by the National Parks Service visitor centre at the battlesite entitled, *Key Original Sources: Outline for the Battle of Guilford Courthouse*.

243 *'Webster's brigade had lost some of its order'*: the movement to the left by the 33rd is described by Stedman and others, Saumarez of the 23rd talks about them having to go around the 'brushwood' obstruction.

— *'After "severe firing", the Virginians began to break'*: Calvert's journal.

— *'Holcombe's Regiment and ours broke off'*: letter of Major St George Tucker to his wife, 18 March 1781. His papers are kept in the College of William and Mary, Williamsburg VA.

245 *'As they pressed on, Kirkwood's riflemen started to pick them off'*: Seymour's journal, Force Papers, LOC, makes clear that Kirkwood's Marylanders and Lynch's Virginian riflemen were principally engaged at this point and charged after the 33rd when they retreated. Lieutenant Colonel John Howard of the 1st Maryland Regiment, in a letter many years after the battle to John Marshal, suggests Webster's first attack ran out of steam, 'he did not press us hard, nor did we defeat or charge upon him'.

— *'pouring in a very heavy fire on them'*: Seymour describes this reception in his journal.

— *'impatient to signalise themselves'*: Stedman, using language almost identical to that of Cornwallis in his dispatch. We may see this as coded criticism of the rashness of the 2nd Guards' advance.

— *'at the 2nd Regiment, which immediately gave way'*: Howard to Marshal again.

246 *'The conflict between the ... Guards and the first regiment of Marylanders'*: Nathaniel Slade of the NC militia.

— *'charged them so furiously that they either killed or wounded almost every man'*: Seymour journal, Force Papers, LOC.

— *'the enemy's cavalry was soon repulsed by a well-directed fire'*: this is from Cornwallis's own dispatch (in Ross). Many accounts of the battle have Cornwallis ordering MacLeod quite deliberately to fire into the melee of the 2nd Guards, Marylanders and Washington's cavalry. The sole basis from any participant for this claim is a line from Lee's *Memoir* that the British artillery, 'opened upon friends as well as foes ... every ball levelled at [Washington and Howard] must pass through the flying Guards'. This was steadily embroidered over the years by American writers, for example, Eli W. Carruthers in *The Old North State* (first published 1854 and 1856 but since re-published by the Guilford Genealogical Society in 1985) who claims that O'Hara remonstrated with Cornwallis not to do such a thing. It is hard to avoid the conclusion that these myths, that started appearing in early nineteenth-century American histories of these events, were intended to show what a ruthless character Cornwallis was. Although Lee was not present on the sector of the field where this incident allegedly happened, I do find it credible that the British artillery fired through 'the flying Guards', i.e., fugitives running or stumbling back from the melee atop the hill. However, parties of unfortunates meandering about were a normal part of any battlefield at this time, and MacLeod could reasonably have engaged Washington without a significant danger of cutting many men down. The position of the guns should cast further doubt on the idea that MacLeod fired into the melee – since the battery was far from the hilltop (200–300 yards when the optimum range for grape from MacLeod's little three pounders might have been 100–150 yards, i.e., as Washington's men were coming down the ridge towards them, as Cornwallis's dispatch suggests) and it is likely that the hand-to-hand fighting was obscured by the brow of that feature. Of the invented disagreement between O'Hara and Cornwallis, there is no evidence in various letters from the two men, even though O'Hara writes to Grafton of the British line being beaten at various points during the action.

246 'The 23rd formed...with several dozen men': Calvert's journal.

247 'Cornwallis's casualties had been shockingly high': return in TNA: PRO 30/11/103.

— 'unfortunate': Greene used this word in orders on the 16th (ed. Showman).

— 'deserted the most advantageous post I ever saw': Greene to Morgan, 20 March 1781 (ed. Showman).

— 'nothing could behave better than the 23rd': Cornwallis to Balfour, 5 April 1781, TNA: PRO 30/11/85.

— 'Lord Cornwallis desires the officers and Soldiers': Calvert's journal.

248 'No zeal or courage is equal to the constant exertions': O'Hara to Grafton, 20 April 1781 (in Rogers), a phenomenally interesting account of the North Carolina campaign.

— 'remained on the very ground on which it had been fought': ibid.

— 'For Surgeon Hill and his mates tip-toeing between the groaning bodies': his report, giving details of all the injuries to the men left behind is in TNA: PRO 30/11/5.

249 'Thomas Parks, a private from Birmingham': details of his wound and service, Discharge Papers, TNA: PRO WO 97/431.

250 'the army was barefooted and in the utmost want of necessaries': Cornwallis to Balfour, 5 April 1781, TNA: PRO 30/11/85.

251 'I am quite tired of marching about the country': Cornwallis to Phillips, 10 April 1781, in Ross.

— 'If our plan is to be defensive': ibid.

— 'the attempt is exceedingly hazardous': Cornwallis to Phillips, 24 April 1781, TNA: PRO 30/11/85

— 'The campaign in North Carolina had ground down Earl Cornwallis's army': figures from TNA: PRO 30/11/5.

252 'Here has been the field for the exercise of genius': Greene to Joseph Reed, 18 March 1781 (ed. Showman).

TWENTY The Beginning of the End

253 'a guarded, cautious, manner': Balfour to Cornwallis, 26 April 1781, TNA: PRO 30/11/6.

— 'Universal disaffection must moulder us away': Balfour to Lewis, 17 January 1781, LOC.

254 'They have adopted the system of murdering every militia officer': Balfour to Cornwallis, 26 April 1781, TNA: PRO 30/11/6.

254 *'impaling the severed heads of suspected spies'*: see for example the case of Harry, Lord Rawdon's slave spy, as described in Major Doyle's letter of 27 November 1782 in TNA: AO 13/4.
— *'were executed five of our deserters'*: Seymour journal, Force Papers, LOC.
— *'Balfour ordered more than 130 American militia'*: the order was given on 17 May, *History of South Carolina in the Revolution 1775–1780*, 2 vols, by Edward McCrady, New York 1901.
255 *'in June 1781 there was a general exchange of prisoners'*: ibid., including numbers of survivors, etc.
— *'these vessels were in general infected with small pox'*: Peter Fayssoux quoted by McCrady.
— *'Clinton started firing off letters about his grievances against the commanding officer'*: these can be found in TNA: PRO 30/55/29 and 30. Clinton's *American Rebellion* contains many criticisms of Balfour's conduct.
— *'I find the Commander in Chief has been a good deal displeased'*: Mackenzie's diary.
256 *'I therefore think it my duty to exculpate Lt Col Balfour'*: Cornwallis to Clinton, 26 April, 1781, TNA: PRO 30/55/30.
— *'I can be the only proper judge'*: Clinton to Cornwallis, 15 June 1781, TNA: PRO 30/55/30.
— *'Clinton harboured ideas of conquering a peninsula'*: see his *American Rebellion*, for example.
257 *'It is the King's firm purpose to recover these [southern] provinces'*: Germain to Cornwallis, 4 June 1781, in Ross.
— *'How great was my disappointment'*: Clinton's *Rebellion* again.
258 *'The marches up into Virginia passed virtually without incident'*: details of march, Calvert's journal.
259 *'he showed up the mediocrity and lassitude of those few British officers'*: Mackenzie's diary.
— *'Words can ill describe the admiration'*: *Memoir of General Graham, With Notices of the Campaigns in Which he was Engaged from 1779 to 1801*, edited by his son Colonel James J. Graham, Edinburgh 1862.
— *'I can testify that every soldier had his negro'*: Ewald.
260 *'desultory expeditions'*: the phrase is used in a couple of letters, including Cornwallis to Leslie, 28 June 1781, TNA: PRO 30/11/87.
— *'As the General's plan is only defensive in this quarter'*: Cornwallis to Balfour, 16 July 1781, TNA: PRO 30/11/88.
— *'determined to throw all blame on me'*: Cornwallis to Rawdon 23 July 1781, TNA: PRO 30/11/88.
261 *'the number of Fusiliers shrank from over 400 on paper'*: return of 15 August 1781, TNA: PRO CO 5/103, gives the breakdown of all the different detachments.
— *'a vacant commission... was given to Watson'*: Cornwallis to Clinton, 10 April 1781, TNA: PRO 30/55/29.
262 *'How will this look to the loyal subjects there?'*: Ewald.
— *'hundreds of wretched negroes that are dying'*: O'Hara's letters from

Portsmouth, including an explanation of the 23rd's mission in the evacuation, are in TNA: PRO 30/11/70.

263 'For six weeks the heat has been so unbearable': Ewald.

— 'only negroes could labour under such conditions': this view is expressed in a letter from Cornwallis to O'Hara, 4 August 1781, in Ross.

264 'On 5 September, the 23rd were given custody': Calvert's journal.

— 'I am now busy fortifying a harbour': Cornwallis to Grant, 24 August 1781, from the James Grant of Ballindalloch Papers, NAS, GD 494/1/46. This is the same Grant who led the 23rd's division at Long Island.

265 'proceeded from the noble Earl's misconception': Tarleton, History.

— 'some better prospects than have of late presented': Balfour to Lewis, 17 January 1781, LOC.

266 'make the most striking example of such': Balfour to Clinton, 6 May 1781, TNA: PRO 30/11/109.

— 'Balfour sought support, writing to Colonel Lord Rawdon': Rawdon's version of the Hayne affair, in a letter of 1813, is in Lee's Memoirs.

— 'He had hanged five men in Camden': although Garden suggests Rawdon hanged men frequently in Camden, searches by the local chapter of the Sons of the American Revolution indicates just five: Sam Andrews, Josiah Gayle, John Miles, Eleazar Smith, and Richard Tucker.

— 'In October 1780 ... he had executed a deserter from his own regiment': Calvert journal. I have found no evidence of any other execution of this type while Cornwallis was in charge.

267 'By all the recognised laws of war': Rawdon in Lee.

— 'Hayne was the only person executed while Balfour was Commandant of Charleston': this is asserted by Garden and I have found no evidence to contradict him.

— 'the prime offenders in dispensing this type of execution were loyalist Americans': the journal of George Nase, now in the University of New Brunswick, suggests that there were six executions in South Carolina and Georgia after Cornwallis quit the state. Most occurred in loyalist regiments. I am grateful to Todd Braisted for bringing these facts to my attention. The most serious accusation of 'British' barbarity during these southern campaigns, that of executing thirteen surrendered defenders of a fortified house in September 1780 at Augusta, Georgia, was also attributable to a loyalist American, Colonel Thomas Brown.

— 'Humanity ... ought to be as dear in a soldier's estimation': Rawdon's letter of 21 February 1782 to the Duke of Richmond, in Fortescue, vol. V.

— 'The more he is beaten, the farther he advances': Mackenzie's diary.

TWENTY-ONE Yorktown

269 'a brief exchange of musketry': Calvert notes the driving in of the regiment's pickets. His journal notes of the siege are scant, perhaps indicating sickness. Lamb and Saumarez from the regiment have a little more to say.

— 'two 12-pounder cannon and some small mortars called coehorns': Ewald.

— 'signs of the French establishing works': personal survey at battle site plus use of the accounts and maps in *The American Campaigns of Rochambeau's Army 1780, 1781, 1782, 1783*, 2 vols, translated and edited by Howard Rice, Jr, and Anne S. K. Browne, Princeton 1972. This is a very useful collection of journals, sketches and maps.

270 'This...*gave us the greatest possible advantage*': Clermont-Crevecoeur's journal in Rice and Browne cited above.

269 '*all horses except those belonging to the cavalry*': Ewald.

271 '*Charles Mair, an officer serving with the 23rd's light company*': Graham of the 76th, who, confusingly, calls Mair Moore.

— '*A rocket rose from the redoubt at once*': Prechtel.

— '*Six of the Touraine regiment's grenadiers were hurt*': Clermont-Crevecoeur in Rice and Brown.

272 '*four 12-pounders; two 24-pounders*': ibid.

— '*three of his twenty-nine years at the Metz artillery school*': the Rice and Browne volumes contain a later memorial by this officer, outlining his career, as well as much other interesting information.

— '*We are certainly now at the most critical period of the war*': Mackenzie's diary.

273 '*An initial estimate of 5 October was given*': Clinton's *American Rebellion* spells out these discussions.

— '*The Fusiliers in the redoubt received their rude awakening*': many accounts describe the stepping up of fire and the driving off of the *Guadeloupe*; however, Ewald gets a little confused about dates at this point and I have relied more on the French journals in describing this episode.

275 '*People were to be seen lying everywhere, fatally wounded*': Dohla. This German private's account of the siege is remarkably good – too bad there is no equivalent from a British ranker.

— '*were greatly exposed to the fire of a battery of nine guns*': Lamb (ed. Hagist). His estimate of guns is one fewer than Clermont-Crevecoeur's, but close enough.

— '*With such works on disadvantageous ground*': Cornwallis to Clinton, 11 October 1781, in *American Rebellion*.

— '*I am doing everything in my power to relieve you by a direct move*': Clinton to Cornwallis, 30 September, ibid.

276 '*On the evening of 12 October, the 23rd were ordered out*': Ewald.

— '*scarcely a gun could be fired from our works*': Graham.

278 '*As the oarsmen pulled away... other redcoats filed down*': Calvert.

— '*The British paid the Americans seemingly but little attention*': Martin.

— '*As the Fusiliers passed, he recognised quite a few faces*': according to a Hewitt family account. Since the 1st New Hampshire were not there at Yorktown as a full regiment, it is possible Hewitt was serving in their light company, which did take part.

279 '*made a poor appearance, ragged and tattered*': Dohla.

— '*May you never get so good a master!*': Graham.

— '*Our ministers will I hope be now persuaded that America is irretrievably lost*': O'Hara to Grafton, 20 October 1781.

279 *'officers throughout Cornwallis's army had drawn lots'*: the Orderly Book of the 43rd shows that this procedure was officially directed, BL, ADD MS 42,449.

280 *'Peter detached the 23rd's two colours from their staffs'*: Peter's role is described in an old regimental record, TNA: PRO WO 76/218. This note and the subsequent regimental histories give the honour of saving the colours to Peter and *another officer*. Mackenzie is the source for Champagne and Apthorpe's overland journey.

— *'He took some pay he was owed and donned a private's uniform'*: Lamb's own memoirs give an extensive account of his odyssey after the fall of Yorktown.

281 *'The serjeant major of the 33rd spotted John Shaw'*: Shaw.

— *'a large detention compound near Lancaster in Pennsylvania'*: details of the camp come from Corporal Fox, a prisoner of the 47th from Saratoga, 'Corporal Fox's Memoir of Service, 1766–1783', by J. A. Houlding and G. Kenneth Yates, *Journal for the Society of Army Historical Research,* vol. 68, 1990. Graham also gives some details.

282 *'Thomas Eyre was an American-born subaltern'*: details of Eyre's case are in a memorial he gave to General Howe after arriving in Philadelphia, now at TNA. Howe writing to Washington on 8 January 1778 (in TNA: PRO 30/55/7) made clear that he still regarded Eyre as an American prisoner, despite his arrival in British lines, and would send an equivalent American over in exchange. Washington's reply on 20 January (PRO 30/55/8) cannily plays on Howe's discomfort over the matter: 'If you suppose Mr Eyre's representation to be just, and that he escaped from a rigorous confinement, under no obligation to his parole, I cannot conceive upon what principle you still consider him my prisoner.'

— *'Of all the situations of life, that of having no pursuit is the worst'*: Hughes of the 53rd, another Convention Army detainee, *Journal.*

284 *'As to the situation of affairs here they are as bad as can be'*: Dansey letter of 27 March 1782, reprinted in *Iron Duke.*

TWENTY-TWO Going Home

285 *'The Fusiliers' imprisonment ended at 8 a.m.'*: details of prisoners' departure, Gordon to Carleton, 8 May 1783, TNA: PRO 30/55/68.

— *'The joyful news'*: Dohla.

— *'not many other captains left to dispute the honour'*: for Saumarez's advocacy, see for example the petition of 12 April 1783 in TNA: PRO CO 5/109. The same file at TNA contains a return of freed prisoners of 28 May that shows the number of the captains, and the Guards being without officers. Experts on the period will wonder about Captain Charles Asgill and two other officers of the Guards, who drew lots to see whether they should be executed in retaliation for the hanging of Captain Huddy, a defected loyalist killed by his former colleagues when they recaptured him in 1782. Some officers of the Guards, to be clear, had gone into captivity at Yorktown but none remained by the time peace was declared.

286 'bonfires were lit, feux de joie echoed across the landscape': there are many
   accounts of the celebrations, but Dohla gives a good sense of the
   atmosphere.
— 'absurd orders to the detainees not to sing their national anthem': Hughes
   describes arguments with the prison guards over the national anthem, albeit
   at an earlier date.
— 'thirty-three deserted, twenty-four died of natural causes': pay lists, TNA:
   PRO WO 12/3597, give their fate and returns, CO 5 gives the overall picture.
— 'Much civility has been shewn them on their march through the country':
   Carleton to Townsend, 28 May 1783, TNA: PRO 30/55/70.
287 'a different procession of petitioners to headquarters': hundreds of the
   petitions survive in TNA: PRO 30/55 class of papers.
288 'a gentleman of character and the head of a respectable family': Carleton to
   Lord North, 31 October 1783, TNA: PRO CO 5/111. North was still a
   minister but no longer prime minister.
— 'Those who would dare to remain in New York': Ewald.
289 'Between 26 May and 17 June': return in TNA: PRO 30/55/72.
— 'Each man has received two pair of stockings': Carleton to Fox
   29 September 1783, TNA: PRO 30/55/82.
— 'the transport of 3,436 people to Nova Scotia': figures from estimates of 24
   September 1783 in TNA: PRO 30/55/82.
— 'Lieutenant Colonel Balfour had in March heard': it was in General Orders
   on 20 March 1783, TNA: PRO WO 28/9. Balfour left America well before his
   regiment.
290 'saved Mason from the hardships of the southern campaigns': these details
   from the pay lists. Major Dansey's letters (HSD) refer to the difficulties of
   keeping musicians in the 33rd at the end of the war.
— 'I am pleased to find that our groundwork': Dansey letter of 11 July 1783, HSD.
— 'having for sometime past had the 23rd Regiment': petition of 15 July 1783,
   TNA: PRO 30/55/75.
291 'encroachments by rebel patrols from Connecticut': Ewald.
— 'around 1,250 men had served in the 23rd': these figures are the product of
   extensive work on the pay lists in TNA: PRO WO 12. However, the later ones,
   for example about combat deaths, are gleaned from a variety of sources
   including returns in CO 5 and even journals.
293 'Some eighty-eight served there during the war': these figures exclude the
   chaplains and surgeons but include the adjutant and quartermaster. They are
   gleaned from a wide variety of sources ranging from pay lists to journals to
   death announcements in the New York press.
294 'It was never said of Burgoyne's army that they ran away': Lamb's scrapbook in Hagist in Journal for the Society of Army Historical Research
   (forthcoming).
— 'Many other British veterans felt the same way': for example Harry Calvert,
   who wrote after the French drove back British troops in Flanders in 1794
   that he had never been in a beaten army before – this episode will be dealt
   with later.

294 'We must not only move as machines, but be as insensible too': Balfour to Lord Polwarth, 2 May 1779, LBRO L30/12/3/10.
— 'bartered away by turbulence and faction': Dansey, 11 July 1783, HSD.
— 'The desertion of the loyalists is looked upon by all of us': Dansey, HSD. I make no apology for taking a couple of quotations from his letters, since he is one of the few writers who reflected deeply on the war's outcome.
— 'four Americans among its depleted corps of officers': they were Apthorpe, McEvers, Skinner and Innis. They were described as 'foreigners' in the review of 1784, TNA: PRO WO 27/51, and I have gleaned other details of their origins. Another American officer of the 23rd, Leverett Saltonstall, died of natural causes in December 1782.
— 'Charles Apthorpe's family in particular': Major Hutcheson in his letters in the BL alludes to Apthorpe properties in Boston, New York city and upstate New York.
295 'Men of all parties consider another revolution as inevitable': Carleton to North 13 October 1783, TNA: PRO CO 5/111.
— 'Although I shuddered at the distress of these men': Ewald.
— 'Washington executed more of his soldiers than the British': in The Morale of the American Revolutionary Army, Allen Bowman says there is definitive proof that Washington's army executed forty soldiers but that the actual number was likely more than that given that 225 death sentences were passed. I have collated British executions from many sources. General Orders contain some reports of executions, but equally most incidents of capital punishment reported in them were not carried out. I have sought confirmation of executions from eye-witnesses and TNA: PRO WO 12 Muster Roll information. A return in the Clinton Papers, WLCL, drawn up on that general's orders, shows that just five men were executed during his years as commander-in-chief, 1778–83. A similar number were executed before Clinton, and another seven to ten in summary proceedings in the south (a journal by Serjeant Major George Nase of the King's American Regiment in the University of New Brunswick proves to be an unusually good source of information on the ones carried out in the south, often at a colonel's whim). Even allowing for one of two cases that I may have failed to detect, a figure of 'about two dozen' British military executions during these wars seems reasonable.

TWENTY-THREE Home Service

298 'The sight greeting Lieutenant General James': details of the review, TNA: PRO WO 27/51.
— 'a very pretty effect when saluting': ibid.
299 'always behaved like a father to me': this phrase occurs in Lamb's letter to the War Office of 26 September 1808, and is reproduced in Hagist, Journal for the Society of Army Historical Research (forthcoming).
— 'kindly and humanely reasoned with me': Lamb described the scene in his memoirs, see Hagist.
— 'Lamb ... felt that his affections had not been returned': Lamb did not mention that award of the serjeant majorship to another man in his

published memoirs, presumably because of his wounded pride over the matter. His hurt feelings over the affair emerge in his unpublished scrapbook.

300 *'I left London on the 15th March'*: ibid.

— *'In all 142 men of the 23rd were discharged'*: Muster Rolls, TNA: PRO WO 12/3960.

— *'seventy-three of those still in the 23rd...were more than thirty years old'*: TNA: PRO WO 27/51; the Inspection Return is source of much useful information, including the subsequent facts about the location of various officers.

301 *'on the morning of 19 August 1785'*: Colonel Dundas's report on his trip to Prussia sits in the BL as 'Remarks on the Prussian Troops and their Movements', KING'S MS 241. This report contains the following quote about twenty-nine battalions in line.

302 *'the facility with which these troops manoeuvre'*: ibid.

303 *'his military ideas are those of a wild boy of the Guards'*: Cornwallis to Ross, 5 October 1785 in Ross. The same letter contains the damning assessment of the Prussian manoeuvres quoted subsequently.

— *'never was attempted before...it succeeded surprisingly well'*: York to George III, 7 October 1785, quoted in Alfred H. Burne *The Noble Duke of York*, London 1947.

— *'much slower in their movements'*: letter to Ross, cited above.

304 *'Instead of being considered as an accessory to the battalion'*: Colonel David Dundas, *Principles of Military Movements, Chiefly Applied to Infantry*, 1788.

— *'all young men, great martinets, but so completely Germanised'*: Hughes.

305 *'actions not to be paralleled in antiquity'*: Dundas, also the following quote.

306 *'gave their fire and retired'*: this fascinating description of the fighting in St Lucia came in a letter from Serjeant Major Thorne of the 5th to Earl Percy, 31 July 1779, DON.

TWENTY-FOUR An Army Re-born

307 *'These were frenetic, suspicious days in British headquarters'*: the primary source for the early part of this chapter is *Journals and Correspondence of General Sir Harry Calvert, Adjutant General of the forces of HRH the Duke of York, Comprising the Campaigns in Flanders and Holland in 1793–4*, edited by his son Sir Harry Verney, London 1853.

308 *'attachment to my person, to your country'*: George to Cornwallis, 28 March 1782, in vol. V of Fortescue.

— *'born to be the honour and salvation'*: in Verney papers.

309 *'I found myself in a situation'*: ibid.

310 *'He found me out'*: Lamb's remarks about his religious conversion, Burgess and some other matters are in 'Memoir of Mr Roger Lamb', by J. O. Bonsall, *Wesleyan-Methodist Magazine*, November 1831.

312 *'neither the Prussian army nor the Austrians found satisfactory tactical answers'*: for a good discussion of the shock of the Flanders campaign, see

David Gates, *The British Light Infantry Arm, c. 1790–1815*, London 1987.

314 'The system of David Dundas': Cornwallis in Ross.

— *'means of rendering the movements of the regiments more simple'*:
Cornwallis to Ross 21 January 1800, in Ross.

314 *'I am indeed to flatter myself that some steps will* speedily *be taken'*:
Calvert's letter of 23rd March 1798 in TNA: PRO WO 1/619. It is not entirely
clear who it is addressed to, but most probably it was the Secretary at War.

— *'General Howe...stepped forward'*: his letter to the Duke of York, offering
his services, has the same date and is in the same file as Calvert's above.

315 *'another Bunker Hill'*: Money, Gen. J., *To the Right Honourable William
Windham on a Partial Reorganisation of the British Army*, London 1799.

316 *'Calvert had Mackenzie appointed as secretary to the Royal Military
College'*: Calvert's role emerges in a letter of 13 March 1807 from
Mackenzie to General Sir Richard Grenville (then colonel of the 23rd),
Dropmore Papers, BL, ADD MS 58897.

317 *'on 7 January 1809, Lamb wrote once more to his old comrade'*: Lamb's
letter is in TNA: PRO WO 121/93. Lamb's scrapbook supplies earlier parts of
this narrative.

318 *'Attachments of persons in the army to each other'*: this passage appears in
Lamb's published memoir.

Bibliography

Adye, Stephen Payne *A Treatise on Courts Martial*, London 1778. An officer of
the Royal Artillery, Adye was Judge Advocate in America at a crucial period.
Anderson, Lieutenant Thomas Journal of Lieutenant Thomas Anderson of the
Delaware Regiment 1780–1782, *Historical Magazine*, April 1867.
Andre, Major, *Andre, Major Andre's journal. An authentic record of the
movements and engagements of the British Army in America from June 1777
to November 1778 as recorded from day to day by Major John Andre*, ed. by
Henry Cabot Lodge, Boston 1933. This journal was kept meticulously and
features some excellent maps of the 1777 campaign.
Anon. *The Detail and Conduct of the American War Under Generals Gage,
How and Burgoyne and Vice Admiral Lord Howe . . .*, London 1780.
Anon. 'Letter of a Hessian Officer to the Landgrave of Hesse-Kassel' reproduced
in *Militair-Wochenblatt*, 18, Berlin 1833.
Anon. 'A Contemporary British Account of General Sir William Howe's
Military Operations in 1777', *Proceedings of the American Antiquarian
Society*, vol. 40, 1930. Factual account by a staff officer attached to
Knyphausen's division, posibly Onslow Beckwith of the 23rd.
Askham, Francis *Those Gay Delavals*, London 1955.
Atkinson, C. T. *The Organisation of the British Army in the American
Revolution,* New Haven 1926.
Balderston, Marion and David Syrett (eds) *The Lost War, Letters from British
Officers during the American Revolution*, Horizon Press, New York 1975.
The letters come mainly fom Lt Feilding of the Marines, and deal with the
early war period.
Bamford, Captain William 'Bamford's Diary', in *Maryland Historical Magazine,*
vols 27 and 28, 1932 and 1933.
Barker, John *The British in Boston, Being the Diary of Lieutenant John Barker
of the King's Own Regiment*, ed. Elizabeth Ellery Dana, Cambridge MA 1924.
Serving in the 4th and then 10th Foot, Barker gives a valuable account of

events in 1775–76.

Baurmeister, Adjutant General *Revolution in America, Confidential Letters and Journals 1776–1784 of Adjutant General Major Baurmeister of the Hessian Forces*, trs and ed. by Bernhard Uhlendorf, New Brunswick 1957.

Bell, J. *Military Almanack*, London 1782.

Bickley, Francis (ed.) *HMC, Report on the Manuscripts of the late Reginald Rawdon Hastings*, HMSO 1934.

Bland, Lieutenant General Humphrey *A Treatise of Military Discipline: In which is Laid down and Explained The Duty of the Officer and Soldier, Through the several Branches of the Service*, London 1762. A standard text for officers, it sold through several editions.

Boatner, Mark M. III *Encyclopedia of the American Revolution*, Mechanicsburg PA 1994.

Bonsall, J. O. 'Memoir of Mr Roger Lamb', *Wesleyan-Methodist Magazine*, November 1831.

Boswell, James *Boswell's London Journal*, ed. by Fredrick A. Pottle, London 1950. The great diarist was a cousin of James Webster of the 33rd.

Bowman, Allen *The Morale of the American Revolutionary Army*, Washington 1943.

Brown, Captain and Ensign de Berniere *Transactions of the British Troops previous to, and at the Battle of Lexington*, Massachusetts Historical Society Collections, series 2, vol. 4, 1816. An account of the reconaissance to Concord carried out by Brown, 52nd, and de Berniere of the 10th, as well as de Berniere's hair-raising account of the action of 19 April 1775.

Buchanan, John *The Road to Guilford Courthouse*, New York 1997.

Burgoyne, Bruce E. (trs) *The Diary of Lieutenant Bardleben and other von Donop Regiment Documents*, Bowie MD 1998.

Burne, Alfred H. *The Noble Duke of York*, London 1947.

Calvert, Harry *Journals and Correspondence of General Sir Harry Calvert, Adjutant General of the forces of HRH the Duke of York, Comprising the Campaigns in Flanders and Holland in 1793–4*, ed. by his son Sir Harry Verney, London 1853.

Cannon, Richard (ed.) *Historical Record of the Twenty Third Regiment, or Royal Welch Fusiliers*, London 1850.

Carruthers, Eli W. *The Old North State*, first published 1854 and 1856; re-published by the Guilford Genealogical Society in 1985.

Cary A. D. L. and Stouppe McCance (eds) *Regimental Records of the Royal Welch Fusiliers*, vol. I, 1689–1815, London 1921.

Cecere, Michael *An Officer of Very Extraordinary Merit: Charles Porterfield and the American War for Independence, 1775–1780*, Westminster MD, 2004.

Clinton, Sir Henry 'Sir Henry Clinton's Journal of the Siege of Charleston 1780', ed. William Bulger, *South Carolina Historical Magazine*, vol. 66, no. 3, July 1965.

Clinton, Sir Henry *The American Rebellion*, ed. William B. Willcox, Hamden CT 1971.

Coffin, Charles (ed.) *History of the Battle of Breed's Hill, by Major Generals*

BIBLIOGRAPHY

William Heath, Henry Lee, James Wilkinson and Henry Dearborn, Portland 1835.

Cooper, Captain T. H. *The Military Cabinet*, 3 vols, London 1809.

Cornwallis, General Lord *The Correspondence of Charles, First Marquess of Cornwallis*, ed. Charles Derek Ross, London 1859.

Cresswell, Nicholas *The Journal of Nicholas Cresswell 1774–1777*, New York 1924.

Cunningham, Peter (ed.) *The Letters of Horace Walpole*, London 1891.

Curtis, Edward E. *The Organisation of the British Army in North America*, Yale 1926.

Cuthbertson, Bennet *System for the Compleat Interior Management and Oeconomy of a Battalion of Infantry*, Dublin 1768. As one-time adjutant of the 5th Foot, Cuthbertson's book was widely read in the army.

Dalrymple, Lieutenant Colonel *William Tacticks*, Dublin 1782.

Dann, John C. (ed.) *The Revolution Remembered, Eyewitness Accounts of the War for Independence*, London 1980.

De Fonblanque, Edward Barrington *Political and Military Episodes in the Latter Half of the Eighteenth Century Derived from the Life and Correspondence of The Right Hon. John Burgoyne, General, Statesman, Dramatist*, London 1876.

Digby, Lieutenant William *The British Invasion from the North, The Campaigns of Generals Carleton and Burgoyne with the Journal of Lieut William Digby*, with notes by James Phinney Baxter, Albany 1887. Digby fought in the 53rd Grenadier Company, giving a lively account of the Saratoga campaign.

Dohla, Johann Conrad *A Hessian Diary of the American Revolution*, trs and ed. Bruce. E. Burgoyne, Norman OK 1990.

Donkin, Robert *Military Collections and Remarks*, New York 1777. A curious volume that deals only in passing with Donkin's personal experience but contains an interesting esssay on *petite guerre* as it should be applied in America.

Downman, Francis *The Services of Lieutenant Colonel Francis Downman, RA*, ed. Colonel F. A. Whinyates, London 1898.

Drake, Samuel Adams *Historic Mansions and Highways Around Boston*, Cambridge MA 1899.

Duer, William Alexander *The Life of William Alexander, Earl of Stirling*, New York 1847.

Dundas, Sir David *Principles of Military Movements, Chiefly Applied to Infantry*, London 1788 (reprinted London 2004).

Ehwald, Col. [Johann von] *Treatise upon the Duties of Light Troops*, English edn 1803 (reprinted Huntingdon 2006).

Enys, Lieutenant John *The American Journals of Lt John Enys*, ed. Elizabeth Cometti, Syracuse NY 1976. Journals of an officer of the 29th in Canada who participated in raids on American frontier settlements.

Evelyn, W. Glanville *Memoirs and Letters of Captain W. Glanville Evelyn*, ed. G.D. Scull, Oxford 1879. A Tory enthusiast for the war, Evelyn served in the

4th Light Company until killed in action just after the fall of New York.

Ewald, Johann von *Diary of the American War: a Hessian Journal*, trs and ed. Joseph P. Tustin, New Haven and London 1979.

Field, Thomas W. *The Battle of Long Island*, Brooklyn 1869.

Fischer, David Hackett, *Washington's Crossing*, Oxford 2004.

Fitzpatrick, John C. (ed.) *The Writings of George Washington*, 39 vols, Washington, 1931–34.

Force, Peter *American Archives, Containing a Documentary History of The English Colonies in North America*, 4th series, 9 vols, Washington 1837–[1853].

Foreman, Amanda *Georgiana, Duchess of Devonshire*, London 1998.

Fortescue, Hon. Sir John (ed.) *The Correspondence of King George the Third, From 1760 to 1783*, 6 vols, London 1928.

Fortescue, Sir John *A History of the British Army*, 13 vols, London 1899–1930.

Fox, Corporal 'Corporal Fox's "Memoir of Service", 1766–1783', ed. J. A. Houlding and G. Kenneth Yates in *Journal for the Society of Army Historical Research*, vol. 68, 1990. Fox served as a corporal in the 47th during the Saratoga campaign and then endured long captivity; his narrative is in note form, not easily followed but important nevertheless.

French, Allen *The Day of Lexington and Concord*, Boston 1925.

French, Allen *The First Years of the American Revolution*, New York 1934.

Gates, David *The British Light Infantry Arm, c. 1790–1815*, London 1987.

Garden, Alexander *Anecdotes of the Revolutionary War in America*, Charleston 1822.

Gardiner, Robert (ed.) *Navies and the American Revolution 1775–1783*, London 1996.

Glover, Richard *Peninsular Preparation, The Reform of the British Army 1795–1809*, Cambridge 1963.

Graham, Col. James J. (ed.) *Memoir of General Graham, With Notices of the Campaigns in Which he was Engaged from 1779 to 1801*, Edinburgh 1862.

Gordon, William 'Letter Written by an American Clergyman', article in *Journal of American History*, vol. 4 (January–March 1910).

Grant, Alistair Macpherson *General James Grant of Ballindalloch*, London [1930].

Greene, Nathaniel *Sketches in the Life and Correspondence of General Nathaniel Greene*, 2 vols, ed. William Johnson, Charleston SC 1822.

Hadden, Lieutenant James M. *A Journal Kept in Canada and Upon Burgoyne's Campaign*, Freeport NY 1884. A lieutenant in the Royal Artillery, Hadden's journal is excellent, as is the additional material included in this edition.

Hagist, Don *A British Soldier's Story: Roger Lamb's narrative of the American Revolution*, Baraboo WI 2004.

Hamilton, Alexander *The Papers of Alexander Hamilton*, vols 1–27, ed. Harold C. Syrett, New York 1961–87.

Hanger, George *The Life, Adventures and Opinions of Col George Hanger, written by Himself*, 2 vols, London 1801. A picaresque memoir dealing more with Hanger's family and financial woes than his service in the British Legion.

Hargreaves, Reginald *The Bloodybacks; the British Serviceman in North America and the Caribbean 1655–1783*, London 1968.

Harvey, Edward *A New Manual and the Platoon Exercise: With an Explanation*, London 1764.

Haslewood, Captain William 'Journal of a British Officer During the Revolution', *Mississippi Valley Historical Review*, vol. 7, June 1920. The journal of this officer of the 63rd covers 1776–7.

Henley, David *Proceedings of a Court Martial Held at Cambridge by Order of Major General Heath, Commanding the American Troops for the Northern District, for the Trial of Colonel David Henley, Accused by General Burgoyne of Ill Treatment of the British Soldiers &c'*, taken in shorthand by an officer who was present, London 1778.

Hughes, Thomas *A Journal by Thos Hughes, For his Amusement, and Designed only for his Perusal by the time he attains the Age of 50 if he lives so long*, intro. E. A. Benians, Cambridge 1947. The author was serving in the 53rd when captured near Ticonderoga in September 1777; the memoir deals mainly with his years in captivity.

Hunter, A. *The Journal of Gen. Sir Martin Hunter*, Edinburgh 1894. This provides an excellent insight into the 52nd Light Company (2nd LI battalion), notably during the 1777 campaign.

Inman, Lieutenant George 'George Inman's Narrative of the American Revolution', *Pennsylvania Magazine of History and Biography*, vol. VII, no 3, 1883. Inman fought initially as a volunteer in the 4th Light Company and was later commissioned into the 17th.

Johnson, Joseph *Traditions and Reminiscences chiefly of the American revolution in the South*, Charleston 1851.

Kemble, Stephen 'Journal of Stephen Kemble, 1773–1789; and British Army Orders' in *The Kemble papers*, New-York Historical Society Collections, New York 1884 (reprinted Boston 1972). These journals over an initial period (1775–79) as a senior staff officer followed by Caribbean service in the 60th.

Kirby, Major E. L. (ed.) *Officers of the Royal Welch Fusiliers (23rd Regiment of Foot) 16 March 1689 to 4 August 1914*, privately published for the regiment in the 1990s.

Knox, Captain John *Historical Journal of the Campaigns in North America*, Toronto 1914.

Lamb, Roger *An Original and Authentic Journal of Occurences During the Late American War from its Commencement to the Year 1783*, Dublin 1809.

Lamb, Roger *Memoir of His Own Life*, Dublin 1811.

[Lambart, Major General Richard] *A New System of Military Discipline, Founded Upon Principle*, 'by A General Officer', London 1773.

Lee, Charles *The Lee Papers*, New-York Historical Society Collections, New York 1872–1875.

Lee, Robert E. (ed.) *The Revolutionary War Memoirs of General Henry Lee*, 1869, facsimile edition New York 1998.

Lister, Ensign Jeremy *Concord Fight*, Cambridge MA 1931.

Lushington, Stephen R. *The Life and Service of General, Lord Harris*, London

1840. Harris was an excellent letter writer from the 5th Foot who served in America 1775–78.

McCrady, Edward   *History of South Carolina in the Revolution 1775–1780*, 2 vols, New York 1901.

Mackenzie, Frederick   *The Diary of Frederick Mackenzie*, 2 vols, Cambridge MA 1930.

Mackenzie, Frederick   *A British Fusilier in Revolutionary Boston*, ed. Allen French, Boston 1926.

Mackenzie, Roderick   *Strictures of Lieut. Colonel Tarleton's History*, London 1787.

Mackesy, Piers   *War For America 1775–1783*, London 1964.

McGuire, Thomas J.   *The Surprise of Germantown*, Germantown PA 1994.

Martin, J. P.   *Private Yankee Doodle*, New York 1962.

Melville, Lewis   *Farmer George*, 2 vols, London 1907.

Money, Gen. J.   *To the Right Honourable William Windham on a Partial Reorganisation of the British Army*, London 1799.

Montresor, Capt. John   *The Journal of Captain John Montresor*, New-York Historical Society Collections, New York 1881.

Morrissey, Brendan   *Boston 1775, The Shot Heard Around the World*, London 1993.

Morrissey, Brendan   *Yorktown 1781, The World Turned Upside Down*, Oxford 1997.

Morrissey, Brendan   *Monmouth Courthouse 1778, The Last Great Battle in the North*, Oxford 2004.

Morton, Robert   'Diary of Robert Morton', *Pennsylvania Magazine of History and Biography*, vol. I, 1877.

Mowday, Bruce E.   *September 11th 1777, Washington's Defeat at Brandywine Dooms Philadelphia*, Shippensburg PA 2002.

Muenchhausen, Friedrich von   *At General Howe's Side, 1776–1778: The Diary Of General William Howe's Aide De Camp, Captain Friedrich Von Muenchhausen*, trs Ernst Kipping, Monmouth Beach NJ 1974.

Murray, Sir James   *Letters From America 1773 to 1780, Being the Letters of a Scots Officer, Sir James Murray, to his home during the War of American Independence*, ed. Eric Robson, Manchester 1951. Murray provides good colour; serving initially in the 57th Light Company, he later purchased Nisbet's Balfour's majority in the 4th.

Nelson, Paul David   *William Tryon and the Course of Empire: A Life in British Imperial Service*, London 1990.

Nelson, Paul David   *Sir Charles Grey, First Early Grey Royal Soldier, Family Patriarch*, London 1996.

Newsome, A. R.   'A British Orderly Book 1780–1781', *The North Carolina Historical Review*, vol. IX, 1932, nos 1, 2 and 3.

New-York Historical Society   *Revolutionary Muster Rolls*, 2 vols, New York 1914.

O'Hara, Charles   'Letters of Charles O'Hara to the Duke of Grafton', ed. George C. Rogers Jr, *South Carolina Historical Magazine*, vol. 65, no. 3, July

1964. O'Hara was an excellent letter-writer, but sadly only some of his O'Hara's dispatches have survived.

Pattison, Brigadier 'A New York Diary of the Revolutionary War', ed. Carson I. A. Ritchie in *Narratives of the Revolution in New York*, New-York Historical Society, 1975.

Peebles, John 'John Peebles' American War 1776–1782', ed. Ira D. Gruber, Stroud 1998. Serving with the 42nd, much of the time in its grenadier company, Peebles is an excellent source from 1776 to early 1782.

Pausch, George *Journal of Captain George Pausch*, New York 1971.

Percy, Hugh *Letters of Hugh Earl Percy from Boston and New York 1774–1776*, ed. Charles Knowles Bolton, Boston 1902.

Prechtel, Lieutenant Johann Ernst *A Hessian Officer's Diary of the American Revolution*, Bowie MD 1994.

Rice, Howard Jr and Anne S. K. Browne (trs and ed.) *The American Campaigns of Rochambeau's Army 1780, 1781, 1782, 1783*, 2 vols, Princeton 1972.

Robertson, Archibald *Archibald Robertson, His Diaries and Sketches in America 1762–1780*, ed. Henry Miller Lydenberg, New York 1930. As an engineer, Robertson's observations are most useful on matters of fortification and topography.

Rottenburg, Colonel *Regulations for the Exercise of Riflemen and Light Infantry and Instructions for Their Conduct in the Field*, London 1803.

Sackville, Viscount George Germain and Caroline Harriet Stopford-Sackville (eds) *HMC, Reports on the Manuscripts of Mrs Stopford-Sackville of Drayton House Northamptonshire*, vol II, London 1910.

Sampson, Richard *Escape in America, The British Convention Prisoners 1777–1783*, Chippenham, 1995.

Sargent, Winthrop *The life and career of Major John Andre: adjutant-general of the British Army in America*, Boston 1861.

Schama, Simon *Rough Crossings*, London 2006.

Scharf, J. Thomas *The chronicles of Baltimore: being a complete history of 'Baltimore town' and Baltimore city from the earliest period to the present time*, Baltimore 1874.

Schecter, Barnett *The Battle for New York*, New York NY 2002.

Serle, Ambrose *The American Journal of Ambrose Serle, Secretary to Lord Howe 1776–1778*, ed. by Edward H. Tatum, San Marino CA 1940. Serle, a civilian secretary working for Lord Howe, gives insights into relations within the higher command.

Shaw, John Robert *John Robert Shaw, an Autobiography of Thirty Years 1777–1807*', ed. Oressa M. Teagarden, Athens OH 1992. A ranker's memoir from the 33rd, evidently recorded many years later.

Showman, Richard K. (ed.) *The Papers of Nathaniel Greene*, 7 vols, Chapel Hill NC 1976–1994.

Shy, Silvia *The British Soldier in America, A Social History of Military Life in the Revolutionary Period*, Austin TX 1981.

Smith, Samuel S. *The Battle of Brandywine*, Monmouth Beach NJ 1976.

Stedman, C. *History of the Origin, Progress and Termination of the American*

War, 2 vols, London 1794.

Stevens, Benjamin Franklin (ed.)   *General Sir William Howe's Orderly Book 1775–1776*, London 1890.

Stevenson, Roger   *Military Instruction for Officers Detached in the Field*, Philadelphia 1775.

Stirke, Henry   'A British Officer's Revolutionary War Journal 1776–1778', ed. S. Sydney Bradford, *Maryland Historical Magazine*, no. 56, June 1961. Stirke served with the 10th Light Company and provides useful testimony at the time it and the 1st Battalion Light Infantry were busiest.

Sullivan, Thomas   *From Redcoat to Rebel: The Thomas Sullivan Journal*, ed. Joseph Lee Boyle, Westminster MD, 2004. A rare ranker's view of the war, Sullivan served in both light and battalion companies of the 49th durng 1775 to 1778, when he deserted.

Tarleton, Banastre   *A History of the Campaigns of 1780 and 1781 in the Southern Provinces of North America'*, London 1781.

Tielke, Captain J. G.   *The Field Engineer*, (English edition) London 1784.

Ward, Christopher L.   *The Delaware Continentals 1776–1783*, Wilmington DE 1941.

Ward, Christopher   *The War of the Revolution*, 2 vols, New York 1952.

Watkins, John   *A Biographical Memoir of his late Royal Highness Frederick Duke of York and Albany*, London 1827.

Wickwire, Franklin and Mary   *Cornwallis and the War of Independence*, London 1970.

Wilkin, Walter Harold   *Some British soldiers in America*, London 1914.

Williams, Lieutenant   *Discord and Civil Wars, being a Journal Kept by Lieutenant Williams*, ed. Walter S. Merwin, Buffalo NY 1954.

Williamson, John   *The Elements of Military Arrangement; Comprehending the Tactick, Exercises, Manoeuvres, and Discipline of the British Infantry*, London 1781.

Wolfe, Major General James   *Instructions to Young Officers*, London 1768.

Wortley, the Hon Mrs E. Stuart (ed.)   *A Prime Minister and His Son From the Correspondence of the 3rd Earl of Bute and of Lt General The Hon. Sir Charles Bute*, London 1925.

Index

Figures in italics indicate maps

[375]